Microsoft® Macintosh® QuickBASIC: A Structured Approach

Harvey M. Deitel
Boston College

Paul J. Deitel

PRENTICE HALL, Englewood Cliffs, New Jersey 07632

Library of Congress Cataloging-in-Publication Data

Deitel, Harvey M.
    Microsoft Macintosh QuickBASIC : a structured approach / Harvey M.
Deitel, Paul J. Deitel.
        p.   cm.
    Includes bibliographical references.
    ISBN 0-13-583501-1 :
    1. Macintosh (Computer)--Programming. 2. Microsoft QuickBasic
(Computer program) I. Deitel, Paul J. II. Title.
QA76.8.M3D452 1990
005.265--dc20   89-25489
                                                        CIP

The author and publisher of this book have used their best efforts in preparing this book. These efforts include the development, research, and testing of the theories and programs to determine their effectiveness. The author and publisher make no warranty of any kind, expressed or implied, with regard to these programs or the documentation contained in this book. The author and publisher shall not be liable in any event for incidental or consequential damages in connection with, or arising out of, the furnishing, performance, or use of these programs.

Cover design: *Lundgren Graphics, Ltd.*
Cover photo: *Slide Graphics of New England*
Manufacturing buyer: *Margaret Rizzi*

Microsoft QuickBASIC is a trademark of Microsoft Corporation, Bellevue, Washington.
Apple is a registered trademark of Apple Computer Inc.
Macintosh is a trademark of Apple Computer Inc.
Microsoft is a registered trademark of Microsoft Corporation, Bellevue, Washington

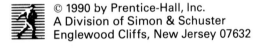 © 1990 by Prentice-Hall, Inc.
A Division of Simon & Schuster
Englewood Cliffs, New Jersey 07632

Printed in the United States of America

10 9 8 7 6 5 4 3 2 1

ISBN 0-13-583501-1

PRENTICE-HALL INTERNATIONAL (UK) LIMITED, *London*
PRENTICE-HALL OF AUSTRALIA PTY. LIMITED, *Sydney*
PRENTICE-HALL CANADA INC., *Toronto*
PRENTICE-HALL HISPANOAMERICANA, S.A., *Mexico*
PRENTICE-HALL OF INDIA PRIVATE LIMITED, *New Delhi*
PRENTICE-HALL OF JAPAN, INC., *Tokyo*
SIMON & SCHUSTER ASIA PTE. LTD., *Singapore*
EDITORA PRENTICE-HALL DO BRASIL, LTDA., *Rio de Janeiro*

Contents

Preface, ix

1 Computer Concepts, 1
   1.1 Introduction, 1
   1.2 What Is a Computer? 1
   1.3 Computer Organization, 2
   1.4 Batch Processing, Multiprogramming, and Timesharing, 2
   1.5 Computer Programming, 3
   1.6 Computer Programming Languages, 3
   1.7 Machine Languages, 4
   1.8 Assembly Languages, 4
   1.9 High-level Languages, 5
   1.10 BASIC, 5
   1.11 Other High-level Languages, 5
   1.12 Structured Programming, 6
   1.13 Microsoft Macintosh QuickBASIC, 7
   1.14 Using the Macintosh and Microsoft QuickBASIC, 7
        Concepts, 15
        Problems, 16

2 Introduction To BASIC Programming, 19
   2.1 Introduction, 19
   2.2 A Simple BASIC Program, 19
   2.3 Some Elements of BASIC, 22
   2.4 Storage Concepts, 23
   2.5 Arithmetic in BASIC, 25
   2.6 Looping, 28
   2.7 Transfers of Control, 31
        Concepts, 32
        Problems, 33

3 Structured Program Development, 37
   3.1 Introduction, 37
   3.2 Algorithms, 37
   3.3 Pseudocode, 38
   3.4 Control Structures, 38
   3.5 The Selection Structure: IF/THEN, 39
   3.6 The Selection Structure: IF/THEN/ELSE, 40

3.7 The Repetition Structure: WHILE/WEND, 41
3.8 Formulating Algorithms, 42
3.9 Top-down, Stepwise Refinement, 43
3.10 Structured Flowcharting, 46
3.11 Developing a Program Flowchart, 49
3.12 Flowcharting: Observations and Guidelines, 51
3.13 A Complete Example, 53
    Concepts, 59
    Problems, 60

4 Program Control, 62
4.1 Introduction, 62
4.2 The Essentials of Looping, 62
4.3 Counter-controlled Loops, 63
4.4 The FOR and NEXT Statements, 63
4.5 The FOR and NEXT Statements: Notes and Observations, 65
4.6 Examples Using the FOR and NEXT Statements, 66
4.7 The READ and DATA Statements, 68
4.8 The DATA List and the DATA List Pointer, 70
4.9 The READ and DATA Statements: Notes and Observations, 71
4.10 A Complete Example with FOR/NEXT and READ/DATA, 72
4.11 The SELECT/CASE Statement, 73
4.12 Logical Operators, 75
    Concepts, 77
    Problems, 78

5 Functions, Subroutines, and Subprograms 82
5.1 Introduction, 82
5.2 Program Modules in BASIC, 82
5.3 Intrinsic Functions, 83
5.4 Applications of the INT Intrinsic Function, 85
5.5 Programmer-defined Functions, 87
5.6 Subroutines, 88
5.7 Subroutines: Notes and Observations, 91
5.8 Subprograms, 91
5.9 Subprogram Definitions, 92
5.10 Passing Arguments by Reference or by Value, 93
5.11 Recursion, 93
    Concepts, 97
    Problems, 97

6 Arrays, 103
6.1 Introduction, 103
6.2 Arrays, 103

6.3 Dimensioning Arrays, 105
6.4 Examples Using Arrays, 105
6.5 Double Subscripted Arrays, 118
Concepts, 120
Problems, 120
Special Section: Building Your Own Computer, 126

7 String Manipulation, 131
7.1 Introduction, 131
7.2 Fundamentals of Strings, 131
7.3 Assigning Strings to String Variables, 132
7.4 READ/DATA with String Variables, 132
7.5 String Variables: Notes and Observations, 133
7.6 A Simple Example Using String Variables, 133
7.7 String Arrays, 137
7.8 Comparing Character Strings, 148
7.9 Internal Numeric Code Representations of Characters, 149
7.10 Manipulating the Individual Characters in a String: MID$, 151
7.11 LEFT$, RIGHT$, INSTR, 152
7.12 Other String Manipulation Functions and Techniques, 154
Concepts, 156
Problems, 157
Special Section: A Compendium of More Advanced String
Manipulation Exercises, 159
Text manipulation, 159
Text Analysis, 159
Word Arrangements, 160
Telephone Number Word Generator, 160
A Songwriting Program, 161
Dealing a Deck of Cards, 161
Word Processing, 161
Business applications, 161
Printing Dates in Various Formats, 161
Check Protection, 162
Writing the Word Equivalent of a Check Amount, 162
Cryptography and symbolic coding schemes, 163
Cryptography, 163
Morse Code, 163
Roman Numerals, 164
Graphical outputs, 164
A Banner Printing Program, 164
Printing a Calendar, 165
Points of the Compass, 165
Face of a Clock, 165

Automatic 10-Pin Bowling Scorekeeper, 165
More business-related problems, 166
A Metric Conversion Program, 166
Dunning Letters, 166
A challenging string manipulation project, 166
A Crossword Puzzle Generator, 166

8 Random Numbers and Simulation, 167
8.1   Introduction, 167
8.2   The RND Intrinsic Function, 167
8.3   The RANDOMIZE Statement, 171
8.4   Scaling and Shifting RND, 172
8.5   A Game of Chance, 174
8.6   A Simple Simulation Model, 174
8.7   A Card Shuffling and Dealing Simulation, 176
      Concepts, 182
      Problems, 182

9 Formatted Outputs, 187
9.1   Introduction, 187
9.2   The PRINT USING Statement, 187
9.3   Integer Image Specifications, 188
9.4   More On Integer Image Specifications, 189
9.5   Image Specifications: Some Notes and Observations, 191
9.6   Decimal Image Specifications, 192
9.7   PRINT USING and E-Notation, 193
9.8   Comma Insertion with PRINT USING, 194
9.9   Insertion of Trailing Minus Signs with PRINT USING, 194
9.10 Insertion of Leading Asterisks with PRINT USING, 195
9.11 Insertion of Floating Dollar Signs with PRINT USING, 196
9.12 String Image Specifications, 197
9.13 Printing Characters, 199
      Concepts, 200
      Problems, 200

10 Sequential Files, 204
10.1 Introduction, 204
10.2 The Data Hierarchy, 204
10.3 Creating a Sequential File Using BASIC, 206
10.4 Obtaining Data from a Sequential File, 207
10.5 Rereading Data from a Sequential File, 208
      Concepts, 209
      Problems, 211

11 Random Access Files, 214

11.1 Introduction, 214
11.2 Creating a Random Access File, 214
11.3 The FIELD Statement, 215
11.4 The LSET and RSET Statements, 215
11.5 The PUT # Statement, 216
11.6 Single-precision, Double-precision, Integer, and Long Integer Numbers, 216
11.7 The MKS$, MKD$, MKI$, and MKL$ Functions, 217
11.8 The CLOSE # Statement, 217
11.9 The CVS, CVD, CVI, and CVL Functions, 218
11.10 The GET # Statement, 219
11.11 The LOF Function, 220
11.12 The EOF Function, 220
  Concepts, 225
  Problems, 225

12 The Mouse, Event Trapping, and Elementary Graphics, 227

12.1 Introduction, 227
12.2 The MOUSE(0) Function, 227
12.3 The MOUSE(1) and MOUSE(2) Functions, 228
12.4 Dragging the Mouse, 229
12.5 Event Trapping and the Mouse, 231
  Concepts, 236
  Problems, 236

13 Menus, 238

13.1 Introduction, 238
13.2 Creating a Menu, 238
13.3 The MENU(0) Function, 240
13.4 The MENU(1) Function, 241
13.5 The MENU RESET Statement and Removing BASIC Default Menus, 242
13.6 Event Trapping with Menus, 244
  Concepts, 250
  Problems, 250

14. Buttons, 252

14.1 Introduction, 252
14.2 The BUTTON Statement, 252
14.3 The BUTTON CLOSE n Statement, 253
14.4 Determining and Changing the State of a Button, 254
14.5 The DIALOG(0) Function, 255
14.6 The DIALOG(1) Function, 255
14.7 Event Trapping with Buttons, 257
  Concepts, 262
  Problems, 262

15. Windows, Dialog Boxes, and Edit Fields, 264
15.1 Introduction, 264
15.2 Windows, 264
15.3 The WINDOW Statement, 264
15.4 The WINDOW Statements, 265
15.5 The WINDOW Functions, 267
15.6 Refreshing Windows, 267
15.7 Using Windows as Dialog Boxes, 271
15.8 The EDIT FIELD Statement, 271
15.9 Using an Edit Field, 272
   Concepts, 276
   Problems, 277

16 QuickDraw, 278
16.1 Introduction, 278
16.2 The CALL Statement, 278
16.3 The CALL TEXT Statements, 279
16.4 The MOVETO, LINETO, MOVE, and LINE Statements, 281
16.5 Changing the Size of the QuickDraw Pen, 284
16.6 Drawing Patterns with the Pen, 284
16.7 The PENMODE Statement, 286
16.8 Drawing Shapes with QuickDraw, 286
   Concepts, 293
   Problems, 294

17 Sights and Sounds, 295
17.1 Introduction, 295
17.2 Animation, 295
17.3 Music in QuickBASIC, 298
   Concepts, 301
   Problems, 301

Appendix, 303
A.1 Introduction, 303
A.2 Compiling QuickBASIC Programs, 303
A.3 Include Files and the $INCLUDE Metacommand, 304
A.4 Debugging, 305
A.5 QuickBASIC Menus, 305
A.6 Other Features, 307
A.7 A Summary of Additional QuickBASIC Statements, 307
   Bibliography, 309

Index, 310

Preface

This text is designed for use in introductory computer science courses featuring the BASIC computer programming language. The book contains a rich collection of examples, exercises, and projects drawn from many fields to provide the student with a chance to solve interesting real-world problems. The book is specifically applicable in educational institutions using Microsoft Corporations powerful QuickBASIC language for Apple's Macintosh line of computers. Users of other powerful versions of BASIC will find the book useful as well.

Each chapter concludes with an alphabetized listing of important terms and a large collection of problems. The exercises range from simple recall questions, to lengthy programming problems, to major projects. Instructors who require substantial term projects of their students will find many appropriate problems listed in the exercises for Chapters 5 through 17.

The book is divided into two portions. The first nine chapters contain the more conventional topics such as introductory explanations of computer concepts, programming, and flowcharting. A thorough description of the elementary features of the BASIC language is presented. The last eight chapters contain advanced material unique to the Apple Macintosh line of computers.

Chapter 1, "Computer Concepts," discusses what computers are, how they work, and how they are programmed. It introduces the notion of structured programming and explains why this set of techniques has fostered a revolution in the way programs are written. The chapter gives a brief history of the development of programming languages form machine languages, to assembly languages, to high-level languages. The origin of the BASIC high-level programming language is discussed, and the development of the powerful Macintosh QuickBASIC dialect of BASIC by Microsoft Corporation is considered. The chapter includes an introduction to the QuickBASIC programming environment.

Chapter 2, "Introduction to BASIC Programming," gives a concise introduction to the writing, editing, and running of BASIC programs. A detailed treatment of decision making and arithmetic operations in BASIC is presented. After studying this chapter, the reader will understand what programming is, what BASIC is, and why BASIC is such an appealing programming language. The chapter presents BASIC as it was originally intended to be used—as an essentially unstructured high-level programming language.

Chapter 3, "Structured Program Development," is probably the most important chapter in the text, especially for the serious student of computer science. It introduces the notion of algorithms (procedures) for solving problems. It explains the importance of structured programming in producing programs that are understandable, debuggable, maintainable, and more likely to work properly on the first try. It introduces the fundamental control structures of structured programming, namely the sequence, selection (IF/THEN and IF/THEN/ELSE), and repetition (WHILE/WEND) structures. It explains the important technique of top-down, stepwise refinement that is critical to the production of properly structured programs. It presents the two most popular program design aids, namely structured flowcharting and structured pseudocode. The methods and approaches used in Chapter 3 are applicable to structured programming in any programming language, not just Microsoft Macintosh QuickBASIC. This chapter helps the student develop good programming habits in preparation for dealing with the more substantial programming tasks in the remainder of the text.

Chapter 4, "Program Control," refines the notions of structured programming and introduces additional control structures. It examines the process of looping in detail and compares the alternatives of counter-controlled loops and sentinel-controlled loops. The FOR/NEXT structure is introduced as a convenient means for implementing counter-controlled loops. The READ and DATA statements are introduced as a means of supplying programs with data as they execute. The WHILE/WEND looping structure is presented for controlling indefinite looping. The SELECT/CASE decision structure is presented. The chapter concludes with a discussion of logical operators.

Chapter 5, "Functions, Subroutines and Subprograms," discusses the design and construction of program pieces. Since the late 1960's, BASIC has "lost ground" in the universities to various structured programming languages, especially Pascal. This trend could be reversed by the very powerful structured programming capabilities in Microsoft Macintosh QuickBASIC. This version of BASIC includes intrinsic functions, programmer-defined functions, subroutines, subprograms, recursion, call-by-reference capabilities, and call-by-value capabilities. The techniques presented in chapter 5 are essential to the production and appreciation of properly structured programs, especially the kinds of larger programs and software systems programmers are likely to develop in real-world applications. The "divide and conquer" strategy is presented as an effective means for solving complex problems; BASIC functions, subroutines, and subprograms enable the programmer to divide complex programs into simpler interacting components. The exercises at the end of the chapter include several classical recursion problems such as the Towers of Hanoi.

Chapter 6, "Arrays," discusses the structuring of data into arrays or groups of related data items. The chapter presents numerous examples of both single-subscripted arrays (lists) and double-subscripted arrays (tables or grids). It is widely recognized that structuring data is just as important as using control structures in the development of properly structured programs. Examples in the chapter investigate various common array manipulations, printing histograms, sorting data, and an introduction to the field of survey data analysis. The end-of-chapter exercises include an especially large selection of interesting and challenging problems. These include improved sorting techniques, the design of an airline reservations system, an introduction to the concept of turtle graphics (made famous in the LOGO language), and the Knight's Tour and Eight Queens problems that introduce the notions of heuristic programming so useful in the field of artificial intelligence. A special section entitled "Building Your Own Computer" is included. This section explains the notion of machine language programming and proceeds with a project involving the design and implementation of a computer simulator that will allow the reader to write and run machine language programs. This unique feature of the text will be especially useful to the reader who wants to understand how computers really work.

Chapter 7, "String Manipulation," is perhaps the most complete treatment of character string processing that has ever appeared in an introductory programming text. The techniques presented here are at the heart of today's popular word processing systems. The chapter contains many interesting examples and exercises, including printing the song "The Twelve Days of Christmas," printing the song "Old MacDonald Had a Farm," printing the numbers from one to ninety-nine in words, printing all possible two-letter words, printing all possible arrangements of a five-letter word, spelling phrases backwards, and converting English phrases to pig Latin. It is followed by a unique selection entitled "A Compendium of More Advanced String Manipulation Exercises," which suggests many possible term projects. The projects include text analysis, word arrangements, a telephone number word generator, a songwriting program, dealing a deck of cards, word processing, printing dates in various formats, check protection, writing the word equivalent of a check amount, cryptography, Morse code, Roman numerals, a banner printing program, printing a calendar, points of the compass, face of a clock, automatic 10-pin bowling scorekeeper, a metric conversion program, and dunning letters. This section concludes with a project suggesting the development of a crossword puzzle generator program; this is an extremely difficult task and one that may usefully be approached by a team of programmers.

Chapter 8, "Random Numbers and Simulation," explains how randomness or the "element of chance" may be introduced into BASIC programs. Randomness adds interest and excitement to programs. It is the essence of enabling computers to play the so-called "games of chance" that depend on coin tossing, dice rolling, card dealing, and the like. The case study on the card shuffling and dealing simulation is the capstone example of the text; it exemplifies the best principles of top-down, stepwise refinement in the development of structured programs. Many intriguing and challenging projects are suggested for the reader's enjoyment. These include a group of projects on computer-assisted instruction (CAI) and several increasingly difficult card playing programs. Several exercises develop the notion of randomly choosing words and phrases to perform creative writing, to write limericks, and to write whodunnit mysteries. The exercises end with a delightful simulation of the classical race of the tortoise and the hare; after you try this exercise you might develop your own original simulations of other "great moments" in history.

Chapter 9, "Formatted Outputs," discusses how data are "polished" or "prettied up" for presentation to users. The chapter focuses on the powerful capabilities of the PRINT USING statement that enable the programmer to specify how "raw" data inside the computer are to be edited to produce neatly formatted user reports. The features discussed in this chapter are quite similar to the data editing capabilities of COBOL, the most commonly used language for commercial data processing applications.

Chapter 10, "Sequential Files," introduces the notions of sequential file processing that are essential in business data processing. An informative section on the data hierarchy explains how data are stored and organized into increasingly more powerful structures inside computer systems. The end-of-chapter problems introduce many of the file manipulations commonly used in commercial data processing.

Chapter 11, "Random Access Files," discusses the kinds of files that make possible the rapid access of individual facts. Random access files are essential to the success of today's interactive transaction processing systems such as airline reservation systems in which individual facts must be located within a fraction of a second from among a massive collection of information.

Chapter 12, "The Mouse, Event Trapping, and Elementary Graphics," is the first of six chapters devoted to the unique features of the Apple Macintosh. The mouse is an extraordinarily simple device, yet it has ushered in a whole new era of user-friendly interactive computing. This chapter explains how the mouse works and how BASIC enables the user to keep track of mouse activity. The examples use some of Microsoft QuickBASIC's elementary graphics capabilities to produce some conceptually simple yet visually pleasing artwork.

Chapter 13, "Menus," discusses the use of pulldown menus, an important component of the Macintosh's user-friendly interface. Before the Macintosh appeared, most systems required their users to memorize long lists of options and commands, and to know when each was appropriate. The Macintosh instead displays all relevant options in pulldown menus and allows the user to select options quickly with the mouse rather than having to key in lengthy command words. This chapter explains how to create menus, how to determine when a user has made a menu selection, and how to determine what selection has been made.

Chapter 14, "Buttons," discusses the use of buttons, yet another important component of the Macintosh's user-friendly interface. Most people are comfortable with pushing buttons to make selections. This chapter explains how to create and label buttons, how to determine when a button has been pushed, and how to determine which of several buttons has been pushed.

Chapter 15, "Windows, Dialog Boxes, and Edit Fields," discusses additional components of the Macintosh's user-friendly interface. Windows enable users to view their work. One window may contain a program listing, while another contains the program's textual output, and yet another contains a program's graphic output. The chapter discusses the various types of windows, how to create them and position them on the screen, and how to determine when activity occurs in a window. Dialog boxes enable communication with the user, both with the mouse and the keyboard; here, too, we explain the types of dialog boxes, how to create them, how to position them on the screen, and how to determine when user activity occurs in them. Edit fields enable users to enter text into dialog boxes and to edit text that is already in place.

Chapter 16, "QuickDraw," discusses some of the built-in graphics capabilities of the Macintosh. QuickDraw enables us to draw rectangles, ovals, rounded rectangles, and many other shapes as well. It can fill these shapes with patterns, invert the background pattern within a shape, paint a new pattern in a shape, and erase a shape from the screen It enables us to draw with a "pen" of any width, height, and pattern. It enables us to set text fonts, sizes, faces, and modes. This chapter discusses many key features of QuickDraw and provides numerous visual examples of its capabilities.

Chapter 17, "Sights and Sounds," discusses methods of animation using the GET and PUT graphics statements. These statements allow the user to retrieve a picture from the screen, and place it repeatedly anywhere on the screen. This chapter also discusses QuickBASIC's music capabilities using the SOUND and WAVE statements.

It is important to note here that full Microsoft Macintosh QuickBASIC is one of the more powerful, general-purpose, high-level programming languages ever developed; it contains many more features than can be discussed in an introductory text. The reader who wants to learn more about Microsoft Macintosh QuickBASIC should consult the documentation available from Microsoft Corporation of Redmond, Washington.

Every textbook author must deal with the problem of cramming every last detail into a book. We were constantly "frustrated" by the richness of Microsoft Macintosh QuickBASIC. It has so many powerful features that we wanted to discuss in the main text, but could not because of the time limitations of a typical one-semester course. Therefore, we have included an Appendix that discusses many of the powerful features of QuickBASIC that we could not include in the main text. In particular, we discuss compiling in the QuickBASIC environment, "include files" and the $INCLUDE metacommand, debugging, descriptions of the various QuickBASIC menu choices, and a summary of the remaining QuickBASIC statements not presented in the text.

One of the great pleasures of writing a textbook is acknowledging the efforts of people whose names may not appear on the cover, but without whose hard work producing this text would have been impossible. We are fortunate to have been able to work on this project with the talented and dedicated team of publishing professionals at Prentice Hall. This book happened because of the encouragement, enthusiasm, and persistence of Marcia Horton, Editor-in-chief of Prentice Hall's College Technical and Reference Division, who combines patience and professionalism with drive and energy in just the right mix. Debbie Young did a marvelous job as production editor.

We appreciate the efforts of our reviewers including Robert Matthews of University of Puget Sound, Leonard Presby of William Paterson College, and James Leon Fuller of Oregon Institute of Technology. These people scrutinized every aspect of the text and made dozens of valuable suggestions for improving the accuracy and completeness of the presentation.

The authors would like to express their appreciation to Mr. Ray Kanemori of Microsoft Corporation. Mr. Kanemori suggested that we write this book and he helped us immeasurably throughout the writing effort. Mr. Kanemori is truly one of those special people who make things happen.

Last, but certainly not least, we would like to thank Barbara Deitel, for her love and understanding, and for her enormous efforts in helping prepare the manuscript. She tested every program in the text, assisted in every phase of the manuscript preparation, and proofread every draft of the text through to publication. Her sharp eye prevented innumerable errors from finding a home in the manuscript.

We assume complete responsibility for any remaining flaws in this text. We would greatly appreciate your comments, criticisms, corrections, and suggestions for improving the text. Please address all correspondence to:

Harvey M. Deitel and
Paul J. Deitel (authors)
c/o Computer Science Editor
College Book Editorial/Production
Prentice Hall
Englewood Cliffs, New Jersey 07632

We will respond by return mail immediately. Harvey M. Deitel is Chairman of the Computer Science Department at Boston College. Paul J. Deitel is a student at the Massachusetts Institute of Technology concentrating in Management Information Systems in the Sloan School of Management.

Harvey M. Deitel
Chestnut Hill, Massachusetts
Paul J. Deitel
Cambridge, Massachusetts

Chapter 1
Computer Concepts

1.1 Introduction

This text provides an introduction to the Apple Macintosh computer and to programming the Macintosh in the world's most popular programming language, namely Microsoft QuickBASIC. Use of computers is increasing in almost every field of endeavor. A decade ago, students might have taken a computer course as an "exotic" elective. Today, many academic institutions require that their students take one or more computer courses.

In an era of steadily rising costs, computing costs have been decreasing dramatically because of exciting developments in electronics and other technologies. Computers that might have weighed many tons, filled large rooms, and cost millions of dollars 25 years ago can now be inscribed on the surface of silicon chips that are smaller than a fingernail and costs perhaps a few dollars. Ironically, silicon is one of the most abundant materials on the earth—it is an ingredient in common sand. Silicon chip technology has made computing so economical that millions of people are able to afford their own personal computers.

1.2 What Is a Computer?

A *computer* is a device capable of performing computations and making logical decisions at speeds thousands and even millions of times faster than human beings can. For example, many current computer models can easily perform one million additions per second. A person operating a desk calculator might require a year to complete the same number of calculations. Today's fastest *supercomputers* can actually perform one billion additions per second—about as many calculations as one thousand people could perform in one year!

Computers process data under the control of sets of instructions called *computer programs*. These computer programs guide the computer through orderly sets of steps to ensure that the data are processed according to procedures defined by people called *computer programmers*.

The various devices that comprise a computer system are referred to as *hardware*. The computer programs that run on a computer are referred to as *software*. This text focuses on preparing computer software with the Macintosh dialect of Microsoft QuickBASIC.

1

1.3 Computer Organization

Regardless of differences in physical appearance, virtually every computer may be envisioned as being divided into five *logical units* or sections. These are:

1. *Input unit.* This is the "receiving" section of the computer. It obtains information (data and computer programs) from various *input devices* and places this information at the disposal of the other units so that the information may be processed. Most information is entered into computers today through typewriter-like keyboards.
2. *Output unit.* This is the "shipping" section of the computer. It takes information that has been processed by the computer and places it on various *output devices* to make the information available for use outside the computer. Most information is output from computers today by printing it on paper or by displaying it on screens.
3. *Storage unit.* This is the "warehouse" section of the computer. It retains information which has been entered through the input unit so that the information may be made available for processing when it is needed. The storage unit also retains information which has already been processed until that information can be placed on output devices by the output unit. The storage unit is often called either *main storage* or *primary storage.*
4. *Arithmetic and logic unit (ALU).* This is the "manufacturing" section of the computer. It is responsible for performing calculations such as addition, subtraction, multiplication, and division. It contains the decision mechanisms that allow the computer, for example, to compare two items from the storage unit to determine whether or not they are equal.
5. *Central processing unit (CPU).* This is the "administrative" section of the computer. It is the computer's coordinator and is responsible for supervising the operation of the other sections. The CPU thus tells the input unit when information should be read into the storage unit, tells the ALU when information from the storage unit should be utilized in calculations, and tells the output unit when to send information from the storage unit to certain output devices.

1.4 Batch Processing, Multiprogramming, and Timesharing

Early computers were capable of performing only one *job* or *task* at a time. This form of computer operation is often called single-user *batch processing*. The computer runs a single program at a time while processing data in groups or *batches*. In these early systems, users generally submitted their jobs to the computer center on decks of punched cards. The users often had to wait hours or even days before printouts were returned to their desks.

As computers became more powerful, it became evident that single-user batch processing rarely utilized the computer's resources efficiently. Instead, it was thought that many jobs or tasks could be made to *share* the resources of the computer to achieve better utilization. This is called *multiprogramming*. Multiprogramming involves the "simultaneous" operation of many jobs on the computer—the computer shares its resources among the jobs which are competing for its attention. With early multiprogramming systems, users still submitted jobs on decks of punched cards and waited hours or days for results.

In the early 1960s, several groups in industry and the universities pioneered the concept of *timesharing*. Timesharing is a special case of multiprogramming in which users access the computer through relatively slow input-output devices or *terminals*. In a typical timesharing computer system, there may be dozens or even hundreds of users sharing the computer at once. The computer does not actually run all the users simultaneously. Rather, it runs a small portion of one user's job and then moves on to service the next user. The computer does this so quickly that it may provide service to each user several times per second. Thus the users *appear* to be running simultaneously.

Timesharing computers operate at speeds that are thousands of times faster than the printing or display speeds of the terminals. Thus the computer can solve a significant portion of the problem specified by User 1, and begin printing some information on User 1's terminal. As the printout occurs on the terminal, the computer can service other users and return to User 1 in time to receive User 1's next request. Thus, User 1 is not kept waiting even though many other users are sharing the computer at the same time.

1.5 Computer Programming

Computers are essentially unintelligent devices. They do not automatically know how to solve particular problems. They merely contain the mechanisms that may ultimately be used in the solution of problems.

The computer has to be told how to solve specific problems. *Computer programming* is the process of instructing the computer to utilize its various mechanisms to solve specific problems. After a computer program is prepared, it is then *loaded* into the computer's main storage. The computer, under the control of its CPU, then processes this *stored program* to achieve the desired results.

1.6 Computer Programming Languages

Computers are programmed by programmers, who write instructions in various languages acceptable to the computer. Some of these *programming languages* are directly understandable by the computer, while others require intermediate *translation* steps.

There are hundreds of computer languages in use today. These may be divided into three general types:

1. Machine languages
2. Assembly languages
3. High-level languages

1.7 Machine Languages

Any computer is capable of directly understanding only one computer language, namely its own *machine language*. Machine language is the natural language of a particular computer. It is closely related to the actual electromechanical construction of that computer. Machine languages generally consist of strings of numbers (ultimately reduced to strings of 1s and 0s) that cause the computer to perform its most elementary operations one at a time. Machine languages are *machine-dependent*, i.e., a particular machine language can be used on only one type of computer. Machine languages are fine for the computer, but are cumbersome for human beings. On one particular computer, the following machine language instructions cause two numbers to be added together and the sum to be saved for future use:

```
+1300042774
+1400593419
+1200274027
```

1.8 Assembly Languages

Early in the development of modern computers, all programs were written in machine languages. As computers became more popular, it became apparent that machine language programming was simply too slow and tedious for most programmers.

Instead of using the strings of numbers that computers could directly understand, programmers began using English-like abbreviations to represent the elementary operations of the computer. Languages consisting of these English-like abbreviations are called *assembly languages*.

Since computers cannot directly read and understand assembly language programs, it is necessary to translate these programs into machine language before the computer can perform the instructions. Computer programs were developed that could read assembly language programs and translate them into machine language at computer speeds. Such *translator programs* are called *assemblers*.

The following section of an assembly language program adds overtime pay to base pay and stores the result in gross pay:

```
ZA1   BASEPAY
A1    OVERPAY
ST1   GROSSPAY
```

1.9 High-level Languages

Computer usage began to increase rapidly with the advent of assembly languages. Once again, however, it became evident that faster and more convenient methods for programming computers were needed. Assembly languages still required that many instructions had to be written to accomplish even the simplest tasks on a computer.

To speed the process of programming computers even further, *high-level languages* were developed in which single statements could be written to accomplish tasks that might require many machine language or assembly language statements. High-level language programs must also be translated into machine language before the programs can be performed by the computer. The programs that translate high-level language programs into machine language are called *compilers*.

High-level languages allow programmers to write instructions that look almost like everyday English and contain commonly used mathematical notations. A payroll program written in a high-level language might contain a statement such as:

```
GROSSPAY = BASEPAY + OVERTIMEPAY.
```

Obviously, high-level languages are much more desirable from the programmer's standpoint than other types of computer languages. High-level languages are easy to learn and easy to use. This book describes the BASIC programming language, one of the simplest high-level languages in use today, one of the most powerful, and by far the most widely used. We present the version of BASIC designed by Microsoft Corporation for use with Apple's highly successful Macintosh computers.

1.10 BASIC

The *BASIC* (**B**eginner's **A**ll-purpose **S**ymbolic **I**nstruction **C**ode) language was developed by John Kemeny and Thomas Kurtz at Dartmouth College in the mid-1960s. BASIC was designed for use in teaching the elementary principles of computer programming in a straightforward manner. The language is particularly well suited for timesharing computers and personal computers. It is concise, easy to learn, and useful for most computer applications that a novice programmer might care to implement.

Like other high-level languages, BASIC is *machine-independent*. BASIC programs written on one computer will run (with little or no modification) on many other types of computers, even though they may have different machine languages.

1.11 Other High-level Languages

Hundreds of high-level languages have been developed, but only a few have achieved broad acceptance. *FORTRAN* (**FOR**mula **TRAN**slator) was developed by IBM Corporation between 1954 and 1957 to be used for scientific and industrial applications that require complex mathematical computations.

COBOL (**CO**mmon **B**usiness **O**riented **L**anguage) was developed in 1959 by a group of computer manufacturers and government and industrial computer users. COBOL is used primarily for commercial applications that require precise and efficient manipulation of large amounts of data.

PL/1 (**P**rogramming **L**anguage **O**ne) was introduced by IBM in the mid-1960s coincident with its System/360 family of computers. PL/1 contains the better features of FORTRAN and COBOL along with many powerful features not available in either of these languages. PL/1 was designed to be a "universal" language useful for both scientific and commercial applications, but the language never gained the wide acceptance for which IBM had hoped.

1.12 Structured Programming

During the 1960s, many large software development efforts encountered severe difficulties. The software was produced late, costs greatly exceeded budget estimates, and the finished products were cumbersome and unreliable. This called attention to the complexities of software development. During the mid-to-late 1960s, a flurry of research activity resulted in the evolution of what has come to be called *structured programming*— a disciplined approach to writing programs that are clear, demonstrably correct, and easy to modify. Chapter 3 presents an overview of the general principles of structured programming. The remainder of the text discusses the development of structured BASIC programs.

One of the more tangible results of this research was the development of the *Pascal* programming language by Nicklaus Wirth in 1971. Pascal, named after the seventeenth-century mathematician and philosopher Blaise Pascal, was specifically designed to facilitate teaching structured programming in academic environments, and was rapidly accepted as the programming language of choice in most universities. Unfortunately, the language lacks many features needed to make it useful in commercial, industrial, and government applications, so it has not been widely accepted in these environments. History may well record that the real significance of Pascal was its selection as the base of the *Ada* programming language.

Ada was developed under the sponsorship of the United States Department of Defense (DOD) during the 1970s and early 1980s. DOD observed that hundreds of separate languages were being used to produce its massive software systems. DOD wanted a single language that would fulfill most of its needs, so it sponsored the development of Ada. Pascal was chosen as a base from which to begin, but the final Ada language is very different from Pascal. The language was named after Lady Ada Lovelace, daughter of the poet Lord Byron. Lady Lovelace is generally believed to have written the world's first computer program in the early 1800s. One important capability of Ada is called *multitasking*. This capability allows programmers to specify that many activities are to occur in parallel. The other widely used high-level languages we have discussed generally allow the programmer to specify that programs perform only one activity at a time. It remains to be seen if Ada will meet its goals of producing reliable software and substantially reducing development and maintenance costs.

1.13   Microsoft Macintosh QuickBASIC

Because of its popularity on timesharing and personal computers, BASIC has become the world's leading general-purpose programming language.   Unfortunately,   no acceptable standard for the language has emerged, and a very large number of separate "dialects" have been developed.   An ANSI (American National Standards Institute) "minimal BASIC" standard has received much discussion, but virtually every version of BASIC in use today offers much more powerful features than this minimal BASIC provides.   It is not likely that a comprehensive standardized version of BASIC will emerge in the foreseeable future.

This text discusses the dialect of BASIC developed by Microsoft Corporation for Apple's highly successful Macintosh computers.   Microsoft Macintosh QuickBASIC is an extremely powerful language that facilitates the writing of well-structured programs and makes it possible to solve substantial computing problems quickly and efficiently.

1.14   Using the Macintosh and Microsoft QuickBASIC

In this section we describe how to get Microsoft Macintosh QuickBASIC installed and running on a Macintosh computer.   In many cases, the reader will be working with a system on which QuickBASIC has already been installed, so the steps described here may be skipped.

The Microsoft QuickBASIC package includes two double-sided disks.   These disks contain two versions of Microsoft QuickBASIC, namely the *binary* version and the *decimal* version.   The two versions can be distinguished by the way they handle noninteger numbers.   The binary version does faster calculations, and is primarily used for scientific and engineering applications.   The decimal version does not produce round-off errors in dollars and cents calculations, and is therefore used for business and financial applications in which the users must literally "account for every penny."   In the examples in this text, we use the binary version.   The reader may wish to experiment with the decimal version to see how these versions differ.

To begin the process of learning BASIC, turn on the Macintosh.   If your system has a hard disk, the computer will boot (start up) with the *System* located in the *System Folder* on the hard disk.   Due to the size of QuickBASIC, if you do not have a hard disk, you will need a Macintosh with two 800K disk drives, and a startup disk which includes a System Folder and the version of QuickBASIC you prefer to use (see the QuickBASIC manual for details).   The disk in the second disk drive will be the location to which you will save your programs.   The remainder of this section assumes that you are working with a reasonably powerful Macintosh with a hard disk.   If you have any questions, consult the Microsoft QuickBASIC literature that came with the software, or, if you are taking a course, ask your instructor.

Now that the computer has been booted, what appears on the screen is the *Macintosh desktop* (see Figure 1.1).   The *icon* (picture) for the hard disk appears in the upper-right corner of the screen.   Normally a gray background appears when the

Macintosh is started. Using the *control panel* found in the *apple menu*, it is possible to change this pattern; for clarity of publication, we have chosen a white background. Click once on the icon if it is not already darkened. Then use the *mouse* to move the *mouse pointer* (the arrow on the screen) to the `File` *menu* in the *menu bar* at the top of the screen. Press the button on the mouse and hold it down to display the menu. While holding the button down, *drag* the mouse down until the `Open` option is blackened, then release the mouse; this opens the disk and allows the user to view all the files and folders on the disk. We have placed all the files and folders from the two QuickBASIC disks into a folder labeled "QuickBASIC" on the hard disk. By opening the folder in the same manner as we opened the disk, we see the window in Figure 1.2. This window contains everything needed to get started with Microsoft QuickBASIC. Now move the pointer to the small square in the upper-left corner of the window and click the mouse; the window disappears. This square is called the *close box*, and it can be used to close any window of this type. Now click the mouse twice quickly on the folder, and the window

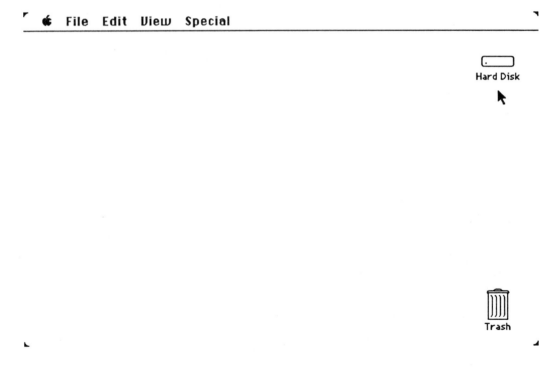

Figure 1.1 The Macintosh desktop

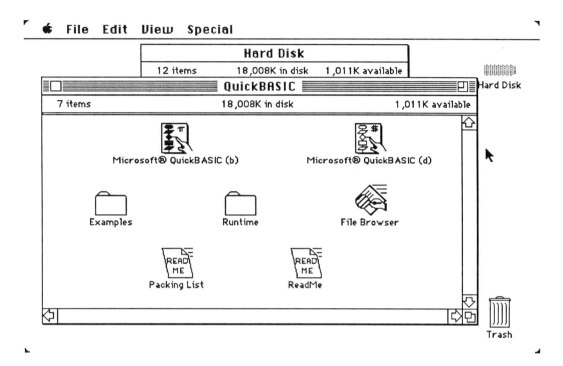

Figure 1.2 The window containing the QuickBASIC files

reappears. Both these methods for opening a disk icon or a folder may be used to open individual files as well.

It is important that the QuickBASIC disks be *backed up* (i.e., security copies made) immediately. To do this, insert the QuickBASIC disk and a blank disk. If the blank disk has not already been initialized, the computer will ask you to do so. To copy the QuickBASIC disk, press the mouse button and hold it down on the QuickBASIC disk icon. Now drag this icon over the blank disk icon and release the mouse button. The Macintosh will then ask if everything on the blank disk should be replaced with the contents of the QuickBASIC disk. Respond **Yes**, and the computer will back up the QuickBASIC disk. Repeat this process for the second disk as well. Always work with the backup copy if you are using the disk drives to run QuickBASIC, and keep the original in a safe place.

Click on the icon labeled "Microsoft® QuickBASIC (b)" in the window, and open it. The screen of Figure 1.3 appears. Notice that there are three windows. The large window is labeled **Untitled**. This is called the *output window*. All output from a program will be displayed in this window, unless the program specifically states otherwise. The window at the bottom of the screen is the *command bar*. This is where

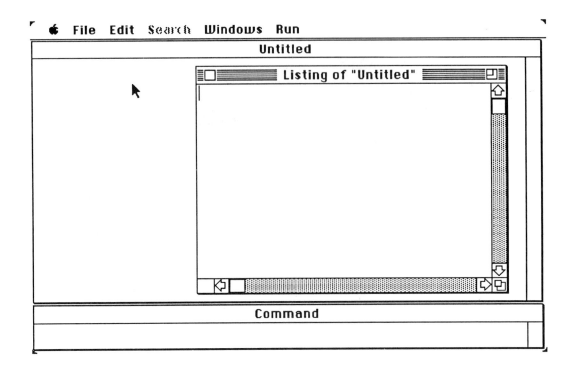

Figure 1.3 The screen in the binary version of Microsoft QuickBASIC

any commands are typed whose outputs are to go directly to the output window. For instance, to determine the product of two numbers quickly, position the pointer in the command bar and click the mouse button. This makes the window active, and a flashing vertical bar appears. The bar is called the *cursor*; it shows the point of insertion of the next character. Then type a statement like the following:

```
print 12 * 17
```

Press the *Return key* located on the right side of your keyboard. The answer, 204, will appear in the upper-left corner of the output window. Finally, the last window on the screen is called the *list window*. This is where a program is typed and displayed. After using the command bar, click inside the list window to make it active.

Type the following BASIC program (which will be explained in detail in Chapter 2) into the list window:

```
rem  Addition program
print "Enter the first number"
input x
print "Enter the second number"
input y
let z = x + y
print "Sum is"; z
end
```

The screen should now appear as in Figure 1.4. Notice that the program does not appear this way on the screen. As each line is typed and the Return key is pressed, certain words are automatically converted to bold uppercase text; these are called *reserved words*, and they have special meaning to Microsoft QuickBASIC as we shall see in the coming chapters.

Now let us save the program so we do not lose it. Move the mouse to the `File` menu at the top of the screen. Press the mouse button and hold it; the list of options in the menu appears (see Figure 1.5). Notice that there are two choices for saving, `Save` and `Save As`. When saving a program that has previously been saved, the `Save` option simply updates the file. The `Save As` option displays the *dialog box* shown in Figure 1.6. For now, either option may be chosen because they operate essentially the same when a program is being saved for the first time. Type the title `Addition program` in the box, then press the `Save` *button* with the mouse, or press the Return key. This box also gives you the ability to tell the computer which disk you would like to save the program on by pressing the `Drive` button if you have more than one disk drive; if you have only one disk drive, you can eject the present disk using the `Eject` button and then save the program on another disk.

The `File` menu has some other options. The `New` option displays a blank output window and an empty list window so that a new program may be entered. If the previous program has not been saved, QuickBASIC will ask if it should be saved. The `Open` option opens another file on the disk. The `Close` option closes the active window. The `Print` option prints the program on the Macintosh's printer. The `Transfer` option transfers to another program, for instance, from binary QuickBASIC to decimal QuickBASIC. The `Quit` option returns to the Macintosh desktop.

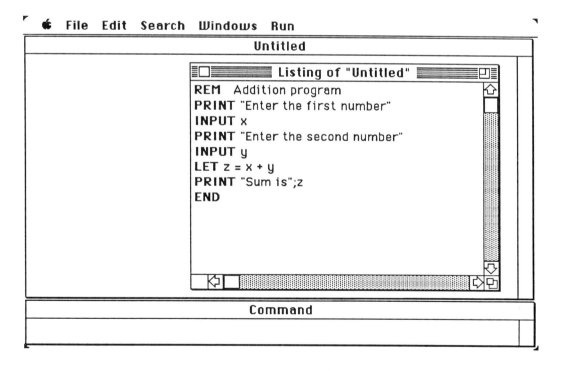

Figure 1.4 The program in the List window

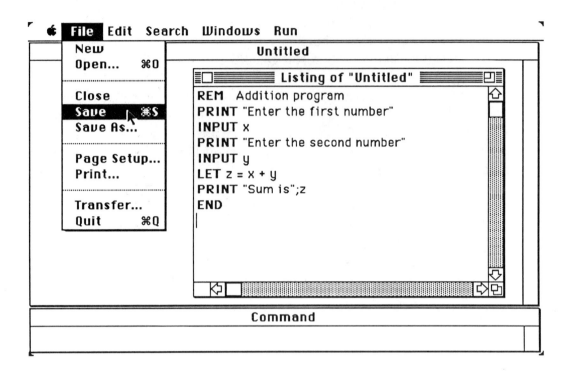

Figure 1.5 Selecting the Save option from the File menu

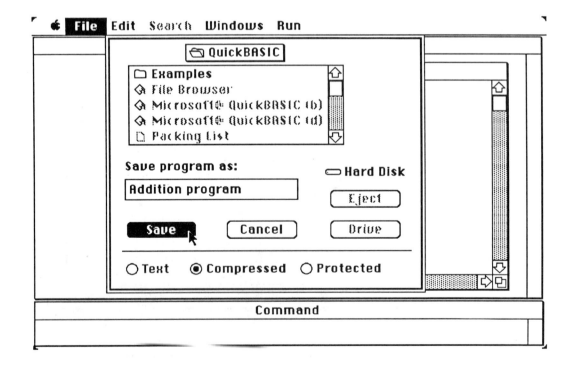

Figure 1.6 The Save As dialog box

To run a program, pull down the `Run` menu and select the `Run` option. The `List` window disappears, and the program starts executing. Now go to the `File` menu and select `Stop`. The program stops and the `List` window reappears. The `List` window will always reappear unless it is closed manually using the close box before the program is run. Now run the program again, and let it run to completion. The `List` window once again reappears.

The `Continue` option in the `Run` menu restarts the program from the statement where the program was stopped. If the program stopped by itself, the `Continue` option cannot be chosen. The `Step`, `Breakpoint ON/OFF`, and the `Trace All` options are used for debugging (correcting) programs; these options are particularly important when developing large and complex programs. Choosing `Options...` from the `Run` menu displays the list of compiling features available in QuickBASIC. The `Compile` option compiles the program, and the `Compile As...` option allows the user to input a specific file name before compiling the program.

Up to this point, everything has (it is hoped) worked correctly. We will now learn to edit a program, and will intentionally make a mistake. Place the cursor in the first `PRINT` statement by clicking the mouse button with the text pointer placed just after the `I` in `PRINT`. Backspace over the letter `I` with the Backspace key (see Figure 1.7). This is one way of deleting text.

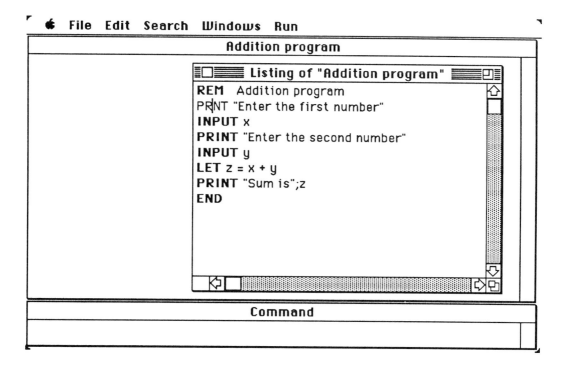

Figure 1.7 Program listing with edited line

Now run the program. An error message appears, and the line with the error has a box around it in the `List` window (see Figure 1.8). This happens because QuickBASIC cannot understand the program at this point. Now place the cursor where the `I` in `PRINT` belongs and type an `I` to correct the program. This is how text can be inserted in a program line. Another way to delete text is to select it by holding the mouse button down and dragging the mouse across the text to be deleted; then either hit backspace to erase the text, or type any new text to be inserted at that point.

At times, you may want to copy a part of your program without having to retype it. This is done with the options in the `Edit` menu. Select the text to be copied, and choose `Copy` from the `Edit` menu. A copy of the selected text is placed on the Macintosh *Clipboard*, a temporary holding area. With the `Paste` option, this text can now be placed anywhere in the program. The text that was put on the clipboard will remain there until something else is cut or copied from the file. The `Cut` option works like `Copy` except that the selected text is removed from the program, so `Cut` is used for moving text.

The options of the `Search` menu locate text in a program. This is particularly useful when working with large programs.

The `Windows` menu allows you to open a window that might be closed such as the list window.

Now select `Quit` from the `File` menu. QuickBASIC asks if the program should be saved before proceeding. Press the `Yes` button. A save dialog box appears on the screen. Press the `Save` button, and QuickBASIC will ask if the existing program should be replaced with the updated version. Click the `Yes` button again; QuickBASIC

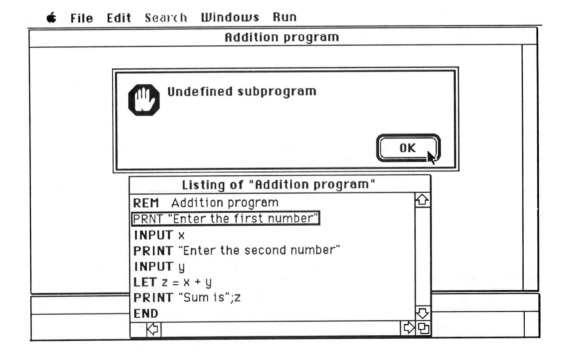

Figure 1.8 Error message and box around erroneous program line

saves the program and returns to the Desktop. It is wise to save a program often while it is being developed or modified; otherwise a considerable amount of work could be lost if there is a power failure, for example.

Notice that the program we just created now appears as an icon in the QuickBASIC window (see Figure 1.9). Clicking twice on this new icon will cause the Macintosh to enter QuickBASIC and run the program automatically.

To terminate a Macintosh session, eject any disks currently in the computer by selecting `Eject` from the `File` menu, and power down the computer.

In Chapter 2 we will introduce the fundamentals of programming in Microsoft Macintosh QuickBASIC.

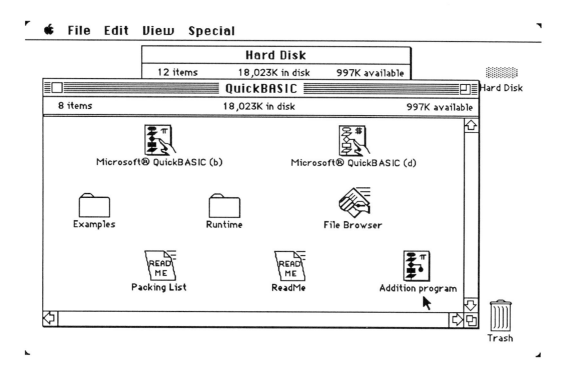

Figure 1.9 Macintosh desktop with Addition program icon in window

Concepts

Ada	button
ALU	central processing unit
ANSI	clipboard
ANSI minimal BASIC	COBOL
apple menu	command bar
arithmetic and logic unit	compiler
assembler	computer
assembly language	computer programmer
BASIC	computer programming
batch processing	control panel

`Copy`
CPU
cursor
data
dialog box
drag the mouse
`Edit` menu
`File` menu
FORTRAN
hardware
high-level languages
icon
input device
input-output device
input unit
list window
logical units
machine-dependent
machine-independent
machine language
Macintosh
Macintosh Desktop
main storage
menu
menu bar
mouse
mouse pointer
multiprogramming
multitasking

natural language of a computer
`Open`
output device
output unit
output window
Pascal
`Paste`
personal computer
primary storage
programming language
`Quit`
reserved words
Return key
`Save`
`Save As...`
`Search` menu
"simultaneous" operation
software
storage unit
stored program
structured programming
supercomputer
task
terminal
timesharing
translator program
window
`Windows` menu

Problems

1.1. Many of today's computers can perform one million additions in one second for a small fraction of a penny. A clerk can perform about one million additions in approximately one year of full-time labor. Why then, do you suppose, are clerks still employed to add numbers?

1.2. As computing costs continue to decrease dramatically over the next several years, "computing power" will become even more readily available. Explain how this trend might affect you in your career and your personal life.

1.3. Categorize each of the following items as either hardware or software:
  (a) CPU
  (b) FORTRAN compiler
  (c) ALU
  (d) COBOL compiler
  (e) input unit
  (f) a user-written payroll program

1.4. Why might you want to write a program in a machine-independent language instead of a machine-dependent language? Why might a machine-dependent language be more appropriate for writing certain types of programs?

1.5. Translator programs such as assemblers and compilers convert programs from one language (referred to as the *source* language) to another language (referred to as the *object* language). Determine which of the following statements are true and which are false:
  (a) A compiler translates high-level language programs into object language programs.
  (b) An assembler translates source language programs into machine language programs.
  (c) A compiler converts source language programs into object language programs.
  (d) High-level languages are generally machine-dependent.
  (e) A machine language program requires translation before the program can be run on a computer.

1.6. Of the many high-level languages in existence today, FORTRAN, COBOL, and BASIC are three of the most popular. Which language was designed specifically for teaching the elementary principles of computer programming on a timesharing computer system? Which language is most widely used for applications requiring complex mathematical calculations? Which language is particularly useful in commercial applications such as payroll, accounts receivable, and inventory control?

1.7. Fill in the blanks in each of the following statements:
  (a) Devices from which users access timesharing computer systems are normally called _____.
  (b) A computer program that converts assembly language programs to machine language programs is called _____.
  (c) Which logical unit of the computer receives information from outside the computer for use by the computer _____.
  (d) The process of instructing the computer to solve specific problems is called _____.
  (e) What type of computer language uses English-like abbreviations for machine language instructions? _____.
  (f) What are the five logical units of the computer? _____.
  (g) Which logical unit of the computer sends information which has already been processed by the computer to various devices so that the information may be used outside the computer? _____.
  (h) The general name for a program that converts programs written in a certain computer language into machine language is _____.
  (i) Which logical unit of the computer retains information? _____.
  (j) Which logical unit of the computer performs calculations? _____.
  (k) Which logical unit of the computer makes logical decisions? _____.
  (l) The commonly used abbreviation for the computer's control unit is _____.
  (m) The level of computer language most convenient to the programmer for writing programs quickly and easily is _____.
  (n) In general, computer use is (increasing/decreasing). _____.
  (o) The most common business-oriented language in wide use today is _____.
  (p) The only language that a computer can directly understand is called that computer's _____.
  (q) Which logical unit of the computer coordinates the activities of all the other logical units? _____.

1.8. State whether each of the following is true or false. Explain your answers.
  (a) Machine languages are generally machine-dependent. _____.
  (b) Timesharing truly runs several users simultaneously on a computer. _____.
  (c) Like other high-level languages, BASIC is generally considered to be machine-independent. _____.

1.9. Fill in the blanks in each of the following statements.
  (a) When the Macintosh is first turned on and a disk is inserted, the disk _____ appears in the upper-right corner of the screen.
  (b) A menu appears in the _____.
  (c) When the BASIC disk icon is clicked twice with the mouse, a _____ appears.

    (d) The _____ is used to type commands that will display their output immediately in the output window.

    (e) All BASIC programs are typed in the _____ window.

1.10. Explain how to accomplish each of the following tasks related to the Macintosh and to Microsoft Macintosh BASIC.

    (a) Open a disk. Give two methods.

    (b) Close a window.

    (c) Make a security copy of a disk.

    (d) Make a window active.

    (e) Save a new version of an existing file under the same name.

    (f) Save a file under a new name while preserving the original copy.

    (g) While using the Save dialog box, tell the Macintosh to make a different disk active.

    (h) While using the Save dialog box, tell the Macintosh to eject a disk so that a different disk may be inserted.

    (i) Using the File menu, indicate that a new program is to be entered.

    (j) Using the File menu, indicate that an existing file is to be opened.

    (k) Using the File menu, close the active window.

    (l) Print the current program.

    (m) Transfer from having one program active to having another program active.

    (n) Return from working with the current active program to the Macintosh Desktop.

    (o) Run a program that has just been entered.

    (p) Terminate execution of a running program.

    (q) Restart a program from the statement where the program was stopped.

    (r) Delete text from a BASIC program. Give two methods.

    (s) Insert text in a BASIC program.

    (t) Move text from one section of a BASIC program to another.

    (u) Copy text from one section of a BASIC program to another.

    (v) Place text on the clipboard.

    (w) Use a menu to make a window active.

    (x) Use a menu to locate text in a program.

    (y) Place text from the clipboard into a designated location in a BASIC program.

Chapter 2
Introduction to BASIC
Programming

2.1 Introduction

In this chapter we introduce BASIC programming and present examples that rapidly familiarize the reader with many important features of BASIC. An *unstructured* approach is used here—BASIC is presented as it was originally intended to be used by its creators. But BASIC has evolved into a far more powerful language that allows and facilitates a *structured* and disciplined approach to program design. In Chapter 3 we present an introduction to *structured programming* in BASIC. We then use the structured approach throughout the remainder of the text.

2.2 A Simple BASIC Program

BASIC is a straightforward computer programming language and is easy to learn. Students can usually begin writing simple but complete programs after a single introductory lesson. The following example program illustrates just how simple the language is.

Example 2.1 An addition program
The BASIC program in Figure 2.1 obtains two values typed by a user at the keyboard of the Macintosh, adds the two values together, and displays the result on the Macintosh screen.

```
REM    Addition program
PRINT "Enter first number"
INPUT x
PRINT "Enter second number"
INPUT y
LET z = x + y
PRINT "Sum is"; z
END
```

Figure 2.1 Addition program

19

Even though this program is simple, it illustrates many important features of the BASIC language:

1. The program contains eight BASIC *statements*.
2. Each statement normally begins with a BASIC command (REM, PRINT, INPUT, PRINT, INPUT, LET, PRINT, END).
3. The remainder of each BASIC statement contains information relevant to the particular BASIC command used in that statement.

Now let us consider each statement of the program in detail:

```
REM Addition program
```

The REM command indicates that this statement contains a *remark*. Remarks are to *document* a program and improve its readability. Remarks do not cause the computer to perform any action when the program is run. The remark Addition program in this statement describes the purpose of the program. Remarks are especially useful when other people must understand your program. A programmer may use many REM statements in a large program to document the purposes of the different sections of the program.

```
PRINT "Enter first number"
```

This PRINT command instructs the computer to print (actually to display) the words Enter first number on the Macintosh's screen. This instruction tells the user to take a specific action, namely, to enter a number. (Note: To make the message print on the computer's printer rather than on the screen, the user should type LPRINT rather than PRINT.)

```
INPUT x
```

This INPUT command instructs the computer to obtain a value for x from the user. When the computer executes this statement, the INPUT command prints a question mark (?) on the screen. The computer then waits for the user to enter a value for x. The user responds by typing a number and then pressing the *Return key*. This sends the number to the computer. The computer then assigns this number to the variable x. Any subsequent references to x in the program will use this same number. The INPUT command facilitates the interaction between the user and the computer. Because this interaction resembles a dialogue, it is often called *conversational computing*. It is also commonly called *interactive computing*.

```
PRINT "Enter second number"
```

This PRINT command instructs the computer to print the words Enter second number on the screen.

`INPUT` y

This *INPUT* command instructs the computer to obtain a value for y from the user.

`LET` z = x + y

This *LET* command instructs the computer to calculate the sum of x and y and assign the result to z.

`PRINT "Sum is"; z`

This *PRINT* command instructs the computer to print the message Sum is followed by the numerical value of z on the screen.

`END`

The *END* command informs the computer that the end of the program has been reached. The **END** statement may be located anywhere in a program to indicate that the program is to terminate. Placing an **END** statement at the end of a program is optional.

No discussion of a BASIC program is complete without consideration of how the computer actually *executes* (or *runs* or *performs*) the program. When our addition program is executed, we obtain the screen output shown in Figure 2.2.

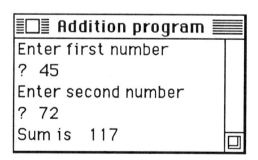

Figure 2.2 Addition program output

Notice that the *semicolon* (;) *separator* or *delimiter* used in the last **PRINT** statement causes the identifying message Sum is and the actual value of z to be printed adjacent to one another. Several other print delimiters exist that allow the programmer to format printed outputs in other useful ways. These will be discussed later in the text.

2.3 Some Elements of BASIC

Now that we have examined a complete BASIC program in detail, consider the following:

1. The computer generally performs BASIC programs one statement at a time in order beginning with the first statement in the program. (Exceptions to this will be discussed later.)
2. **REM** statements are ignored by the computer when it runs a program. (The apostrophe (') may also be used to insert remarks.)
3. To instruct the Macintosh to print words or phrases on the screen, enclose the information to be printed in *quotation marks*. Information contained within quotation marks is called a *literal* because it is interpreted literally—exactly as it appears between the quotes. Literals are also called *messages* or *strings*.
4. To instruct the computer to print the value of a variable, do not enclose the variable name in quotes. Notice the differences between the following BASIC statements (assume z = 117):

BASIC statement	Printed output
`PRINT z`	117
`PRINT "z"`	z
`PRINT "z =";z`	z = 117

5. The **LET** command is used to perform a calculation and to assign the result to a *variable name* (such as x, y, or z). (Actually, the word **LET** is optional and may be omitted. Thus **LET** a = b + 5 may be written as a = b + 5.)
6. The **INPUT** command displays a question mark (?) on the screen, and then waits for the user to respond. We have preceded the **INPUT** commands by **PRINT** commands that describe precisely what information should be entered by the user in response to the question mark typed by the **INPUT**. In fact, the **PRINT** and the **INPUT** may be combined into a single statement as follows:

```
INPUT "Enter first number"; x
```

This version of **INPUT** first prints the literal "Enter first number" and then prints a question mark and accepts a value for x from the user. The question mark may be suppressed by replacing the semicolon with a comma.

7. In Macintosh BASIC, variable names for numeric variables must begin with a letter and may be as long as 40 characters. Variable names may contain letters, digits, and periods; they may not contain spaces. Because variable names can be so long, the BASIC programmer is encouraged to choose meaningful variable names such as total (instead of simply t), and largestearnings (instead of simply l). Some programmers use periods to separate the words in multiword

variable names. BASIC does not distinguish between uppercase and lowercase letters in variable names, so NUMBER, Number, number, and nUmBeR are all equivalent. Some valid variable names for numeric variables are x, total, Count, Week1, and summer.months. Some invalid variable names for numeric variables are 7, 66screwdrivers, and THISVARIABLENAMEISMUCHTOOLONGTO-BEVALIDINBASIC.

8. When an equal sign (=) is used in a **LET** statement, it has a different meaning than in algebra; it denotes *replacement*. The BASIC statement

      LET z = x + y

should be read "**LET** the value of z (regardless of what it currently is) *be replaced by* the sum of the values of x and y."

9. Statements such as

      LET c = c + 1

which are algebraically inconsistent are perfectly reasonable in BASIC. This statement says "**LET** the value of c be replaced by the value of c plus 1," or more simply "add 1 to c."

2.4 Storage Concepts

Variable names such as x, y, and z used in BASIC programs actually correspond to *locations* in the computer's primary storage. Every location in the computer's storage has a *name* and a *value*.

In the addition program of Figure 2.1, when the statement

      INPUT x

is performed, the *value* typed by the user is placed into a *location* to which the computer has assigned the *name* x. Suppose the user types the number 45 in response to the **INPUT** x. Then the computer will place the value 45 into location x, and the storage will appear as shown in Figure 2.3.

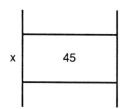

Figure 2.3 A storage location showing name and value

Whenever a new value is placed into a storage location, it overrides the previous value in that location. Since this previous information is no longer available for use by the computer, the process of reading information into a storage location is called *destructive readin.*

Returning to our addition program again, when the statement

INPUT y

is performed, suppose the user types the value 72. The machine will then place the value 72 into location y (by the process of destructive readin), and the storage will appear as shown in Figure 2.4.

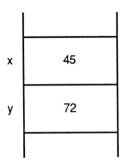

Figure 2.4 Storage locations after INPUT of variables

Once the program has obtained values for x and y, it adds the values together and places the result into variable z. The statement

LET z = x + y

which performs the addition also involves destructive readin. This occurs when the calculated sum of x and y is placed into location z (without regard to what value may already be in z). After z is calculated, the storage appears as shown in Figure 2.5.

Note that the values of x and y appear exactly as they did before they were used in the calculation of z. These values were used by the Macintosh which performed the calculation without destroying the values of x and y. Thus when a value is read out of a storage location, the process is referred to as *nondestructive readout.*

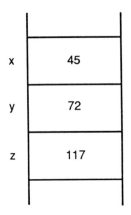

Figure 2.5 Storage locations after a calculation

2.5 Arithmetic In BASIC

Most BASIC programs perform arithmetic calculations. Figure 2.6 summarizes the BASIC *arithmetic operators*. Note that multiplication and exponentiation require special symbols not used in ordinary algebraic notation. The asterisk (*) indicates multiplication, and the caret (^) denotes exponentiation.

Operation	BASIC operator	Sample algebraic expression	Sample BASIC expression
Addition	+	$f + 7$	f + 7
Subtraction	−	$p - c$	p − c
Multiplication	*	bm	b * m
Division	/	x / y	x / y
Exponentiation	^	a^2	a ^ 2

Figure 2.6 Basic arithmetic operators

Arithmetic expressions in BASIC must be written in *straight-line form* to facilitate entering programs into the computer. Thus, expressions such as "a divided by b" and "r squared" must be written as a/b and r ^ 2, respectively, so that all constants, variables, and operators appear in a straight line.

Parentheses are used in BASIC expressions in much the same manner as in algebraic expressions. To multiply a times the quantity b + c we write:

$$a \; * \; (b \; + \; c)$$

BASIC evaluates arithmetic expressions in a precise sequence determined by the following *rules of operator precedence,* which are generally the same as those followed in algebra:

1. Expressions or portions of expressions contained within pairs of parentheses are evaluated first. Thus, *parentheses may be used to force the order of evaluation to occur in any sequence desired by the programmer.* Parentheses are said to be at the "highest level of precedence." In cases of embedded (or *nested*) parentheses, the innermost pairs are evaluated first.
2. Exponentiation operations are evaluated next. If an expression contains several exponentiation operations, evaluation proceeds from left to right.
3. Multiplication and division operations are evaluated next. If an expression contains several multiplication and division operations, evaluation proceeds from left to right. Multiplication and division are said to be on the same level of precedence.

4. Addition and subtraction operations are evaluated last. If an expression contains several addition and subtraction operations, evaluation proceeds from left to right. Addition and subtraction are also said to be on the same level of precedence.

Figure 2.7 summarizes these rules of operator precedence.

Operator(s)	Operation(s)	Order of evaluation or precedence
()	Parentheses	Evaluated first
^	Exponentiation	Evaluated second. (If several operators, they are evaluated left to right.)
* or /	Multiplication Division	Evaluated third. (If several operators, they are evaluated left to right.)
+ or -	Addition Subtraction	Evaluated last. (If several operators, they are evaluated left to right.)

Figure 2.7 Precedence of arithmetic operators

Now let us consider several expressions in light of the rules of operator precedence.

Example 2.2 Writing arithmetic expressions in BASIC
(a)   Straight-line depreciation:

$$d = \frac{c - s}{l} \qquad \begin{matrix} c & = \text{cost of asset} \\ s & = \text{salvage value} \\ l & = \text{life} \end{matrix}$$

BASIC: `depreciation = (cost - salvage) / life`

Note that the parentheses are required because division has a higher precedence than subtraction. The entire quantity (`cost - salvage`) is to be divided by `life`. If the parentheses are erroneously omitted, we obtain `cost - salvage / life`, which evaluates incorrectly as

$$\text{cost} - \frac{\text{salvage}}{\text{life}}$$

(b)   Arithmetic mean of five terms:

$$m = \frac{a + b + c + d + e}{5}$$

BASIC: `m = (a + b + c + d + e) / 5`

Again, the parentheses are required so that the sum of all five terms is divided by 5. Without the parentheses only the e would be divided by 5.

(c)   Equation of a straight line:

$$y = mx + b$$

BASIC: `y = m * x + b`

No parentheses are required. The multiplication is evaluated first, because multiplication has a higher precedence than addition.

(d)   Second-degree polynomial:

$$y = ax^2 + bx + c$$

BASIC: `Y = a * x ^ 2 + b * x + c`
         2   1   4   3   5

The outlined numbers indicate the order in which BASIC evaluates the operators. The exponentiation, `x ^ 2`, is performed first. This leaves two multiplications and two additions. Since multiplication has a higher level of precedence than addition, the multiplications are performed first in left-to-right order. Finally, two additions remain. These are also performed left to right.

(e)   One root of a quadratic equation:

$$x = \frac{-b + \sqrt{b^2 - 4ac}}{2a}$$

BASIC: `x = (-b + (b ^ 2 - 4 * a * c) ^.5)) / (2 * a)`

This complex example combines all the BASIC arithmetic operators. Note that the parenthesized quantity (b ^ 2 - 4 * a * c) is contained within an outer set of parentheses. This is an example of nested parentheses. Remember that when nested parentheses occur in an arithmetic expression, BASIC evaluates the quantity within the innermost set of parentheses first. It is important to note that the quantity (2 * a) must be parenthesized. Otherwise, the entire quantity to the left of the "/" would be divided by 2, and the result would be multiplied by a (in the numerator), which would yield an erroneous result.

Not all expressions with several pairs of parentheses contain nested parentheses. The expression

```
a * (b + c) + c * (d + e)
```

does not contain nested parentheses. Instead, the parentheses are said to be on the same level. In this situation, BASIC evaluates the parenthesized expressions from left to right.

To develop a better understanding of the rules of operator precedence, let us see how BASIC evaluates a second-degree polynomial.

Example 2.3 Detailed BASIC evaluation of an arithmetic expression
Consider the second-degree polynomial

```
y = a * x ^ 2 + b * x + c
        2   1     4     3   5
```

The outlined numbers indicate the order in which BASIC performs the operations. Suppose $a = 2$, $b = 3$, $c = 7$, and $x = 5$. The following illustrates how BASIC evaluates this expression.

Step 1. y = 2 * 5 ^ 2 + 3 * 5 + 7
                    5 ^ 2 = 25   (Exponentiation is performed first)

Step 2. y = 2 * 25 + 3 * 5 + 7
                    2 * 25 = 50   (Leftmost multiplication is next)

Step 3. y = 50 + 3 * 5 + 7
                    3 * 5 = 15   (Multiplication before addition)

Step 4. y = 50 + 15 + 7
                    50 + 15 = 65   (Leftmost addition)

Step 5. y = 65 + 7
                    65 + 7 = 72   (Last remaining operation)

2.6 Looping

If programmers had to write separate instructions for each of the operations to be performed in a program, it would probably be more efficient to solve problems manually than to use a computer. In fact, most programs are designed to reuse certain instructions many times. The process of reusing statements repeatedly is called *looping*. The program of Figure 2.8 illustrates a BASIC program that utilizes looping to produce an interesting printout.

Example 2.4 Printing tabular information by looping

```
REM    Program that prints a table of values
PRINT "X", "X-Squared", "X-Cubed"
LET x = 1
Calculating:
   PRINT x, x^2, x^3
   IF x = 10 THEN END
   LET x = x + 1
   GOTO Calculating
```

Figure 2.8 Printing tabular information by looping

When this program is run, it produces the output shown in Figure 2.9.

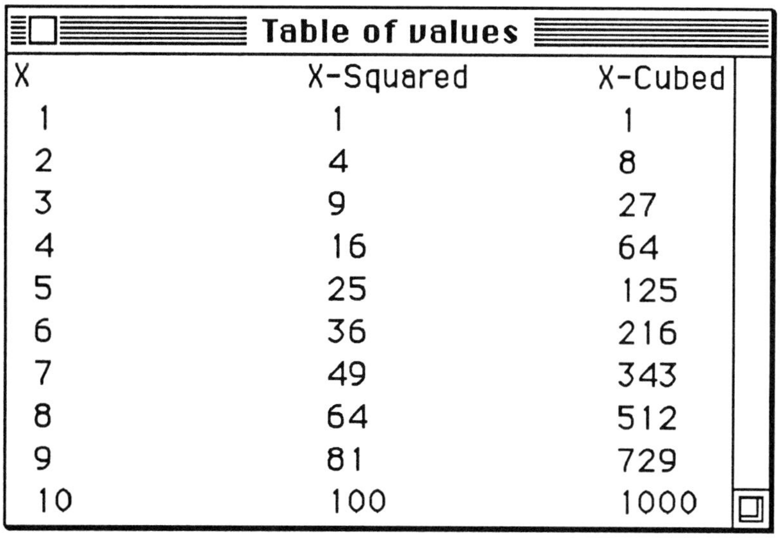

X	X-Squared	X-Cubed
1	1	1
2	4	8
3	9	27
4	16	64
5	25	125
6	36	216
7	49	343
8	64	512
9	81	729
10	100	1000

Table of values

Figure 2.9 Tabular information

Discussion: The **REM** statement

```
REM    Program that prints a table of values
```

documents the purpose of the program and is ignored by the computer when the program is run.

```
PRINT "X", "X-Squared", "X-Cubed"
```

This **PRINT** statement prints the *title* line of the table (i.e., the *headings* of the columns). The commas (,) separating the three literals cause the literals to print in a column format. BASIC divides each output line into columns. Thus the first literal, "X", prints in column 1. The second literal, "X-Squared", prints in column 2. The third literal, "X-Cubed", prints in column 3.

```
LET x = 1
```

This **LET** statement sets x to its *initial value* of 1. In this example x begins at 1 and is repeatedly incremented by 1 until 10 lines of the table have been printed. BASIC automatically initializes all numeric variables to zero. It is nevertheless considered a good programming practice to specify initial values for all variables even if they are zero, especially because most other languages that the programmer is likely to use do not initialize variables automatically.

```
PRINT x, x ^ 2, x ^ 3
```

This **PRINT** statement prints a line of the table depending upon the current value of x. Note once again that the commas cause column skips or column tabs. Note, too, that **PRINT** statements can contain arithmetic expressions that are evaluated before printing occurs. When this statement is performed, the computer prints the current value of x, squares x and prints the result, and cubes x and prints the result. The three values are printed on the same line in column format because of the commas.

```
IF x = 10 THEN END
```

The **IF** command is the primary *decision-making* command in BASIC. This **IF** command tests to see if the variable x is equal to 10. If it is, then all lines of the table have been printed, and the remainder of the command is performed causing the computer to **END** the program. If x is not equal to 10, then the computer ignores the remainder of the **IF** statement, and proceeds to perform the next statement. The **IF** command is discussed in detail in the next section.

```
LET x = x + 1
```

If the **IF** statement finds that the value of x has not reached 10, then the **LET** statement is performed. This **LET** statement adds 1 to x in preparation for printing the next line of the table. Note that the variable x is being used to count the number of lines printed. A variable that is used to tally the number of times an event has occurred is called a *counter*. Most large computer programs contain many counters.

```
GOTO Calculating
```

This **GOTO** statement instructs the computer to go back to the program *label* Calculating and continue processing from that point. Thus, instead of writing ten separate **PRINT** statements to print the individual lines of the table, we go back and reuse the **PRINT** at Calculating repeatedly until the **IF** statement determines that the entire table has been printed. The program is said to contain a *loop* beginning with the label Calculating and ending with the **GOTO** statement. To illustrate the power of looping, consider that the preceding program could easily be modified to print a table of 1000 lines without adding additional statements. It is merely necessary to rewrite the **IF** statement as follows:

```
IF x = 1000 THEN END
```

2.7 Transfers Of Control

The previous section introduced several BASIC commands that will now be discussed more thoroughly. With both the **GOTO** statement and the **IF** statement, the computer may be instructed to perform a statement other than the next statement in sequence. The process of altering the normal sequence in which statements are performed is called *transfer of control*.

The **IF** statement causes a transfer of control only when a certain *condition* is met. In Figure 2.8, the **IF** statement transfers control (in this case, ends the program) only when the condition x = 10 is true. When x is not equal to 10, the computer proceeds to the **LET** statement. Thus the **IF** statement may be said to cause a *conditional transfer of control*.

The **GOTO** statement always transfers control (without first determining if any conditions are met). Thus the **GOTO** statement is said to cause an *unconditional transfer of control*. The **GOTO** statement in Figure 2.8 always transfers control to the label Calculating.

Standard algebraic relational operator	BASIC relational operator	Example of BASIC condition	Meaning of BASIC condition
=	=	A = B	A is equal to B
≠	<>	A <> B	A is not equal to B
>	>	A > B	A is greater than B
<	<	A < B	A is less than B
≥	>=	A >= B	A is greater than or equal to B
≤	<=	A <= B	A is less than or equal to B

Figure 2.10 BASIC relational operators

Conditions in **IF** statements are formed by using the *relational operators,* which are summarized in Figure 2.10. The result of using these operators is always simply the observation of "true" or "false" with the appropriate conditional transfer or not.

Example 2.5 Using relational operators

For each of the following assume a = 3 and b = 2. State whether the condition is true or false. Which statement will be performed immediately after the **IF** statement?

(a)   **IF** a = b **GOTO** Beginloop
        PRINT "a not equal to b"

Answer. Since 3 is not equal to 2, the condition is false, and therefore a conditional transfer of control does not occur. The next statement performed after the **IF** is the **PRINT** statement.

(b)   **IF** a > b **GOTO** Processtotals
        PRINT z ^ 2

Answer. Since 3 is indeed greater than 2, the condition is true and therefore a conditional transfer of control to Processtotals occurs.

(c)   **IF** a <= b **GOTO** Summarizeresults
        GOTO Continueloop

Answer. Since 3 is not less than or equal to 2, no transfer of control occurs in the **IF** statement. The **GOTO** statement is performed next because the condition is false, and control is transferred to the label Continueloop.

Concepts

arithmetic operators
asterisk (*)
BASIC commands
caret (^)
column format
comma (,) separator
condition
conditional transfer of control
conversational computing
counter
destructive readin
END
equal sign (=)
GOTO
heading
highest level of precedence
IF

initial value
INPUT
interactive computing
left-to-right evaluation
LET
literal
loop
message
nested parentheses
nondestructive readout
numeric variable
parentheses ()
PRINT
question mark (?)
relational operators
  = "is equal to"
  <> "is not equal to"

> "is greater than"
< "is less than"
>= "is greater than or equal to"
<= "is less than or equal to"
REM
replacement
Return key
rules of operator precedence
semicolon (;) separator
statement
storage location
storage location name

storage location value
straight-line form
string
structured programming
THEN
title
transfer of control
unconditional transfer of control
variable name
variable
value

PROBLEMS

2.1. Fill in the blanks in each of the following:
   (a) Each BASIC statement normally begins with a _____.
   (b) The BASIC statement that is used to document a program and improve its readability is
   _____.
   (c) The BASIC statement that is used to display messages on the Macintosh screen is _____.
   (d) The BASIC statement that causes an unconditional transfer of control is _____.
   (e) The BASIC statement _____ indicates that a program should terminate.
   (f) The BASIC command that is used to perform most calculations is _____.
   (g) The BASIC command that is used to make decisions is _____.
   (h) The BASIC command that is used to obtain a value from the Macintosh keyboard is
   _____.
   (i) Which key on the keyboard must be pressed in order to enter each BASIC statement into the
   computer? _____.
   (j) The BASIC command that sometimes causes a conditional transfer of control is _____.

   Note: In the above, the words "statement" and "command" are used somewhat
   interchangeably. Of course, we know that it is more proper to state that

   LET

   is a BASIC command, whereas

   LET a = b + 2

   is a BASIC statement.

2.2. Write a single BASIC statement that accomplishes each of the following:
   (a) Write a single BASIC statement that prints the message "Enter two numbers".
   (b) Write a single BASIC statement that assigns the sum of variables b and c to variable a.
   (c) Write a single BASIC statement that causes a conditional transfer of control to statement
   Calculateratio if the value of the numeric variable t is greater than or equal to 4.237.
   (d) Write a single BASIC statement which states that the program in the remaining statements
   performs a sample payroll calculation (i.e., use a statement that helps to document a
   program).
   (e) Write a single BASIC statement that obtains two numerical values from the Macintosh
   keyboard.

2.3. State which of the following are true and which are false. For those that are false, state why.
  (a) The computer sometimes evaluates BASIC expressions from right to left.
  (b) The following are all valid names for numeric variables in BASIC: a, b, c, z, z2, t5, j7.
  (c) The BASIC statement **PRINT "LET** a = 5**"** is a typical example of an assignment statement.
  (d) The BASIC statement **IF** a = b + 6 **GOTO** Nextitem always causes a transfer of control if a has a value greater than b.
  (e) The following two statements are equivalent:

```
LET a = b ^ .5
LET a = b ^ 1/2
```

  (f) The computer always performs BASIC statements one after the other sequentially in order as written.
  (g) A valid BASIC expression containing no parentheses is evaluated from left to right.
  (h) The following are all invalid names for numeric variables in BASIC:

```
a46, b938, 3g, 87, 67h2, h222, h22, 2h.
```

  (i) In BASIC arithmetic expressions, exponentiation is always performed before subtraction.
  (j) If a BASIC statement contains **GOTO**, then the next statement is never performed immediately after the **GOTO** statement.

2.4. Fill in the blanks in each of the following:
  (a) The last executed statement in every BASIC program should normally be _____.
  (b) The process of going back and reusing statements in a BASIC program repeatedly is called _____.
  (c) The exponentiation operator is _____.
  (d) What arithmetic operation is on the same level of precedence as multiplication? _____.
  (e) What arithmetic operations are on a lower level of precedence than exponentiation? _____.
  (f) When parentheses are nested, which set of parentheses is evaluated first in an arithmetic expression? _____.
  (g) A location in the computer's storage that may contain different values at various times throughout the execution of a program is called a _____.
  (h) Which print spacing character causes items to print in "column format?" _____.
  (i) What is the meaning of the symbol "=" when used in a **LET** statement? _____.
  (j) What is the meaning of the symbol "=" when used in an **IF** statement? _____.

2.5. What, if anything, prints when each of the following BASIC statements is performed? If nothing prints, then answer "nothing." Assume x = 2 and y = 3.
  (a) **PRINT** x
  (b) **PRINT** x + x
  (c) **PRINT** "x="
  (d) **PRINT** "x="; x
  (e) **PRINT** x + y; "="; y + x
  (f) **LET** z = x + y
  (g) **INPUT** x, y
  (h) **IF** x = y **GOTO** Sameitems
  (i) **REM PRINT** "x + y": "="; x + y
  (j) **PRINT**

2.6. Which, if any, of the following BASIC statements contain variables involved in destructive readin?
  (a) **PRINT "Destructive readin"**
  (b) **PRINT "LET** a = 5**"**
  (c) **INPUT** b, c, d, e, f
  (d) **LET** p = i + j + k + 7
  (e) **IF** a = 7 **GOTO** Endofweek

2.7. Given the equation

$$y = ax3 + 7$$

which of the following, if any, are correct BASIC statements for this equation?
(a) `LET y = a * x ^ 3 + 7`
(b) `LET y = a * x * x * x + 7`
(c) `LET y = (a) * (x) ^ 3 + (7)`
(d) `LET y = (((a) * (x) ^ (3)) + (7))`
(e) `LET y = (((a) * (x) ^ (3)) + (7)))`

2.8. Show the value of x after each of the following BASIC statements is performed.
(a) `LET x = 7 + 3 * 6 / 2 - 1`
(b) `LET x = 2 ^ 2 * 2 + 2 - 2 / 2`
(c) `LET x = (2 + 2 * 2 ^ 2) / (2 * 2 - 2 / 2)`
(d) `LET x = (3 * 9 * (3 + (9 * 3/ (3))))`

2.9. Write a BASIC program that asks the user to enter two numbers, obtains the two numbers from the user, and prints the product of the two numbers.

2.10. Write a BASIC program that prints the numbers 1 to 10. Do not use a loop.

2.11. Write a BASIC program that utilizes looping to print the numbers from 1 to 10.

2.12. Write a BASIC program that asks the user to enter two numbers, obtains the two numbers from the user, and then prints the larger of the two numbers. If the two numbers are equal, then print the message "These numbers are the same."

2.13. Write a BASIC program that utilizes looping to print the following table of values:

N	10 * N	100 * N	1000 * N	10000 * N
1	10	100	1000	10000
2	20	200	2000	20000
3	30	300	3000	30000
4	40	400	4000	40000
5	50	500	5000	50000
6	60	600	6000	60000
7	70	700	7000	70000
8	80	800	8000	80000
9	90	900	9000	90000
10	100	1000	10000	100000

2.14. Write a BASIC program that utilizes looping to produce the following table of values:

A	A + 2	A + 4	A + 6
3	5	7	9
6	8	10	12
9	11	13	15
12	14	16	18
15	17	19	21

2.15. Write a BASIC program that **INPUT**s five numbers from a user at a Macintosh, and then prints the sum and the average of these numbers. Write this program using several different methods, as follows:

(a) Use five separate **INPUT** statements and no loop.
(b) Use a single **INPUT** statement of the form **INPUT** x and use a loop.
(c) Use a single **INPUT** statement and no loop.

2.16. The process of finding the largest number in a group of numbers is used frequently in computer applications. For example, a program that determines the winner of a sales contest would **INPUT** the number of units sold by each salesperson. The salesperson who sells the most units wins the contest. Write a BASIC program that **INPUT**s a series of 10 numbers, and determines and prints the largest of the numbers. *Hint:* Your program should use three variables as follows:

counter: A counter to count to 10 (i.e., to keep track of how many numbers have been **INPUT**, and to determine when all 10 numbers have been processed).
number: The current number **INPUT** to the program.
largest: The largest number found so far.

Using these variables, your program should then operate as follows:

Step 1: **INPUT** the first number directly into the variable largest. (*Note:* This makes sense, because after you have looked at only the first number, it is perfectly reasonable to say that this is the "largest number found so far.")
Step 2: Set counter to 2 (to indicate that you are now going to look at the second number).
Step 3: **INPUT** a number into the variable number.
Step 4: Compare number to largest to determine if number is larger than largest. If it is not, then go to *Step 6*.
Step 5: Replace the value of largest with the value of number (i.e., use the BASIC statement **LET** largest = number).
Step 6: If counter is now 10 (i.e., all 10 numbers have been processed) go to *Step 9*.
Step 7: Add one to counter.
Step 8: Go back to *Step 3*.
Step 9: At this point, the value in largest is the largest of the 10 numbers. Print this value, preceded by the literal "Largest is".
Step 10: End of program.

The preceding procedure uses an unstructured approach to finding the largest of a series of numbers. In Chapter 3 we discuss structured programming, and we present a structured version of this procedure.

Chapter 3
Structured Program Development

3.1 Introduction

Before writing a BASIC program to solve a particular problem, it is essential to have a thorough understanding of the problem, and a carefully planned approach to solving the problem. This chapter discusses several techniques that facilitate the development of structured computer programs.

3.2 Algorithms

The solution to any computing problem involves performing a series of *steps* (or operations) in a specific *order*. A *procedure* for solving a problem in terms of

1. the *steps* to be executed
2. the *order* in which these steps should be executed

is called an *algorithm*. The following example demonstrates that correctly specifying the order in which the steps are to be executed is important.

Example 3.1 The rise and shine algorithm

Consider the algorithm followed by one junior executive for getting out of bed and going to work in the morning:

Turn off alarm clock.
Get out of bed.
Take off pajamas.
Brush teeth.
Take a shave.
Take a shower.
Put on $500 suit.
Eat breakfast.
Carpool to work.

This routine gets the executive to work well prepared to make critical decisions. Suppose, however, that the same steps are performed in a slightly different order:

Turn off alarm clock.
Get out of bed.
Take off pajamas.
Brush teeth.
Take a shave.
Put on $500 suit.
Take a shower.
Eat breakfast.
Carpool to work.

In this case, our junior executive will show up for work in a soaking wet business suit! Specifying the order in which statements are to be executed in a computer program is called *program control*. In this and the next chapter, we investigate the program control capabilities of BASIC.

3.3 Pseudocode

Pseudocode is an artificial and informal language that helps programmers develop algorithms. The pseudocode we present here is particularly useful for developing algorithms that will be converted to BASIC programs. Pseudocode is similar to everyday English; it is a convenient and user-friendly language.

Pseudocode programs are not actually run on computers. Rather, they merely help the programmer to "think out" a program before attempting to write it in a programming language such as BASIC. In this chapter, we present a discussion of pseudocode, and give several examples of how pseudocode may be used effectively in developing structured BASIC programs.

Pseudocode consists purely of characters, and therefore programmers may type pseudocode programs into the computer, edit them, and save them. The computer can display or print a fresh copy of a pseudocode program for us at any time. If a small number of changes are made, we need only type those changes; the computer will then retype the complete pseudocode program.

3.4 Control Structures

Normally, statements in a BASIC program are executed one after the other in the order in which they are written. Both the GOTO and the IF/THEN statements enable the programmer to specify that the next statement to be executed may be other than the next statement in sequence. This is called *transfer of control*.

During the 1960s, it became clear that the indiscriminate use of transfers of control was the root of a great deal of difficulty experienced by software development groups. The finger of blame was pointed to the GOTO, and the notion of structured programming became almost synonymous with "GOTO elimination."

The research of Bohm and Jacopini[1] had demonstrated that programs could indeed be written without any GOTO statements. The challenge of the era became for programmers to shift their styles to "GOTO-less programming." It was not until well into the 1970s that the programming profession at large started taking structured programming seriously. The results have been impressive as software development groups have reported reduced development times, more frequent on-time delivery of systems, and more frequent within-budget completion of software projects. The key to these successes is simply that programs produced with structured techniques are clearer, easier to debug and modify, and more likely to be bug-free in the first place.

Bohm and Jacopini's work demonstrated that all programs could be written in terms of only three *control structures*, namely *sequence*, *selection*, and *repetition*. The *sequence structure* is essentially built into BASIC. Unless directed otherwise, the computer automatically performs BASIC statements one after the other in the order in which they are written.

3.5 The Selection Structure: IF/THEN

The *selection structure* is used to choose from alternative courses of action. For example, suppose the passing grade on an exam is 60. The pseudocode statement

```
IF student's grade is greater than 59 THEN print "passed"
```

determines if the condition (see Section 2.7) "student's grade is greater than 59" is true or false. If the condition is true, then "passed" is printed, and the next pseudocode statement in order is performed. If the condition is false, the printing is ignored, and the next pseudocode statement in order is performed. Notice that the keywords of the control structure (in this case IF and THEN) are capitalized. This helps improve the readability of the algorithm, but such capitalization is optional. This statement may be written on more than one line as follows:

```
IF student's grade is greater than 59 THEN
   print "passed"
END IF
```

Whenever the IF statement is written on several lines, the END IF is used to eliminate any confusion about where the statement ends, especially if several statements are to be performed when the condition is true. Note that the second line is indented. Indentation

---

[1] C. Bohm and G. Jacopini, "Flow Diagrams, Turing Machines, and Languages with Only Two Formation Rules," *Communications of the ACM*, Vol. 9, No. 5 (May 1966), pp. 336-371.

can greatly improve the readability of a program. Such indentation is optional, but it is highly recommended as it helps emphasize the inherent structure of structured programs.
The preceding single-line IF/THEN statement may be written in BASIC as

```
IF grade > 59 THEN PRINT "passed"
```

The multiple-line version may be written in BASIC as

```
IF grade > 59 THEN
   PRINT "passed"
END IF
```

Notice that the BASIC statements correspond closely to the pseudocode statements. This is one of the properties of pseudocode that makes it such a useful program development tool. To keep the pseudocode informal, we will adopt the convention that commands such as PRINT which are normally capitalized in BASIC programs will not be capitalized in pseudocode.

3.6 The Selection Structure: IF/THEN/ELSE

The IF/THEN selection structure performs an indicated action only when the condition is true. The IF/THEN/ELSE allows the programmer to specify separate actions to be performed when the condition is true and when the condition is false. For example, the pseudocode statement

```
IF student's grade is greater than 59 THEN print "passed" ELSE print "failed"
```

will print "passed" if the student's grade is greater than 59, and will print "failed" if the student's grade is not greater than 59. In either case, after printing occurs, the next pseudocode statement in sequence is performed. The preceding pseudocode statement may be written in multiline format as follows:

```
IF student's grade is greater than 59
   THEN print "passed"
   ELSE print "failed"
END IF
```

The preceding single-line IF/THEN/ELSE statement may be written in BASIC as

```
IF grade > 59 THEN PRINT "passed" ELSE PRINT "failed"
```

The multiple-line version may be written in BASIC as

```
IF grade > 59 THEN
   PRINT "passed"
   ELSE
      PRINT "failed"
END IF
```

A multiple line **IF/THEN/ELSE**, or block **IF/THEN/ELSE**, can test for many different cases by using the **ELSEIF** statement. If more than one test is valid, then only the statements after the first valid test will be executed. For example, the pseudocode statement

```
IF student's grade is greater than 90 THEN
   print "A"
   ELSEIF student's grade is greater than 80 THEN
      print "B"
      ELSEIF student's grade is greater than 70 THEN
         print "C"
         ELSEIF student's grade is greater than 60 THEN
            print "D"
            ELSE
               print "F"
END IF
```

The preceding pseudocode may be written in BASIC as

```
IF grade > 90 THEN
   PRINT "A"
   ELSEIF grade > 80 THEN
      PRINT "B"
      ELSEIF grade > 70 THEN
         PRINT "C"
         ELSEIF grade > 60 THEN
            PRINT "D"
            ELSE
               PRINT "F"
END IF
```

If the variable grade is greater than 90, the first four conditions will be true, but only the **PRINT** statement after the first test will be executed.

3.7 The Repetition Structure: WHILE/WEND

The *repetition structure* allows the programmer to specify that some action is to be repeated until some *terminating condition* occurs. The pseudocode statement

```
WHILE there are more items on my shopping list
   purchase next item and cross it off my list
WEND
```

where WEND designates "while END," describes the repetition that occurs during a shopping trip. The condition, "there are more items on my shopping list" may be true or false. If it is true, then the action, "purchase next item and cross it off my list" is performed. This action will be performed repeatedly as long as the condition remains true.

Eventually, the condition will become false (when the last item on the shopping list has been purchased and crossed off the list). At this point, the loop terminates, and the first pseudocode statement after the WEND statement is performed.

The statement(s) contained between the WHILE statement and the WEND statement constitute the *scope* or the *body* of the loop. Some action specified within the body of the WHILE/WEND must eventually cause the condition to become false. Otherwise, the loop will never terminate—a common programming error called an *infinite loop*.

As an example of an actual WHILE/WEND in BASIC, consider a program designed to find the first power of 2 larger than 1000. Suppose the variable product has been initialized to 2. When the following WHILE/WEND finishes looping, product will contain the desired answer:

```
WHILE product <= 1000
   product = 2 * product
WEND
```

Another repetition structure, the FOR/NEXT, is presented in Chapter 4. The FOR/NEXT is particularly convenient for creating loops that repeat program statements a specific number of times.

3.8 Formulating Algorithms

To illustrate how algorithms are developed, let us consider several examples.

Example 3.2 Class average on a quiz (assuming ten students)

A class of ten students took a quiz. The grades for this quiz are available to you. Determine the class average on the quiz.

Discussion: The class average is equal to the sum of the grades divided by the number of students. The algorithm for solving this problem on a computer must input each of the grades into the computer, perform the averaging calculation, and print the result. Let us use pseudocode, list the steps, and indicate the order in which these steps should be performed. We use counter-controlled looping to input the grades one at a time. The pseudocode algorithm is shown in Figure 3.1.

```
Set totaler to zero
Set grade counter to one

WHILE grade counter is less than or equal to ten
    Input the next grade
    Add the grade into the totaler
    Add one to the grade counter
WEND

Set the class average to the totaler divided by ten
Print the class average

END
```

Figure 3.1   Pseudocode algorithm that uses counter-controlled
looping to solve the class average problem of Example 3.2

Note the reference to a totaler. A *totaler* is a location (just like any other) in the computer's storage which is used to accumulate the sum of a series of numbers. Any such location should always be initialized to zero before being used in a program; otherwise the total would include the previous number which resided in that location. BASIC does initialize all numeric variables to zero automatically in a program, but this is not the case in most other computer languages. It is considered a good programming practice to initialize all totalers in all programs.

3.9 Top-down, Stepwise Refinement

Let us now generalize the class averaging problem.

Example 3.3 Class average on a quiz (arbitrary number of students)

Develop a class averaging program that will process an arbitrary number of grades each time the program is run.

Discussion: In Example 3.2, the number of grades was known in advance. In this example, no indication is given of how many grades are to be entered. The problem statement specifies that the program must process an arbitrary number of grades. How will the program determine when to stop the input of grades? How will it know when to calculate and print the class average?

One way to solve this problem is to use a special value called a *sentinel value* (also called a *signal value* or *dummy value*) to indicate "end of data entry." The user of the program types in the various grades until all legitimate grades have been entered. The user then types the sentinel value to indicate that the last grade has been entered.

Clearly, the sentinel value must be carefully chosen so that it cannot be confused with an acceptable input value. Since grades on a quiz are normally positive numbers, -1 is an acceptable sentinel value for this problem. Thus, a run of the class average program might obtain an input stream such as 95, 96, 75, 74, 89, -1. The program would then compute and print the class average for the grades 95, 96, 75, 74, and 89 (-1 is the sentinel value, so it does not enter into the averaging calculation).

Let us approach the class average program with a technique called *top-down, stepwise refinement,* a technique that is essential to the development of well-structured programs. We begin with a pseudocode representation of the *top:*

```
Calculate and print the class average for the quiz grades
```

The top is a single statement that conveys the overall function of the program. We now begin the refinement process.

```
Initialize variables
Input and sum up the quiz grades
Calculate and print the class average
END
```

Here, only the sequence structure has been used—the steps listed are to be executed in order, one after the other. It is important to note that each refinement, as well as the top itself, is a complete specification of the algorithm; only the level of detail varies.

To proceed to the next level of refinement, we must commit to specific variables. We will need a running total of the numbers, a count of how many numbers there are, and a variable to hold the calculated average. The pseudocode statement

```
Initialize variables
```

may be refined as follows:

```
Set total to zero
Set counter to zero
```

Notice that only the counter and the totaler need to be initialized; the variable used to represent the average need not be initialized because its calculation does not depend on its previous value. The pseudocode statement

```
Input and sum up the quiz grades
```

will require a loop that successively inputs each grade. Since we do not know in advance how many grades there are, we will use a sentinel-controlled loop. The user will type in each legitimate grade one at a time. After the last legitimate grade is typed, the user will type the sentinel value. The program will test for this value after each grade is input, and will terminate the loop when the sentinel is entered. The refinement of the preceding pseudocode statement is then

```
Input the first grade

WHILE the user has not as yet entered the sentinel value
    Add this grade into the running total
    Add one to the grade counter
    Input the next grade (possibly the sentinel)
WEND
```

The pseudocode statement

```
Calculate and print the class average
```

may be refined as follows:

```
Set the average to the total divided by the counter
Print the average
```

The complete *second refinement* is shown in Figure 3.2

```
Set total to zero
Set counter to zero

Input the first grade
WHILE the user has not as yet entered the sentinel value
    Add this grade into the running total
    Add one to the grade counter
    Input the next grade
WEND

Set the average to the total divided by the counter
Print the average

END
```

Figure 3.2 Pseudocode algorithm that uses sentinel-controlled looping to solve the class average problem of Example 3.3

In Figure 3.2, we have included some completely blank lines in the pseudocode for readability. Actually, the blanks separate the various phases of this program by function: an initialization phase that clears the program variables, a looping phase that inputs each grade and adjusts the program variables accordingly, and a termination phase that calculates and prints the final results.

The algorithm in Figure 3.2 implements the procedure for solving the more general class averaging problem of Example 3.3. Once the algorithm has been specified in sufficient detail (as above), the process of implementing a working BASIC program is relatively straightforward; the BASIC program and a sample execution are shown in Figure 3.3.

```
REM   Class average program
total = 0
counter = 0

INPUT "Enter Grade"; grade
WHILE grade <> -1
    total = total + grade
    counter = counter + 1
    INPUT "Enter Grade"; grade
WEND

average = total / counter
PRINT "Class average is"; average
END
```

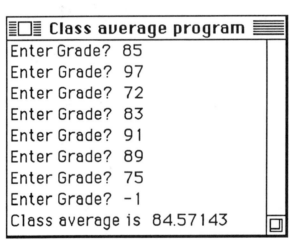

```
≣□≣ Class average program ≣≣≣
Enter Grade?  85
Enter Grade?  97
Enter Grade?  72
Enter Grade?  83
Enter Grade?  91
Enter Grade?  89
Enter Grade?  75
Enter Grade?  -1
Class average is  84.57143
```

Figure 3.3   BASIC program and sample execution for the class
average problem of Example 3.3

3.10 Structured Flowcharting

Another useful technique for developing and representing algorithms is called flowcharting. A *flowchart* is a graphical representation of an algorithm. We draw flowcharts using certain special symbols such as ovals, diamonds, rectangles, circles, and others connected together by arrows called *flowlines*. The flowchart symbols indicate the steps to be performed; a description of each step is written inside its appropriate symbol. The flowlines indicate the order in which the steps are to be performed. Figure 3.4 is the flowchart that corresponds to the pseudocode algorithm of Figure 3.2.

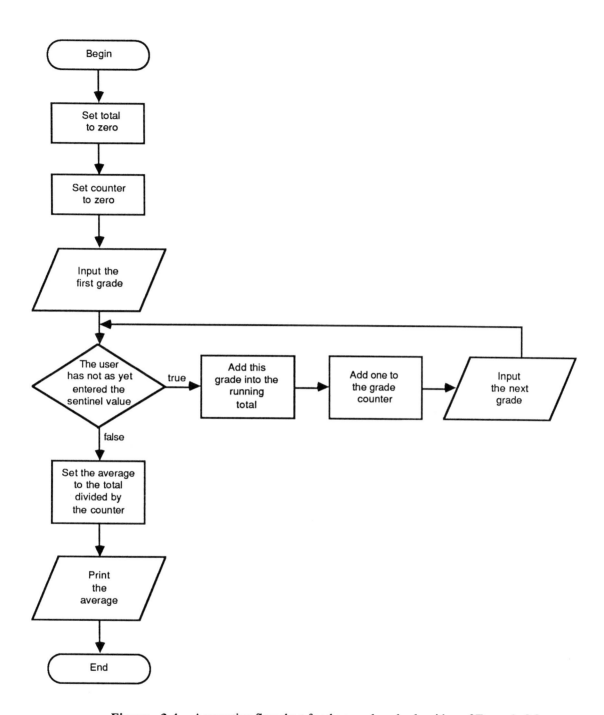

Figure 3.4 A narrative flowchart for the pseudocode algorithm of Example 3.3

The flowchart of Figure 3.4 is called a *narrative flowchart* because of the liberal use of English phrases in the flowchart symbols. Before a BASIC program is written, it may be helpful to draw another flowchart that contains the symbolic notations of the BASIC language instead of the English phrases. This additional flowchart is called a *program flowchart.* Program flowcharts are discussed in Section 3.11.

Let us now discuss each of the flowcharting symbols used in Figure 3.4. The oval symbol, also called the *termination symbol,* is used to indicate the beginning and end of every algorithm (Figure 3.5). The oval symbol containing the word "Begin" is always the first symbol used in a flowchart. The oval symbol containing the word "End" is always the last symbol used in a flowchart.

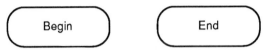

Figure 3.5   Oval or termination symbols

The rectangle symbol (Figure 3.6), also called the *process symbol,* is used to indicate any type of calculation. Process symbols correspond to the steps that are normally performed by LET statements in BASIC. Notice that this narrative flowchart contains many process symbols, each of which contains some calculation required by the algorithm.

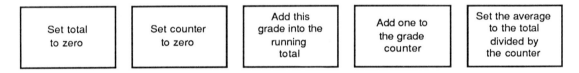

Figure 3.6   Rectangle or process symbols

Every computer implementation of an algorithm requires that information be communicated to the computer in some manner. The parallelogram symbol, also called the *input/output symbol,* is used to indicate that information is to be entered into the computer, or that the computer is to output information. Input/output symbols correspond to the steps that are normally performed by INPUT statements and PRINT statements in BASIC. The narrative flowchart contains several input/output symbols (see Figure 3.7)

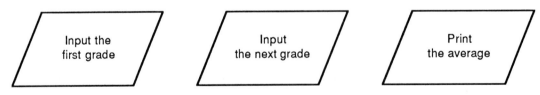

Figure 3.7   Parallelogram or input/output symbols

Perhaps the most important flowcharting symbol is the diamond symbol, also called the *decision symbol,* which indicates that a decision is to be made at a certain point in a flowchart. The decision symbol contains a condition that can be either true or false.

The decision symbol has two flowlines emerging from it. One flowline indicates the direction to be taken when the condition written inside the symbol is true; the other indicates the direction to be taken when the condition is false. The narrative flowchart of Figure 3.4 contains one decision symbol (see Figure 3.8).

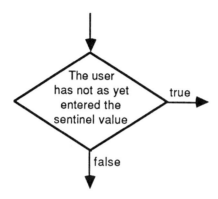

Figure 3.8   Diamond or decision symbol

Figure 3.9 illustrates flowchart segments that correspond to each of the three control structures, namely sequence, selection, and repetition.

3.11 Developing a Program Flowchart

A program flowchart is constructed by replacing the English phrases of the narrative flowchart with the symbolic notations required in BASIC programs. Once the program flowchart has been constructed, writing the actual BASIC program is usually straightforward. The program flowchart for the class average problem appears in Figure 3.10. The reader should compare each symbol in the narrative flowchart of Figure 3.4 with the corresponding symbol in this program flowchart. The following points should be considered:

1. The same flowcharting symbols are used to specify the corresponding operations in each flowchart.
2. The program flowchart uses actual BASIC notations for variables and calculations.
3. The program flowchart uses actual BASIC commands **INPUT** and **PRINT** in input/output symbols.

Flowchart   BASIC

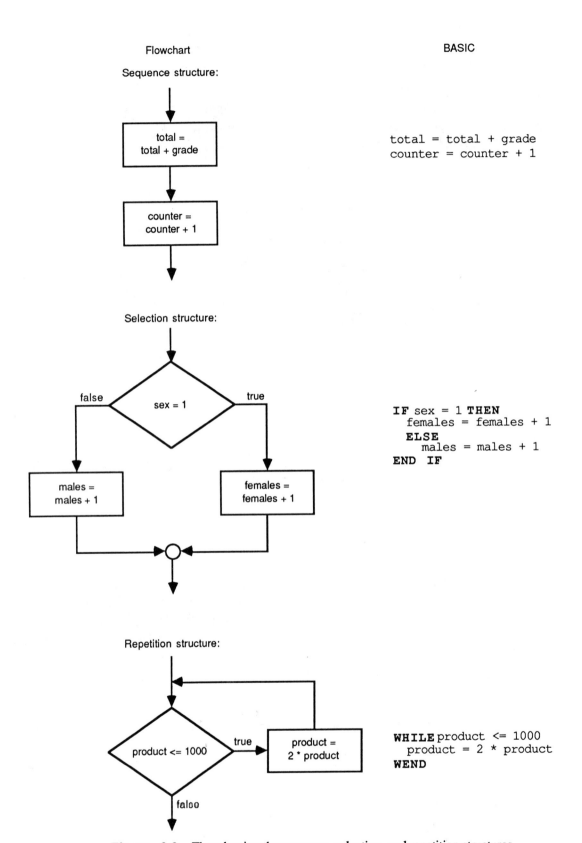

Figure 3.9   Flowcharting the sequence, selection, and repetition structures

4. We recall from Chapter 2 that the equals sign (=) when used to indicate calculations really means "is replaced by." Thus the calculation

```
total = total + grade
```

   is read "let `total` be replaced by the sum of its current value plus `grade`" or more simply "add `grade` to `total`." The calculation

```
counter = counter + 1
```

   is read "let `counter` be replaced by the sum of its current value plus `1`" or more simply "add `1` to `counter`."

5. The BASIC program for the class average problem was presented in Figure 3.3. Each BASIC statement corresponds closely to a particular symbol in the program flowchart.

In general, to develop a computer solution to any problem, it is useful to perform the following steps:

1. Read the problem statement carefully.
2. Develop an approach to solving the problem, and formulate the algorithm as a series of steps to be performed in a specific order. Some people prefer to use pseudocode for this purpose; others prefer to develop structured flowcharts.
3. Write a BASIC program by carefully referencing either the structured flowcharts or the pseudocode.

3.12 Flowcharting: Observations and Guidelines

Experience has shown that the most difficult part of solving a problem on a computer is developing the algorithm for the solution. Once a correct algorithm has been specified, the process of producing a working BASIC program is normally straightforward. Flowcharts help the programmer develop algorithms, particularly those with complex decision making. Flowcharts provide a visual representation of the logic required to solve a problem.

Many programmers write programs without ever writing flowcharts (or using pseudocode). They feel that their ultimate goal is to solve the problem on a computer, and that drawing flowcharts merely delays the production of final outputs. Flowcharts provide useful documentation for working programs long after the programs are first written. Flowcharts are particularly useful for helping others understand the logic of your programs.

Every flowchart should begin with the oval symbol containing the word Begin. Every flowchart should end with the oval symbol containing the word End. Avoid crossing flowlines. Use a flowcharting template if possible. (A flowcharting template is a plastic sheet with the flowchart symbols punched out. A particular flowchart symbol is drawn by tracing around the edges of the punched-out shape.)

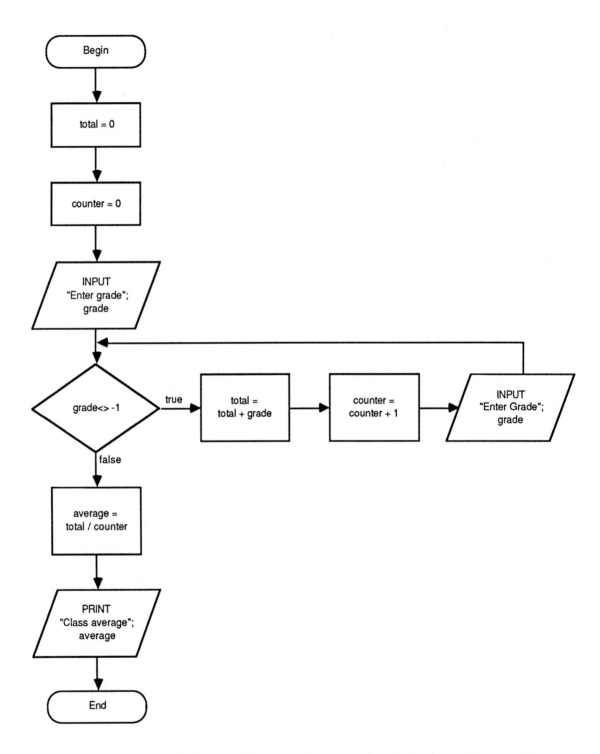

Figure 3.10 A program flowchart for the pseudocode algorithm of Example 3.3

3.13 A Complete Example

Now that we have covered the fundamental principles of algorithms, pseudocode, and flowcharting, let us attempt to work a complete problem. We will
1. Formulate the algorithm using pseudocode and top-down, stepwise refinement.
2. Draw a narrative flowchart.
3. Draw a program flowchart.
4. Write a BASIC program.

Example 3.4 Examination results

One local college offers a course that prepares students for the state licensing exam for real estate brokers. Last year, several of the students who completed this course took the licensing examination. Naturally, the college wants to know how well its students did on the exam. A questionnaire has been sent to each of the 10 students who took the exam, and the director of the program has asked you to summarize the results. You have been given a list of these 10 students. Next to each name, one of the following codes has been written:

Code	Meaning
1	Passed the exam
2	Failed the exam

Write a BASIC program to analyze the results of the exam as follows:
(a) Input each of the 10 test results (i.e., a 1 or a 2). Each time the program requests another test result, it is to display the message "Enter result" on the screen.
(b) Count the number of test results of each type.
(c) Display a summary of the test results indicating the number of students who passed and the number of students who failed.
(d) If more than 8 students passed the exam, print the message "Raise tuition."

Discussion: First, we read the problem statement carefully, and make the following observations:

1. The program must process 10 test results. A counter-controlled loop will be used.
2. Each test result is simply a number, either a 1 or a 2. Each time the program inputs a test result, the program must determine if the number is a 1 or a 2. We will explicitly test for a 1 in our algorithm. If the number is not a 1, we will assume that it is a 2. (The reader should consider the consequences of this assumption.)

3. Two more counters will be used. One will count the number of students who passed the exam; the other will count the number of students who failed the exam.
4. After the program has processed all of the results, it will decide if more than 8 students passed the exam.

Let us proceed with top-down, stepwise refinement. We begin with a pseudocode representation of the top:

```
Analyze exam results and decide if tuition should be raised
```

Once again, it is important to emphasize that the top is a complete representation of the program, but several refinements are still necessary before the pseudocode naturally evolves into a BASIC program. The first refinement is

```
Initialize variables
Input the ten quiz grades and count passes and failures
Print a summary of the exam results and decide if tuition
    should be raised
END
```

Here, too, even though we have a complete representation of the entire program, further refinement is still necessary. We must now commit to specific variables. Counters are needed to record the passes and failures, and a counter will be used to control the looping process. The pseudocode statement

```
Initialize variables
```

may be refined as follows:

```
Set passes to zero
Set failures to zero
```

The pseudocode statement

```
Input the ten quiz grades and count passes and failures
```

will require a loop that successively inputs the result of each exam. Here it is known in advance that there are precisely ten exam results, so counter-controlled looping is appropriate. Inside the loop, a selection structure will determine whether each exam result is a pass or a failure, and will increment the appropriate counters accordingly. The refinement of the preceding pseudocode statement is then

```
Set student counter to one

WHILE student counter is less than or equal to ten
    Input the next exam result

    IF the student passed
        THEN add one to passes
        ELSE add one to failures
    END IF

    Add one to student counter
WEND
```

Notice the use of blank lines to set off the `WHILE/WEND` and `IF/THEN/ELSE` control structures to improve program readability. The pseudocode statement

```
Print a summary of the exam results and decide if tuition
    should be raised
```

may be refined as follows:

```
Print the number of passes
Print the number of failures
IF eight or more students passed THEN print "Raise tuition"
```

The complete second refinement appears in Figure 3.11.

```
Set passes to zero
Set failures to zero

Set student counter to one

WHILE student counter is less than or equal to ten
    Input the next exam result

    IF the student passed
        THEN add one to passes
        ELSE add one to failures
    END IF

    Add one to student counter
WEND

Print the number of passes
Print the number of failures
IF eight or more students passed then print "Raise tuition"

END
```

Figure 3.11 Pseudocode for examination results problem

This pseudocode is now sufficiently refined to be easily converted to BASIC. Figure 3.12 shows the narrative flowchart that corresponds to this pseudocode program. Figure 3.13 shows the corresponding program flowchart. The BASIC program and several sample executions are shown in Figure 3.14.

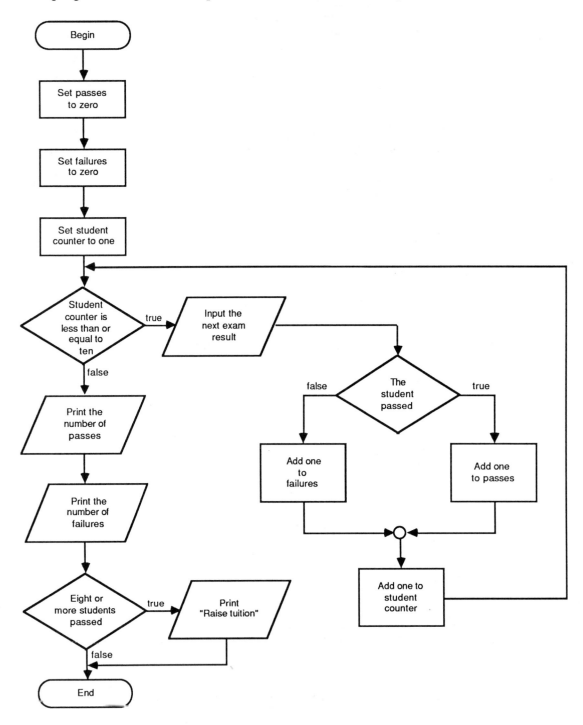

Figure 3.12 Narrative flowchart for the examination results program

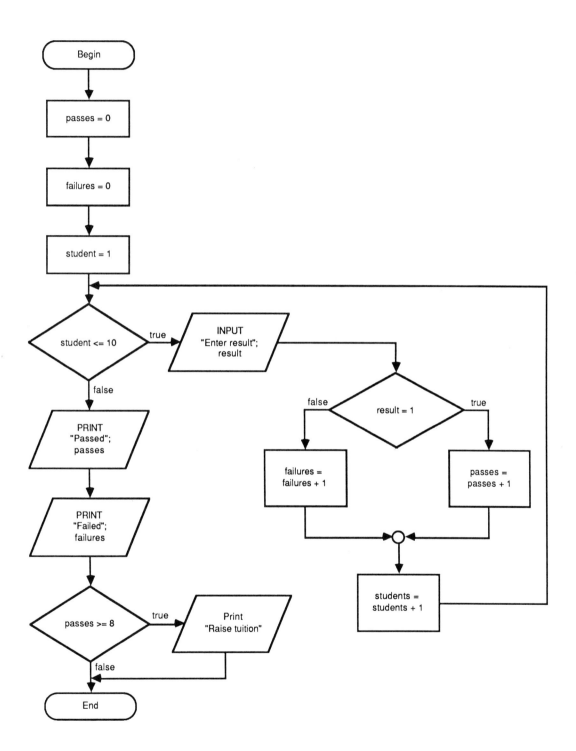

Figure 3.13   Program flowchart for the examination results program

```
REM    Analysis of Examination Results
passes = 0
failures = 0
student = 1

WHILE student <= 10
    INPUT "Enter result (1=pass,2=fail)"; result
    IF result = 1 THEN
       passes = passes + 1
       ELSE
          failures = failures + 1
    END IF
    student = student + 1
WEND
PRINT "Passed"; passes
PRINT "Failed"; failures
IF passes >= 8 THEN PRINT "Raise tuition"
END
```

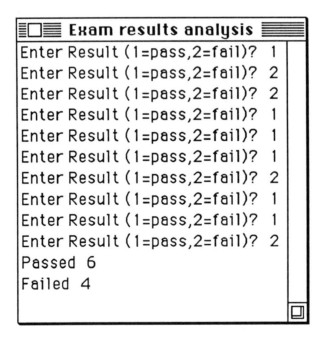

Figure 3.14 BASIC program and several sample executions for examination results problem

continued

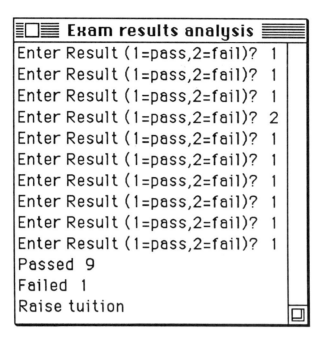

Figure 3.14 *continued*

Concepts

algorithm	narrative flowchart
arrow symbol	order of steps
block `IF/THEN/ELSE`	oval symbol
body of a loop	process symbol
calculation symbol	program flowchart
control structure	pseudocode
counter	rectangle symbol
decision symbol	scope of a loop
diamond symbol	selection structure
dummy value	sentinel value
"end of data entry"	sequence structure
end symbol	signal value
flowchart	steps
flowchart symbol	stepwise refinement
flowcharting template	structured programming
flowline	terminating condition
`FOR/NEXT` repetition structure	termination symbol
`GOTO`-less programming	top
`IF/THEN` selection structure	top-down, stepwise refinement
`IF/THEN/ELSE` selection structure	totaler
infinite loop	`WHILE/WEND` repetition structure
initialization	
input/output symbol	

Problems

3.1. Fill in the blanks in each of the following:
  (a) The solution to any problem involves performing a series of steps in a specific _____.
  (b) Another term for procedure is _____.
  (c) The general name for a location in the computer's storage that is used to accumulate the sum of a series of numbers is _____.
  (d) The process of setting certain numeric variables to zero at the beginning of a program is called _____.
  (e) A special value that is used to indicate "end of data entry" is called a _____, a _____, or a _____.
  (f) A graphical representation of an algorithm is called a _____.
  (g) What symbol is used in a flowchart to indicate the order in which the steps should be performed? _____.
  (h) A flowchart that makes liberal use of English phrases in the flowchart symbols is called a _____ flowchart.
  (i) A flowchart that uses notations very similar to those used in actual programs is called a _____ flowchart.
  (j) The termination symbol is used to indicate the _____ and _____ of every algorithm.
  (k) The last symbol in every flowchart is the _____ shape which contains the word _____.
  (l) The rectangle symbol corresponds to steps that are normally performed by the _____ command in BASIC.
  (m) The _____ symbol is used to indicate the entry of information into the computer via a terminal device.
  (n) The item that is written inside a decision symbol is called a _____.

3.2. Draw a single flowchart symbol that indicates each of the following:
  (a) The message "Enter two numbers" is to be typed on a terminal.
  (b The sum of variables x, y, and z is to be assigned to variable p.
  (c) If the current value of variable m is greater than twice the current value of variable v, then the algorithm should proceed to a flowchart symbol with the label `Calculating`. (*Note:* You need merely draw the symbol that tests the above condition.)
  (d) Values for variables s, r, and t are to be obtained from the user.
  (e) An algorithm is to terminate.

3.3. For each of the following, formulate the algorithm as a series of steps to be performed in a certain order:
  (a) Obtain two numbers from the keyboard, compute the sum of the numbers, and then display the result.
  (b) Obtain two numbers from the keyboard, and determine and display which (if either) is the larger of the two numbers.
  (c) Obtain a series of positive numbers from the keyboard, and determine and display the sum of the numbers. Assume that the user types the sentinel value -1 to indicate "end of data entry."

3.4. State which of the following are true and which are false:
  (a) Experience has shown that the most difficult part of solving a problem on a computer is producing a working BASIC program.
  (b) A sentinel value must be a value that cannot be confused with a legitimate data value.
  (c) In a flowchart, the flowlines indicate the steps to be performed.
  (d) Conditions written inside decision symbols always contain arithmetic operators (i.e., +, -, *, /, and ^).
  (e) The narrative flowchart uses actual BASIC notation for variables and arithmetic calculations.
  (f) In top-down, stepwise refinement, each refinement is a complete representation of the algorithm.

For the following problems, perform each of these steps:

1. Read the problem statement.
2. Formulate the algorithm using pseudocode and top-down, stepwise refinement.
3. Draw a narrative flowchart.
4. Draw a program flowchart.
5. Write a BASIC program.
6. Run the BASIC program.

3.5. Because of the high price of gasoline, drivers are concerned with the mileage obtained by their automobiles. One driver has kept track of several tankfuls of gasoline by recording miles driven and gallons used for each tankful. Develop a BASIC program that will input the miles driven and gallons used for each tankful. The program should calculate and display the miles per gallon obtained for each tankful. After processing all input information, the program should calculate and print the combined miles per gallon obtained for all tankfuls.

3.6. Develop a BASIC program that will determine if a department store customer has exceeded the credit limit on a charge account. For each customer, the following facts are available:

1. Account number
2. Balance at the beginning of the month
3. Total of all items charged by this customer this month
4. Total of all credits applied to this customer's account this month
5. Allowed credit limit

The program should input each of these facts, calculate the new balance (= beginning balance + charges - credits), and determine if the new balance exceeds the customer's credit limit. For those customers whose credit limit is exceeded, the program should display the customer's account number, credit limit, new balance, and the message "Credit limit exceeded."

3.7. One large chemical company pays its salespeople on a commission basis. The salespeople receive $200 per week plus 9 percent of their gross sales for that week. For example, a salesperson who sells $3000 worth of chemicals in a week receives $200 plus 9 percent of $3000, or a total of $470. Develop a BASIC program that will input each salesperson's gross sales for last week, and will calculate and display that salesperson's earnings. Process one salesperson's figures at a time.

omit step 4

3.8. The simple interest i on a loan of p dollars at a rate of r percent for a period of t days is calculated by the formula

$$i = p * r * t / 365$$

The above formula assumes that the rate r is the annual interest rate, and therefore includes the division by 365 (days). Develop a BASIC program that will **INPUT** p, r, and t for several loans, and will calculate and display the simple interest for each loan, using the above formula.

3.9. Develop a BASIC program that will determine the gross pay for each of several employees. The company pays "straight-time" for the first 40 hours worked by each employee, and pays "time-and-a-half" for all hours worked in excess of 40 hours. You are given a list of the employees of the company, the number of hours each employee worked last week, and the hourly rate of each employee. Your program should input this information for each employee, and should determine and display the employee's gross pay.

Chapter 4
Program Control

4.1 Introduction

At this point in the text, the reader should be comfortable with the process of writing simple but complete BASIC programs. In this and subsequent chapters, many of the more powerful features of the BASIC language are introduced. Looping is considered in greater detail, and several BASIC statements that facilitate loop control are presented.

4.2 The Essentials of Looping

Most programs involve repetition or *looping*. A *loop* is a group of instructions the computer executes repeatedly until some *terminating condition* is satisfied. We have discussed two means of loop control:

1. Counter-controlled looping
2. Sentinel-controlled looping

A loop counter is used to count the number of times a group of instructions should be repeated. It is incremented (usually by 1) each time the group of instructions is performed. When the value of the counter indicates that the correct number of repetitions has been performed, the loop is terminated and the computer proceeds to execute the next section of the program.

Sentinel values are generally used to control looping when:

1. The precise number of repetitions is not known in advance.
2. The loop includes statements that obtain data each time the loop is performed.

The sentinel value indicates "end of data." The sentinel is entered after all valid data items have been supplied to the program. Sentinels must be chosen carefully so that there is no possibility of confusing them with valid data items.

4.3 Counter-controlled Loops

Counter-controlled loops require the following items:

1. The *name* of the loop counter
2. The *initial value* of the loop counter
3. The *increment* or *step* by which the loop counter is modified each time through the loop
4. The *final value* of the loop counter.

Consider the simple program shown in Figure 4.1, which prints the numbers from 1 to 15. The statement counter = 1 *names* the loop counter (counter) and sets it to its *initial value* of 1. The statement counter = counter + 1 *increments* the loop counter by 1 each time the loop is performed. The **IF** statement tests if the value of the loop counter has exceeded its *final value* of 15. It is important to note here that this loop is performed for the final value of the loop counter. The loop terminates when the loop counter exceeds its final value of 15.

```
REM   A program with a loop counter
counter = 1

Counting:
    IF counter > 15 THEN END
    PRINT counter
    counter = counter + 1
    GOTO Counting

1
2
3
4
5
6
7
8
9
10
11
12
13
14
15
```

Figure 4.1 Looping with a loop counter

4.4 The FOR and NEXT Statements

Because looping is so important in computer programs, most computer languages provide special statements for conveniently implementing loops. In BASIC, the **FOR** and **NEXT** statements (also called the **FOR/NEXT** structure) may be used to handle all the details of counter-controlled looping automatically. The **FOR** and **NEXT** statements allow BASIC programmers to form loops with fewer statements than would ordinarily be required with the techniques of Section 4.3. Even more importantly, the **FOR/NEXT** structure makes programs clearer. This helps the programmer write programs that are easier to debug and modify. To illustrate the power of **FOR** and **NEXT**, let us rewrite the program of Section 4.3 that prints the numbers from 1 to 15; the result is shown in Figure 4.2.

```
REM    Using FOR and NEXT to implement looping
FOR counter = 1 TO 15 STEP 1
   PRINT counter
NEXT counter
END
```

Figure 4.2 Looping with the FOR and NEXT statements

The program in Figure 4.2 operates as follows. When the **FOR** statement is performed, the variable counter is *defined* to be the loop counter or the *control variable*. The statement initializes the control variable to its *initial value* of 1 and specifies the *final value* of the control variable to be 15. The **FOR** statement also specifies the *increment* or *step* for the control variable to be 1. The **PRINT** statement then prints the first value of counter, namely 1. The **NEXT** counter statement causes the control variable to be incremented by the value specified in the **STEP** portion of the **FOR** statement (in this case, 1). The control variable is then tested to determine if it exceeds the final value of 15 specified in the **FOR** statement. Since the control variable is now equal to 2, the final value is not exceeded, so the program performs the first statement after the **FOR** statement. This process continues until the **NEXT** statement causes the control variable to be incremented to the first value exceeding the final value (in this case, 16). When this value is reached, the program continues by performing the first statement after the **NEXT** (in this case, **END**). Let us take a closer look at the **FOR** statement in this program (see Figure 4.3).

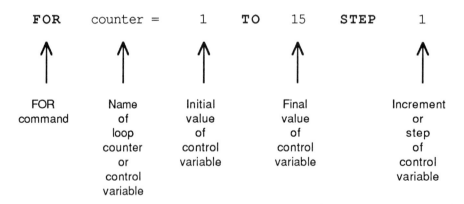

Figure 4.3 Detailed format of the FOR statement

Notice that in a sense the **FOR** statement "does it all"—it specifies each of the four items needed for looping with a loop counter. The **NEXT** statement is required to define

the *scope* or *body* of the loop, i.e., the statements to be repeated each time the loop is performed. Thus to utilize the **FOR** and **NEXT** statements to implement a loop, the programmer:
1. Writes a **FOR** statement defining the various items required by the loop counter.
2. Writes the instructions comprising the scope or the body of the loop.
3. Writes a **NEXT** statement in which the name of the control variable follows the word **NEXT**; the **NEXT** statement closes the loop.

4.5 The FOR and NEXT Statements: Notes and Observations

1. The **FOR** and **NEXT** statements must occur in matching pairs. For example, if a program contains a **FOR** x statement, the program must also contain a corresponding **NEXT** x.

2. If the increment or step is +1, it is not necessary to include the phrase **STEP** 1 in the **FOR** statement. Thus the statement

        FOR i = 1 TO 10

   assumes a **STEP** of +1 and is identical to the statement

        FOR i = 1 TO 10 STEP 1

3. The initial value, the final value, and the step can all be arithmetic expressions. If we assume that x = 2 and y = 5, the statement

        FOR j = x TO 4 * y ^ x STEP x * y

   is equivalent to the statement

        FOR j = 2 TO 100 STEP 10

4. If the initial value, the final value, and/or the step are given in the **FOR** statement as expressions, these expressions are evaluated immediately upon entering the **FOR** statement. The initial value is assigned to the control variable. If the values of any of the variables in these expressions should change after entering the **FOR** statement, the initial value, final value, and the step will remain as they were upon entering the **FOR** statement.
5. The step may be negative (in which case the loop actually counts "backwards").
6. If the step is positive, the **FOR/NEXT** loop terminates when the value of the control variable becomes greater than the final value. If the step is negative, the loop terminates when the value of the control variable becomes less than the final value.

7. Upon entering a **FOR/NEXT** loop, if the initial value of the control variable is greater than the final value (less than the final value for a negative step), the body portion of the loop is not performed. Instead, the computer proceeds to the statement following the **NEXT** statement.
8. The value of the control variable can be changed in the body of a loop, but this is generally considered to be a poor programming practice.
9. The control variable is frequently printed or used in calculations in the body of a loop, but it does not need to be. It is perfectly acceptable to use the control variable for controlling looping while never mentioning it within the body of the loop at all.
10. Because the computer's internal representation of numbers containing decimal fractions is often approximate and not precise, it is wise to avoid using decimal fractions to control **FOR** statements. Use integer values to control counting loops; otherwise, strange results may be obtained.
11. The **FOR/NEXT** structure is flowcharted in much the same manner as the **WHILE/WEND** structure discussed in Chapter 3 (see Figure 4.4).

```
FOR counter = 1 TO 15 STEP 1
    PRINT counter
NEXT counter
```

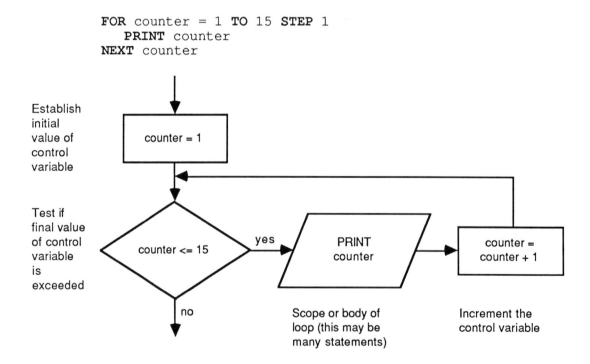

Figure 4.4 Flowcharting the FOR and NEXT statements

4.6 Examples Using the FOR and NEXT Statements

Example 4.1 Writing FOR statements
(a) Write a **FOR** statement that varies a control variable from 1 to 100 in steps of 1.

Answer.   `FOR i = 1 TO 100 STEP 1`

or

`FOR i = 1 TO 100`

(Remember that the `STEP` need not be specified if it is 1.)

(b)   Write a `FOR` statement that varies a control variable from 7 to 77 in steps of 7.

Answer.   `FOR i = 7 TO 77 STEP 7`

(c)   Write a `FOR` statement that varies a control variable from 20 to 2 in steps of −2.

Answer.   `FOR i = 20 TO 2 STEP -2`

(d)   Write a `FOR` statement that varies a control variable over the following sequence of values: 2, 5, 8, 11, 14, 17, 20.

Answer.   `FOR j = 2 TO 20 STEP 3`

(e)   Write a `FOR` statement that varies a control variable over the following sequence of values: 99, 88, 77, 66, 55, 44, 33, 22, 11, 0.

Answer.   `FOR j = 99 TO 0 STEP -11`

Example 4.2 Summation with FOR/NEXT
Write a BASIC program that calculates and prints the sum of all the even integers from 2 to 100. (See Figure 4.5.)

```
REM    Summation with FOR/NEXT
sum = 0
FOR number = 2 TO 100 STEP 2
    sum = sum + number
NEXT number
PRINT "Sum is"; sum
END

Sum is 2550
```

Figure 4.5 Summation with FOR/NEXT

Example 4.3 Compound interest with FOR/NEXT
A person invests $1000.00 in a savings account yielding 5 percent interest. Assuming that all interest is left on deposit in the account, calculate and print the

amount of money in the account at the end of each year for 10 years. Use the following formula for determining these amounts:

$$a = p(1 + r)^n$$

where

p is the original amount invested (i.e., the principal)
r is the annual interest rate
n is the number of years
a is the amount on deposit at the end of the Nth year.

Discussion: This problem involves a loop that performs the indicated calculation for each of the ten years the money remains on deposit. Observe Figure 4.6. A **FOR/NEXT** pair is used to implement the loop by varying a control variable from 1 to 10 in steps of 1.

```
REM    Compound interest problem
PRINT "Year", "Amount on Deposit"
principal = 1000
rate = .05

FOR year = 1 TO 10 STEP 1
    PRINT year, principal * (1 + rate) ^ year
NEXT year
END
```

▤▢▦ Compound Interest ▦▦▦	
Year	Amount on Deposit
1	1050
2	1102.5
3	1157.625
4	1215.506
5	1276.281
6	1340.095
7	1407.1
8	1477.455
9	1551.328
10	1628.894

Figure 4.6 Compound interest program with FOR/NEXT

4.7 The READ and DATA Statements

BASIC provides many different statements that allow programmers to assign values to variables. The **INPUT** statement obtains values directly from the user's terminal, and the

LET statement obtains values by performing calculations and assigning the results to specific variables.

BASIC also provides the **READ** and **DATA** statements for assigning values to variables. The various values that will be needed by a program are entered into **DATA** statements. Thus, the data effectively become a portion of the program itself. Using **DATA** statements, the programmer actually enters data values before the program is run, thus eliminating the need for the user interaction required by the **INPUT** statement. When the program is run, the values are assigned to variables by the **READ** statements in the program.

Consider the BASIC program shown in Figure 4.7, which calculates the area of a rectangular parcel of land. The program begins by performing the **READ** statement. This statement obtains values for the variables parcellength and parcelwidth from the **DATA** statement.

```
REM    Simple area program using READ/DATA
READ parcellength, parcelwidth
PRINT "Area is"; parcellength * parcelwidth
END

DATA 10, 20

Area is 200
```

Figure 4.7 Simple area program with READ/DATA

The **READ/DATA** combination assigns values to the variables precisely in the order in which the variable names appear in the **READ** statement and in the order in which the values appear in the **DATA** statement. In Figure 4.7, when the **READ** is performed, the value 10 is assigned to the variable parcellength and the value 20 is assigned to the variable parcelwidth.

A more interesting application of the **READ/DATA** pair occurs when the **READ** is used inside a loop. Let us modify the program of Figure 4.7 so that it calculates the area of five different parcels of land; we obtain Figure 4.8.

```
REM    Area program with looping
FOR parcel = 1 TO 5
      READ parcellength, parcelwidth
      PRINT "Area is"; parcellength * parcelwidth
NEXT parcel
END

DATA 10,20,10,30,20,20,20,30,30,30

Area is 200
Area is 300
Area is 400
Area is 600
Area is 900
```

Figure 4.8 Area program with READ/DATA and FOR/NEXT

The program in Figure 4.8 performs the READ statement five times. Each time the READ is performed, a pair of values is obtained from the DATA statement. Notice that the first time the READ is performed, the first two values are obtained from the DATA statement, causing `parcellength` to be 10, `parcelwidth` to be 20, and the calculated area to be 200. The second time the READ is performed, the next two values are obtained from the DATA statement, causing `parcellength` to be 10, `parcelwidth` to be 30, and the calculated area to be 300. Subsequent READs obtain succeeding pairs of values from the DATA statement.

4.8 The DATA List and the DATA List Pointer

DATA values are entered into a BASIC program before the program is run on the computer. A program may contain many READ statements that obtain values for many different variables. Some programs require many DATA statements to be entered.

To control the handling of DATA items, BASIC treats all the items in the DATA statements as a single list called the *DATA list*. When the program is run, the computer maintains a pointer to the next item in the DATA list. When the program first begins executing, the *DATA list pointer* points to the first item in the DATA list. Each time a READ statement is performed, the computer advances the DATA list pointer to point to subsequent DATA items.

Consider the BASIC program of Figure 4.9, which calculates the area of an arbitrary number of land parcels. The first READ statement obtains the first data value (in this case, the value 3 in the first DATA statement). This tells the program how many parcels of land are to be processed. The value obtained is assigned to the variable `number`, which is then used as the final value in the FOR statement. The FOR statement is now set to loop three times (from 1 to 3 in steps of +1), which means that the second READ statement will be performed three times. Thus, three successive pairs of values will be obtained from the second DATA statement.

```
REM    Area program with arbitrary number of parcels
READ number
FOR parcel = 1 TO number
   READ parcellength, parcelwidth
   PRINT "Area is"; parcellength * parcelwidth
NEXT parcel
END

DATA 3
DATA 10,20,30,40,50,60

Area is 200
Area is 1200
Area is 3000
```

Figure 4.9 Area program for arbitrary number of parcels

To see precisely how the **DATA** list and the **DATA** list pointer operate, consider Figure 4.10, which shows the **DATA** list at various times throughout the execution of the program in Figure 4.9. The **DATA** list pointer is indicated by an arrow.

(a) When the program first begins to run:

3   10   20   30   40   50   60   (number = 0, parcellength = 0, parcelwidth = 0)
↑

(b) After the program performs the first READ statement:

3   10   20   30   40   50   60   (number = 3, parcellength = 0, parcelwidth = 0)
     ↑

(c) After the program performs the second READ statement the first time:

3   10   20   30   40   50   60   (number = 3, parcellength = 10, parcelwidth = 20)
               ↑

(d) After the program performs the second READ statement the second time:

3   10   20   30   40   50   60   (number = 3, parcellength = 30, parcelwidth = 40)
                         ↑

(e) After the program performs the second READ statement the third time:

3   10   20   30   40   50   60   (number = 3, parcellength = 50, parcelwidth = 60)
                              ↑

Figure 4.10 Operation of the DATA list and the DATA list pointer

4.9 The READ and DATA Statements: Notes and Observations

1. **DATA** statements are nonexecutable—they are ignored when a program is run.
2. **DATA** statements may be placed anywhere in a BASIC program. Some programmers prefer to place all **DATA** statements together, whereas others prefer to place **DATA** statements near the respective **READ** statements that reference the **DATA**.

3. **DATA** statements cannot perform calculations. They must contain only constants separated by commas.
4. If a program attempts to **READ** more data than have been provided in the **DATA** statements, the error message "Out of data" will be displayed on the screen.
5. The **READ** statement is flowcharted with the same parallelogram or input/output symbol used to flowchart the **INPUT** and **PRINT** statements.
6. There is no flowcharting symbol for the **DATA** statement for much the same reason as there is no flowcharting symbol for the values actually obtained by an **INPUT** statement when a program is run.
7. The **RESTORE** statement resets the **DATA** list pointer to the beginning of the **DATA** list so that subsequent **READ** statements will begin reading from the first value in the **DATA** list. The following **RESTORE** statement resets the **DATA** list pointer to the beginning of the **DATA** list.

```
RESTORE
```

8. The **READ** statement cannot perform calculations. It must contain only variable names separated by commas.
9. The **READ** statement may also read nonnumeric information. For example, the statement

```
READ name$
```

could read the value "Sammy Jones" from the statement

```
DATA "Sammy Jones"
```

Information contained in a pair of quotation marks is called a string. A variable name followed by a dollar sign is called a *string variable*. Chapter 7 discusses strings and string variables in detail.

4.10 A Complete Example with FOR/NEXT and READ/DATA

Example 4.4 Straight-line depreciation
For income tax purposes, the government allows businesses to deduct a certain amount of money from gross income to reflect the depreciation (or deterioration in value) of the business's assets. Since it is impossible to calculate the precise amount of physical depreciation that an asset actually suffers each year, accountants use various methods to estimate depreciation.

To calculate straight-line depreciation, the accountant estimates the useful life of the asset (i.e., the expected number of years for which the asset may effectively be used to perform its intended function), and the asset's salvage value (i.e., the estimated value of the asset at the end of its useful life). The straight-line depreciation is then calculated by subtracting the salvage value from the original cost of the asset, and then dividing the result by the asset's useful life (in years). For example, an asset that cost $10,000 and has a useful life of five years with an estimated salvage value of $2000 would have a straight-line depreciation per year of (10,000 - 2000)/5, or $1600.

Write a BASIC program that calculates straight-line depreciation for five assets. For each asset you are given an identification number, original cost, salvage value, and estimated useful life. Use **READ/DATA** and **FOR/NEXT**. Print the results in a neat tabular format. The program is shown in Figure 4.11.

```
REM    Straight line depreciation
PRINT "Asset", "Cost", "Salvage", "Life", "Depreciation"
FOR asset = 1 TO 5
    READ identification, cost, salvage, life
    PRINT identification, cost, salvage, life, (cost-salvage)/life
NEXT asset
END

DATA 203,5000,1000,4
DATA 314,4000,1500,5
DATA 411,10000,3000,7
DATA 514,9000,2600,8
DATA 749,6000,1500,5
```

Asset	Cost	Salvage	Life	Depreciation
203	5000	1000	4	1000
314	4000	1500	5	500
411	10000	3000	7	1000
514	9000	2600	8	800
749	6000	1500	5	900

Figure 4.11 Straight-line depreciation with READ/DATA and FOR/NEXT

4.11 The SELECT/CASE Statement

The **IF** statement introduced in Chapter 2 is the primary decision-making command in BASIC. Occasionally, an algorithm will contain a series of decisions in which a particular variable or expression is tested for each of the values it may assume, and different actions are taken. BASIC provides the **SELECT/CASE** statement to handle this kind of decision making. The following example illustrates the use of the **SELECT/CASE** statement.

Example 4.5 Piecework payroll with the SELECT/CASE statement
Many manufacturing concerns pay their employees on a piecework basis instead of hourly—employees are paid for the number of units they manufacture. Since different items involve different amounts of effort and skill to produce, different piecework rates are paid for each type of item.

Write a BASIC program that will calculate the gross pay for an employee on a piecework basis. This employee is paid the following rates for each item produced:

Item#	Rate
1	.22 (i.e., 22 cents)
2	.30
3	.35
4	.37

Your program should read from a series of tickets for the employee. Each ticket contains two pieces of data:

(a) An item number (1, 2, 3, or 4).
(b) The quantity of that item produced by this employee.

The employee's supervisor fills out a new ticket every time the employee begins working on a different type of item. Thus, it is possible to have several tickets for this employee with the same item number.

For each ticket processed, your program should print the item number, quantity, piecework rate, and the amount earned by this employee for this ticket. Your program should add up the amounts on each of this employee's tickets and should print the employee's gross pay. Include as the first item in your data an integer that tells the program how many tickets to process.

Discussion: The BASIC program and a sample execution appear in Figure 4.12. This program incorporates many of the techniques of this chapter. It uses **FOR/NEXT**, **READ/DATA**, and **SELECT/CASE**.

The **SELECT/CASE** statement determines which rate should be paid for each ticket. Depending on the item number, item, this statement **SELECT**s the appropriate rate. Five **CASE**s are shown. The first four handle the **SELECT**ion of a rate for a valid item number. When the item number is invalid, the **CASE ELSE** causes an error message to be printed. Note that in this example each of the **CASE**s causes only a single statement to be performed. In general, however, each **CASE** may cause many statements to be performed.

CASEs may be specified for single items (e.g., **CASE** 2 as in our example), for lists of items (e.g., **CASE** 1, 3, 5, 7, 9), for ranges of items (e.g., **CASE** 5 TO 10), and for conditions (e.g., **CASE IS** >= 7). It is possible to combine items, ranges, and conditions in a single **CASE** (e.g., **CASE** 1, 3 TO 7, IS > 10). The **CASE ELSE** is optional, and is executed only when none of the listed **CASE**s applies. If **CASE ELSE** is omitted and none of the **CASE** clauses are true, an error will occur.

The first **DATA** statement specifies the number of tickets to be processed. The subsequent **DATA** statements contain the information for each of the tickets. The first value in each **DATA** statement is the item number; the second value is the quantity produced.

4.12 Logical Operators

BASIC makes decisions by evaluating conditions and then choosing different paths of execution. So far we have studied only *simple conditions* such as counter <= 10, total > 1000, and number <> sentinelvalue. We have expressed these conditions in terms of the relational operators =, <>, >, <, >=, and <=. Each decision tested precisely one condition. If we wanted to test multiple conditions in the process of making a decision, we had to perform these tests in separate statements.

```
REM    Piecework payroll program
PRINT "Item", "Quantity", "Rate", "Amount"
READ tickets
FOR counter = 1 TO tickets
    READ item, quantity
    SELECT CASE item
        CASE 1
            rate = .22
        CASE 2
            rate = .3
        CASE 3
            rate = .35
        CASE 4
            rate = .37
        CASE ELSE
            PRINT "Invalid item = "; item, "quantity = "; quantity
    END SELECT
    pay = pay + rate * quantity
    PRINT item, quantity, rate, rate * quantity
NEXT counter
PRINT
PRINT "Total pay is",,,"$";pay
END

DATA 7
DATA 1,80
DATA 3,40
DATA 2,100
DATA 1,20
DATA 3, 200
DATA 2, 30
DATA 4, 200
```

Figure 4.12 Piecework payroll with FOR/NEXT, READ/DATA, and SELECT/CASE
continued

Item	Quantity	Rate	Amount
1	80	.22	17.6
3	40	.35	14
2	100	.3	30
1	20	.22	4.4
3	200	.35	70
2	30	.3	9
4	200	.37	74
Total pay is			$ 219

Payroll

Figure 4.12 *continued*

BASIC provides a set of *logical operators* that may be used to form more complex conditions by combining conditions. The most commonly used logical operators are *AND*, *OR*, and *NOT*.

Suppose we wish to ensure at some point in a program that two conditions are both true before we choose a certain path of execution. In this case we use the AND logical operator as in the following program segment:

```
IF sex = 1 AND age >= 65 THEN
     seniorfemales = seniorfemales + 1
```

This **IF** statement contains two simple conditions. The condition sex = 1 is evaluated to determine if the person is a female. The condition age >= 65 is evaluated to determine if the person is a senior citizen. The **IF** statement then considers the combined condition

```
sex = 1 AND age >= 65
```

This is considered to be true if both of the simple conditions are true. Finally, if this combined condition is indeed true, then the count of seniorfemales is incremented by 1. Note that if either or both of the simple conditions are false, then the program skips the incrementing and proceeds to the statement following the **IF**.

Now let us consider the OR logical operator. Suppose we wish to ensure at some point in a program that either or both of two conditions are true before we choose a certain path of execution. In this case we use the OR logical operator as in the following program segment:

```
IF semesteraverage >= 90 OR finalexam >= 90 THEN
     PRINT "Student grade is A"
```

This statement also contains two simple conditions. The variable `semesteraverage >= 90` is evaluated to determine if the student deserves an "A" in the course because she has maintained a high average throughout the semester. The condition `finalexam >= 90` is evaluated to determine if the student deserves an "A" in the course because of an outstanding performance on the final examination. The **IF** statement then considers the combined condition

```
semesteraverage >= 90 OR finalexam >= 90
```

and awards the student an "A" if either or both of the simple conditions are true. Note that the message "Student grade is A" is not printed only when both of the simple conditions are false.

BASIC provides the **NOT** logical operator to enable a programmer to "reverse" the meaning of a condition. Unlike **AND** and **OR**, which combine two conditions (and are therefore called *binary operators*), **NOT** affects only a single condition (and is therefore called a *unary operator*). **NOT** is placed before a condition when we are interested in choosing a path of execution if the original condition (without the **NOT**) is false, such as in the following program segment:

```
IF NOT (grade = sentinelvalue) THEN
    PRINT "The next grade is"; grade
```

In most cases, the programmer can avoid using **NOT** by expressing the condition differently with an appropriate relational operator. For example, the preceding statement may be written without the **NOT** as follows:

```
IF grade <> sentinelvalue THEN
    PRINT "The next grade is"; grade
```

BASIC provides three other logical operators for combining parts of conditions. These are **XOR** (exclusive **OR**), **EQV** (equivalence), and **IMP** (implication). The **XOR** of two conditions is true if either condition is true, but not if both are true or both are false. The **EQV** of two conditions is true only if both conditions are true or both are false. The **IMP** of two conditions is false only if the first condition is true and the second is false. The novice programmer will rarely need to use **XOR**, **EQV**, or **IMP**. Problem 4.18 examines logical operators in detail and introduces the concept of truth tables.

Concepts

AND	**EQV**
binary operator	final value of control variable
body of a loop	first statement after the **FOR**
control variable	first statement after the **NEXT**
DATA list	**FOR/NEXT** structure
DATA list pointer	**IMP**
DATA statement	increment or step of control variable

infinite loop
initial value of control variable
logical operators
loop
loop control
loop counter
loop termination
negative step
nonexecutable statement
NOT
optional STEP 1
OR
"Out of data" error message
positive step

READ statement
repetition
RESTORE statement
scope of the loop
SELECT/CASE statement
sentinel value
simple condition
statement modifiers
terminating condition
unary operator
WHILE/WEND structure
XOR

Problems

4.1. State which values of the control variable x are generated by each of the following **FOR** statements:
  (a)   **FOR** x = 2 **TO** 13 **STEP** 3
  (b)   **FOR** x = 5 **TO** 22 **STEP** 7
  (c)   **FOR** x = 3 **TO** 15 **STEP** 3
  (d)   **FOR** x = 1 **TO** 5 **STEP** 7
  (e)   **FOR** x = 12 **TO** 2 **STEP** -3

4.2. Write **FOR** statements that generate the following sequences of values:
  (a)   1, 2, 3, 4, 5, 6, 7
  (b)   3, 8, 13, 18, 23
  (c)   20, 14, 8, 2, -4, -10
  (d)   19, 27, 35, 43, 51
  (e)   No values at all

4.3. State which of the following statements are valid and which are invalid. For those statements that are invalid, specify why:
  (a)   **DATA** 8 9, 10
  (b)   **DATA** 6, 4.5, 77
  (c)   **DATA** 16, 6/4*3, 14.2
  (d)   **DATA** 19, 37 64 82
  (e)   **DATA** A, B, C$

4.4. State which of the following statements are valid and which are invalid. For those statements that are invalid, specify why:
  (a)   **READ** i j, k
  (b)   **READ** j5, k6, 8, 9.5
  (c)   **READ** a4, a8, c9
  (d)   **READ** j$, a4
  (e)   **READ** a + 5, b - 6

4.5. Determine which of the following statements are true and which are false. For those statements that are false, state why:
  (a)   If a program contains a **FOR** statement, it must contain a **NEXT** statement.
  (b)   If a program contains five **FOR** statements, each of these **FOR** statements must have a corresponding **NEXT** statement.
  (c)   If a program contains five **READ** statements, it must also contain five **DATA** statements.
  (d)   If a program contains five **READ** statements, it may also contain ten **DATA** statements.
  (e)   If a program contains ten **READ** statements, it may also contain a single **DATA** statement.

4.6. Write a BASIC program that sums all the values in a **DATA** statement. Assume that the first value in the **DATA** statement specifies the number of values remaining in the **DATA** statement.

4.7. Write a BASIC program that calculates and prints the average of all the values in a **DATA** statement. Assume the last value in the **DATA** statement is the sentinel value 999999.

4.8. Write a BASIC program that finds the smallest value in a **DATA** statement. Assume that the first value in the **DATA** statement specifies the number of values remaining in the **DATA** statement.

4.9. Write a BASIC program that calculates and prints the sum of the even integers from 2 to 30.

4.10. Write a BASIC program that calculates and prints the product of the odd integers from 1 to 15.

4.11. The factorial function is used frequently in simple probability problems. The factorial of a positive integer *n* (written *n!* and pronounced "n factorial") is equal to the product of the positive integers from 1 to n. Write a BASIC program that evaluates the factorials of the first ten positive integers from 1 to 10. Print the results in a neat tabular format.

4.12. Modify the compound interest problem of Example 4.6 to repeat its steps for interest rates of 5 percent, 6 percent, 7 percent, 8 percent, 9 percent, and 10 percent. Use a **FOR/NEXT** loop to vary the interest rate.

4.13. Write a BASIC program that prints the following patterns. Use **FOR/NEXT** loops to generate the patterns. All asterisks (*) should be printed by a single **PRINT** statement of the form **PRINT "*";** (this causes them to print side by side).

```
      (A)              (B)              (C)              (D)
   *              **********        **********                   *
   **             *********          *********                  **
   ***            ********            ********                 ***
   ****           *******              *******                ****
   *****          ******                ******               *****
   ******         *****                  *****              ******
   *******        ****                    ****             *******
   ********        ***                     ***            ********
   *********        **                      **           *********
   **********        *                       *          **********
```

4.14. Collecting money becomes increasingly difficult during periods of recession, so companies may tighten their credit limits to prevent their accounts receivable (money owed to them) from becoming too large. In response to a prolonged recession, one company has cut its customer's credit limits in half. Thus, if a particular customer had a credit limit of $1000, this customer's credit limit is now $500. If a customer had a credit limit of $5000, this customer's credit limit is now $2500. Write a BASIC program that analyzes the credit status of ten customers of this company. For each customer you are given:

1. The customer's account number
2. The customer's credit limit before the recession
3. The customer's current balance (i.e., the amount the customer owes the company)

Your program should calculate and print the new credit limit for each customer, and should determine (and print) which customers have current balances that exceed their new credit limits.

4.15. Modify the straight-line depreciation program of Figure 4.11 to print a table for each depreciation, indicating the value of the asset at the end of each year of its useful life. The value of an asset at the end of the first year, for example, is the original cost minus the first year's straight-line depreciation.

4.16. One interesting application of computers is drawing graphs and bar charts (sometimes called "histograms"). Write a BASIC program that obtains five numbers (each between 1 and 30) from a **DATA** statement. For each number read, your program should print a line containing that number of adjacent asterisks. For example, if your program reads the number seven, it should print *******.

4.17. A mail order house sells seven different products whose retail prices are shown in the following table:

Product number	Retail price
1	$ 2.98
2	4.50
3	9.98
4	4.49
5	6.87
6	3.49
7	19.99

Write a BASIC program that reads a series of pairs of numbers as follows:

1. Product number
2. Quantity sold for one day

Your program should use a **SELECT/CASE** statement to help determine the retail price for each product. Your program should calculate and display the total retail value of all products sold last week.

4.18. The following charts are called "truth tables"—they show all possible results when conditions are combined and reversed with logical operators. Complete these tables by filling in each blank with "true" or "false."

Condition1	Condition2	Condition1 AND Condition2
false	false	false
false	true	false
true	false	_____
true	true	_____

Condition1	Condition2	Condition1 OR Condition2
false	false	false
false	true	true
true	false	_____
true	true	_____

Condition1	NOT Condition1
false	true
true	_____

Condition1	Condition2	Condition1 XOR Condition2
false	false	false
false	true	true
true	false	_____
true	true	_____

Condition1	Condition2	Condition1 EQV Condition2
false	false	true
false	true	false
true	false	_____
true	true	_____

Condition1	Condition2	Condition1 IMP Condition2
false	false	true
false	true	true
true	false	_____
true	true	_____

Chapter 5
Functions, Subroutines, and Subprograms

5.1 Introduction

Most computer programs designed to solve commercial and scientific problems are much larger than the example programs presented in the first few chapters of this text. For this reason, most computer languages contain features that facilitate the design, implementation, and operation of large programs.

Experience has shown that the best way to handle a large program is to divide it into several smaller *program pieces* or *modules* each of which is more manageable than the original program. This technique is often called *divide and conquer*. This chapter describes the many features of the BASIC language that assist programmers in writing and using modular programs.

5.2 Program Modules in BASIC

The BASIC language provides the programmer with the ability to use several important types of program modules. These are:

1. Intrinsic functions
2. Programmer-defined functions
3. Subroutines
4. Subprograms

Intrinsic functions provide the programmer with a built-in repertoire of routines for performing common mathematical calculations and many other useful operations. These routines are a part of the BASIC language itself.

Programmer-defined functions are written by the programmer. They allow the programmer to define calculations that may be used at many points in a program. Once such a calculation is defined in detail, the programmer can insert the calculation at other points in the program merely by referencing the function by name. The actual statements defining the calculations to be performed by the function are written only once. As we will see, each function, whether intrinsic or user-defined, returns a value to the program "in the place of the function name itself."

Subroutines are also supplied by the programmer. A subroutine is a series of BASIC statements which is written once in a program, but which may be called upon from many points throughout a BASIC program.

Subprograms are supplied by the programmer, and like subroutines, can be called upon any number of times from within the program. Subprograms are critical to the development of large, correct, and reliable software systems, the kind that students are likely to implement as they enter computing careers.

Subroutines as used in early versions of BASIC are discussed here for completeness. The programmer is advised to use subprograms rather than subroutines, to construct large programs.

5.3 Intrinsic Functions

Some of the intrinsic functions in BASIC are summarized in Figure 5.1. These particular functions allow the programmer to perform certain common mathematical calculations.

Intrinsic functions are normally used in a program by writing the name of the function followed by a left parenthesis followed by the *argument* of the function followed by a right parenthesis. For example, a programmer desiring to calculate and print the square root of 900 might write

```
PRINT SQR(900)
```

When this statement is executed, the computer uses the intrinsic function `SQR` to calculate the square root of the number contained in the parentheses (900). The number 900 is the argument of the `SQR` function.

The argument of a function does not have to be a constant; it may be a variable or an expression. The statement

```
a = SQR(b)
```

is perfectly valid as long as the variable `b` has been assigned a (nonnegative) value. The statement

```
PRINT SQR(c1 + d * f)
```

is also perfectly valid as long as `c1`, `d`, and `f` have been assigned values before the computer performs the statement (and the value of the expression is nonnegative). If we assume that `c1 = 13`, `d = 3`, and `f = 4`, then the preceding statement would calculate and print the square root of `13 + 3 * 4 = 25`, which is, of course, 5.

Function	Meaning	Explanation
SQR(x)	square root of x	SQR(900) is 30 SQR(9) is 3
EXP(x)	exponential function e^x	EXP(1) is 2.71828 EXP(2) is 7.38906
LOG(x)	natural logarithm of x (base e)	LOG(2.71828) is 1 LOG(7.38906) is 2
ABS(x)	absolute value of x	if x>0 then ABS(x) is x if x=0 then ABS(x) is 0 if x<0 then ABS(x) is -x
FIX(x)	signed integer portion of x	FIX(86.4) is 86 FIX(-86.4) is -86
SGN(x)	algebraic sign of x	if x>0 then SGN(x) is 1 if x=0 then SGN(x) is 0 if x<0 then SGN(x) is -1
INT(x)	the greatest integer not greater than x (or "integer part of x")	INT(7.5) is 7 INT(3) is 3 INT(0) is 0 INT(-5.6) is -6
RND	produces a random number between 0 and 1	
SIN(x)	trigonometric sine of x (x in radians)	
COS(x)	trigonometric cosine of x (x in radians)	
TAN(x)	trigonometric tangent of x (x in radians)	
ATN(x)	the angle (in radians) with trigonometric tangent x	

Figure 5.1 Intrinsic functions in BASIC

Some other useful intrinsic functions are `DATE$`, `TIME$`, and `TAB`. The BASIC statement

```
PRINT DATE$, TIME$
```

would print the date and the time as follows:

```
05-27-1989       15:07:37
```

The `TAB` function is used in `PRINT` statements to specify the precise column in which information should be printed. The operation of the `TAB` function is shown in Figure 5.2.

```
REM    Using the TAB function to control print positioning
PRINT "123456789"
FOR column = 1 TO 9
   PRINT TAB(column); "*"
NEXT column
END
```

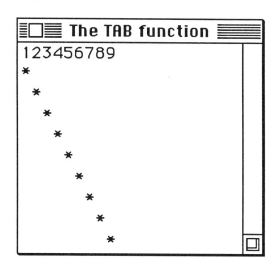

Figure 5.2 The TAB function used to control print positioning

5.4 Applications of the INT Intrinsic Function

The `INT` intrinsic function is useful in many types of programs. `INT` is particularly useful in conjunction with the `RND` function (as we will see in Chapter 8). Other uses of `INT` include:

1. Determining if a number is an integer.
2. Rounding a number to a particular decimal place.

3. Determining if one number is a multiple of another.
4. Determining if a number is even or odd.

The following example illustrates the use of the **INT** function.

Example 5.1 Car towing agency

A car towing agency charges $10.00 minimum to tow a car up to two miles. The agency charges $1.00 per mile for each additional mile in excess of two miles. If the total miles towed is not an integer, then the towing charge is calculated for the next higher integer number of miles (i.e., if the tow is for 3.4 miles, for example, then the charge is calculated for a 4-mile tow). Write a BASIC program that will read miles towed for each of 10 tows, and will calculate and print the towing charge for each tow.

Discussion: This problem requires that towing charges be calculated for three different situations:

1. The miles towed is two miles or less. In this case the minimum charge of $10.00 applies.
2. The miles towed is larger than two miles and is an integer. In this case, the charge is $10.00 for the first two miles and $1.00 per mile for all miles in excess of two miles.
3. The number of miles towed is larger than two miles and is not an integer. In this case, the charge is $10.00 for the first two miles and $1.00 per mile or part thereof for all miles towed in excess of two miles.

The program must determine if the number of miles towed is an integer. The **INT** function makes this determination straightforward. The program need merely test if the number of miles towed is equal to the "integer part" of the miles towed:

```
IF miles = INT (miles) ...
```

Why does this test work? If the number is an integer, it must be equal to its integer part. If the number is not an integer, it will not be equal to its integer part.

Figure 5.3 shows the BASIC program and a sample execution for the car-towing problem. Note that if the number of miles towed is greater than two miles but is not an integer, then the program "rounds up" (i.e., it adds 1 to the miles towed and takes the integer part of the result). For example, if the number of miles towed is 8.4, then the towing charge is calculated for a tow of 9.0 miles. The 9.0 figure is obtained by adding 1.0 to 8.4 to get 9.4, and then taking the integer part of the result to obtain 9.0. This method of rounding the number of miles upward works equally well for all tows in which the number of miles towed is greater than two miles but is not an integer.

```
REM    Car-towing Program
PRINT "Tow", "Miles", "Charge"
FOR tow = 1 TO 10 STEP 1
   READ miles
   PRINT tow, miles,
   IF miles <= 2 THEN
      PRINT 10
      ELSEIF miles = INT(miles) THEN
         PRINT 10 + 1 * (miles - 2)
         ELSE
            PRINT 10 + 1 * (INT(miles - 2) +1)
   END IF
NEXT tow
END

DATA .5, 1, 1.4, 2, 2.3, 3, 3.2 , 4, 4.1, 5
```

Car-towing program		
Tow	Miles	Charge
1	.5	10
2	1	10
3	1.4	10
4	2	10
5	2.3	11
6	3	11
7	3.2	12
8	4	12
9	4.1	13
10	5	13

Figure 5.3 BASIC program and sample run for car-towing problem

5.5 Programmer-defined Functions

Programmers may define their own functions by using the *DEF command* in BASIC. Suppose, for example, that the area of a circle is to be calculated several times throughout a program. The programmer may define a function to do this as follows:

```
DEF FNArea(radius) = 3.1416 * radius ^ 2
```

The command **DEF** indicates that the statement contains a *function definition*. Immediately after the **DEF**, the programmer writes the name of the function. Function names for programmer-defined functions in BASIC must begin with the letters FN.

Following the function name, the programmer writes a list of one or more *formal parameters* enclosed by parentheses. Formal parameters are variable names used in the function definition to indicate the calculation to be performed. The programmer then writes an equals sign followed by the arithmetic expression defining the calculation to be performed in terms of the formal parameters.

Once the programmer has defined `FNArea` as in the preceding `DEF` statement, `FNArea` may then be used throughout the program in the same manner as an intrinsic function. For example, to calculate and print the area of a circle of radius 7, the programmer might write a statement such as

```
PRINT FNArea(7)
```

Function definitions can be placed anywhere in a BASIC program before they are used. It is considered good practice to place all `DEF` statements at the beginning of the program.

Function definitions may reference other functions. Thus, a statement such as

```
DEF FNx(a) = FNy(a) * FNz(a)
```

is perfectly reasonable as long as `FNy` and `FNz` have been defined.

Function definitions may include more than one formal parameter, but functions can return only a single value. The statement

```
DEF FNa(b, c, d) = 3 * b + 2 * c + 5 * d
```

uses three formal parameters (`b`, `c`, and `d`), but whenever `FNa` is used in a program it nevertheless returns only a single value. For example, if `b` is 2, `c` is 3, and `d` is 4, then `FNa (b, c, d)` would perform the calculation

```
3 * 2 + 2 * 3 + 5 * 4
```

and would return the value 32.

5.6 Subroutines

Once again, a subroutine is a series of BASIC statements which is written once in a program, but which may be called upon from many points throughout a BASIC program. To use subroutines, the programmer needs the BASIC statements *GOSUB* and *RETURN*. `GOSUB` causes an unconditional transfer of control to a subroutine; this is referred to as *invoking* or *calling* the subroutine. **RETURN** causes an unconditional transfer of control back to the *main program*. If a programmer wants to perform the subroutine `Grandtotal`, the programmer writes

```
GOSUB Grandtotal
```

This statement causes the computer to transfer control to the subroutine at label `Grandtotal`. The computer then performs the various statements in the subroutine. The last executable statement to be performed in a subroutine must always be **RETURN**. When the **RETURN** is performed, control is transferred back to the first statement after the **GOSUB** that invoked the subroutine and the program resumes execution at that point.

A particular subroutine is written only once in a BASIC program, but may be invoked from many points throughout the program. The **RETURN** statement must therefore be capable of transferring control back to many different points in the program depending on which of several **GOSUB**s invoked the subroutine.

When the computer performs a **GOSUB** statement, two actions are actually performed:

1. The location of the statement following the **GOSUB** is automatically stored in a variable in the computer's primary storage. This is called the *return location*.
2. The computer then performs a simple unconditional transfer of control to the first statement in the subroutine.

When the computer reaches the **RETURN** statement at the end of this subroutine, the following actions are performed:

1. The return location is retrieved from primary storage.
2. The computer performs a simple unconditional transfer of control back to the return location.

Example 5.2 Flow of control using subroutines

Consider the outline of a BASIC program illustrated in Figure 5.4. Show how the various **GOSUB** statements and the **RETURN** statement cooperate to allow the program to perform the statements of subroutine `ShowTotals` from many different places throughout the program. Assume that the program contains no transfers of control other than those effected by the **GOSUB**s and the **RETURN**.

Discussion: The computer begins at line 1 and executes the next several statements sequentially. When the computer gets to line 4, it performs the first **GOSUB** statement. The computer remembers that line 5 is the return location; this enables the subroutine to return to the proper place in the *main program* after the subroutine is performed. The computer then transfers control to the `ShowTotals` subroutine and performs the various statements in the subroutine. When the computer gets to the **RETURN** statement at line 21, it transfers control to the return location, in this case line 5.

The computer then performs the next several BASIC statements sequentially (because the problem statement said there were no other transfers of control). Then the computer arrives at the **GOSUB** statement at line 8. It remembers line 9 as the return location, and transfers control to the `ShowTotals` subroutine. It then performs the statements of the subroutine until it reaches the **RETURN**. The computer then transfers control to the return location, line 9, and continues performing statements until it comes to the **GOSUB** at line 12. The computer remembers line 13 as the return location, and then transfers control to `ShowTotals` and performs the subroutine. When the computer gets to the

```
      _____                              'line 1
      _____                              'line 2
      _____                              'line 3

      GOSUB ShowTotals                       'line 4
      _____                              'line 5
      _____                              'line 6
      _____                              'line 7

      GOSUB ShowTotals                       'line 8
      _____                              'line 9
      _____                              'line 10
      _____                              'line 11

      GOSUB ShowTotals                       'line 12
      _____                              'line 13
      _____                              'line 14
      _____                              'line 15
      END                                    'line 16

ShowTotals:
      REM The subroutine                     'line 17
      _____                              'line 18
      _____                              'line 19
      _____                              'line 20

      RETURN                                 'line 21
```

Figure 5.4 Outline of a BASIC program, illustrating the use of GOSUB/RETURN
with a subroutine

RETURN, it transfers control to line 13, and performs the remaining statements in
the program until it reaches **END**.

A word of caution is in order here. As the computer executes these
remaining statements, it will eventually reach line 16, the statement before the
subroutine. Unless line 16 ends the program or causes a transfer of control, the
computer will "fall into" the subroutine. Subroutines must be invoked only by
GOSUBs. Programs should not be allowed to enter a subroutine accidentally.
Because subroutines end with **RETURN**, it is meaningless to perform a subroutine
unless a GOSUB has previously saved the return location.

In Example 5.2, it was necessary to remember only a single return location
because each subroutine returned directly to the main program without invoking other
subroutines. BASIC does, however, allow subroutines to invoke other subroutines, so it
provides a mechanism called a *stack* in which multiple return locations may be saved in
the proper sequence for invoking and returning from subroutines. Items are placed in a
stack in *last-in-first-out (LIFO)* order, so that the *most recent* item placed there is the first

one retrieved. Thus, when a main program calls a subroutine, it places (or *pushes*) a return location on top of the stack; when the subroutine calls another subroutine, it places a second return location on the stack on top of the first location. When the second subroutine reaches its RETURN, BASIC automatically fetches its return location (to the first subroutine) from the top of the stack (this is called *popping* the stack). Now the stack contains only a single return location because the pop operation *fetches* and then *discards* the top element of the stack. When the first subroutine reaches its RETURN, BASIC pops the stack to obtain the return location (to the main program), and execution resumes in the main program. At this point the stack is empty. All these pushing and popping operations are handled automatically by BASIC and are transparent to the user.

5.7 Subroutines: Notes and Observations

1. Subroutines must be invoked or called only via the GOSUB.
2. The last statement to be executed in every subroutine must be RETURN.
3. Subroutines may invoke other subroutines. BASIC automatically keeps track of the return locations.
4. Subroutines may reference intrinsic functions and programmer-defined functions.
5. Many programmers group all their subroutines together at the end of their programs.
6. A subroutine can return many values to a program (in contrast to a function, which can return only a single value to a program).
7. A subroutine may access all variables in the main program.

5.8 Subprograms

Subprograms, like subroutines, allow the programmer to work with separate program pieces or "logical units." Each logical unit can be developed, tested and debugged independently.

However, as we will soon see, subprograms are far better than subroutines for building correct, reliable, and maintainable large-scale programs. This is true primarily because all variables within a subprogram definition are *local variables*. A local variable is only accessible in the subprogram in which it is defined. This makes it impossible for local variables to be changed accidentally by "misbehaving" portions of a large program. Such changes are often called *side effects*; these have been responsible for many problems in software systems built over the last several decades. Subprograms cannot be accidentally entered (as subroutines unfortunately can); they must be properly "called" in order to use them. Every subprogram has a list of formal parameters. These allow the main program and the subprogram to transfer values back and forth.

5.9 Subprogram Definitions

The format for a subprogram definition is

```
SUB Subname (parameterlist) STATIC
    first part of subprogram body
    EXIT SUB
    remaining part of subprogram body
END SUB
```

SUB and **END SUB** mark the beginning and end of the subprogram definition. Subname is any valid variable name. The parameterlist is a list of formal parameters. The parameter list must include parameters for any data that will be passed back to the main program. **STATIC** causes all local variables to be preserved between calls to the subprogram; when **STATIC** is omitted, variables are *automatic* (i.e., numeric variables are initialized to zero, and string variables are initialized to null each time the subprogram is called.) **EXIT SUB** provides an alternate means of leaving the subprogram and is optional. All subprograms should be placed at the end of the main program.

The exponentiation subprogram of Figure 5.5 inputs two numbers from the user, a for the base, and b for the exponent. A subprogram is used to multiply a by itself b times.

Subprograms are invoked with the **CALL** statement which has the format

```
CALL Subname (argumentlist)
```

where argumentlist is a list of variables or values that will replace the formal parameters in the subprogram definition. The Power subprogram in Figure 5.5 is invoked using the **CALL** statement as follows

```
CALL Power (a, b, total)
```

```
REM    The Power subprogram
INPUT "Enter the base"; a
INPUT "Enter the exponent"; b
CALL Power (a, b, total)
PRINT total
END

SUB Power (x, y, returntotal) STATIC
    returntotal = 1
    FOR c - 1 TO y
        returntotal = returntotal * x
    NEXT c
END SUB
```

Figure 5.5 An exponentiation subprogram

5.10 Passing Arguments by Reference or by Value

There are two ways to pass arguments to a subprogram in QuickBASIC, namely *pass by reference* and *pass by value*. When an argument is passed by reference, the address of the argument in the computer's memory is passed; any changes to the argument in a subprogram actually change the value of the passed argument in the calling program. When a variable is passed by value, a *copy* of the variable is made and the address of the copy is passed. Changes to the copy do not affect the variable's value in the calling program. To pass by value, an expression must be passed to the subprogram. QuickBASIC evaluates the expression and passes the address of a temporary location in memory where the value of the expression is stored.

Passing by reference and passing by value are two of the most important concepts in the construction of good programs. Ideally, the programmer should use the pass by value whenever the subprogram or function does not need to modify the value of a variable in the calling program. This prevents the accidental side effects that so greatly hinder the development of correct and reliable large-scale software systems.

The program in Figure 5.6 illustrates the differences between pass by value and pass by reference. We use a simple subprogram, add1, that increments the supplied value by 1 and prints the result. The subprogram then returns to the calling program which prints the value of the variable involved in the call.

The program is divided into two sections. In the first section, the subprogram is called with a pass by value of an expression, in this case the simple expression (x). The subprogram adds 1, prints 8, and returns to the calling program which then prints the value of x. Because x was enclosed in parentheses in the call, the pass was by value. Thus, the original value of x remains unchanged at 7, and this value is printed.

In the second section, the subprogram is called with a pass by reference of a variable, in this case the variable x. The subprogram adds 1, prints 8, and returns to the calling program which then prints the value of x. Because x was not enclosed in parentheses in the call, the pass was by reference. Thus, the original value of x becomes 8, and this is printed.

Arrays (see Chapter 6) may also be passed to a subprogram or function. An array is passed with the name of the array and an empty set of parentheses following the name. In the parameter list of the subprogram, an array formal parameter must appear in the same fashion. Single array elements may be passed by value, however, an entire array may not.

5.11 Recursion

A *recursive subprogram* is a subprogram that either directly or indirectly calls itself. Recursion is a complex topic discussed at length in upper-level computer science courses. In this section, a simple example of recursion is presented.

Example 5.3 Using recursion to calculate factorials
The factorial of a nonnegative integer n, written $n!$ (and pronounced "*n* factorial"), is defined mathematically as the product

```
REM    Understanding pass by reference and pass by value
x = 7
PRINT "EXAMPLE OF PASS BY VALUE WITH AN EXPRESSION"
PRINT "x is assigned the value "; x
PRINT "Actual parameter passed is (x)"
PRINT "Value printed by add1 is ";
CALL add1((x))
PRINT "Value of x in main program after add1 is "; x
PRINT
PRINT
x = 7
PRINT "EXAMPLE OF PASS BY REFERENCE WITH A VARIABLE"
PRINT "x is assigned the value "; x
PRINT "Actual parameter passed is x"
PRINT "Value printed by add1 is ";
CALL add1(x)
PRINT "Value of x in main program after add1 is "; x
END

SUB add1 (number) STATIC
   number = number + 1
   PRINT number
END SUB
```

```
╔══════════ Passing-Reference vs. Value ══════════╗
║ EXAMPLE OF PASS BY VALUE WITH AN EXPRESSION      ║
║ x is assigned the value  7                       ║
║ Actual parameter passed is (x)                   ║
║ Value printed by add1 is  8                      ║
║ Value of x in main program after add1 is  7      ║
║                                                  ║
║                                                  ║
║ EXAMPLE OF PASS BY REFERENCE WITH A VARIABLE     ║
║ x is assigned the value  7                       ║
║ Actual parameter passed is x                     ║
║ Value printed by add1 is  8                      ║
║ Value of x in main program after add1 is  8      ║
╚══════════════════════════════════════════════════╝
```

Figure 5.6 Understanding pass by reference and pass by value

$$n * (n - 1) * (n - 2) * \ldots * 1$$

with 1! defined to be 1. For example, 5! is the product 5 * 4 * 3 * 2 * 1, which is equal to 120.

The factorial of an integer, number, greater than 0 can be calculated (nonrecursively) using a **FOR/NEXT** as follows:

```
factorial = 1
FOR counter = number TO 1 STEP -1
   factorial = counter * factorial
NEXT counter
```

A recursive definition of factorial is arrived at by observing the relationship

$$n! = n * (n - 1)!$$

For example, 5! is clearly equal to 5 * 4!. Recursive subprograms typically result in a succession of subprogram calls leading to a simple result. For example, the evaluation of 5! would proceed as follows:

$$5! = 5 * 4!$$
$$5! = 5 * (4 * 3!)$$
$$5! = 5 * 4 * (3 * 2!)$$
$$5! = 5 * 4 * 3 * (2 * 1!)$$
$$5! = 5 * 4 * 3 * 2 * 1$$

Here the succession of recursive calls proceeds until 1! has to be evaluated. Since 1! is defined to be 1, no further recursion is necessary.

Thus, there are two components to any recursive subprogram. One component expresses the problem as a recursive call that evaluates a slightly simpler problem. The other component provides a means for the recursion to terminate by evaluating the simplest case.

Example 5.4 A recursive factorial subprogram

Write a recursive subprogram that calculates factorials, and incorporate it into a program that prints the factorials of 1 to 10.

Discussion: The program and a sample execution are shown in Figure 5.7. The subprogram `Factorial` first tests to see if the terminating condition is true, i.e., is `number` equal to 1. If `number` is 1, `result` is set to 1, no recursion is necessary, and a `result` of 1 is returned to the caller. If `number` is greater than 1, then the statements

```
CALL Factorial ((number - 1), result)
result = number * result
```

express the problem as the product of `number` and the `result` of a recursive call to `Factorial` evaluating the simpler factorial of `number - 1`.

Let us see how this subprogram calculates the factorial of 3. While processing the first call, `Factorial` determines that 3 is not equal to 1 (i.e., the terminating condition is false). It therefore calculates `result` as 3 times the factorial of 2; it recursively calls `Factorial` to calculate this `result`. This call finds that 2 is not equal to 1. It therefore calculates its own `result` as 2 times the factorial of 1; it recursively calls `Factorial` to calculate this `result`. This call

```
REM    Calculating factorials with a recursive subprogram
FOR i = 1 TO 10
    CALL Factorial ((i), theresult)
    PRINT theresult
NEXT i
END

SUB Factorial (number, result)
    IF number = 1 THEN
        result = 1
        ELSE
            CALL Factorial ((number - 1), result)
            result = number * result
    END IF
END  SUB
```

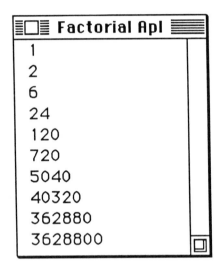

Figure 5.7 Calculating factorials with a recursive subprogram

indeed finds that 1 is equal to 1 so Factorial returns the result, 1, to its caller which calculates 2 times 1 and returns the result, 2, to its caller which calculates 3 times 2 and returns the *final* result, 6, to the calling main program.

Notice that the Factorial subprogram does not use the keyword **STATIC**, and thus all variables are assumed to be *dynamic*. Dynamic variables are used in recursive programs because they are saved onto the *stack* each time the subprogram calls itself.

Unfortunately, it is not possible to run recursive programs directly from the QuickBASIC environment; recursive programs must first be compiled. Compiling takes some extra time, but it makes the program execute much faster because the computer no longer needs to interpret (or translate) each instruction every time it is executed. To compile the Factorial program, select the Compile option from the **Run** menu. This will compile the program and run it. Compiling creates a new file with "Apl" (meaning "application") appended to the file name. This file can then be run at any time from the Macintosh Desktop by selecting it and opening it exactly as you would the QuickBASIC program or any other application. See the Appendix for a detailed explanation of the compiling features.

Concepts

ABS
argument of a function
ATN
automatic variable
call a subroutine
COS
DATE$
DEF
divide and conquer
dynamic variable
EXP
factorial
first statement after the GOSUB
FIX
FN
formal parameter
function
function definition
GOSUB
greatest integer not greater than
INT
integer part of
intrinsic function
invoke a subroutine
is a number an integer?
last-in-first-out
LIFO
local variable
LOG
main program

modular programming
module
pass by reference
pass by value
pop
program piece
programmer-defined function
push
recursion
recursive call
recursive subprogram
RETURN
return a single value
return location
return multiple values
RND
round a number
SGN
side effects
SIN
SQR
stack
STATIC
STATIC variable
SUB/END SUB
subprogram
subroutine
TAB
TAN

Problems

5.1. Show the value of x after each of the following BASIC statements is performed:
   (a)   LET x = ABS(7.5)
   (b)   LET x = INT(7.5)
   (c)   LET x = SGN(7.5)
   (d)   LET x = ABS(0.0)
   (e)   LET x = INT(0.0)
   (f)   LET X = SGN(0.0)
   (g)   LET x = ABS(-6.4)
   (h)   LET x = INT(-6.4)
   (i)   LET x = SGN(-6.4)
   (j)   LET x = INT(SGN(-ABS(-8+INT(-5.5))))

5.2. A parking garage charges a $2.00 minimum fee to park for up to three hours. The garage charges an additional $0.50 per hour for each hour *or part thereof* in excess of three hours. The maximum charge for any given 24-hour period is $10.00. Assume that no car parks for longer than 24 hours at a time. Write a BASIC program that will calculate and print the parking charges for each of 16 customers who parked their cars in this garage yesterday. You should enter the hours parked for each customer in **DATA** statements. Your program should print the results in a neat tabular format, and should calculate and print the total of yesterday's receipts. Use the following format for your outputs:

Car	Hours	Charge
1	1.5	2
2	4	2.5
3	3.5	2.5
4	24	10
etc.		
TOTAL	98	DOLLARS

5.3. One important application of the **INT** system-defined function is rounding a number to the nearest integer. The BASIC statement

LET y = **INT** (x + .5)

will round off the number x to the nearest integer, and assign the result to y. Write a BASIC program that reads several numbers from **DATA** statements and uses the above statement to round off each of these numbers to the nearest integer. For each number processed, print both the original number and the rounded number.

5.4. The **INT** system-defined function may also be used to round a number to a particular decimal place. The BASIC statement

LET y = **INT** (x * 10 + .5) / 10

will round the number x to the tenths position (i.e., the first position to the right of the decimal point). The BASIC statement

LET y = **INT** (x * 100 + .5) / 100

will round the number x to the hundredths position (i.e., the second position to the right of the decimal point).
   Write a BASIC program that defines four functions to round a number x to
(a) The nearest integer
(b) The nearest tenth
(c) The nearest hundredth
(d) The nearest thousandth
   Your program should read values from **DATA** statements. For each value your program should print the original value, the number rounded to the nearest integer, the number rounded to the nearest tenth, the number rounded to the nearest hundredth, and the number rounded to the nearest thousandth. Print the results in a neat tabular format with appropriate headings.

5.5. Examine the following program carefully. Note that there are two groups of identical statements. Rewrite the program, eliminating one of the sets of four statements and defining the other set as a subroutine. Use **GOSUB** and **RETURN**. The new program should yield the same results as the original program when it is run.

```
REM   A BASIC program to be rewritten with subroutines
PRINT "Enter two numbers"
INPUT x, y
PRINT "The sum is"; x + y
PRINT "The product is"; x * y
PRINT "The difference is"; x - y
PRINT "Enter two numbers"
INPUT x, y
PRINT "The sum is"; x + y
PRINT "The product is"; x * y
END
```

5.6. Describe an acceptable use of the **GOTO** statement in programs containing subroutines.

5.7. Define a single-line function, **FN**Hypotenuse, that calculates the length of the hypotenuse of a right triangle when the other two sides are given. Use this function in a program to determine the length of the hypotenuse for each of the following triangles.

Triangle	Side 1	Side 2
1	3	4
2	5	12
3	8	15

5.8. Write a function FNPower (Base, Exponent) that when invoked returns

$$\text{Base}^{\text{Exponent}}$$

For example, FNPower (3, 4) = 3 * 3 * 3 * 3. Assume that exponent is a positive, nonzero integer.

5.9. Use the **INT** function to write a program that inputs a series of pairs of numbers and determines for each pair whether the second is a multiple of the first.

5.10. Use the **INT** function to write a program that inputs a series of numbers and determines which are even and which are odd.

5.11. Develop a subprogram that will display at the left margin of the page a solid square of asterisks whose side is contained in variable side. For example, if side is 4, the subroutine should display

```
****
****
****
****
```

5.12. Write a subprogram that functions like the subroutine of Problem 5.11 except that it forms the square out of whatever character is contained in "string variable" Fillcharacter$. (*Note:* String variables are discussed in depth in Chapter 7.) Thus if side is 5 and Fillcharacter$ is "#" then a **GOSUB** to this subroutine should print

```
#####
#####
#####
#####
#####
```

5.13. Use techniques similar to those developed in Problems 5.11 and 5.12 to produce a program that graphs a wide range of shapes and positions these shapes at various locations across the screen.

5.14. Show precisely what the output of the following program will be when the program is run:

```
GOSUB FirstSub
GOSUB SecondSub
GOSUB ThirdSub
GOTO WrapUp
FirstSub:
    PRINT "A"; "B";
    RETURN
SecondSub:
    PRINT "C"; "D",
    RETURN
ThirdSub:
    PRINT "E", "F"
    RETURN
WrapUp:
    END
```

Enter the program and run it to determine if your answer is correct. Now delete the **GOTO** statement and run the program. What happens? Why?

5.15. Write program segments that accomplish each of the following:
   (a) Calculate the integer part of the quotient when integer a is divided by integer b.
   (b) Calculate the integer remainder when integer a is divided by integer b.
   (c) Use the program pieces developed in (a) and (b) to write a subroutine that **INPUT**s an integer and prints it as a series of digits, each pair of which is separated by two spaces. For example, if the number 4562 is entered, then your subroutine should print

   4   5   6   2

5.16. Write a subprogram that will take the time as three integers (for hours, minutes, and seconds), and will return the number of seconds since the last time the clock "struck 12." Then use this subprogram to calculate the amount of time in seconds between two times, both of which are within one "12-hour cycle" of the clock.

5.17. Implement the following integer functions:
   (a) Write a function **FNCelsius** that returns the Celsius equivalent of a Fahrenheit temperature.
   (b) Write function **FNFahrenheit** that returns the Fahrenheit equivalent of a Celsius temperature.
   (c) Use these functions to write a program that prints charts showing the Fahrenheit equivalents of all Celsius temperatures from 0 to 100 degrees, and the Celsius equivalents of all Fahrenheit temperatures from 32 to 212 degrees.

5.18. Write a subprogram that returns the largest of three integers.

5.19. A number is said to be a *perfect number* if its factors, including 1, sum to the number itself. For example, 6 is a perfect number because 6 = 1 + 2 + 3. Write a subprogram that determines if a number is a perfect number. Use this subprogram in a program that determines and prints all the perfect numbers between 1 and 10,000.

5.20. An integer is said to be *prime* if it is divisible only by 1 and itself. Thus 2, 3, 5, and 7 are prime, but 4, 6, 8, and 9 are not. Write a subprogram that determines if `number` is prime. Use this subprogram in a program that determines and prints all the prime numbers between 1 and 10,000. How many of these 10,000 numbers do you really have to test before being sure that you have found all the primes?

5.21. Write a subprogram that takes an integer value and prints the number with the digits reversed. For example, given the number 7631, the subprogram should print 1367.

5.22. The *greatest common divisor* (GCD) of two integers is the largest integer that evenly divides each of the two numbers. Write a subprogram that determines the greatest common divisor of `first` and `second`.

5.23. Write a subprogram that prints 4 if a student's average is 90-100, 3 if the average is 80-89, 2 if the average is 70-79, 1 if the average is 60-69, and 0 if the average is lower than 60.

5.24. Write a recursive subprogram `power (base, exponent, result)` that when invoked returns

$$base^{exponent}$$

For example, `power (3, 4, result)` = $3 \wedge 4$ or $3 * 3 * 3 * 3$. Assume that `exponent` is a positive, nonzero integer. *Hint:* The recursion step would use the relationship

$$base^{exponent} = base * base^{exponent - 1}$$

and the terminating condition occurs when `exponent` is equal to 1 because

$$base^1 = base$$

5.25. The Fibonacci series

$$0, 1, 1, 2, 3, 5, 8, 13, 21, ...$$

begins with the terms 0 and 1 and has the property that each succeeding term is the sum of the two preceding terms.
(a) Write a subprogram `fibonacci (n, result)` that calculates the nth Fibonacci number using a nonrecursive approach.
(b) Write a recursive subprogram `rfibonacci (n, result)` that calculates the nth Fibonacci number. Use the following relationships:

fib (n) = fib (n - 1) + fib (n - 2)
fib (1) = 1
fib (0) = 0

(c) Develop a test program that will help you determine which of these programs executes more efficiently. (*Hint:* Calculate a large number of large Fibonacci numbers and check for any noticeable difference in execution speed.)

5.26. (Towers of Hanoi) Every budding computer scientist must grapple with certain classic problems, and the Towers of Hanoi (see Figure 5.10) is one of the most famous of these. Legend has it that in a temple in the Far East, priests are attempting to move a stack of disks from one peg to another. The initial stack had 64 disks threaded onto one peg and arranged from bottom to top by decreasing size. The priests are attempting to move the stack from this peg to a second peg

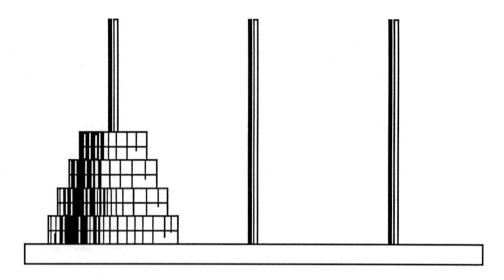

Figure 5.10 The Towers of Hanoi for the case with four disks

under the constraints that exactly one disk is moved at a time, and at no time may a larger disk be placed above a smaller disk. A third peg is available for temporarily holding the disks.

Supposedly the world will end when the priests complete their task (and thus there is little incentive for us to facilitate their efforts).

Let us assume that the priests are specifically attempting to move the disks from peg 1 to peg 3. We wish to develop an algorithm that will print the precise sequence of disk-to-disk peg transfers.

If we were to approach this problem with conventional methods, we would rapidly find ourselves hopelessly knotted up in managing the disks. Instead, if we attack the problem with recursion in mind, it immediately becomes tractable. Moving n disks can be viewed in terms of moving only $n - 1$ disks (and hence the recursion) as follows:

1. Move $n - 1$ disks from peg 1 to peg 2, using peg 3 as a temporary holding area.
2. Move the last disk (the largest) from peg 1 to peg 3.
3. Move the $n - 1$ disks from peg 2 to peg 3, using peg 1 as a temporary holding area.

The process ends when the last task involves moving $n = 1$ disk, and this is accomplished by trivially moving the disk without the need for a temporary holding area.

Write a program to solve the Towers of Hanoi problem. Use a recursive subprogram with four parameters:

1. The number of disks, n, to be moved
2. The peg on which these disks are initially threaded
3. The peg to which this stack of disks is to be moved
4. The peg to be used as a temporary holding area

Your program should print the precise instructions it will take to move the disks from the starting peg to the destination peg. For example, to move a stack of three disks from peg 1 to peg 3, your program should print the following series of moves:

       1 --> 3 (This means move one disk from peg 1 to peg 3)
       1 --> 2
       3 --> 2
       1 --> 3
       2 --> 1
       2 --> 3
       1 --> 3

Chapter 6
Arrays

6.1 Introduction

There are many applications in which data items are conveniently organized into lists and tables of values. This chapter introduces the features of BASIC that assist the programmer in creating, storing, and manipulating lists and tables of values.

6.2 Arrays

BASIC stores lists of values in *arrays*. An array is a group of related memory locations. These locations are related by the fact that they all have the same name. To refer to a particular location or element within the array, we specify the name of the array and the position of the particular element within the array.

Figure 6.1 shows an array called c. This array contains twelve *elements*. Any one of these elements may be referred to by giving the name of the array followed by the *position number* of the particular element. The position number is contained in parentheses. Thus, the first element of array c is referred to as c(1), the seventh element of array c is referred to as c(7), and, in general, the *i*th element of array c is referred to as c(i).

Array names in BASIC follow the same conventions as other variable names. The position number contained within parentheses is often called a *subscript*. A subscript may be a number or an expression. Thus, to refer to the eighth element of array c, we write c(8), where c is the array name and 8 is the subscript. If a program uses an expression as a subscript, then the expression is evaluated to determine the particular position number within the array. For example, if a = 5 and b = 6, then the statement

```
c(a + b) = c(a + b) + 1
```

results in array element c(11) being incremented by 1.

Let us examine array c in Figure 6.1 more closely. The *name* of the array is c. Its twelve elements are referred to as c(1), c(2), c(3), . . ., c(12). The *value* of c(1) is 45, the value of c(2) is 6, the value of c(3) is 117, the value of c(8) is 62,

Name of array (Note that
all elements of this array
have the same name, c)

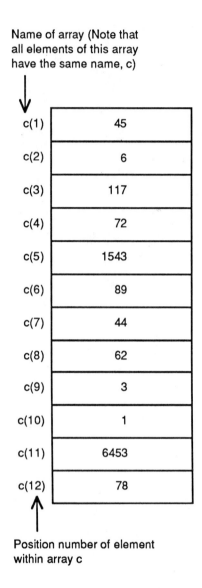

Position number of element
within array c

Figure 6.1 A 12-element array

and the value of c(12) is 78. To print the sum of the values contained in the first three elements of array c, we would write

        PRINT c(1) + c(2) + c(3)

To divide the value of the seventh element of array c by 2 and assign the result to the variable x, we would write

        x = c(7) / 2

6.3 Dimensioning Arrays

Arrays take up space in the computer's memory. The programmer specifies the number of locations required by each array so that the computer may reserve the appropriate amount of space; the *DIM* ("dimension") statement is used for this purpose. To tell the computer to reserve 12 elements for array c, the programmer writes

```
DIM c(12)
```

Space may be reserved for several arrays with a single **DIM** statement. To reserve 100 elements for array b and 27 elements for array x, the programmer writes

```
DIM b(100), x(27)
```

For arrays containing 10 or fewer elements it is not necessary to use the **DIM** statement. BASIC automatically reserves 10 locations for an array when the **DIM** statement is omitted. Nevertheless, it is considered a good programming practice to dimension every array regardless of its size.

Note that BASIC automatically reserves space for the zeroth (0th) element of every array. Thus, the statement

```
DIM a(100)
```

actually reserves 101 locations, one for each of the array elements a(0), a(1), a(2), ..., a(100). We shall often ignore the zeroth element of each array in our discussions.

6.4 Examples Using Arrays

Example 6.1 Initializing an array to zeros
Write a BASIC program that will initialize the elements of a ten-element array n to zeros, and then print the array in neat tabular format.

Discussion: The solution is presented in Figure 6.2. BASIC initializes its numeric arrays to zero at the beginning of each program, but arrays are often reused many times in a program, so the programmer will have to initialize an array to zeros occasionally. Also, many people consider it a good programming practice to initialize all arrays anyway. Note that the use of the **DIM** statement in this program is optional.

```
REM   Initialize elements of array to zero; print the array
DIM n(10)

FOR i = 1 TO 10
   n(i) = 0
NEXT i

PRINT "Element", "Value"
FOR i = 1 TO 10
   PRINT i, n(i)
NEXT i
END
```

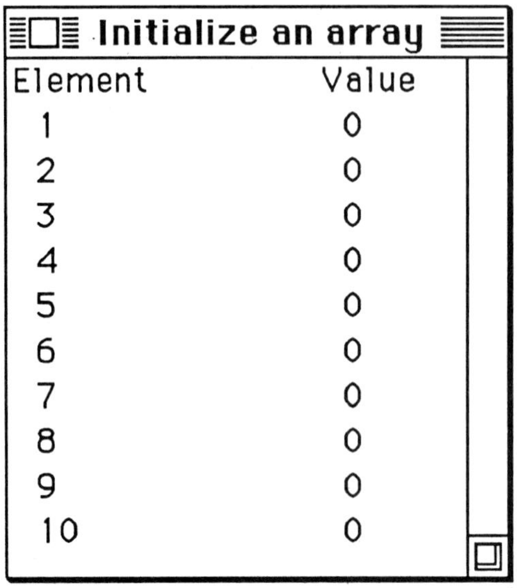
Initialize an array
Element Value
1 0
2 0
3 0
4 0
5 0
6 0
7 0
8 0
9 0
10 0

Figure 6.2 Initializing the elements of an array to zeros

Example 6.2 Reading the elements of an array from DATA statements

Write a BASIC program that will read ten values from **DATA** statements, place these values into the elements of array n, and then print the array in neat tabular format.

Discussion: The solution is presented in Figure 6.3. Note once again that the use of the **DIM** statement is optional in this program because BASIC would automatically reserve ten locations for n.

```
REM   Read elements of an array from
REM   DATA statements and print the array

DIM n(10)

FOR i = 1 TO 10
   READ n(i)
NEXT i
PRINT "Element", "Value"
FOR i = 1 TO 10
   PRINT i, n(i)
NEXT i
END

DATA 32, 27, 64, 18, 95, 14, 90, 70, 60, 37
```

Array READ/DATA	
Element	Value
1	32
2	27
3	64
4	18
5	95
6	14
7	90
8	70
9	60
10	37

Figure 6.3 Reading the elements of an array from DATA statements

Example 6.3 Fill the elements of an array with a series of generated values

Write a BASIC program that will initialize the elements of a ten-element array s to the values 2, 4, 6, . . ., 20, and then print the array in neat tabular format.

Discussion: The solution is presented in Figure 6.4. The values are generated by multiplying the loop counter by 2. At this point, the reader should begin to recognize the power of the **FOR/NEXT** combination in array manipulations. The first **FOR/NEXT** loop could also be used to fill a 1000-element array by changing the 10 in the **FOR** statement to 1000. (What other changes to the program would be necessary to enable it to process a 1000-element array?)

```
REM    Initialize the elements of array s to the
REM    even integers from 2 to 20 and print the array
DIM s(10)

FOR j = 1 TO 10
   s(j) = 2 * j
NEXT j
PRINT "Element", "Value"
FOR j = 1 TO 10
   PRINT j, s(j)
NEXT j
END
```

Initialize array s	
Element	Value
1	2
2	4
3	6
4	8
5	10
6	12
7	14
8	16
9	18
10	20

Figure 6.4 Generating the values to be placed into elements of an array

Example 6.4 Totaling the elements of an array

Write a BASIC program that will total the values contained in the elements of the twelve-element array a.

Discussion: The solution is presented in Figure 6.5. The statement in the body of the second **FOR/NEXT** loop does the totaling. Note that the **DIM** statement in this problem is required because the array contains more than 10 elements.

Example 6.5 Summarizing the results of an opinion poll

Forty students were asked to rate the quality of the food in the student cafeteria on a scale of 1 to 10 (1 means awful and 10 means excellent). Read the forty responses from **DATA** statements and summarize the results of the poll.

```
REM    Read elements of array from DATA statements
REM    then compute the sum of these elements
DIM a(12)
total = 0

FOR i = 1 TO 12
   READ a(i)
NEXT i
FOR i = 1 TO 12
   total = total + a(i)
NEXT i
PRINT "Total of array elements is"; total
END

DATA 1, 3, 5, 4, 7, 2, 99, 16, 45, 67, 89, 45


Total of array elements is 383
```

Figure 6.5 Computing the sum of the elements of an array

Discussion: This is a typical array application (See Figure 6.6). We wish to summarize the number of responses of each type (i.e., 1 through 10). We use a ten-element array, frequency. The first **FOR/NEXT** loop reads the responses one at a time and increments one of the ten counters in the frequency array. The key statement in the loop is

```
frequency(rating) = frequency(rating) + 1
```

This statement increments the appropriate counter depending on the value of rating. If rating is 1, then this statement is actually interpreted as

```
frequency(1) = frequency(1) + 1
```

If rating is 7, then the statement is interpreted as

```
frequency(7) = frequency(7) + 1
```

Note that regardless of how many responses are processed in the survey, we will still need only a ten-element array to summarize the results. Notice also that this statement assumes that the data contain legitimate values from 1 to 10. If the data contained a 13, then the statement would attempt to add 1 to frequency(13), which is nonexistent, and an error message would be printed.

It is considered a good programming practice to have programs check all input values for validity so that erroneous information may be rejected before it enters into a program's calculations.

```
REM    Student poll program
REM    read the responses and
REM    count the number of each type
FOR response = 1 TO 40
   READ rating
   frequency (rating) = frequency (rating) + 1
NEXT response

PRINT "Rating", "Frequency"
FOR rating = 1 TO 10
   PRINT rating, frequency (rating)
NEXT rating
END

DATA 1, 2, 6, 4, 8, 5, 9, 7, 8, 10
DATA 1, 6, 3, 8, 6, 10, 3, 8, 2, 7
DATA 6, 5, 7, 6, 8, 6, 7, 5, 6, 6
DATA 5, 6, 7, 5, 6, 4, 8, 6, 8, 10
```

Student poll	
Rating	Frequency
1	2
2	2
3	2
4	2
5	5
6	11
7	5
8	7
9	1
10	3

Figure 6.6 A simple student poll analysis program

Example 6.6 Printing histograms

Write a BASIC program that reads numbers from **DATA** statements and graphs the information in the form of a bar chart or histogram—each number should be printed, and then a bar consisting of that many asterisks should be printed beside the number. (See Problem 4.16.)

Discussion: The solution is presented in Figure 6.7. The nested **FOR/NEXT** loop actually draws the bars. Note the use of the blank **PRINT** to end a histogram bar.

```
REM    Histogram printing program
DIM n(10)

FOR i = 1 TO 10
    READ n(i)
NEXT i

PRINT "Element", "Value", "Histogram"
FOR i = 1 TO 10
    PRINT i, n(i),

    FOR j = 1 TO n(i)
        PRINT "*";
    NEXT j

    PRINT
NEXT i
END

DATA 1, 3, 5, 7, 9, 11, 13, 15, 17, 19
```

Histogram program		
Element	Value	Histogram
1	1	*
2	3	***
3	5	*****
4	7	*******
5	9	*********
6	11	***********
7	13	*************
8	15	***************
9	17	*****************
10	19	*******************

Figure 6.7 A program that prints histograms

Example 6.7 Sorting the elements of an array into ascending sequence

Sorting data (i.e., placing the data into some particular order) is one of the most important computer applications. A bank must sort all the checks it processes so that it can prepare individual bank statements at the end of each month. Virtually every business must sort some data into order to facilitate the processing of information. Write a BASIC program that sorts the values in the elements of the ten-element array A into ascending order.

Discussion: The solution is shown in Figure 6.8. The technique we use is called the *bubble sort* because the smaller values gradually "bubble" their way upward to the top of the array (like air bubbles rising in water), while the larger values sink to the bottom of the array. The technique is to make several passes through the array. On each pass, successive pairs of elements are compared. If a pair is in increasing order (or if the values are identical), we leave it as it is. If a pair is in decreasing order, we swap the values.

First we compare a(1) to a(2), then a(2) to a(3), then a(3) to a(4), and so on until we complete the pass by comparing a(9) to a(10). Note that though there are 10 elements, only nine comparisons are performed. Because of the way the successive comparisons are made, a large value may move down the array many positions on a single pass, but a small value may move up only one position. On the first pass, the largest value will sink all the way to the bottom element of the array, a(10). On the second pass, the second largest value will sink to the second element from the bottom of the array, a(9). On the ninth pass, the ninth largest value will sink to the ninth element from the bottom of the array, a(2). This, of course, will leave the smallest value sitting in a(1), so only nine passes of the array are actually needed to sort the array even though there are ten elements in the array.

```
REM    This program reads data items into an array,
REM    sorts the data items into ascending order,
REM    and prints the resulting array.
FOR i = 1 TO 10
    READ a(i)
NEXT i

PRINT "Data items in original order"
FOR i = 1 TO 10
    PRINT a(i);
NEXT i
PRINT

FOR pass = 1 TO 9
    FOR i = 1 TO 9
        IF a(i) > a(i+1) THEN
            hold = a(i)
            a(i) = a(i+1)
            a(i+1) = hold
        END IF
    NEXT i
NEXT pass

PRINT "Data items in ascending order"
FOR i = 1 TO 10
    PRINT a(i);
NEXT i
PRINT
END

DATA 2, 6, 4, 8, 10, 12, 89, 68, 45, 37
```

Figure 6.8 BASIC program for sorting an array *(continued)*

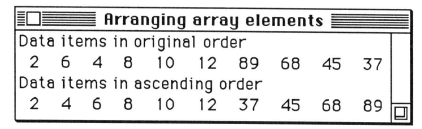

Figure 6.8 *(continued)*

The sorting is performed by the nested **FOR/NEXT** loop. If a swap is necessary, it is performed by the three assignments

```
hold = a(i)
a(i) = a(i + 1)
a(i + 1) = hold
```

where the extra variable `hold` temporarily stores one of the two values being swapped. The swap cannot be performed with only the two assignments

```
a(i) = a(i + 1)
a(i + 1) = a(i)
```

Let us see why. Suppose a(i) is 7 and a(i + 1) is 5. After the first assignment both values will be 5 and the value 7 will be lost. Hence the need for the extra variable `hold`.

BASIC provides the **SWAP** statement to enable us to exchange the values of two variables of the same type. For example, the preceding swap may also be accomplished with the single statement

```
SWAP a(i), a(i + 1)
```

For small arrays this version of the bubble sort is fine, but for larger arrays it is inefficient. We leave it to the exercises to develop a more efficient version of the bubble sort. More advanced computer science textbooks discuss a wide variety of powerful sorting techniques.

Example 6.8 Introduction to survey data analysis
Computers are commonly used to compile and analyze the results of surveys and opinion polls. Write a BASIC program that will read 99 responses to a survey from **DATA** statements. Each of the responses is a number from 1 to 10. The program should compute the mean, median, and mode of the 99 values.

Discussion: The mean is the arithmetic average of the 99 values. The `ComputeMean` subprogram in Figure 6.10 computes the mean by totaling the 99 elements and dividing the result by 99.

The median is the "middle value." The `ComputeMedian` subprogram in Figure 6.10 determines the median by first sorting the array of responses into ascending order, and then picking the middle element, `workarray(50)`, of the sorted array. Note that when there is an even number of elements, the median should be calculated as the mean of the two middle elements.

The mode is the value that occurs most frequently among the 99 responses. The `ComputeMode` subprogram in Figure 6.11 determines the mode by first tabulating the number of responses of each type, and then selecting the value that occurred the greatest number of times. This subprogram also produces a histogram to aid in determining the mode graphically.

Figure 6.12 contains a sample run of this program. The reader is urged to study the program and its outputs carefully. This example includes most of the common manipulations usually required in array problems.

```
REM   This program introduces the topic of survey data analysis.
REM   It reads 99 responses from a survey, and then computes the mean,
REM   the median, and the mode of the survey data

DIM response(99), frequency(10)

CALL ReadResponse(response())
CALL ComputeMean(response(), returnmean)
CALL ComputeMedian(response(), returnmedian)
CALL ComputeMode(frequency(), response(), returnmode)

LPRINT
LPRINT "The mean was "; returnmean
LPRINT "The median was "; returnmedian
LPRINT "The mode was "; returnmode
END

DATA 6, 7, 8, 9, 8, 7, 8, 9, 8, 9
DATA 7, 8, 9, 10, 9, 8, 7, 8, 7, 8
DATA 6, 7, 8, 9, 10, 9, 8, 7, 8, 7
DATA 7, 8, 9, 8, 9, 8, 9, 10, 8, 9
DATA 6, 7, 8, 7, 8, 7, 9, 8, 9, 10
DATA 7, 8, 9, 8, 9, 8, 9, 7, 5, 3
DATA 5, 6, 7, 2, 5, 3, 9, 4, 6, 4
DATA 7, 8, 9, 6, 8, 7, 8, 9, 7, 8
DATA 7, 4, 10, 2, 5, 3, 8, 7, 5, 6
DATA 4, 5, 6, 1, 6, 5, 7, 8, 7
```

Figure 6.9 Survey data analysis program (part 1 of 3)

```
SUB ComputeMean (workarray(), workmean) STATIC
   LPRINT "******"
   LPRINT " Mean "
   LPRINT "******"
   total = 0
   FOR j = 1 TO 99
      total = total + workarray(j)
   NEXT j
   workmean = total / 99

   LPRINT "The mean is the average value of all the data items."
   LPRINT "The mean is equal to the total of all the data items divided"
   LPRINT "by the number of data items (99)."
   LPRINT "The mean of the values in this run is ..."
   LPRINT total; "/ 99 = "; total/99
   LPRINT
END SUB

SUB ComputeMedian (workarray(), workmedian) STATIC
   LPRINT "******"
   LPRINT "Median"
   LPRINT "******"

   LPRINT "The unsorted array of response is"
   FOR j = 1 TO 99
      LPRINT workarray(j);
   NEXT j
   LPRINT

   FOR Pass = 1 TO 98
      FOR j = 1 TO 98
         IF workarray(j) > workarray(j + 1) THEN
            SWAP workarray(j), workarray(j + 1)
         END IF
      NEXT j
   NEXT Pass
   LPRINT

   LPRINT "The sorted array is"
   FOR j = 1 TO 99
      LPRINT workarray(j);
   NEXT j
   LPRINT

   LPRINT "The median is the 50th element of the sorted 99 element array."
   LPRINT "For this run the median is "; workarray(50)
   LPRINT
   workmedian = workarray(50)
END SUB
```

Figure 6.10 Survey data analysis program (part 2 of 3)

```
SUB ComputeMode (workarray1(), workarray2(), workmode) STATIC
   LPRINT "******"
   LPRINT " Mode "
   LPRINT "******"

   FOR rating = 1 TO 10
      workarray1(rating) = 0
   NEXT rating

   FOR j = 1 TO 99
      workarray1(workarray2(j)) = workarray1(workarray2(j)) + 1
   NEXT j

   LPRINT "Response", "Frequency", "Histogram"
   LPRINT
   LPRINT,,"          1   1   2   2   3"
   LPRINT,,"     5    0   5   0   5   0"
   LPRINT

   largest = 0
   modevalue = 0
   FOR rating = 1 TO 10
      LPRINT rating, workarray1(rating),
      IF workarray1(rating) > largest THEN
         largest = workarray1(rating)
         modevalue = rating
      END IF
      FOR h = 1 TO workarray1(rating)
         LPRINT "*";
      NEXT h
      LPRINT
   NEXT rating
   workmode = modevalue

   LPRINT "The mode is the most frequent value."
   LPRINT "For the run the mode is"; modevalue
   LPRINT "which occurred"; largest; "times"
   LPRINT
END SUB

SUB ReadResponse(workarray()) STATIC
   FOR j = 1 TO 99
      READ workarray(j)
   NEXT j
END SUB
```

Figure 6.11 Survey data analysis program (part 3 of 3)

```
******
 Mean
******
```

The mean is the average of all the data items.
The mean is equal to the total of all the data
items divided by the number of data items (99).
The mean of the values in this run is ...
 710 / 99 = 7.17172

```
******
Median
******
```

The unsorted array of responses is
6 7 8 9 8 7 8 9 8 9 7 8 9 10 9 8 7 8 7 8 6 7 8 9 10
9 8 7 8 7 7 8 9 8 9 8 9 10 8 9 6 7 8 7 8 7 9 8 9 10
7 8 9 8 9 8 9 7 5 3 5 6 7 2 5 3 9 4 6 4 7 8 9 6 8
7 8 9 7 8 7 4 10 2 5 3 8 7 5 6 4 5 6 1 6 5 7 8 7

The sorted array is
1 2 2 3 3 3 4 4 4 4 5 5 5 5 5 5 5 6 6 6 6 6 6 6 6
6 7 7 7 7 7 7 7 7 7 7 7 7 7 7 7 7 7 7 7 7 7 7 8 8
8 8 8 8 8 8 8 8 8 8 8 8 8 8 8 8 8 8 8 8 8 8 8 8 8
9 9 9 9 9 9 9 9 9 9 9 9 9 9 9 9 9 9 9 10 10 10 10

The median is the 50th element of the
sorted 99 element array. For this run
the median is 8.

```
******
 Mode
******
```

Response	Frequency	Histogram
		1 1 2 2 3
		5 0 5 0 5 0
1	1	*
2	2	**
3	3	***
4	4	****
5	7	*******
6	9	*********
7	22	**********************
8	27	***************************
9	19	*******************
10	5	*****

The mode is the most frequent value.
For this run the mode is 8
which occurred 27 times.

The mean was 7.17172
The median was 8
The mode was 8

Figure 6.12 Sample run for the survey data analysis program

6.5 Double-Subscripted Arrays

Arrays may also be used in BASIC to represent *tables* of values consisting of information arranged in *rows* and *columns*. To identify a particular element of such a table, we must specify *two position numbers* or *subscripts*: the first (by convention) identifies the row in which the element is contained, and the second (by convention) identifies the column in which the element is contained. Tables or arrays that require two subscripts to identify a particular element are called *double-subscripted arrays*.

Figure 6.13 illustrates a double-subscripted array, a. The array contains three rows and four columns, so it is said to be a "3 by 4" array. In general, an array with *m* rows and *n* columns is called an *m by n array*.

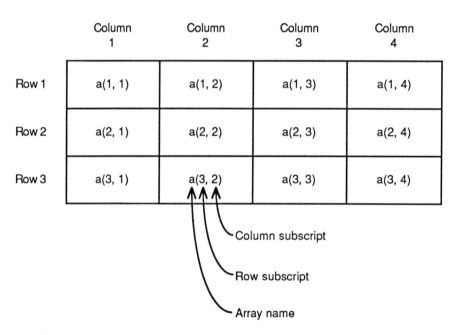

Figure 6.13 A double-subscripted array with three rows and four columns

Every element within array a has been identified in the figure by a name of the form a(i, j); a is the name of the array, and i and j are the subscripts that uniquely identify each element within array a. Notice that the names of the elements in the first row all have a first subscript of 1; the names of the elements in the fourth column all have a second subscript of 4.

Double-subscripted arrays must also be dimensioned by using the **DIM** statement, but only if the array is larger than 10 by 10. BASIC automatically provides space for a 10-by-10 array if the programmer does not specify the dimensions in a **DIM** statement. (Because of the zeroth row and zeroth column, BASIC actually provides 121 elements, because there are 11 rows and 11 columns.)

Example 6.9 Introduction to double-subscripted arrays
Refer to the double-subscripted array in Figure 6.13. Answer each of the following questions:
(a) How many rows does the array contain?
Answer. 3
(b) How many columns does the array contain?
Answer. 4
(c) How many elements does the array contain?
Answer. 12
(d) Write a BASIC statement that sets the element in row 2 and column 3 to zero.
Answer.   `a(2,3) = 0`
(e) Write a **FOR/NEXT** loop that sets all the elements in the third row to zero.
Answer.

```
FOR column = 1 TO 4
      a(3,column) = 0
NEXT column
```

Explanation. We specified the *third* row, and therefore we know that the first subscript is always 3. The **FOR/NEXT** loop varies only the second subscript (i.e., the column subscript). The preceding **FOR/NEXT** loop is equivalent to:

```
a(3,1) = 0
a(3,2) = 0
a(3,3) = 0
a(3,4) = 0
```

(f) Write a set of BASIC statements that will determine and print the total of all the elements in array `a`. You may assume that values have already been placed into the array.

Answer.
```
total = 0
FOR row = 1 TO 3
   FOR column = 1 TO 4
      total = total + a(row,column)
   NEXT column
NEXT row
PRINT "Total is"; total
```

Explanation. The first statement initializes `total` to zero. The program then proceeds to total the elements of the array one row at a time. The first **FOR** statement begins by setting `row` (i.e., the row subscript) to 1 so that the elements of the first row may be totaled by the nested **FOR/NEXT** statement. The second **NEXT** statement then causes the row subscript to be incremented to 2. The elements of the second row are then totaled. Then row three is totaled and the result is displayed.

Concepts

a(i)	name of an array
a(i,j)	position number
array	row of a double-subscripted array
automatic reservation of space for an array	row subscript
bar chart	single-subscripted array
column of a double-subscripted array	sorting items into order
column subscript	sorting pass
DIM statement	sorting the elements of an array
dimension an array	subscript
double-subscripted array	survey data analysis
expression as a subscript	SWAP statement
histogram	table of values
initialize an array	temporary area for exchange of values
m-by-n array	totaling the elements of an array
mean	value of an element
median	
mode	

Problems

6.1. Fill in the blanks in each of the following:

    (a)   BASIC stores lists of values in _____.

    (b)   The locations in an array are related by the fact that they _____.

    (c)   The position number contained within parentheses is often called a _____.

    (d)   A position number may be a(n) _____ or a(n) _____.

    (e)   The names of the five elements of array P are _____, _____, _____, _____, and _____.

    (f)   The number contained in a particular element of an array is called the _____ of that element.

    (g)   The programmer reserves space for arrays by using the _____ statement.

    (h)   The process of reserving space for an array in the computer's memory is called _____ the array.

    (i)   If the programmer does not explicitly reserve space for a single-subscripted array, then how many locations will the computer automatically reserve? _____.

    (j)   The process of placing the elements of an array into some particular order is called _____.

    (k)   The sorting scheme in which smaller values are forced to the top of the array while larger values are forced to the bottom is called _____.

    (l)   The process of using the computer to assist in the analysis of surveys and opinion polls is called _____.

    (m)   The arithmetic average of a series of values is called _____.

    (n)   In a double-subscripted array, the first subscript (by convention) identifies the _____.

    (o)   An m-by-n matrix contains _____ rows, _____ columns, and _____ elements.

    (p)   The name of the element in the third row and the fifth column of array d is _____.

6.2. State which of the following are true and which are false:

    (a)   To refer to a particular location or element within an array, we specify the name of the array and the value of the particular element.

    (b)   The programmer must explicitly reserve space for all arrays by using the DIM statement.

(c) To tell the computer to reserve 100 locations for array p, the programmer writes

```
DIM p
```

(d) For arrays containing 10 or fewer elements it is not necessary to use the **DIM**.
(e) **DIM** is a nonexecutable statement and may therefore be placed anywhere in a BASIC program.
(f) A BASIC program that initializes the elements of a 15-element array to zero must contain one **FOR** statement.
(g) A BASIC program that totals the elements of a double-subscripted array must contain two **NEXT** statements.
(h) If the elements of an array are already in proper order, then a bubble sort of that array will still require two passes.
(i) The mean, median, and mode of the following set of values are 5, 6, and 7, respectively: 1, 2, 5, 6, 7, 7, 7.

6.3. Write BASIC statements to accomplish each of the following:
    (a) Write a single BASIC statement that will display the value of the seventh element of array f.
    (b) Write a single BASIC statement that will **INPUT** a value into the fourth element of single-subscripted array b.
    (c) Write a set of BASIC statements that will initialize each of the values of single-subscripted array g to have the value 8. Assume that g has 5 elements.
    (d) Write a set of BASIC statements that will total the elements of array c of **DIM** c(100).
    (e) Write a set of BASIC statements that will copy array a into the first portion of array b. Assume **DIM** a(11), b(34).
    (f) Write a set of BASIC statements that will find the smallest and largest values contained in 99-element array w.

6.4. Consider a 2 by 5 array t.
    (a) Write a dimension statement for t.
    (b) How many rows does t have?
    (c) How many columns does t have?
    (d) How many elements does t have?
    (e) Write the complete names of all the elements in the second row of t.
    (f) Write the complete names of all the elements in the third column of t.
    (g) Write a single BASIC statement that sets the element of t that is in the first row and the second column to zero.
    (h) Write a series of BASIC statements that initializes each element of t to zero. Do not use **FOR/NEXT**.
    (i) Write a series of BASIC statements that initializes each element of t to zero. Use **FOR/NEXT**.
    (j) Write a series of BASIC statements that **INPUT**s the values for the elements of t.
    (k) Write a series of BASIC statements that determines and prints the smallest value in array t.
    (l) Write a series of BASIC statements that displays the elements of the first row of t.
    (m) Write a series of BASIC statements that totals only the elements of the fourth column of t.

6.5. Use a single-subscripted array to solve the following problem. One large chemical company pays its salespeople on a commission basis. The salespeople receive $200 per week plus 9 percent of their gross sales for that week. For example, a salesperson who sells $3000 worth of chemicals in a week receives $200 plus 9 percent of $3000, or a total of $470. Write a BASIC program (using an array of counters) that determines how many of the salespeople earned salaries in each of the following ranges (assume that each salesperson's salary is truncated to an integer amount):
    1. $200-$299
    2. $300-$399
    3. $400-$499
    4. $500-$599
    5. $600-$699

6. $700-$799
7. $800-$899
8. $900-$999
9. $1000 and over

6.6. In the text it was stated that the bubble sort presented in Example 6.7 was inefficient for large arrays. Make the following simple modifications to improve the performance of the bubble sort.
 (a) After the first pass, the largest number is guaranteed to be in the highest-numbered element of the array; after the second pass, the two highest numbers are "in place," and so on. Therefore, instead of making nine comparisons on every pass, modify the bubble sort to make eight comparisons on the second pass, seven on the third pass, and so on.
 (b) The data in the array may already be in the proper order or near proper order, so why make nine passes if fewer will suffice? Modify the sort to check at the end of each pass if any swaps have been made. If none has been made, then the data must already be in the proper order, so the program should terminate. If swaps have been made, then at least one more pass is needed.

6.7. Write single statements that perform each of the following array operations:
 (a) Initialize the 10 elements of array `counts` to zeros.
 (b) Add 1 to each of the 15 elements of array `bonus`.
 (c) Read the 12 values of array `monthlysales` from **DATA** statements.
 (d) Print the 5 values of array `bestscores` in column format across a single line.

6.8. Use a single-subscripted array to solve the following problem. A set of **DATA** statements contains a list of 30 numbers, each of which is between 100 and 1000. Your program is to read each number and then print it only if it is not a duplicate of a number already read. Provide for the "worst case" in which all 30 numbers are different. Use the smallest possible array to solve this problem.

6.9. Label the elements of 3-by-5 double-subscripted array `sales` to indicate the order in which they are set to zero by the following program segment:

```
FOR row = 1 TO 3
    FOR column = 1 TO 5
        sales(row, column) = 0
    NEXT column
NEXT row
```

6.10. (Airline Reservations System) A small airline has just purchased a computer for its new automated reservations system. The president has asked you to program the new system in BASIC. You are to write a program to assign seats on each flight of the airline's only plane (capacity: 30 seats).
 Your program should display the following menu of alternatives:

  Please type 1 for "smoking"
  Please type 2 for "nonsmoking"

If the person types 1, then your program should assign a seat in the smoking section (seats 1-15). If the person types 2, then your program should assign a seat in the nonsmoking section (seats 16-30). Your program should then print a boarding pass indicating the person's seat number and whether it is in the smoking or nonsmoking section of the plane.
 Use a single-subscripted array to represent the seating chart of the plane. Initialize all the elements of the array to 0 to indicate that all seats are empty. As each seat is assigned, set the corresponding elements of the array to 1 to indicate that the seat is no longer available.
 Your program should, of course, never assign a seat that has already been assigned. When the smoking section is full, your program should ask the person if it is acceptable to be placed in the nonsmoking section (and vice versa). If yes, then make the appropriate seat assignment. If no, then print the message "Next flight leaves in 3 hours."

6.11. Use a double-subscripted array to solve the following problem. A company has four salespeople (1 to 4) who sell five different products (1 to 5). Once a day, each salesperson passes in a slip for each different type of product sold. Each slip contains:
        1. The salesperson number
        2. The product number
        3. The total dollar value of that product sold that day
Thus, each salesperson passes in between 0 and 5 sales slips per day. Assume that the information from all of the slips for last month has been entered into **DATA** statements. Write a program that will read all this information, and summarize the total sales by salesperson by product. All totals should be stored in the double-subscripted, 5-by-4 array `sales`. After processing all the information for last month, print the results in neat tabular format with each of the four columns representing a particular salesperson, and each of the five rows representing a particular product. Cross total each row to get the total sales of each product for last month; cross total each column to get the total sales by salesperson for last month.

6.12. (Turtle Graphics) The Logo language, which is particularly popular among personal computer users, made the concept of *turtle graphics* famous. Imagine a mechanical turtle that walks around the room under the control of a BASIC program. The turtle holds a pen in one of two positions, up or down. While the pen is down, the turtle traces out shapes as it moves; while the pen is up, the turtle moves about freely without writing anything. In this problem you will simulate the operation of the turtle and create a computerized sketchpad as well.

    Use a 50-by-50 array `floor` which is initialized to zeros. Read commands from **DATA**. Keep track of the current position of the turtle at all times and whether the pen is currently up or down. Assume that the turtle always starts at position 1,1 of the floor with its pen up. The set of turtle commands your program must process are as follows:

Command	Meaning
1	Pen up
2	Pen down
3	Turn right
4	Turn left
5,10	Move forward 10 spaces (or a number other than 10)
6	Print the 50-by-50 array
9	End of data (sentinel)

Suppose that the turtle is somewhere near the center of the floor. The following "program" would draw and print a 12-by 12-square:

        2
        5,12
        3
        5,12
        3
        5,12
        3
        5,12
        1
        6
        9

As the turtle moves with the pen down, set the appropriate elements of array `floor` to 1s. When the 6 command (print) is given, wherever there is a 1 in the array, display an asterisk, or some other character you choose. Write a BASIC program to implement the turtle graphics capabilities discussed here. Write several turtle graphics programs to draw interesting shapes. Add other commands to increase the power of your turtle graphics language.

6.13. (Knight's Tour) One of the more interesting puzzlers for chess buffs is the Knight's Tour problem, originally proposed by the mathematician Euler. The question is, quite simply, this: Can the chess piece called the knight move around an empty chessboard and touch every one of the 64 squares once and only once? We will study this intriguing problem in depth here.

   The knight makes L-shaped moves (over two in one direction and then over one more in a perpendicular direction). Thus, from a square in the middle of an empty chessboard, the knight can make eight different moves as shown in Figure 6.14.

(a)   Draw an 8-by-8 chessboard on a sheet of paper and attempt a Knight's Tour by hand. Put a 1 in the first square you move to, a 2 in the second square, a 3 in the third, and so on. Before starting the tour, estimate how far you think you will get, remembering that a full tour consists of 64 moves. How far did you get? Were you even close to your estimate?

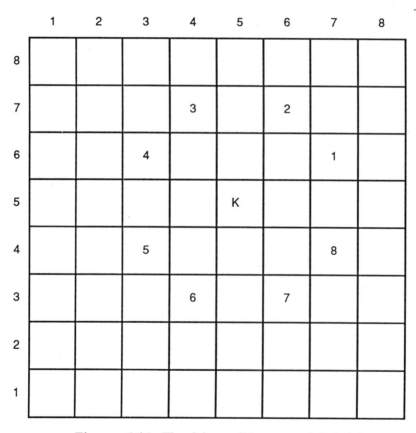

Figure 6.14   The eight possible moves of the knight

(b)   Now let us develop a program that will move the knight around a chessboard. The board itself is represented by an 8-by-8 double-subscripted array, board. Each of the squares is initialized to zero to indicate that no moves have yet been made. We describe each of the eight possible moves in terms of both their horizontal and vertical components. For example, move 1 consists of moving two squares horizontally to the right and one square vertically upward. Move 2 consists of moving one square horizontally to the right and two squares vertically upward. Horizontal moves to the left and vertical moves downward are indicated with negative numbers. The eight moves may then be described by two single-subscripted arrays, horizontal and vertical, as follows:

```
horizontal(1) = +2
horizontal(2) = +1
horizontal(3) = -1
horizontal(4) = -2
horizontal(5) = -2
horizontal(6) = -1
horizontal(7) = +1
horizontal(8) = +2
vertical(1) = +1
vertical(2) = +2
vertical(3) = +2
vertical(4) = +1
vertical(5) = -1
vertical(6) = -2
vertical(7) = -2
vertical(8) = -1
```

Let the variables currentrow and currentcolumn indicate the row and column of the knight's current position. To make a move type movenumber, where movenumber is between 1 and 8; your program uses the statements

```
currentrow = currentrow + vertical(movenumber)
currentcolumn = currentcolumn + horizontal(movenumber)
```

Keep a counter that varies from 1 to 64. Record the latest count in each square that the knight moves to. Remember to test each square to see if the knight has already been there. And, of course, test every move to make sure that the knight does not land off the chessboard. Now write a program to move the knight around the chessboard. Run the program. How far does the knight go before it runs out of potential moves?

(c) After attempting to write and run a Knight's Tour program, you have probably developed some valuable insights. We will use these to develop a heuristic or a (strategy) for moving the knight. Heuristics do not guarantee success, but a carefully developed heuristic greatly improves the chance of success. You may have observed that the outer squares are in some sense more troublesome than the squares nearer to the center of the board. In fact, the most troublesome, or inaccessible, squares are the four corners.

Intuition may suggest to you that you should attempt to move to the most troublesome squares first, and leave open those that are easiest to get to so that when the board gets congested near the end of your tour you will have a greater chance of success.

We may develop an "accessibility heuristic" by classifying each of the squares according to how accessible they are, and then always moving the knight to the square (within the knight's L-shaped moves, of course) that is most inaccessible. We label a double-subscripted array accessibility with numbers indicating from how many squares each particular square is accessible. On a blank chessboard, the center squares therefore are rated as 8s, the corner squares are rated as 2s, and the other squares have accessibility numbers of 3, 4, or 6 as follows:

```
2  3  4  4  4  4  3  2
3  4  6  6  6  6  4  3
4  6  8  8  8  8  6  4
4  6  8  8  8  8  6  4
4  6  8  8  8  8  6  4
4  6  8  8  8  8  6  4
3  4  6  6  6  6  4  3
2  3  4  4  4  4  3  2
```

Now write another Knight's Tour program, using the accessibility heuristic. At any time, the knight should move to the square with the lowest accessibility number. In case of a tie, the knight may be moved to any of the tied squares. Therefore, the tour may begin in any of the four corners. (*Note:* As the knight moves around the chessboard, your program should reduce the accessibility numbers as more and more squares become occupied. In this way, at any given time during the tour, each available square's accessibility number will remain equal to precisely the number of squares from which that square may be reached.) Run this version of your program. Did you get a full tour? Now modify the program to run 64 tours, one from each square of the chessboard. How many full tours did you get?

(d)   In the program of part (c) there was little that you could do in the case of a tie except to pick a square essentially at random. Actually, there is something you could do here that intuitively should improve your chances of success. This is called lookahead and is a valuable technique in various kinds of game playing programs. Write one last version of your Knight's Tour program which, when encountering a tie between two or more squares, decides what square to choose by looking ahead to those squares reachable from the "tied" squares. Your program should move to the square for which the next move would arrive at a square with the lowest accessibility number.

6.14.   (Eight Queens) Another puzzler for chess buffs is the Eight Queens problem. Simply stated: Is it possible to place eight queens on an empty chessboard so that no queen is "attacking" any other, that is, so that no two queens are in the same row, the same column, or along the same diagonal? Use the kind of thinking developed in Problem 6.13 to formulate a heuristic for solving the Eight Queens problem. Run your program. (*Hint:* It is possible to assign a numeric value to each square of the chessboard indicating how many squares of an empty chessboard are "eliminated" once a queen is placed in that square. For example, each of the four corners would be assigned the value 22, as can be seen from the diagram in Figure 6.15.)

```
* * * * * * * *
* *
*   *
*     *
*       *
*         *
*           *
*             *
```

Figure 6.15 The 22 squares eliminated by placing a queen in the upper left corner

Once these "elimination numbers" are placed in all 64 squares, the heuristic might dictate that the next queen always be placed in the square with the smallest elimination number. Why is this strategy intuitively appealing?

Special Section: Building Your Own Computer

In the next several problems, we take a temporary diversion away from the world of high-level language programming. We will "peel open" a computer and look at how it is constructed on the inside. We will introduce machine language programming and write several machine language programs. To make this an especially valuable experience, we will then build a computer (through the technique of *simulation*) on which you will actually be able to execute your machine language programs!

6.15.   (Machine Language Programming) Let us create a hypothetical computer which we will call the Simpletron. As its name implies, it is a simple machine, but, as we will soon see, a powerful one as well. The Simpletron runs programs written in the only language it directly understands, that is, Simpletron Machine Language, or SML for short (see Figure 6.16).

The Simpletron contains an *accumulator* —a "special register" in which information is put before we use that information in calculations or examine it in various ways. All information in the Simpletron is handled in terms of *words*. A word is a signed four-digit decimal number such as +3364, −1293, +0007, −0001, etc. The Simpletron is equipped with a 99-word memory, and these words are referenced by their location numbers 01, 02, ..., 99.

Before running the SML program, we must *load* or place it into Simpletron's memory. The first instruction (or statement) of every SML program is always placed in location 01. SML is briefly summarized in Figure 6.16.

Operation Code	Meaning
10	Read a word from the terminal into memory
	(Print a "?" on the terminal as BASIC's **INPUT** does)
11	Write a word from memory to the terminal
20	Load a word from memory into the accumulator
21	Store a word from the accumulator into memory
30	Add a word from memory to the word in the accumulator
31	Subtract a word from memory from the word in the accumulator
32	Divide a word from memory into the word in the accumulator
33	Multiply a word from memory by the word in the accumulator
40	Branch to a specific location in memory
41	Branch to a specific location in memory if the accumulator is negative
42	Branch to a specific location in memory if the accumulator is zero
43	Halt, i.e., the program has completed its task

Figure 6.16 A summary of Simpletron Machine Language (SML)

Each instruction written in SML occupies one word of the Simpletron's memory and hence is a signed four-digit decimal number. We shall assume that the sign of an SML instruction is always plus, but the sign of a data word may be either plus or minus. The first two digits of an instruction are the *operation code*, which tells the Simpletron what operation is to be performed. The last two digits of an instruction are the *operand*, which is the address of the memory location containing the word to which the operation applies. Now let us consider several simple SML programs.

Example 1

Location	Number	Instruction
01	+1008	(Read A)
02	+1009	(Read B)
03	+2008	(Load A)
04	+3009	(Add B)
05	+2110	(Store C)
06	+1110	(Write C)
07	+4300	(Halt)
08	+0000	(Variable A)
09	+0000	(Variable B)
10	+0000	(Result C)

This SML program reads two numbers from the keyboard and then computes and prints their sum. The instruction +1008 reads the first number from the keyboard and places it into location 08 (which we have initialized to zero). Then +1009 reads the next number into location 09. The load instruction, +2008, then puts the first number into the accumulator, and the add instruction, +3009, adds the second number to the number in the accumulator. *All SML arithmetic instructions leave their result in the accumulator,* so the store instruction, +2110, places the result back into memory location 10 from which the write instruction, +1110, takes it and prints it (as a signed four-digit decimal number). The halt instruction, +4300, terminates the execution of the program.

Example 2

Location	Number	Instruction
01	+1010	(Read A)
02	+1011	(Read B)
03	+2010	(Load A)
04	+3111	(Subtract B)
05	+4108	(Branch negative to 08)
06	+1110	(Write A)
07	+4300	(Halt)
08	+1111	(Write B)
09	+4300	(Halt)
10	+0000	(Variable A)
11	+0000	(Variable B)

This SML program reads two numbers from the keyboard and then determines and prints the larger value. Note the use of the instruction +4108 as a conditional transfer of control, much the same as BASIC's **IF** statement.

Now write SML programs to accomplish each of the following tasks.

(a) Use a sentinel-controlled loop to read 10 positive numbers and compute and print their sum.

(b) Use a counter-controlled loop to read seven numbers, some positive and some negative, and compute and print their average.

(c) Read a series of numbers and determine and print the largest number. The first number read indicates how many numbers should be processed.

6.16. (A Computer Simulator) It may at first seem outrageous, but in this problem you are going to build your own computer. No, you will not be soldering components together. Rather, you will use the powerful technique of simulation to create a software *model* of the Simpletron. You will not be disappointed. Your Simpletron simulator will turn the computer you are using into a Simpletron, and you will actually be able to run, test, and debug the SML programs you wrote in Problem 6.15. You are to write a BASIC program that operates according to the following description. Then run each of the SML programs you wrote in Problem 6.15.

When you run your Simpletron simulator, it begins by printing:

```
*** Welcome to Simpletron!                        ***

*** Please enter your program one instruction     ***
*** (or data word) at a time.  I will type the    ***
*** location number and a question mark (?).       ^ ^ ^
*** You then type the word for that location.      ***
*** Type the sentinel -9999 to stop entering      ***
*** your program.                                 ***
```

Simulate the memory of the Simpletron with a single-subscripted array `memory` that has 99 elements. Now assume that we have said RUN, and let us examine the dialog as we enter the program of Example 2 of Problem 6.15:

```
01 ? + 1010
02 ? + 1011
03 ? + 2010
04 ? + 3111
05 ? + 4108
06 ? + 1110
07 ? + 4300
08 ? + 1111
09 ? + 4300
10 ? + 0000
11 ? + 0000
12 ? - 9999


*** Program loading completed ***
*** Program execution begins ***
```

The SML program has now been placed in the `memory` array. Now the Simpletron actually executes your SML program. It begins with the instruction in location 1 and, like BASIC, executes instructions sequentially, unless directed to some other part of the program by a transfer of control.

Your program and data are now in array `memory`. Use the variable `accumulator` to represent the accumulator. Use the variable `instructioncounter` to keep track of the location in memory that contains the instruction being performed. Use the variable `operationcode` to indicate the operation currently being performed, i.e., the left two digits of the instruction word. Use the variable `operand` to indicate the memory location that the current instruction operates upon. Thus, `operand` is the rightmost two digits of the instruction currently being performed. Do not execute the instructions directly from memory. Rather, transfer the next instruction to be performed from memory to a variable called `instructionregister`. Then pick off the left two digits and place them in `operationcode`; pick off the right two digits and place them in `operand`.

When Simpletron begins execution, the special registers are initialized as follows:

```
accumulator          +0000
instructioncounter   01
instructionregister  +0000
operationcode        00
operand              00
```

Now let us "walk through" the execution of the first SML instruction, +1010 in memory location 01. This is called an *instruction execution cycle*.

The `instructioncounter` tells us the location of the next instruction to be performed. We *fetch* the contents of that location from memory by using the BASIC statement

```
instructionregister = memory(instructioncounter)
```

The operation code and the operand are extracted from the instruction register by the statements

```
operationcode = INT(instructionregister / 100)
operand = instructionregister - 100 * operationcode
```

Now the Simpletron must determine that the operation code is actually a Read (versus a Write, a Load, etc.). A nested **IF/THEN/ELSE** statement differentiates among the twelve operations of SML.

Within the nested **IF/THEN/ELSE** statement, the behavior of certain of the SML instructions is simulated as follows (we leave the others to the reader):

Read: **INPUT** memory(operand)
Load: accumulator = memory(operand)
Add: accumulator = accumulator + memory(operand)
Various branch instructions: We'll discuss these shortly.
Halt: This instruction prints the message

*** Simpletron execution terminated ***

and then prints the name and contents of each register as well as the complete contents of memory. This printout is often called a *computer dump* (and, no, a computer dump is not a place where old computers go).

Let us proceed with the execution of our program's first instruction, namely the $+1010$ in location 01. As we have indicated, the nested **IF/THEN/ELSE** statement simulates this by performing the BASIC statement

INPUT memory(operand)

Thus, a question mark (?) is displayed on the screen, and the Simpletron waits for the user to type a value and then press RETURN. The value is then read into location 10.

At this point, simulation of the first instruction is completed. All that remains is to prepare the Simpletron to execute the next instruction. Since the instruction just performed was not a transfer of control, we need merely increment the instruction counter as follows:

instructioncounter = instructioncounter + 1

This completes the simulated execution of the first instruction and the entire process, i.e., the instruction execution cycle, begins anew with the fetch of the next instruction to be executed.

Now let us consider how the branching instructions, i.e., the transfers of control, are simulated. It is really quite simple. All we need to do is to adjust the value in the instruction counter appropriately. Therefore, the unconditional branch instruction (40) is simulated within the nested **IF/THEN/ELSE** as

instructioncounter = operand

The conditional "branch if accumulator is zero" instruction is simulated as

IF accumulator = 0 **THEN**
    instructioncounter = operand

At this point you should implement your Simpletron simulator and run each of the SML programs you wrote in Problem 6.15. If you wish, you may embellish SML with additional features and provide for these in your simulator.

Chapter 7
String Manipulation

7.1 Introduction

With this chapter we begin our study of more advanced topics. At this point in the text, the reader should have a thorough understanding of fundamental programming concepts, and should be well prepared for investigating more substantial programming applications.

String manipulation features of the BASIC language permit the programmer to write programs that process letters, words, sentences, names, addresses, descriptive data, and special symbols (such as +, -, *, /, $, etc.).

String manipulation has been increasing in importance in recent years. Early high-level languages such as FORTRAN had limited string manipulation capabilities. BASIC and PL/1, both developed in the mid-1960s, have more substantial capabilities. Several high-level languages have been developed that contain extremely powerful string manipulation features. These languages include LISP, SNOBOL, SLIP, COMIT, and IPL/V.

The importance of string manipulation has been greatly underscored by recent developments in the area of *word processing*. Word processing involves many office tasks related to automatic letter writing systems, text editing systems, document preparation systems, etc. Because of exciting developments in electronics, it has become possible to apply modern computer technology to the office products industry and thus to achieve significant improvements in office productivity. Using today's word processing systems, a typist prepares an original business letter and edits the text until it is error-free; then the word processing system automatically types as many original letters as are needed. The typist need only supply inserts that vary from letter to letter such as name, address, dollar amounts, etc. This chapter illustrates many of the text manipulation methods that are useful in word processing systems.

7.2 Fundamentals of Strings

A string is a series of characters that is treated as a single unit. A string may include letters, digits, and various special characters such as +, -, *, /, $, and others. *String values* or *string constants* in BASIC are written in quotation marks (single or double) as follows:

"John Q. Doe"	(a name)
"15 Main Street"	(a street address)
"Waltham, Massachusetts"	(a city and state)
"235-27-1752"	(a social security number)

String values were called *literals* in earlier chapters of this text. From this point forward, we shall refer to string values (or string constants) simply as *strings*. BASIC also provides for *string variables* that may contain different strings during a particular run of a program. *String variable names* should end in a dollar sign.

7.3 Assigning Strings to String Variables

Values may be assigned to string variables with the **LET**, **INPUT**, and **READ** statements. To assign the string "blue" to the string variable color$, the **LET** may be used as follows:

```
LET color$ = "blue"
```

To assign the value "yes" to the string variable answer$, the **INPUT** statement would be

```
INPUT answer$
```

In response to the question mark (?) printed by this **INPUT**, the user would type

```
?"yes"  (the question mark was printed by the INPUT)
```

Note that the string may be typed in double quotes, in single quotes, or without quotes.

The **READ/DATA** pair may also be used with strings. To assign the string "January" to the variable month$, the **READ/DATA** would be used as follows:

```
READ month$
DATA "January"
```

Here, too, the quotes are optional. The quotes are necessary when the string being read contains a comma.

7.4 READ/DATA with String Variables

Assigning values to string variables using the **READ/DATA** pair is straightforward. The following rules apply:

1. Numbers and strings may be intermixed in **DATA** statements. Numbers should be assigned to numeric variables, and strings should be assigned to string variables.

BASIC will respond with an error message if a program attempts to assign a string value to a numeric variable. Numbers assigned to string variables are treated as strings.

2. Values in **DATA** statements are separated by commas. Therefore, if a string contains a comma (such as "Waltham, Massachusetts") then the string must be enclosed in quotation marks. This causes the computer to interpret the comma as part of the string instead of as a value separator.

3. Single quotes may be included in a string by quoting the string with double quotes (and vice versa).

4. As with numeric **DATA** values, the **RESTORE** command resets the **DATA** list pointer to reuse string **DATA** values.

7.5 String Variables: Notes and Observations

1. Microsoft QuickBASIC allows strings to be as long as 32,767 characters.
2. Semicolon (;) print spacing causes strings to print adjacent to one another with no intervening spaces.
3. Strings should always be enclosed in quotation marks when used in **LET** or **IF** statements.
4. Strings cannot be used directly in arithmetic calculations. The following statement is invalid:

```
LET a = 5 + "7"
```

7.6 A Simple Example Using String Variables

In this section we put string variables to work. The program that we develop uses only the simplest string variable techniques, yet it still generates an interesting printout.

Example 7.1 "The Twelve Days of Christmas"
The traditional Christmas song "The Twelve Days of Christmas" consists of repetitive verses and an interesting verse structure. Write a BASIC program that prints this song in a neat stanza format.

Discussion: The program appears in Figure 7.1, and a sample printout containing the complete song appears in Figure 7.2. The **FOR/NEXT** loop generates the twelve verses of the song. The **IF/THEN** statements cause the successively larger verses to be printed. The words in the **DATA** statements are used in the first line of each verse to indicate the appropriate day of Christmas. The **READ** statement obtains the word indicating the correct day of Christmas for each verse.

```
REM    Program that LPRINTs the traditional Christmas song
REM    The Twelve Days of Christmas

LPRINT
LPRINT "_____"
LPRINT "The Twelve Days of Christmas"
LPRINT "_____"
LPRINT

FOR day = 1 TO 12
    READ dayname$
    LPRINT "On the "; dayname$; " day of Christmas,"
    LPRINT "My true love sent to me:"

    IF day = 12 THEN LPRINT "      Twelve drummers drumming,"
    IF day >= 11 THEN LPRINT "      Eleven pipers piping,"
    IF day >= 10 THEN LPRINT "      Ten lords a-leaping,"
    IF day >= 9 THEN LPRINT "      Nine ladies dancing,"
    IF day >= 8 THEN LPRINT "      Eight maids a-milking,"
    IF day >= 7 THEN LPRINT "      Seven swans a-swimming,"
    IF day >= 6 THEN LPRINT "      Six geese a-laying,"
    IF day >= 5 THEN LPRINT "      Five gold rings."
    IF day >= 4 THEN LPRINT "      Four calling birds,"
    IF day >= 3 THEN LPRINT "      Three French hens,"
    IF day >= 2 THEN LPRINT "      Two turtle doves, and "
    IF day >= 1 THEN LPRINT "A partridge in a pear tree."

    LPRINT
    LPRINT
NEXT day
END

DATA first, second, third, fourth, fifth, sixth
DATA seventh, eighth, ninth, tenth, eleventh, twelfth
```

Figure 7.1 A program that uses strings to print the traditional
Christmas song "The Twelve Days of Christmas"

```
_____
The Twelve Days of Christmas
_____

On the first day of Christmas,
My true love sent to me:
A partridge in a pear tree.

On the second day of Christmas,
My true love sent to me:
    Two turtle doves, and
A partridge in a pear tree.
```
continued

Figure 7.2 The song "The Twelve Days of Christmas" produced
by the program of Figure 7.1 (part 1 of 3)

```
On the third day of Christmas,
My true love sent to me:
    Three French hens,
    Two turtle doves, and
A partridge in a pear tree.

On the fourth day of Christmas,
My true love sent to me:
    Four calling birds,
    Three French hens,
    Two turtle doves, and
A partridge in a pear tree.

On the fifth day of Christmas,
My true love sent to me:
    Five gold rings.
    Four calling birds,
    Three French hens,
    Two turtle doves, and
A partridge in a pear tree.

On the sixth day of Christmas,
My true love sent to me:
    Six geese a-laying,
    Five gold rings.
    Four calling birds,
    Three French hens,
    Two turtle doves, and
A partridge in a pear tree.

On the seventh day of Christmas,
My true love sent to me:
    Seven swans a-swimming,
    Six geese a-laying,
    Five gold rings.
    Four calling birds,
    Three French hens,
    Two turtle doves, and
A partridge in a pear tree.

On the eighth day of Christmas,
My true love sent to me:
    Eight maids a-milking,
    Seven swans a-swimming,
    Six geese a-laying,
    Five gold rings.
    Four calling birds,
    Three French hens,
    Two turtle doves, and
A partridge in a pear tree.
```
continued

Figure 7.2 The song "The Twelve Days of Christmas" produced by the program of Figure 7.1 (part 2 of 3)

```
On the ninth day of Christmas,
My true love sent to me:
    Nine ladies dancing,
    Eight maids a-milking,
    Seven swans a-swimming,
    Six geese a-laying,
    Five gold rings.
    Four calling birds,
    Three French hens,
    Two turtle doves, and
A partridge in a pear tree.

On the tenth day of Christmas,
My true love sent to me:
    Ten lords a-leaping,
    Nine ladies dancing,
    Eight maids a-milking,
    Seven swans a-swimming,
    Six geese a-laying,
    Five gold rings.
    Four calling birds,
    Three French hens,
    Two turtle doves, and
A partridge in a pear tree.

On the eleventh day of Christmas,
My true love sent to me:
    Eleven pipers piping,
    Ten lords a-leaping,
    Nine ladies dancing,
    Eight maids a-milking,
    Seven swans a-swimming,
    Six geese a-laying,
    Five gold rings.
    Four calling birds,
    Three French hens,
    Two turtle doves, and
A partridge in a pear tree.

On the twelfth day of Christmas,
My true love sent to me:
    Twelve drummers drumming,
    Eleven pipers piping,
    Ten lords a-leaping,
    Nine ladies dancing,
    Eight maids a-milking,
    Seven swans a-swimming,
    Six geese a-laying,
    Five gold rings.
    Four calling birds,
    Three French hens,
    Two turtle doves, and
A partridge in a pear tree.
```

Figure 7.2   The song "The Twelve Days of Christmas" produced
by the program of Figure 7.1 (part 3 of 3)

7.7 String Arrays

A *string array* is an array whose elements are strings. As with numeric arrays, BASIC automatically reserves space for ten elements (or strings) in every string array. If the user desires to place more than ten elements in a string array, then the user must dimension the string array to the appropriate number of elements.

String arrays are named in the same manner as strings. A particular element (or string) within a string array is referred to by giving the name of the string array followed by the subscript (enclosed in parentheses) of the string within the string array. The fifth element or string within array month$ is referred to as month$(5). The Ith element or string within array part$ is referred to as Part$(I). The following example illustrates the use of string arrays.

> **Example 7.2 Processing the names of the months as strings**
> Write a BASIC program that contains the names of the twelve months in **DATA** statements. The program should read these names into the twelve elements of array monthname$, print the names in normal calendar order (i.e., January, February, etc.), and then print the names in reverse calendar order (i.e., December, November, etc.).
>
> *Discussion:* The program and a sample printout appear in Figure 7.3. The statement
>
> ```
> DIM monthname$(12)
> ```

reserves space for array monthname$ to contain twelve strings as elements. The **DATA** statements contain the names of the twelve months. The first **FOR/NEXT** statement reads the names of the months into the appropriate elements of array monthname$. The second **FOR/NEXT** statement prints the month names in calendar order. The third **FOR/NEXT** statements prints the month names in reverse calendar order.

> **Example 7.3 "Old MacDonald Had a Farm"**
> Write a BASIC program that prints the traditional song "Old MacDonald Had a Farm" in neat stanza format.
>
> *Discussion:* The program appears in Figure 7.4, and a sample printout appears in Figure 7.5. The song consists of a repetitive structure with each verse adding lines about an additional animal. Strings for the names of the animals and the sounds they make are contained in **DATA** statements. The last **DATA** statement contains the sentinel values indicating that the song is to terminate. The **DIM** statement dimensions two string arrays, animal$ and sound$, to contain eleven elements each. This provides enough room for information about ten animals. The string animal$ contains the names of the animals, and sound$ contains the sounds the various animals make.

```
REM     Print the months of the year
DIM monthname$(12)

FOR month = 1 TO 12
    READ monthname$(month)
NEXT month

LPRINT "The twelve months in calendar order"
FOR month = 1 TO 12
    LPRINT monthname$(month)
NEXT month
LPRINT

LPRINT "The twelve months in reverse order"
FOR month = 12 TO 1 STEP -1
    LPRINT monthname$(month)
NEXT month
END

DATA January, February, March, April, May, June, July
DATA August, September, October, November, December
```

```
The twelve months in calendar order
January
February
March
April
May
June
July
August
September
October
November
December

The twelve months in reverse order
December
November
October
September
August
July
June
May
April
March
February
January
```

Figure 7.3   A program and sample printout illustrating the processing
of the names of the months as strings

The first WHILE/WEND structure reads the names of the animals and the sounds they make into the appropriate elements of animal$ and sound$. The second WHILE/WEND structure prints a table showing the various animals and sounds. The third WHILE/WEND structure writes the verses of the song. The nested FOR/NEXT reiterates the various animals mentioned so far.

```
REM    Program that writes verses to the traditional
REM    song Old MacDonald Had a Farm
DIM animal$(11), noise$(11)

pet = 1
READ animal$(pet), noise$(pet)
WHILE animal$(pet) <> "End"
   pet = pet + 1
   READ animal$(pet), noise$(pet)
WEND

LPRINT "Animal", "Noise"
LPRINT "_____", "_____"

pet = 1
WHILE animal$(pet) <> "End"
   LPRINT animal$(pet), noise$(pet)
   pet = pet + 1
WEND

verse = 1
WHILE animal$(verse) <> "End"
   LPRINT
   LPRINT "Old MacDonald had a farm, ee-igh, ee-igh, oh."
   LPRINT "And on this farm he had a "; animal$(verse);
   LPRINT ", ee-igh, ee-igh, oh."

   FOR pet = verse TO 1 STEP -1
      LPRINT "With a "; noise$(pet); " "; noise$(pet); " here,";
      LPRINT "and a "; noise$(pet); " "; noise$(pet); " there;"
      LPRINT "Here a "; noise$(pet); ", there a "; noise$(pet);", ";
      LPRINT "everywhere a "; noise$(pet); " "; noise$(pet); ","
   NEXT pet

   LPRINT "Old MacDonald had a farm, ee-igh, ee-igh, oh."
   verse = verse + 1
WEND
END

DATA duck, quack
DATA turkey, gobble
DATA chick, cluck
DATA cow, moo
DATA End, End
```

Figure 7.4 A program that uses strings to print the traditional song "Old MacDonald Had a Farm"

```
Animal      Sound
_____      _____

duck        quack
turkey      gobble
chick       cluck
cow         moo
```

```
Old MacDonald had a farm, ee-igh, ee-igh, oh.
And on this farm he had a duck, ee-igh, ee-igh, oh.
With a quack quack here, and a quack quack there;
Here a quack, there a quack, everywhere a quack quack,
Old MacDonald had a farm, ee-igh, ee-igh, oh.

Old MacDonald had a farm, ee-igh, ee-igh, oh.
And on this farm he had a turkey, ee-igh, ee-igh, oh.
With a gobble gobble here, and a gobble gobble there;
Here a gobble, there a gobble, everywhere a gobble gobble,
With a quack quack here, and a quack quack there;
Here a quack, there a quack, everywhere a quack quack,
Old MacDonald had a farm, ee-igh, ee-igh, oh.

Old MacDonald had a farm, ee-igh, ee-igh, oh.
And on this farm he had a chick, ee-igh, ee-igh, oh.
With a cluck cluck here, and a cluck cluck there;
Here a cluck, there a cluck, everywhere a cluck cluck,
With a gobble gobble here, and a gobble gobble there;
Here a gobble, there a gobble, everywhere a gobble gobble,
With a quack quack here, and a quack quack there;
Here a quack, there a quack, everywhere a quack quack,
Old MacDonald had a farm, ee-igh, ee-igh, oh.

Old MacDonald had a farm, ee-igh, ee-igh, oh.
And on this farm he had a cow, ee-igh, ee-igh, oh.
With a moo moo here, and a moo moo there;
Here a moo, there a moo, everywhere a moo moo,
With a cluck cluck here, and a cluck cluck there;
Here a cluck, there a cluck, everywhere a cluck cluck,
With a gobble gobble here, and a gobble gobble there;
Here a gobble, there a gobble, everywhere a gobble gobble,
With a quack quack here, and a quack quack there;
Here a quack, there a quack, everywhere a quack quack,
Old MacDonald had a farm, ee-igh, ee-igh, oh.
```

Figure 7.5   The song "Old MacDonald Had a Farm" produced by the
program of Figure 7.4

Example 7.4 The numbers from one to ninety-nine in words

Whenever we write a bank check for a certain amount of money, we enter that
amount twice on the face of the check. First the amount is written in numerals,
and then it is written again in words. In this example, we begin to develop the
logic for writing numerical amounts in words. Exercises at the end of this chapter
examine check writing and check protection in detail. Write a BASIC program
that counts from one to ninety-nine in words.

Discussion: The program appears in Figure 7.6 and a sample printout appears in Figure 7.7. Before examining the program in Figure 7.6, the reader is urged to attempt to develop an algorithm. The answer is not immediately obvious. The reader should write down the word equivalents of the many numbers in the range 1 through 99 to determine what patterns exist and how to take advantage of them. Observing the sample printout of Figure 7.7 should be helpful.

After some experimentation the reader should make the following observations:

1. The word equivalents of the numbers from 1 through 9 are useful for representing the numbers 1 through 9, and for representing the rightmost portions of the numbers from 21 through 99 that are not multiples of 10.
2. The word equivalents of the numbers from 10 through 19 are useful only for representing those numbers.
3. The word equivalents of the multiples of 10 from 20 to 90 (i.e., twenty, thirty, forty, fifty, etc.) are useful for representing those multiples of 10, and for representing the leftmost portions of the numbers from 21 to 99 that are not multiples of ten.

Thus to implement a program to solve this problem (see Figure 7.6), we need to place only certain word equivalents of numbers into **DATA** statements to make these word equivalents available for constructing all the numbers from 1 to 99. In particular, we place the word equivalents of the numbers 1 through 9 into the first two **DATA** statements. The word equivalents of the numbers 10 through 19 are contained in the second two **DATA** statements. Finally, the word equivalents of the multiples of 10 from 10 through 90 are contained in the third pair of **DATA** statements.

The program uses three string arrays, each of which contains ten or fewer strings (and therefore no dimensioning is necessary). The first **FOR/NEXT** statement reads the word equivalents of the digits into string array digit$. The second **FOR/NEXT** statement reads the word equivalents of the teens into string array teen$. The third **FOR/NEXT** statement reads the word equivalents of the multiples of ten into string array ten$. The last **FOR/NEXT** statement generates the numbers from 1 to 99. The **SELECT/CASE** statement prints the word equivalent of each value of number generated by the **FOR/NEXT**.

The **SELECT/CASE** statement operates as follows. If number is between 1 and 9 (i.e., number < 10), then the word equivalent of number is obtained by referencing the appropriate element of digit$. If number is between 10 and 19, then the word equivalent of number is obtained by referencing the appropriate element of teen$.

If number is between 20 and 99, then the separate digits of number are calculated: digit1 is the leftmost digit and digit2 is the rightmost digit. If digit2 is zero, then number is a multiple of ten and its word equivalent is obtained from the ten$ array.

If `digit2` is not zero, then `number` is not a multiple of ten. At this point we know that the word equivalent of `number` is made up of three pieces, namely a multiple of ten followed by a dash followed by a digit. The word equivalent for the multiple of ten is obtained from the `ten$` array, and the word equivalent for the digit is obtained from the `digit$` array.

Example 7.4 introduces many of the concepts that are needed in order to be able to print a check amount in words. The logic is not complex, but it is certainly cumbersome. Many computerized check-writing systems do not print the check amount in words, perhaps for this reason.

```
REM    Program that counts from 1 to 99 using words
FOR j = 1 TO 9
   READ digit$(j)
NEXT j

FOR j = 1 TO 10
   READ teen$(j)
NEXT j

FOR j = 1 TO 9
   READ ten$(j)
NEXT j

LPRINT "The numbers from one to ninety-nine in words ..."
LPRINT

FOR number = 1 TO 99
   SELECT CASE number
      CASE IS < 10
         LPRINT digit$(number),
      CASE IS < 20
         LPRINT teen$(number - 9),
      CASE ELSE
         digit1 = INT(number / 10)
         digit2 = number - 10 * digit1
         IF digit2 = 0 THEN
            LPRINT ten$(digit1),
            ELSE
               LPRINT ten$(digit1); "-"; digit$(digit2),
         END IF
   END SELECT
   IF number / 5 = INT(number / 5) THEN LPRINT
NEXT number
END

DATA one, two, three, four, five
DATA six, seven, eight, nine
DATA ten, eleven, twelve, thirteen, fourteen
DATA fifteen, sixteen, seventeen, eighteen, nineteen
DATA ten, twenty, thirty, forty, fifty
DATA sixty, seventy, eighty, ninety
```

Figure 7.6 A program that prints the numbers from one to ninety-nine in words

```
The numbers from one to ninety-nine in words ...

one            two            three          four           five
six            seven          eight          nine           ten
eleven         twelve         thirteen       fourteen       fifteen
sixteen        seventeen      eighteen       nineteen       twenty
twenty-one     twenty-two     twenty-three   twenty-four    twenty-five
twenty-six     twenty-seven   twenty-eight   twenty-nine    thirty
thirty-one     thirty-two     thirty-three   thirty-four    thirty-five
thirty-six     thirty-seven   thirty-eight   thirty-nine    forty
forty-one      forty-two      forty-three    forty-four     forty-five
forty-six      forty-seven    forty-eight    forty-nine     fifty
fifty-one      fifty-two      fifty-three    fifty-four     fifty-five
fifty-six      fifty-seven    fifty-eight    fifty-nine     sixty
sixty-one      sixty-two      sixty-three    sixty-four     sixty-five
sixty-six      sixty-seven    sixty-eight    sixty-nine     seventy
seventy-one    seventy-two    seventy-three  seventy-four   seventy-five
seventy-six    seventy-seven  seventy-eight  seventy-nine   eighty
eighty-one     eighty-two     eighty-three   eighty-four    eighty-five
eighty-six     eighty-seven   eighty-eight   eighty-nine    ninety
ninety-one     ninety-two     ninety-three   ninety-four    ninety-five
ninety-six     ninety-seven   ninety-eight   ninety-nine
```

Figure 7.7 A sample printout of the program of Figure 7.6 that
prints the numbers from one to ninety-nine in words

Example 7.5 Printing all possible two-letter words
Write a BASIC program that generates all possible two-letter words. Carefully examine the printout of the program. Circle all common words.

Discussion: Here is an interesting application of computers to linguistics, the science of language. Suppose you were asked to list all the two-letter words in the English language. How would you go about doing so? Perhaps you would jot down as many as immediately come to mind. Perhaps you would open some mammoth unabridged dictionary and search for two-letter words.

Another approach is presented in the program of Figure 7.8. This program generates every possible two-letter word. Since each letter may be any of the 26 letters of the alphabet, there are 26 times 26, or a total of 676 possible distinct two-letter words.

Before looking at the sample printout in Figure 7.9, the reader is encouraged to attempt to list all possible two-letter words that come to mind. The reader should make up a list and compare it to Figure 7.9. No doubt the reader will omit some common two-letter words.

```
REM    Program that LPRINTs out all two-letter words
DIM alphabet$(26)

FOR letter = 1 TO 26
    READ alphabet$(letter)
NEXT letter

FOR letter = 1 TO 26
    FOR secondletter = 1 TO 26
        LPRINT alphabet$(letter); alphabet$(secondletter); " ";
    NEXT secondletter
    LPRINT
NEXT letter
END

DATA A, B, C, D, E, F, G, H, I, J, K, L, M, N, O, P, Q, R, S, T
DATA U, V, W, X, Y, Z
```

Figure 7.8 Program that prints all two-letter words

```
AA AB AC AD AE AF AG AH AI AJ AK AL AM AN AO AP AQ AR AS AT AU AV AW AX AY AZ
BA BB BC BD BE BF BG BH BI BJ BK BL BM BN BO BP BQ BR BS BT BU BV BW BX BY BZ
CA CB CC CD CE CF CG CH CI CJ CK CL CM CN CO CP CQ CR CS CT CU CV CW CX CY CZ
DA DB DC DD DE DF DG DH DI DJ DK DL DM DN DO DP DQ DR DS DT DU DV DW DX DY DZ
EA EB EC ED EE EF EG EH EI EJ EK EL EM EN EO EP EQ ER ES ET EU EV EW EX EY EZ
FA FB FC FD FE FF FG FH FI FJ FK FL FM FN FO FP FQ FR FS FT FU FV FW FX FY FZ
GA GB GC GD GE GF GG GH GI GJ GK GL GM GN GO GP GQ GR GS GT GU GV GW GX GY GZ
HA HB HC HD HE HF HG HH HI HJ HK HL HM HN HO HP HQ HR HS HT HU HV HW HX HY HZ
IA IB IC ID IE IF IG IH II IJ IK IL IM IN IO IP IQ IR IS IT IU IV IW IX IY IZ
JA JB JC JD JE JF JG JH JI JJ JK JL JM JN JO JP JQ JR JS JT JU JV JW JX JY JZ
KA KB KC KD KE KF KG KH KI KJ KK KL KM KN KO KP KQ KR KS KT KU KV KW KX KY KZ
LA LB LC LD LE LF LG LH LI LJ LK LL LM LN LO LP LQ LR LS LT LU LV LW LX LY LZ
MA MB MC MD ME MF MG MH MI MJ MK ML MM MN MO MP MQ MR MS MT MU MV MW MX MY MZ
NA NB NC ND NE NF NG NH NI NJ NK NL NM NN NO NP NQ NR NS NT NU NV NW NX NY NZ
OA OB OC OD OE OF OG OH OI OJ OK OL OM ON OO OP OQ OR OS OT OU OV OW OX OY OZ
PA PB PC PD PE PF PG PH PI PJ PK PL PM PN PO PP PQ PR PS PT PU PV PW PX PY PZ
QA QB QC QD QE QF QG QH QI QJ QK QL QM QN QO QP QQ QR QS QT QU QV QW QX QY QZ
RA RB RC RD RE RF RG RH RI RJ RK RL RM RN RO RP RQ RR RS RT RU RV RW RX RY RZ
SA SB SC SD SE SF SG SH SI SJ SK SL SM SN SO SP SQ SR SS ST SU SV SW SX SY SZ
TA TB TC TD TE TF TG TH TI TJ TK TL TM TN TO TP TQ TR TS TT TU TV TW TX TY TZ
UA UB UC UD UE UF UG UH UI UJ UK UL UM UN UO UP UQ UR US UT UU UV UW UX UY UZ
VA VB VC VD VE VF VG VH VI VJ VK VL VM VN VO VP VQ VR VS VT VU VV VW VX VY VZ
WA WB WC WD WE WF WG WH WI WJ WK WL WM WN WO WP WQ WR WS WT WU WV WW WX WY WZ
XA XB XC XD XE XF XG XH XI XJ XK XL XM XN XO XP XQ XR XS XT XU XV XW XX XY XZ
YA YB YC YD YE YF YG YH YI YJ YK YL YM YN YO YP YQ YR YS YT YU YV YW YX YY YZ
ZA ZB ZC ZD ZE ZF ZG ZH ZI ZJ ZK ZL ZM ZN ZO ZP ZQ ZR ZS ZT ZU ZV ZW ZX ZY ZZ
```

Figure 7.9 A sample printout of the two-letter word program of Figure 7.8

Example 7.6 Arrangements of a five-letter word
One way of encoding information to disguise its correct meaning is to rearrange the letters of a word. It takes some concentration to realize that HETER is simply a rearrangement of the letters of the word THREE (or THERE). It is not immediately obvious that VIRED is a rearrangement of the letters of DRIVE.

Write a BASIC program that may be used to help decode messages produced by rearranging the letters of individual words. Your program should `INPUT` a five-letter coded word, and should then print all the different five-letter words that can be produced by rearranging the five letters (there are 120 distinct arrangements or *permutations* of five different letters). To complete the decoding of each word, visually scan each of the printed arrangements and then circle the correct word.

Discussion: The program appears in Figure 7.10, and several sample printouts appear in Figure 7.11. The `INPUT` statement asks the user to enter the coded five-letter word. The word is placed in w$.

The involved `FOR/NEXT` structure prints all the arrangements of the five-letter word entered by the user. The `PRINT` statements in the `FOR/NEXT` structure control the printing of the different arrangements of the word. The remainder of the `FOR/NEXT` structure varies the subscripts a, b, c, d, and e that reference particular letters within w$.

The logic here is somewhat complex. Once a value is chosen for variable a, the program proceeds to choose a value for variable b. The first `IF` statement makes certain that the value chosen for variable b differs from a (otherwise the same letter would be printed twice). If b is equal to a, then a different value for b must be chosen.

Once a value of b has been chosen that does differ from a, the program proceeds to choose a value for c. It is necessary to choose a value for c that differs from both a and b. This is accomplished by testing the condition c<>b `AND` c<>a. This condition is true if both c<>b is true and if c<>a is true. (Remember that `AND` is a BASIC logical operator.)

The program then proceeds to choose a value for d (which, of course, must not be equal to any of the values chosen for a, b, or c). Finally, the program proceeds to choose a value for e that differs from a, b, c, and d. The `PRINT` statements display one arrangement of the five-letter word entered by the user.

The `MID$` function selects individual characters from w$. In general, the `MID$` function allows any `number` of characters to be selected beginning with a given `position` of some `basestring$` as follows:

    MID$(basestring$, position, number)

For example, the statement

    PRINT MID$("ABCDEF", 4, 2)

would print DE, the portion of ABCDEF beginning with the fourth position of the string and two characters long. If b is currently 3, then MID$(w$,b,1) selects one character at the third position of w$, the word entered by the user. In each case, visual inspection of the various word arrangements quickly yields the correct word.

```
REM    Program that produces all possible 5-letter words
REM    that can be derived from a given 5-letter word
REM    by rearranging the letters
INPUT "Enter 5-letter word"; w$
PRINT "The arrangements of the word "; w$; " are:"
PRINT

counter = 1

FOR a = 1 TO 5
   FOR b = 1 TO 5
      IF b <> a THEN
      FOR c = 1 TO 5
         IF c <> b AND c <> a THEN
         FOR d = 1 TO 5
            IF d <> c AND d <> b AND d <> a THEN
            FOR e = 1 TO 5
               IF e <> d AND e <> c AND e <> b AND e <> a THEN
                  PRINT MID$(w$, a, 1); MID$(w$, b, 1); MID$(w$, c, 1);
                  PRINT MID$(w$, d, 1); MID$(w$, e, 1); " ";
                  IF counter / 10 = INT(counter / 10) THEN PRINT
                     counter = counter +1
               END IF
            NEXT e
            END IF
         NEXT d
         END IF
      NEXT c
      END IF
   NEXT b
NEXT a
END
```

Figure 7.10 Program for producing all possible arrangements of a five-letter word

```
Enter 5-letter word? sciba
The arrangements of the word sciba are:

sciba  sciab  scbia  scbai  scaib  scabi  sicba  sicab  sibca  sibac
siacb  siabc  sbcia  sbcai  sbica  sbiac  sbaci  sbaic  sacib  sacbi
saicb  saibc  sabci  sabic  csiba  csiab  csbia  csbai  csaib  csabi
cisba  cisab  cibsa  cibas  ciasb  ciabs  cbsia  cbsai  cbisa  cbias
cbasi  cbais  casib  casbi  caisb  caibs  cabsi  cabis  iscba  iscab
isbca  isbac  isacb  isabc  icsba  icsab  icbsa  icbas  icasb  icabs
ibsca  ibsac  ibcsa  ibcas  ibasc  ibacs  iascb  iasbc  iacsb  iabcs
iabsc  iabcs  bscia  bscai  bsica  bsiac  bsaci  bsaic  bcsia  bcsai
bcisa  bcias  bcasi  bcais  bisca  bisac  bicsa  bicas  biasc  biacs
basci  basic  bacsi  bacis  baisc  baics  ascib  ascbi  asicb  asibc
asbci  asbic  acsib  acsbi  acisb  acibs  acbsi  acbis  aiscb  aisbc
aicsb  aicbs  aibsc  aibcs  absci  absic  abcsi  abcis  abisc  abics


Enter 5-letter word? lehiw
The arrangements of the word lehiw are:

lehiw  lehwi  leihw  leiwh  lewhi  lewih  lheiw  lhewi  lhiew  lhiwe
lhwei  lhwie  liehw  liewh  lihew  lihwe  liweh  liwhe  lwehi  lweih
lwhei  lwhie  lwieh  lwihe  elhiw  elhwi  elihw  eliwh  elwhi  elwih
ehliw  ehlwi  ehilw  ehiwl  ehwli  ehwil  eilhw  eilwh  eihlw  eihwl
eiwlh  eiwhl  ewlhi  ewlih  ewhli  ewhil  ewilh  ewihl  hleiw  hlewi
hliew  hliwe  hlwei  hlwie  heliw  helwi  heilw  heiwl  hewli  hewil
hilew  hilwe  hielw  hiewl  hiwle  hiwel  hwlei  hwlie  hweli  hweil
hwile  hwiel  ilehw  ilewh  ilhew  ilhwe  ilweh  ilwhe  ielhw  ielwh
iehlw  iehwl  iewlh  iewhl  ihlew  ihlwe  ihelw  ihewl  ihwle  ihwel
iwleh  iwlhe  iwelh  iwehl  iwhle  iwhel  wlehi  wleih  wlhei  wlhie
wlieh  wlihe  welhi  welih  wehli  wehil  weilh  weihl  whlei  whlie
wheli  wheil  while  whiel  wileh  wilhe  wielh  wiehl  wihle  wihel


Enter 5-letter word? liunt
The arrangements of the word liunt are:

liunt  liutn  linut  lintu  litun  litnu  luint  luitn  lunit  lunti
lutin  lutni  lniut  lnitu  lnuit  lnuti  lntiu  lntui  ltiun  ltinu
ltuin  ltuni  ltniu  ltnui  ilunt  ilutn  ilnut  ilntu  iltun  iltnu
iulnt  iultn  iunlt  iuntl  iutln  iutnl  inlut  inltu  inult  inutl
intlu  intul  itlun  itlnu  ituln  itunl  itnlu  itnul  ulint  ulitn
ulnit  ulnti  ultin  ultni  uilnt  uiltn  uinlt  uintl  uitln  uitnl
unlit  unlti  unilt  unitl  untli  until  utlin  utlni  utiln  utinl
utnli  utnil  nliut  nlitu  nluit  nluti  nltiu  nltui  nilut  niltu
niult  niutl  nitlu  nitul  nulit  nulti  nuilt  nuitl  nutli  nutil
ntliu  ntlui  ntilu  ntiul  ntuli  ntuil  tliun  tlinu  tluin  tluni
tlniu  tlnui  tilun  tilnu  tiuln  tiunl  tinlu  tinul  tulin  tulni
tuiln  tuinl  tunli  tunil  tnliu  tnlui  tnilu  tniul  tnuli  tnuil
```

Figure 7.11 Several sample printouts for the five-letter word
arrangements program of Figure 7.10

7.8 Comparing Character Strings

In string manipulation applications, it is frequently necessary to compare two strings. We have used the equals (=) relational operator in IF statements in this chapter to determine if two strings are identical. In fact, all of the BASIC relational operators may be used to compare strings.

Example 7.7 Comparing strings

Write a BASIC program that inputs two strings and compares them. Print messages to indicate whether the first string "is greater than," "is less than," or "is equal to" the second string.

Discussion: The program and sample printout appear in Figure 7.12.

The first IF statement uses the equals relational operator to determine if the strings are identical. If they are, then an appropriate message is printed. The program then proceeds to read the next pair of strings.

If the strings are not identical, then the program determines if the first string is greater than the second string. If this is the case, then an appropriate message is printed. If not, then the first string must be less than the second string, and an appropriate message is printed.

To understand just what it means for one string to be "greater than" or "less than" another string, consider the process of alphabetizing a series of last names. The reader would, no doubt, place "Jones" before "Smith" because the first letter of "Jones" comes before the first letter of "Smith" in the alphabet. But the alphabet is more than just a list of 26 letters—it is an ordered list. Each of the letters occurs in a specific place within the ordering. "Z" is more than merely a letter of the alphabet. More specifically, it is the twenty-sixth letter of the alphabet.

The sample printout in Figure 7.12 illustrates several examples of string comparisons. The string "a" is considered to be less than the string "b" (because "a" comes before "b" in the alphabet). The string "f" is considered to be greater than the string "e" (because "f" comes after "e" in the alphabet). Note that the computer considers the string "j" to be less than the string "john." This corresponds to the ordering the reader would use in alphabetizing names of different lengths. If one name is equivalent to the leftmost portion of another name, then the shorter name would come before the longer name in an alphabetical sequence.

How does the computer know that one particular letter comes before another? All characters are represented inside the computer as numeric codes; when the computer compares two strings, it actually compares these numeric codes.

```
REM     Program that compares two strings
INPUT "Enter two strings"; first$, second$
WHILE first$ <> "End"
    IF first$ = second$ THEN
        PRINT first$; " is equal to "; second$
        ELSEIF first$ > second$ THEN
            PRINT first$; " is greater than "; second$
        ELSE
            PRINT first$; " is less than "; second$
    END IF
    PRINT
    INPUT "Enter two strings"; first$, second$
WEND
END
```

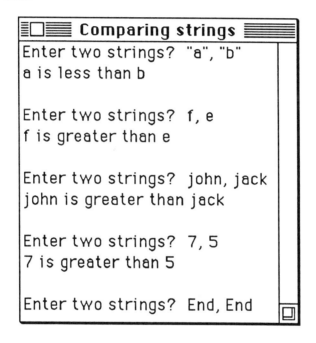

Figure 7.12 A program for comparing strings

7.9 Internal Numeric Code Representations of Characters

The internal numeric codes used to represent characters may vary somewhat on different computers. In an effort at standardizing character representations, most computer manufacturers have designed their machines to utilize one of two popular coding schemes, namely, *EBCDIC* or *ASCII*. EBCDIC stands for "Extended Binary Coded Decimal Interchange Code" and ASCII stands for "American Standard Code for Information Interchange." There are other coding schemes, but these two are certainly the most popular.

EBCDIC and ASCII are called *character codes* or *character sets*. Figure 7.13 shows the numeric code representations for many of the characters in the ASCII character set. String manipulations actually involve the manipulation of the appropriate numeric codes and not the characters themselves.

When the computer compares two strings, it actually compares the numeric codes that make up the characters in the strings. Since it is meaningful to say that one numeric code is greater than, is less than, or is equal to another numeric code, it becomes possible to relate various characters or strings to one another by referring to the table in Figure 7.13. Note that each letter of the alphabet has a higher numeric code than the previous letter. Each digit (when used as a string) has a higher numeric code than the previous digit. Since the ASCII representations of the uppercase letters (i.e., the numbers 65 through 90) are all higher than the ASCII representations of the digits (i.e., 48 through 57), then any computer that uses the ASCII character set will order the digits before the uppercase letters. (EBCDIC-oriented computers actually order the letters before the digits.)

Letters		Numbers	
Character	ASCII representation	Character	ASCII representation
A	65	0	48
B	66	1	49
C	67	2	50
D	68	3	51
E	69	4	52
F	70	5	53
G	71	6	54
H	72	7	55
I	73	8	56
J	74	9	57
K	75		
L	76		
M	77	Special characters	
N	78		
O	79		ASCII
P	80	Character	representation
Q	81		
R	82	!	33
S	83	@	64
T	84	#	35
U	85	$	36
V	86	%	37
W	87	&	38
X	88	'	44
Y	89	.	46
Z	90	*	42
		(	40
		)	41
		-	45
		+	43
		/	47
		:	58
		;	59
		?	63

Figure 7.13 The numeric code representations for many of the characters in the ASCII character set

7.10 Manipulating the Individual Characters in a String: MID$

BASIC provides several different means for referencing the individual characters in a string. The next several examples introduce these techniques.

Example 7.8 Spelling phrases backwards

Write a BASIC program that INPUTs a phrase (i.e., a character string) and then prints the phrase spelled backwards. For example, if the user enters the string "STOP" the program should print POTS.

Discussion: The program and sample run appear in Figure 7.14. In order to be able to spell a word or a phrase backwards, we need the ability to extract one character at a time from a string. In particular, in this example we need to be able to obtain the last character of the string, then the next previous character, then the next, etc. The MID$ function is appropriate for this purpose.

The crux of the program is the FOR/NEXT loop. The loop counts backwards from the highest-numbered position in the string to 1. The function LEN (for "length") is used to determine the length of phrase$. The MID$ function is then used to extract one character at a time from phrase$.

```
REM    Program that spells phrases backwards
INPUT "Enter a word or a phrase"; phrase$
WHILE phrase$ <> "End"
    PRINT phrase$; " ... spelled backwards is ... "
    FOR position = LEN(phrase$) TO 1 STEP -1
        PRINT MID$(phrase$, position, 1);
    NEXT position
    PRINT
    PRINT
    INPUT "Enter a word or a phrase"; phrase$
WEND
END
```

```
Enter a word or a phrase? serutan
serutan ... spelled backwards is ...
natures

Enter a word or a phrase? able was i ere i saw elba
able was i ere i saw elba ... spelled backwards is ...
able was i ere i saw elba

Enter a word or a phrase? a man a plan a canal panama
a man a plan a canal panama ... spelled backwards is ...
amanap lanac a nalp a nam a

Enter a word or a phrase? poor dan is in a droop
poor dan is in a droop ... spelled backwards is ...
poord a ni si nad roop
```

Figure 7.14 A program and a sample printout illustrating spelling words backwards

7.11 LEFT$, RIGHT$, INSTR

Let us consider three additional built-in functions, namely `LEFT$`, `RIGHT$`, and `INSTR`, which are useful for manipulating and searching character strings.

`LEFT$` selects the leftmost portion of a string. For example, the statements

```
a$ = "ABCDEF"
PRINT LEFT$(a$, 4)
```

would select the leftmost four characters of a$, and would print ABCD. `RIGHT$` selects the rightmost portion of a string. For example, the statements

```
a$ = "ABCDEF"
PRINT RIGHT$(a$, 4)
```

would select the rightmost 4 characters of a$, and would print CDEF.

The `INSTR` function is useful for searching through one string, called the *base string,* to see if it contains another string, called the *search string.* For example, the statements

```
a$ = "AEIOU"
b$ = "IOU"
PRINT INSTR(1, a$, b$)
```

would determine that b$ (the search string) is indeed contained within a$ (the base string). The `INSTR` function is set to the starting position of b$ within a$, in this case 3, and so 3 is printed. In this `INSTR` example, the 1 indicates that the search for b$ is to begin in position 1 of a$. It is possible to begin the search at any position within a$. Note that if `INSTR` determines that the search string is not contained within the base string, then `INSTR` returns zero. For example, the following statements would each print zero.

```
PRINT INSTR(1, "aeiou", "aeb")
PRINT INSTR(4, "aeiou", "iou")
PRINT INSTR(1, "aeiou", "aeiouy")
```

Example 7.9 Pig Latin

As a capstone exercise to the study of string manipulation, write a BASIC program that encodes English language phrases into pig Latin. Pig Latin is a form of coded language often used for amusement. Many variations exist in the methods used to form pig Latin phrases. For simplicity, use the following algorithm:

To form a pig Latin phrase from an English language phrase, the translation proceeds one word at a time. To translate an English word into a pig Latin word, place the first letter of the English word at the end of the English word, and add the letters "ay." Thus, the word "jump" becomes "umpjay," the word "the" becomes "hetay," and the word "computer" becomes "omputercay." Blanks between words remain as blanks. Make the following assumptions: the English phrase consists of words separated by blanks, there are no punctuation marks, and all words have two or more letters.

Discussion: A program and sample printout appear in Figures 7.15 and 7.16. The statement **INPUT** phrase$ obtains an English phrase. The **WHILE** statement tests if the user has entered the sentinel value ("Fini" of course). If the user has not entered "Fini," the computer proceeds to the body of the **WHILE**. The position of the first blank in the string is determined, if the string does in fact contain a blank. The nested **WHILE** structure picks off one word at a time from phrase$, places the word in nextword$, and calls the subprogram PrintLatinWord to print the pig Latin equivalent of the word.

```
REM    Pig Latin program
PRINT "Enter a Phrase (Fini to end)"
INPUT phrase$

WHILE phrase$ <> "Fini"
   blankposition = INSTR(1, phrase$, " ")
   WHILE blankposition <> 0
      nextword$ = LEFT$(phrase$, blankposition - 1)
      CALL PrintLatinWord ((nextword$))
      phrase$ = RIGHT$(phrase$, LEN(phrase$) - blankposition)
      blankposition = INSTR(1, phrase$, " ")
   WEND

   nextword$ = phrase$
   CALL PrintLatinWord ((nextword$))

   PRINT
   PRINT
   PRINT "Enter a phrase (Fini to end)"
   INPUT phrase$
WEND
END

SUB PrintLatinWord (workword$) STATIC
   FOR position = 2 TO LEN(workword$)
      PRINT MID$(workword$, position, 1);
   NEXT position
   PRINT LEFT$(workword$, 1);
   PRINT "ay ";
END SUB
```

Figure 7.15 A pig Latin program

```
Enter a phrase (Fini to end)
? pig Latin
igpay atinLay

Enter a phrase (Fini to end)
? to be or not to be that is the question
otay ebay roay otnay otay ebay hattay siay hetay uestionqay

Enter a phrase (Fini to end)
? garbage in garbage out
arbagegay niay arbagegay utoay

Enter a phrase (Fini to end)
? the greatest lemon in the company's history
hetay reatestgay emonlay niay hetay ompany'scay istoryhay

Enter a phrase (Fini to end)
? beginner's all-purpose symbolic instruction code
eginner'sbay ll-purposeaay ymbolicsay nstructioniay odecay

Enter a phrase (Fini to end)
? common business oriented language
ommoncay usinessbay rientedoay anguagelay

Enter a phrase (Fini to end)
? formula translator
ormulafay ranslatortay

Enter a phrase (Fini to end)
? think
hinktay

Enter a phrase (Fini to end)
? Fini
```

Figure 7.16 A sample printout from the Pig Latin program of Figure 7.15

After a word is processed, the program "shrinks" the original English phrase by removing that word from `phrase$`. The next blank is located if there is one. Eventually, `phrase$` will shrink to a single word. This will cause a zero to be assigned to `blankposition`, and will cause termination of the nested **WHILE/WEND** structure.

The program then processes the last word in the phrase, and prints its Pig Latin equivalent. Then the next English phrase is requested for translation.

7.12 Other String Manipulation Functions and Techniques

This section contains a series of short notes describing other string manipulation functions and methods available in BASIC.

1. *String concatenation.* Larger strings can be constructed by placing several smaller strings next to one another. This process is called *string concatenation* and is indicated with the plus sign as follows:

```
a$ = "Pro"
b$ = "gram"
c$ = a$ + b$
PRINT c$
```

The above statements would concatenate (or append) b$ to the right of a$ to create an entirely new string, c$. When this section of the program is run, it would print the string

```
Program
```

2. *VAL function.* The **VAL** function is used to perform calculations with strings containing numbers. The statement

```
PRINT VAL("5") + VAL("7")
```

would print the number 12.

3. *STR$ function.* The **STR$** function complements the **VAL** function. **STR$** is used to obtain a string version of a number. The statements

```
a = 5
c = 9
d$ = STR$(a) + STR$(c)
PRINT d$
```

would print the string

```
59
```

4. *SPACE$ function.* The **SPACE$** function creates a string of blanks consisting of a specific number of blanks. The statement

```
PRINT "A"; SPACE$(10); "B"
```

would print

```
A          B
```

where 10 blank spaces appear between the letters.

5. *STRING$ function.* The **STRING$** function creates a string of characters containing several occurrences of a specified character. The character is specified by its ASCII code. The statement

```
PRINT STRING$(5, 66)
```

would print BBBBB, since 66 is the ASCII code for B.

6.   *ASC function.* The ASC function returns the ASCII code corresponding to a given character. The statement

```
PRINT ASC("a")
```

would print 97, the ASCII code for lowercase "a". If the given string contains more than one character, the ASC function prints the ASCII code of the first character only. The CHR$ function complements the ASC function. CHR$ returns the string corresponding to an ASCII code.

7.   *LINE INPUT command.* The LINE INPUT command is used instead of the INPUT when it is desired to read a string containing quotes, punctuation marks, and certain other special characters. The following program uses LINE INPUT to accept a phrase with several different punctuation marks.

```
LINE INPUT "Enter string?", Sentence$
PRINT Sentence$
END
```

```
≣☐≣═══════════ Using LINE INPUT ≣═════════════
Enter string? to be, or not to be: that is the question
to be, or not to be: that is the question                   ⬜
```

Concepts

ASC
ASCII
base string
character code
character set
CHR$
COMIT
concatenation operator (+)
EBCDIC
INSTR
IPL/V
LEFT$
LEN
LINE   INPUT
LISP
MID$
numeric array representation of a
     string
numeric code representation of a
     character
quotation marks (single or double)

RIGHT$
search string
SLIP
SNOBOL
SPACE$
statement label
string
string array
string concatenation
string constant
string manipulation
string value
string variable
string variable name
STRING$
STR$
VAL
word processing
zeroth element of array representation
     of a string

Problems

7.1. State which of the following are valid variable names and which are invalid:
  (a) month$
  (b) z5$
  (c) q34$
  (d) g$
  (e) 5g$
  (f) 67g$
  (g) string$
  (h) name
  (i) 47
  (j) 5$

7.2. Show three different methods of assigning the string of vowels, "AEIOU," to the string variable vowel$.

7.3. Write a BASIC program that reads the names of the seven days of the week from **DATA** statements and prints these names. Place only some of the names in quotation marks.

7.4. Examine the following section of a BASIC program carefully:

```
     PRINT "Do you want to enter more numbers?"
     INPUT a$
WEND
PRINT "Sum is"; s
PRINT "average is"; s / n
```

  (a) List the string variable names used in the above program segment.
  (b) List the string constants used in the above program segment.
  (c) List the numeric variable names used in the above program segment.

7.5. The following list of values contains some numeric constants and some string constants:

```
5, "7", 8.9, six, 3.14159   "2.087", mc022, "mc365"
```

Write a BASIC program that attempts to read each of these values as numbers. What happens? Now try to read each of these values as strings. What happens?

7.6. What, if anything, prints when each of the following BASIC statements is performed? If the statement contains an error, describe the error and indicate how to correct it.
  (a) **PRINT** "A", "B", "C"
  (b) **PRINT** "I"; "O"; "U"
  (c) **PRINT** "Computer
  (d) **PRINT** "AVG.";"";"I";"S";100/10
  (e) **PRINT** 5 + "5";"="; 10

7.7. When, if ever, must the programmer dimension a string array?

7.8. Write a BASIC program that reads the names of the months into a string array and then prints the names of every second month (i.e., February, April, June, etc.).

7.9. The program of Figure 7.4, which prints the traditional song "Old MacDonald Had a Farm," prints four verses of the song. Show how you would modify the program to print an additional verse for the pig and the sound oink. Note that it is necessary to insert only one additional BASIC statement into the program.

7.10. Suppose that you are interested in determining how many commonly used three-letter words there are in the English language that begin with a particular letter. Modify the program of Figure 7.8 so that it obtains the first letter of the three-letter words from the user, and then generates all possible three-letter words beginning with the letter typed by the user.

7.11. The program of Figure 7.10 produces all possible arrangements of the letters in a five-letter word. Use the techniques of this program to write a program that produces all possible three-letter words that can be derived from the letters of a given five-letter word. For example, the three-letter words produced from the word "bathe" include the commonly used words

            ate   bat   bet   tab   hat   the   tea

7.12. Use the techniques for comparing strings developed in Section 7.8 and the techniques for sorting arrays developed in Chapter 6 to write a program that alphabetizes a list of strings. Use the names of 10 or 15 towns in your area as input data to your program.

7.13. The chart in Figure 7.13 shows the numeric code representations for many of the characters in the ASCII character set. Study this chart carefully and then state whether each of the following is true or false.
   (a) The letter "A" comes before the letter "B."
   (b) The digit "9" comes before the digit "0."
   (c) The commonly used symbols for addition, subtraction, multiplication, and division in BASIC all come before any of the digits.
   (d) The digits come before the letters.
   (e) If a sort program sorts strings into ascending sequence, then the program will place the symbol for a right parenthesis before the symbol for a left parenthesis.

7.14. Write a BASIC program that reads a series of strings from **DATA** statements and prints only those strings beginning with the letter "b."

7.15. Write a BASIC program that reads a series of strings from **DATA** statements and prints only those strings that end with the letters "ED."

7.16. Write a BASIC program that inputs an ASCII code and prints the corresponding character. Use the **CHR$** function. Modify this program so that it generates all possible three-digit codes in the range 000 to 255 and attempts to print the corresponding characters. What happens when this program is run?

7.17. One enterprising young student of BASIC has observed that the program presented in Figure 7.1 to print "The Twelve Days of Christmas" could easily be greatly simplified by the use of string arrays. This student claims that the twelve **IF** statements could be replaced by a single statement with the use of string arrays. Either show how this can be done, or come to the aid of the author.

7.18. Show what, if anything, is printed by each of the following BASIC statements:
   (a) **PRINT** "front" + "wards"
   (b) **PRINT LEN**("abcdefghijklmnopqrstuvwxyz")
   (c) **PRINT VAL**("12") + **VAL**("17")
   (d) **PRINT STR$**(1) + **STR$**(23) + **STR$**(456)
   (e) **PRINT LEFT$**("righthalf", 5)
   (f) **PRINT RIGHT$**("inthemiddle", 6)
   (g) **PRINT MID$**("faretheewell", 2, 3)
   (h) **PRINT** "A" + **SPACE$**(2) + "B" + **SPACE$**(4) + "C"

7.19. Show what, if anything, is printed by each of the following BASIC statements:
   (a) **PRINT ASC**("d")
   (b) **PRINT ASC**("antidisestablishmentarianism")
   (c) **PRINT STRING$**(7, 67)

Special Section

A Compendium of More Advanced String Manipulation Exercises

The preceding exercises are keyed to the text and designed to test the reader's understanding of fundamental string manipulation concepts. This section includes a collection of intermediate and advanced problems. The reader should find these problems challenging yet enjoyable. The problems vary considerably in difficulty. Some require an hour or two of program writing and implementation. Others are useful for lab assignments that might require two or three weeks of study and implementation. Some are challenging term projects.

Text manipulation

7.20. *Text Analysis.* The availability of computers with string manipulation capabilities has resulted in some rather interesting approaches to analyzing the writings of great authors. Much attention has been focused in recent years on the issue of whether or not William Shakespeare ever lived. Some scholars believe that there is substantial evidence that indicates that Christopher Marlowe actually penned the masterpieces normally attributed to Shakespeare. Researchers have used computers in the efforts to find similarities in the writings of these two authors. This exercise examines three methods for analyzing texts with a computer.

(a) Write a BASIC program that reads several lines of text from **DATA** statements and then prints a table indicating the number of occurrences of each letter of the alphabet in the text.

For example, the phrase

To be, or not to be: that is the question:

contains one "a," two "b's," no "c's," etc.

(b) Write a BASIC program that reads several line of text from **DATA** statements and then prints a table indicating the number of one-letter words, two-letter words, three-letter words, etc. appearing in the text.

For example, the phrase

Whether 'tis nobler in the mind to suffer

contains

Word Length	Occurrences
1	0
2	2
3	2
4	1 (including 'tis)
5	0
6	2
7	1

(c) Write a BASIC program that reads several lines of text from **DATA** statements, and then prints a table indicating the number of occurrences of each different word within the text. The first version of your program should include the words in the table in the same order in which they first appear in the text. A more interesting (and useful) printout should then be attempted in which the words are sorted alphabetically.

For example, the lines

> To be, or not to be: that is the question:
> Whether 'tis nobler in the mind to suffer

contain the words "to" three times, the word "be" two times, the word "or" once, etc.

7.21. *Word Arrangements.* Write a BASIC program that INPUTs a five-letter word and then prints all the one-letter, two-letter, three-letter, four-letter, and five-letter words that can be derived from it. Read your program's printout and circle all commonly used English words.

For example, the word "slate" yields the following (among many others):

> one-letter words: "a"
> two-letter words: "as," "at"
> three-letter words: "let," "set"
> four-letter words: "late," "sale," "seal"
> five-letter words: "tales," "steal"

7.22. *Telephone Number Word Generator.* Standard telephone dials contain the digits 0 through 9. The numbers 2 through 9 each have three letters associated with them, as is indicated by the following table:

DIGIT	LETTERS
0	(none)
1	(none)
2	A B C
3	D E F
4	G H I
5	J K L
6	M N O
7	P R S
8	T U V
9	W X Y

Many people find it difficult to memorize phone numbers, so they use the correspondence between digits and letters in the above table to develop seven-letter words that correspond to their phone numbers. For example, a person whose telephone number is 686-2377 might use the correspondence indicated in the above table to develop the seven-letter word "NUMBERS."

Businesses frequently attempt to get telephone numbers which are easy for their clients to remember. If a business can advertise a simple word for its customers to dial, then no doubt the business will receive at least a few more calls.

Any particular seven-letter word corresponds to exactly one seven-digit telephone number. For example, the restaurant wishing to increase its take-home business could surely do so with the number 825-3688 (i.e., "TAKEOUT"). The 825 exchange may or may not be available in that area, and even if it is available, the number may already be in use.

Any particular seven-digit phone number corresponds to a great many separate seven-letter words. Unfortunately, most of these represent unrecognizable juxtapositions of letters. It is possible, however, that the owner of a barber shop would be pleased to know that the shop's telephone number, 424-7288, corresponds to "HAIRCUT." The owner of a liquor store would, no doubt, be delighted to find that the store's telephone number, 233-7226, corresponds to "BEERCAN." A veterinarian with the phone number 738-2273 would be pleased to know that the number corresponds to the letters "PETCARE."

Write a BASIC program that, given a seven-digit number, produces every possible seven-letter word corresponding to that number. There are 2187 (3 to the seventh power) such words. Avoid phone numbers with the digits 0 and 1.

7.23. *A Songwriting Program.* Write a BASIC program that prints verses to the song "A Hundred Bottles of Beer on the Wall." Use the techniques developed in Example 7.4 to generate the word equivalents of the numbers 100, 99, 98, etc. The first two verses of the song are

> A hundred bottles of beer on the wall
> A hundred bottles of beer
> If one of those bottles should happen to fall
> Ninety-nine bottles of beer on the wall.
>
> Ninety-nine bottles of beer on the wall
> Ninety-nine bottles of beer
> If one of those bottles should happen to fall
> Ninety-eight bottles of beer on the wall.

If you have access to a speech synthesizer, connect it to your computer system and let it sing the verses of the song out loud!

7.24. *Dealing a Deck of Cards.* One very important application of computers is in the simulation of real-world situations. Chapter 8 of this text discusses the use of computers in simulation in great detail. In this problem we begin to develop the techniques that will be useful in simulating many "games of chance."

Write a BASIC program that, given a list of the integers 1 to 52 in any order whatsoever, simulates the dealing of a deck of cards. (*Note:* Chapter 8 presents techniques for shuffling a deck of cards.)

Obviously, the reader must assign some correspondence between the numbers from 1 to 52 and the cards in a standard deck of 52 cards. One way to do this is to let the first 13 cards be hearts, the next 13 be diamonds, the next 13 be clubs, and the last 13 be spades. Within each suit of 13 cards, the first 10 cards represent the ace through the ten, and the remaining three cards represent the jack, the queen, and the king of that suit, respectively.

On the basis of the scheme presented above, the number 1 corresponds to the ace of hearts, the number 2 corresponds to the two of hearts, the number 10 corresponds to the ten of hearts, the number 13 corresponds to the king of hearts, the number 26 corresponds to the king of diamonds, the number 39 corresponds to the king of clubs, and the number 52 corresponds to the king of spades.

7.25. *Word Processing.* The detailed treatment of string manipulation in this text is greatly attributable to the exciting growth in word processing in recent years. One important function in word processing systems is sometimes called *type-justification* or the alignment of words to both the left and right margins of a page. This generates a very professional-looking document that gives the appearance of being set in type rather than prepared on a typewriter. Type-justification is normally accomplished on most computer systems by the insertion of one or more blank characters between each of the words in a line so that the rightmost word aligns with the right margin.

Write a BASIC program that reads several lines of text from **DATA** statements, and then prints this text in type-justified format. Assume that the text is to be printed on 8 1/2-inch-wide paper, and that one-inch margins are to be allowed on both the left and right sides of the printed page. Assume that the computer prints 10 characters to the horizontal inch. Therefore, your program should print 6 1/2 inches of text or 65 characters per line.

Business applications

7.26. *Printing Dates in Various Formats.* Dates are commonly printed in several different formats in business correspondence. Two of the more common formats are:

05/27/45 and May 27, 1945

Write a BASIC program that reads a date in the first format and produces a date in the second format.

In commercial data processing applications, the two digits of the day of the month are referred to as DD, the two digits of the month as MM, and the last two digits of the year as YY. Therefore, the above problem can be stated more generally as:

Write a BASIC program that reads a date in the form
MM/DD/YY and produces a date in the form
monthname DD, 19YY

7.27. *Check Protection*. Computers are frequently employed in check-writing systems such as payroll and accounts payable applications. Many strange stories circulate throughout the computer industry regarding weekly paychecks being printed (by mistake) for amounts in excess of $1 million. Many weird amounts are printed by computerized check-writing systems because of human error and/or machine failure. Systems designers, of course, make every effort to build controls into their systems to prevent erroneous checks from being issued.

Another serious problem is the intentional alteration of a check amount by someone who intends to cash a check fraudulently. To prevent a dollar amount from being altered, most computerized check-writing systems employ a technique called *check protection.*

Checks designed for imprinting by computer contain a fixed number of spaces in which the computer may print an amount. Suppose a paycheck contains eight blank spaces in which the computer is supposed to print the amount of a weekly paycheck. If the amount is large, then all eight of those spaces will be filled, for example:

```
        1,230.60      (check amount)
        -----------
        12345678      (position numbers)
```

On the other hand, if the amount is less than $1000, then several of the spaces would ordinarily be left blank. For example,

```
           99.87
        -------------
        12345678
```

contains three blank spaces. If a check is printed with blank spaces, then it is easier for someone to alter the amount of the check. To prevent a check from being altered, many check-writing systems insert *leading asterisks* to protect the amount as follows:

```
        ***99.87
        -----------
        12345678
```

Write a BASIC program that inputs a dollar amount to be printed on a check, and then prints the amount in check-protected format with leading asterisks if necessary. Assume that nine spaces are available for printing an amount. (*Note*: In Chapter 11, "Formatted Outputs," we'll see how the powerful **PRINT USING** statement may be used to accomplish many common types of string editing operations more easily than is possible here.)

7.28. *Writing the Word Equivalent of a Check Amount*. Continuing the discussion of the previous example, we reiterate the importance of designing check-writing systems to prevent alteration of check amounts. One common security method requires that the check amount be written both in numbers, and "spelled out" in words as well. Even if someone is able to alter the numerical amount of the check, it is extremely difficult to change the amount in words.

Many computerized check-writing systems do not print the amount of the check in words. Perhaps the main reason for this omission is the fact that most high-level languages used in commercial applications do not contain adequate string manipulation features. Another reason is that the logic for writing word equivalents of check amounts is somewhat involved.

Write a BASIC program that inputs a numeric check amount and uses the techniques developed in Example 7.4 to write the word equivalent of the amount. For example, the amount 112.43 should be written as

ONE HUNDRED TWELVE and 43/100

Cryptography and symbolic coding schemes

7.29. *Cryptography.* Cryptography is the science of coding and cipher systems. Most people associate cryptography with undercover activities. But cryptography is becoming important in day-to-day computing and data communications.

To establish some degree of protection of business and personal information, coding schemes have been developed for transmitting computerized information. This activity has resulted in renewed interest in cryptography.

Write a BASIC program that uses a simple *substitution coding* scheme to encode English language messages. Your program should replace each letter in the original message with the next higher letter in the alphabet, i.e., A is replaced by B, L is replaced by M, etc. Replace all Z's in the original message with A's. All blanks are to be preserved.

Your program is a *coder* or *encoder*. A program that reads a coded message (*ciphertext*) and converts it to uncoded form (*plaintext*) is called a *decoder*. Discuss how you would write a decoder program for processing the messages produced by your encoder program.

7.30. *Morse Code.* Perhaps the most famous of all coding schemes is the Morse code, developed by Samuel Morse in 1832 for use with the telegraph system. The Morse code assigns a series of dots and dashes to each letter of the alphabet, each digit, and a few special characters (such as the period, comma, colon, and semicolon). In sound-oriented systems, the dot represents a short sound and the dash represents a long sound. Other representations of dots and dashes are used with light-oriented systems and signal flag systems.

Separation between words is indicated by a space, or, quite simply, the absence of a dot or dash. In a sound-oriented system, a space is indicated by a short period of time during which no sound is transmitted. The international version of the Morse code appears in Figure 7.17.

Write a BASIC program that reads an English language phrase and encodes the phrase into Morse code. Also write a BASIC program that reads a phrase in Morse code and converts the phrase into the English language equivalent. Use one blank between each Morse-coded letter and three blanks between each Morse-coded word.

A	.-		N	-.
B	-...		O	---
C	-.-.		P	.--.
D	-..		Q	--.-
E	.		R	.-.
F	..-.		S	...
G	--.		T	-
H	....		U	..-
I	..		V	...-
J	.---		W	.--
K	-.-		X	-..-
L	.-..		Y	-.--
M	--		Z	--..

Figure 7.17 The letters of the alphabet as expressed in international Morse code

7.31. *Roman Numerals.* In the ancient Roman number system, letters are used to represent numbers. The system is awkward compared to the Arabic numerals used today, yet it is still taught to school children and used for certain applications such as pagination and the engraving of building cornerstones.

Certain numbers are represented be a single letter in the Roman numeral system as follows:

Letter	Value
I	1
V	5
X	10
L	50
C	100
D	500
M	1000

Other integers are written according to the following two rules:

1. If one letter is immediately followed by another letter of equal or smaller value, then the two values are added. For example,

XX	=	20 (i.e., 10 plus 10)
VI	=	6 (i.e., 5 plus 1)
XV	=	15 (i.e., 10 plus 5)

2. If one letter is immediately followed by another letter of greater value, then the first is subtracted from the second. For example,

IV	=	4 (i.e., 5 minus 1)
IX	=	9 (i.e., 10 minus 1)
XL	=	40 (i.e., 50 minus 10)

Some other examples of decimal equivalents for Roman numeral representations are

CM	=	900
XLVII	=	47
CXV	=	115
MCMXV	=	1915

Write a BASIC program that prints the Roman numeral equivalents of the decimal numbers from 1 to 100. Write a BASIC program that converts a decimal number into the equivalent Roman numeral representation. Write a BASIC program that converts a Roman numeral into the equivalent decimal number representation. Write a BASIC program that performs the simple arithmetic operations of addition, subtraction, multiplication, and division on Roman numeral expressions entered by the user in the form

(Roman numeral) (arithmetic operator) (Roman numeral)

For example, this last program should accept the expression XV + VI and should print the result XXI.

Graphical outputs

7.32. *A Banner Printing Program.* Write a BASIC program that inputs a phrase and prints it, using very large letters to create a banner. Test your program with the phrase "the quick brown fox jumps over the lazy dog." To allow for long phrases, design your program so that it prints the letters down the page instead of across the page. For example, your program might print the word "ME" as shown in Figure 7.18.

```
            MMMMMMMMMMMMMMMMMMM
            MMMMMMMMMMMMMMMMMMMMM
                       MMMM
                      MMMM
                     MMMM
                    MMMM
                   MMMM
            MMM
              MMMM
                MMMM
                  MMMM
                    MMMM
                      MMMM
            MMMMMMMMMMMMMMMMMMMMM
            MMMMMMMMMMMMMMMMMMMMM


            EEEEEEEEEEEEEEEEEEEE
            EEEEEEEEEEEEEEEEEEEE
            EE        EEE        EE
            EE        EEE        EE
            EE        EEE        EE
            EE        EEE        EE
            EE        EEE        EE
            EE                   EE
            EE                   EE
            EE                   EE
```

Figure   7.18

Experiment with different size letters and different means of representing each letter. The style of a set of letters is called a *type font*. Represent letters in two or three different fonts. The more ambitious reader should try to implement a script font. Your efforts should yield some insight into the complexities of font design and even handwriting analysis.

7.33. *Printing a Calendar.* Write a BASIC program that prints a calendar. Your program should print the year in large letters across the top of the calendar. The name of each month should be printed in large letters across the top of each month's section of the calendar. To generalize your program, allow the user to enter the year and day of the week on which the year begins. This will allow the program to print a calendar for any year. If the year entered by the user is divisible by four, then your program should provide for February 29.

7.34. *Points of the Compass.* Write a BASIC program that prints a table indicating the abbreviations for the major points of the compass (at least three levels deep—such as NNW), and the corresponding readings in degrees (based on a 360-degree circle with north equal to zero degrees).

7.35. *Face of a Clock.* Write a BASIC program that inputs a time such as 11:35 (35 minutes after the hour of 11), and then draws the face of a clock with the hour and minute hands positioned to indicate the time. Incorporate the above program as a subroutine into a larger program that teaches a youngster how to tell time.

7.36. *Automatic 10-Pin Bowling Scorekeeper.* Many bowling establishments offer computerized scorekeeping systems. Write a BASIC program that automatically scores a 10-pin bowling game and prints the scoresheet after each frame. Your program should accept as input the number of pins knocked down by each ball in a frame. Note that every frame has two balls unless a strike is thrown. Be careful to consider any special handling needed if a spare or a strike occurs in the tenth frame.

More business-related problems

7.37. *A Metric Conversion Program.* Write a BASIC program that will assist the user with metric conversions. Your program should allow the user to specify the names of the units as strings (i.e., centimeters, liters, grams, etc. for the metric system and inches, quarts, pounds, etc. for the English system) and should respond to simple questions such as

"How many inches in 2 meters?"
"How many liters in 10 quarts?"

Your program should recognize any invalid conversions. For example, the question

"How many feet in 5 kilograms?"

is not meaningful because "feet" is a unit of length while a "kilogram" is a unit of weight.

7.38. *Dunning Letters.* Many businesses spend a great deal of time and money collecting overdue debts. "Dunning" is the process of making repeated and insistent demands upon a debtor to attempt to collect a debt.

Computers are often used to generate dunning letters automatically and in increasing degrees of severity as a debt becomes older. The theory here is that as a debt becomes older it becomes more difficult to collect, and therefore the dunning letters must become more threatening.

Write a BASIC program that contains the texts of five dunning letters of increasing severity. Your program should accept as input from a user:

1. The debtor's name
2. The debtor's address
3. The debtor's account
4. The amount owed
5. The age of the amount owed (i.e., one month overdue, two months overdue, etc.).

Use the age of the amount owed to select one of the five message texts, and then print the dunning letter inserting the other user-supplied information where appropriate.

A challenging string manipulation project

7.39. *A Crossword Puzzle Generator.* Most people have worked a crossword puzzle at one time or another, but few have ever attempted to generate one. Generating a crossword puzzle is a difficult problem. It is suggested here as a string manipulation project requiring substantial sophistication and effort. There are many issues the programmer must resolve in order to get even the simplest crossword puzzle generator program working.

For example, how does one represent the grid of a crossword puzzle inside the computer? Should one use a series of strings, or should arrays be used? Can a project of this scope be attempted reasonably with single-subscripted arrays, or should double-subscripted arrays (that are more like the grid of a crossword puzzle) be used?

The programmer needs a source of words (i.e., a computerized dictionary) that can be directly referenced by the program. In what form should these words be stored to facilitate the complex manipulations required by the program? The really ambitious reader will want to generate the "clues" portion of the puzzle in which the brief hints for each "across" word and each "down" word are printed for the puzzle worker. Merely printing a version of the blank puzzle itself is not a simple problem.

Chapter 8
Random Numbers and Simulation

8.1 Introduction

This chapter was inspired by the author's stay at Paradise Island, Nassau in the Bahamas. Perhaps the island's most popular attraction (besides perfect sun and sea) is the world-famous Paradise Island Casino.

There is something in the air of a gambling casino that invigorates every type of person from the high-rollers at the plush mahogany-and-felt craps tables to the quarter-poppers at the one-armed bandits. It is the *element of chance,* the possibility that luck will convert a mere pocketful of money into a mountain of wealth.

The element of chance can be introduced into computer applications by the use of the *RND intrinsic function* in BASIC. This chapter describes the use of RND for simulating games of chance and other situations that depend upon an element of uncertainty.

8.2 The RND Intrinsic Function

Consider the following BASIC statement:

```
i = RND
```

The RND built-in function generates a value between 0 and 1 but never exactly 1. This value is then assigned to the variable i.

RND generates numbers *at random,* i.e., every number between 0 and 1 (but never 1) has an equal *chance* (or *probability*) of being chosen each time RND is referenced in a BASIC program.

The limited range of values produced by RND is rarely sufficient in most applications requiring random numbers. For example, a program that simulates the flipping of a coin might require only two integers to be chosen: a 1 might represent "heads" and a 2, "tails." A program that simulates the rolling of a six-sided die would require integers to be chosen at random from the range 1 to 6 inclusive.

To demonstrate the use of RND, let us develop a small program that will simulate 20 rolls of a six-sided die and will print the value of each roll. First we use the RND directly to confirm the range of values produced (see Figure 8.1).

```
REM    Values produced by RND
FOR i = 1 TO 5
   FOR j = 1 TO 4
      k = RND
      PRINT k,
   NEXT j
   PRINT
NEXT i
END
```

.1213501	.651861	.8688611	.7297624
.798853	7.369804E-02	.4903128	.4545189
.1072496	.9505103	.7038702	.531864
.9711614	.3209329	.9561278	.9345151
.5349367	.5644214	.6712188	.7025722

Figure 8.1 Values produced by **RND**

Notice that all these values do fall between 0 and 1. These numbers could be used to simulate the roll of a die by dividing the interval from 0 to 1 into six equal parts. The number generated by **RND** could then be tested to determine in which of the six intervals it belongs, and an integer from one to six could then be assigned. This process would result in a large number of BASIC statements and would be cumbersome to program. Instead, let us demonstrate how a single BASIC statement can be written to choose integers at random from the range 1 to 6.

Because we want to obtain a range of six integers, we must expand the normal range of **RND**. This is accomplished by multiplying the value produced by **RND** by 6. We call this *scaling*, and the multiplier (6 in this case) is called a *scaling factor* (see Figure 8.2).

```
REM    Scaling values produced by RND
FOR i = 1 TO 5
   FOR j = 1 TO 4
      k = 6 * RND
      PRINT k,
   NEXT j
   PRINT
NEXT i
END
```

.7281007	3.911166	5.213167	4.378574
4.793118	.4421883	2.941876	2.727113
.6434973	5.703062	4.223221	3.191184
5.826969	1.925597	5.736767	5.607091
3.20962	3.386528	4.027313	4.215433

Figure 8.2 Scaling values produced by **RND**

By scaling the range (i.e., 0 to 1) produced by **RND** we obtain numbers in a wider range. To determine how wide the new range is, we multiply the extremes of the previous range (again, 0 and 1) by the scaling factor, 6. Thus the low extreme of the new range is 6 times 0, or 0, and the high extreme of the new range is 6 times 1, or 6. But remember that **RND** produces numbers between 0 and 1 but never exactly 1; therefore 6 *

RND produces numbers between 0 and 6 but never exactly 6. The outputs shown in Figure 8.2 confirm the effects of scaling.

Notice that the numbers produced by 6 * RND include decimal fractions. Since we desire only integers to be produced, we must take the integer part of 6 * RND with the INT intrinsic function (see Figure 8.3).

Now we are indeed choosing integers, but one slight problem remains. The range of these integers is 0 to 5 instead of the desired range of 1 to 6. This occurs because all numbers between 0 and 0.999999 are becoming 0 and all numbers between 5 and 5.999999 are becoming 5. This problem is easy to correct. We need merely *shift* the range of numbers produced by +1 (see Figure 8.4).

```
REM    Producing integer random numbers
FOR i = 1 TO 5
    FOR j = 1 TO 5
        k = INT(6 * RND)
        PRINT k,
    NEXT j
    PRINT
NEXT i
END
```

0	3	5	4	4
0	2	2	0	5
4	3	5	1	5
5	3	3	4	4
4	4	2	2	0

Figure 8.3 Producing integer random numbers

```
REM    Shifting a range of random numbers
FOR i = 1 TO 5
    FOR j = 1 TO 5
        k = 1 + INT(6 * RND)
        PRINT k,
    NEXT j
    PRINT
NEXT i
END
```

1	4	6	5	5
1	3	3	1	6
5	4	6	2	6
6	4	4	5	5
5	5	3	3	1

Figure 8.4 Shifting a range of random numbers

Thus we are now choosing integers at random in the range 1 to 6. To show that these numbers are occurring with equal likelihood, let us use our technique to simulate 6000 rolls of a die. If the numbers are indeed being chosen with equal likelihood, then we should obtain each possible integer from 1 to 6 about 1000 times (see Figure 8.5).

```
REM    Roll a six-sided die 6000 times
DIM frequency(6)

FOR face = 1 TO 6
    frequency(face) = 0
NEXT face

FOR roll = 1 TO 6000
    face = 1 + INT(6 * RND)
    frequency(face) = frequency(face) + 1
NEXT roll

PRINT "Face", "Frequency"
FOR face = 1 TO 6
    PRINT face, frequency(face)
NEXT face
END
```

▤▢▦ **Rolling a die** ▦▦▦	
Face	Frequency
1	929
2	1051
3	1011
4	1014
5	980
6	1015

Figure 8.5 Roll a six-sided die 6000 times

Thus by scaling and shifting, and by use of the INT intrinsic function, we have utilized the RND built-in function to simulate realistically the rolling of a six-sided die.

RND may be referenced with a value as in RND(x). If x is greater than zero, or if x is omitted as in our examples so far, then each time RND is referenced it generates the next random number in sequence. If x is less than zero, then the same sequence of random values restarts for the given x. If x is equal to zero, then the reference to RND repeats the last random number generated.

8.3 The RANDOMIZE Statement

Consider again our die-rolling program (Figure 8.6).

```
REM    Die-rolling program
FOR i = 1 TO 5
   FOR j = 1 TO 5
      k = 1 + INT(6 * RND)
      PRINT k,
   NEXT j
   PRINT
NEXT i
END
```

1	4	6	5	5
1	3	3	1	6
5	4	6	2	6
6	4	4	5	5
5	5	3	3	1

Figure 8.6 Die-rolling program

If we run this program again we get:

1	4	6	5	5
1	3	3	1	6
5	4	6	2	6
6	4	4	5	5
5	5	3	3	1

Notice that exactly the same sequence of values was printed for each run. Are we not supposed to get "random" numbers? Ironically, this repeatability is an important characteristic of the RND built-in function, as we shall soon see. To condition a program to produce a different sequence of random numbers for each run, we use the BASIC command *RANDOMIZE* as shown in Figure 8.7. Let us run the program several times and observe the results. Notice that with the inclusion of the RANDOMIZE statement we now obtain a *different* sequence of random numbers each time the program is run and we type a different random number seed.

The RANDOMIZE statement is ordinarily inserted in a program only after the program has been thoroughly debugged. During the debugging stage, however, it is better to omit the RANDOMIZE. This ensures repeatability, which is essential to proving that corrections to a program are working properly.

If we wish to randomize without the need for typing in a seed each time, we use the statement RANDOMIZE TIMER. This causes the Macintosh to read its system clock to obtain the value for the seed automatically. (The number of seconds since midnight is used as the seed.)

```
REM    Randomizing die-rolling program
RANDOMIZE

FOR i = 1 TO 5
   FOR j = 1 TO 5
      k = 1 + INT(6 * RND)
      PRINT k,
   NEXT j
   PRINT
NEXT i
END
```

```
Random Number Seed (-32768 to 32767)?  67
1              6              1              3              1
5              3              5              1              5
5              5              4              6              2
6              4              3              2              6
3              6              1              3              5


Random Number Seed (-32768 to 32767)?  432
5              6              3              3              3
3              1              1              1              6
5              3              5              3              3
2              1              5              3              6
3              3              6              5              2
```

Figure 8.7 Randomizing the die-rolling program

8.4 Scaling and Shifting RND

The values produced directly by RND are always in the limited range:

```
0 <= RND < 1
```

In Section 8.2 we demonstrated how to write a single BASIC statement to simulate the rolling of a six-sided die:

```
face = 1 + INT(6 * RND)
```

This statement always assigns an integer value (at random) to the variable face in the following range:

```
1 <= face <= 6
```

Note that the width of this range (i.e., the number of consecutive integers in the range) is 6 and the starting number in the range is 1. Referring to the preceding statement, we see that the width of the range is determined by the number used to multiply RND and the starting number of the range is equal to the number (i.e., 1) that is added to INT(6 * RND). We can generalize this result as follows:

$$face = a + INT (b * RND)$$

a = "shifting value," which is equal to the first number in the desired range of consecutive integers.

b = "scaling factor," which is equal to the width of the desired range of consecutive integers.

Example 8.1 Choosing integers at random from a range of consecutive integers

Write BASIC statements that assign an integer (at random) to the variable i in each of the following ranges:

(a) $1 <= i <= 2$

Answer. The width of the interval is 2, and the starting number is 1; therefore,

$$i = 1 + INT(2 * RND)$$

(b) $110 <= i <= 119$

Answer. The width of the interval is 10, and the starting number is 110; therefore,

$$i = 110 + INT(10 * RND)$$

(c) $7 <= i <= 14$

Answer. The width of the interval is 8, and the starting number is 7; therefore,

$$i = 7 + INT(8 * RND)$$

(d) $1 <= i <= 100$

Answer. The width of the interval is 100, and the starting number is 1; therefore,

$$i = 1 + INT(100 * RND)$$

Example 8.2 Choosing integers at random from sets of numbers other than ranges of consecutive integers

(a) Write a single BASIC statement that will choose a number at random from the set of integers 3, 6, 9, . . . , 27.

Answer. The set of numbers is not a range of consecutive integers. Therefore, the formula we developed does not apply. However, if we carefully examine the set of numbers, we see that the set consists of the consecutive multiples of 3, from 1 times 3 to 9 times 3. Thus we need to choose an integer at random from 1 to 9 and multiply the result by 3:

```
i = 3 * (1 + INT(9 * RND))
```

(b) Write a single BASIC statement that will choose a number at random from the set of integers 4, 7, 10, 13, 16, 19, 22, 25, 28.

Answer. Once again, the set of numbers is not a range of consecutive integers, and our formula does not apply. Careful examination of this set, however, reveals that it consists of the same set of numbers as in part (a), but each number has been shifted by +1. Thus we need merely add 1 to the result obtained in part (a):

```
i = 1 + 3 * (1 + INT(9 * RND))
```

8.5 A Game of Chance

The RND built-in function may be used to program simulations of many "games of chance." One of the most popular games of chance is known as "craps," which is played in casinos and back alleys throughout the world.

Example 8.3 The game of craps
Write a BASIC program that simulates the game of craps. (See Figures 8.8 and 8.9.) A person designated the player rolls two dice. Each die has six faces. These faces contain one, two, three, four, five, and six spots, respectively.

After the dice have come to rest, the sum of the spots on the two upward faces is calculated. If the sum is 7 or 11 on the first throw, the player wins. If the sum is 2, 3, or 12 on the first throw (called "craps"), the player loses (i.e., the "house" wins).

If the sum is 4, 5, 6, 8, 9, or 10 on the first throw, then that sum becomes the player's "point." To win, the player must continue to throw the dice until he "makes his point." The player loses if he rolls a 7 before making his point. (*Note:* In Problem 8.22 you will be asked to write a program that investigates the game of craps in depth.)

8.6 A Simple Simulation Model

Random numbers are often useful in developing computerized simulation models of real-world situations. Many businesses must maintain inventories of various items. In the next example, we examine how random numbers may be used to develop a simulation model to aid in inventory control.

```
REM    Simulation of the game of craps
RANDOMIZE TIMER

gamestatus = 0
CALL Rolldice (sum)

SELECT CASE sum
   CASE 7, 11
      gamestatus = 1
   CASE 2, 3, 12
      gamestatus = 2
   CASE ELSE
      mypoint = sum
      PRINT "Point is "; mypoint
END SELECT

WHILE gamestatus = 0
   CALL Rolldice (sum)
   IF sum = mypoint THEN
      gamestatus = 1
      ELSEIF sum = 7 THEN
         gamestatus = 2
   END IF
WEND

IF gamestatus = 1 THEN
   PRINT "Player wins"
   ELSE
      PRINT "Player loses"
END IF
PRINT
END

SUB Rolldice (worksum)
   die1 = 1 + INT(6 * RND)
   die2 = 1 + INT(6 * RND)
   worksum = die1 + die2
   PRINT "Player rolled"; die1; "+"; die2; "="; worksum
END SUB
```

Figure 8.8 Program to simulate the game of craps

```
Player rolled 2 + 5 = 7
Player wins


Player rolled 3 + 6 = 9
Point is 9
Player rolled 6 + 6 = 12
Player rolled 3 + 1 = 4
Player rolled 5 + 2 = 7
Player loses
```

Figure 8.9 Sample runs for the game of craps

Example 8.4 A simple inventory simulation model
A local hardware store owner has asked you to develop a computer program to help him study his inventory of galvanized garbage cans. The store owner gives you the following facts:

1. Past experience has shown that in a typical business day the store will sell from one to five galvanized garbage cans with equal likelihood, i.e., the number of galvanized garbage cans sold on a particular day is a random integer chosen from the range 1 through 5.
2. Past experience has shown that in a typical business day customers will return either one or two galvanized garbage cans with equal likelihood, i.e., the number of galvanized garbage cans returned on a particular day is a random integer chosen from the range 1 through 2. (Assume that returned cans may be resold to other customers.)
3. The store now has 64 galvanized garbage cans in stock.
4. Whenever the inventory of galvanized garbage cans is down to 32 or less, it is necessary to reorder from the supplier. (*Note:* Inventory is counted at the end of each business day after all sales and returns have been tallied.)

Write a BASIC program that will determine how many business days will elapse before the store owner will have to reorder galvanized garbage cans. Your program should make this determination 50 times (each time assuming a beginning inventory of 64 galvanized garbage cans). Your program should then calculate and print the average number of business days until reorder is needed. Figures 8.10 and 8.11 contain the program listing and several sample runs.

8.7 A Card Shuffling and Dealing Simulation

We have already used random number generation to simulate the game of craps. Game playing with computers is educational and enjoyable. In this section we shall use random number generation to develop a card-playing simulation program. The reader may modify this program to play specific card games.

Example 8.5 Shuffling and dealing a deck of cards
Using the techniques of top-down, stepwise refinement, develop a BASIC program that will shuffle a deck of 52 playing cards, and then deal each of the 52 cards.

We shall use a 4-by-13 double-subscripted array deck to represent the deck of playing cards. The rows correspond to the suits—row 1 to "Hearts," row 2 to "Diamonds," row 3 to "Clubs," and row 4 to "Spades." The columns correspond to the face values of the cards—columns 1 through 10 correspond to faces "Ace" through "Ten" respectively, and columns 11 through 13 correspond

```
REM    Inventory simulation model
RANDOMIZE TIMER

total = 0

FOR k = 1 TO 10
   FOR j = 1 TO 5
      inventory = 64
      days = 1
      sales = 1 + INT(5 * RND)
      returns = 1 + INT(2 * RND)
      inventory = inventory - sales + returns

      WHILE inventory > 32
         days = days + 1
         sales = 1 + INT(5 * RND)
         returns = 1 + INT(2 * RND)
         inventory = inventory - sales + returns
      WEND
      total = total + days
      PRINT days,
   NEXT j
   PRINT
NEXT k
PRINT "Average days until reorder"; total / 50
END
```

Figure 8.10 Program for inventory simulation problem

23	22	27	25	21
19	36	26	16	15
19	20	22	19	20
17	14	26	21	24
23	26	24	25	20
18	17	21	21	26
17	16	22	23	23
21	24	17	27	26
21	17	24	19	17
21	28	20	16	20

Average days until reorder 21.44

22	29	16	17	30
24	24	20	29	22
20	13	21	21	28
18	20	16	31	15
20	20	14	20	20
23	19	13	28	21
18	18	16	24	15
20	23	27	20	22
23	16	26	24	18
24	15	18	23	14

Average days until reorder 20.76

Figure 8.11 Sample runs for inventory simulation problem

to "Jack," "Queen," and "King." We shall load array `suit$` with the four suits, and array `face$` with the thirteen face values.

This simulated deck of cards may be shuffled as follows. First the array `deck` is cleared to zeros. Then, a `row` (1-4) is chosen at random, and a column (1-13) is chosen at random. Then the number 1 is inserted in array element `deck(row, column)` to indicate that this card is going to be first in the shuffled deck. This process continues with the numbers 2, 3, . . . , 52 being inserted in the `deck` array to indicate which cards are to be placed second, third, . . . , and fifty-second in the shuffled deck. As the `deck` array begins to fill with card numbers, it is possible that a card will be selected twice, i.e., `deck(row, column)` will be nonzero when it is selected. This selection is simply ignored and another `row` and `column` are chosen at random until an unselected card is found. Eventually, the numbers 1-52 will occupy the 52 slots of the `deck` array. At this point, the deck of cards is fully shuffled.

To deal the first card we simply search the array for `deck(row, column)` = 1. This is accomplished with a nested **FOR/NEXT** structure that varies `row` from 1 to 4 and `column` from 1 to 13. What card does that slot of the array correspond to? The `suit$` array has been preloaded with the four suits, so to get the suit we need merely print `suit$(row)`. Similarly, to get the face value of the card, we need merely print `face$(column)`.

Let us proceed with top-down, stepwise refinement. The top is simply

```
Shuffle and deal 52 cards
```

Our first refinement yields:

```
Initialize the suit$ array
Initialize the face$ array
Shuffle the deck
Deal 52 cards
END
```

"Shuffle the deck" may be expanded as follows:

```
FOR each of the 52 cards
    Place card number in randomly selected unoccupied slot
        of deck
NEXT card
```

"Deal 52 cards" may be expanded as follows:

```
FOR each of the 52 cards
    Find card number in deck array and print face and suit
        of card
NEXT card
```

Incorporating these expansions yields our second refinement:

```
Initialize the suit$ array
Initialize the face$ array
FOR each of the 52 cards
    Place card number in randomly selected unoccupied slot
        of deck
NEXT card
FOR each of the 52 cards
    Find card number in deck array and print face and suit
        of card
NEXT card
END
```

"Place card number in randomly selected unoccupied slot of deck" may be expanded as follows:

```
Choose slot of deck randomly
WHILE chosen slot of deck has been previously chosen
    Choose slot of deck randomly
NEXT
Place card number in chosen slot of deck
```

"Find card number in deck array and print face and suit of card" may be expanded as follows:

```
FOR each slot of the deck array
    IF slot doesn't contain card number
        THEN look at next slot
    END IF
    Print the face and suit of the card
NEXT slot of deck array
```

Incorporating these expansions yields our third refinement:

```
Initialize the suit$ array
Initialize the face$ array

FOR each of the 52 cards
    Choose slot of deck randomly
    WHILE chosen slot of deck has been previously chosen
        Choose slot of deck randomly
    NEXT
    Place card number in chosen slot of deck
NEXT card

FOR each of the 52 cards
    FOR each slot of deck array
        IF slot doesn't contain desired card number
            THEN look at next slot
        END IF
        Print the face and suit of the card
    NEXT slot of deck array
NEXT card

END
```

This completes the refinement process. The program is shown in Figure 8.12 and a sample execution is shown in Figure 8.13.

```
REM    Card dealing program
RANDOMIZE TIMER

DIM deck(4,13), suit$(4), face$(13)

CALL ReadSuit (suit$())
CALL ReadFace (face$())
CALL ShuffleDeck (deck())
CALL DealDeck (deck(), face$(), suit$())
END

DATA Hearts, Diamonds, Clubs, Spades
DATA Ace, Deuce, Three, Four, Five, Six, Seven
DATA Eight, Nine, Ten, Jack, Queen, King


SUB DealDeck (workdeck2(), workface$(), worksuit$()) STATIC
   FOR card = 1 TO 52
      FOR row = 1 TO 4
         FOR column = 1 TO 13
            IF workdeck2(row, column) = card THEN
               LPRINT workface$(column); " of "; worksuit$(row)
            END IF
         NEXT column
      NEXT row
   NEXT card
END SUB

SUB ReadFace (workface$()) STATIC
   FOR i = 1 TO 13
      READ workface$(i)
   NEXT i
END SUB

SUB ReadSuit (worksuit$()) STATIC
   FOR i = 1 TO 4
      READ worksuit$(i)
   NEXT i
END SUB

SUB ShuffleDeck (workdeck()) STATIC
   FOR card = 1 TO 52
      row = 1 + INT(4 * RND)
      column = 1 + INT(13 * RND)
      WHILE workdeck(row, column) <> 0
         row = 1 + INT(4 * RND)
         column = 1 + INT(13 * RND)
      WEND
      workdeck(row, column) = card
   NEXT card
END SUB
```

Figure 8.12 Card dealing program

```
Ace of Clubs
Four of Hearts
Nine of Spades
Ace of Hearts
Eight of Diamonds
Ace of Diamonds
Jack of Hearts
Seven of Hearts
Seven of Diamonds
Four of Diamonds
Six of Spades
Five of Spades
King of Diamonds
Ten of Clubs
Queen of Hearts
Four of Clubs
Eight of Clubs
Eight of Hearts
Queen of Diamonds
Three of Clubs
Three of Spades
Jack of Clubs
Seven of Spades
Ace of Spades
Deuce of Hearts
Jack of Diamonds
Nine of Diamonds
Ten of Spades
King of Clubs
King of Spades
Seven of Clubs
Six of Clubs
Deuce of Spades
Five of Hearts
Deuce of Diamonds
Queen of Spades
King of Hearts
Four of Spades
Six of Diamonds
Jack of Spades
Five of Clubs
Six of Hearts
Nine of Hearts
Ten of Hearts
Deuce of Clubs
Three of Hearts
Five of Diamonds
Eight of Spades
Three of Diamonds
Nine of Clubs
Ten of Diamonds
Queen of Clubs
```

Figure 8.13 Sample run of card dealing program

Concepts

element of chance
equal likelihood
games of chance
generate numbers at random
normal range of RND:
  0 <= RND <1
random number
RANDOMIZE
RANDOMIZE TIMER
range
RND built-in function
scaling

scaling factor
shifting
shifting value
simulate roll of a six sided die:
  face = 1 + INT(6 * RND)
simulation
simulation model
starting number of range
uncertainty
width of range

Problems

8.1. What does it mean to choose numbers "at random?"

8.2. Why is the RND built-in function useful for simulating games of chance?

8.3. Why would you include the BASIC command **RANDOMIZE** in a program? Under what circumstances is it desirable to omit the **RANDOMIZE** command?

8.4. Why is it often necessary to scale and/or shift the values produced by RND?

8.5. Why is computerized simulation of real-world situations a useful technique?

8.6. Write BASIC statements that assign an integer (at random) to the variable n in each of the following ranges:

(a)	1 <= n <= 2	**(e)**	100 <= n <= 112
(b)	1 <= n <= 6	**(f)**	1000 <= n <= 1112
(c)	1 <= n <= 100	**(g)**	-1 <= n <= 1
(d)	0 <= n <= 9	**(h)**	-3 <= n <= 11

8.7. Write a single BASIC statement that will choose a number at random from the set of integers 2, 4, 6, 8, 10.

8.8. Write a single BASIC statement that will choose a number at random from the set of integers 3, 5, 7, 9, 11.

8.9. Write a single BASIC statement that will choose a number at random from the set of integers 6, 10, 14, 18, 22.

8.10. Write a BASIC program that simulates the tossing of a coin. For each toss of the coin the program should print "Heads" or "Tails," Let the program toss the coin 100 times, and count the number of times each side of the coin appears. Print the results. *Note:* If the program realistically simulates the tossing of a coin, then each side of the coin should appear approximately half the time for a total of approximately 50 heads and 50 tails.

8.11. Computers are playing an ever-increasing role in education. Write a BASIC program that will assist an elementary school student in learning multiplication. Your program should use **RND** to produce two positive one-digit integers randomly. It should then type a question such as:

```
How much is 6 times 7?
```

The student then types the answer. Your program checks the student's answer. If it is correct, you type "Very good!" and then go on to ask another multiplication question. If the answer is wrong, you type "No. Please try again." and then you let the student try the same question again repeatedly until the student finally gets it right. If the student types -1 in response to any of the program's questions, then the program should print "That's all for now. Bye."

8.12. The use of computers in education is referred to as *computer-assisted instruction* (CAI). One problem that sometimes develops in CAI is student fatigue. This can often be eliminated by varying the computer's dialogue to hold the student's attention. Modify the program of Problem 8.11 so that the computer prints various comments for each correct answer and each incorrect answer. This can be accomplished by setting up several different responses.

Responses to a correct answer:

> Very good!
> Excellent!
> Nice work!
> Keep up the good work!

Responses to an incorrect answer.

> No. Please try again.
> Wrong. Try once more.
> Don't give up!
> No. Keep trying.

Your program should then use the random number generator to choose a number from one to four. This number is then used to select an appropriate response to each answer.

8.13. More sophisticated CAI systems monitor the performance of the student over a period of time to determine if the student is making progress. The decision to begin the next topic is often based upon the student's degree of success with previous topics. Modify the program of Problem 8.12 to count the number of correct and incorrect responses. After the student types -1 to terminate the session, your program should calculate the percentage of correct responses. If this is lower than 75 percent, your program should print "Please ask your instructor for extra help."

8.14. Write a BASIC program that simulates the rolling of two dice. The program should use **RND** to roll the first die, and should use the **RND** again to roll the second die. The sum of the two values should then be calculated. *Note:* Since each die can show an integer value from 1 to 6, then the sum of the two values will vary from 2 to 12. Your program should throw the two dice 36,000 times. Use a single-subscripted array to tally the numbers of times each possible sum appears. Print the results in a tabular fashion.

8.15. The advertising agency employed by a large manufacturing company wants to rename the company to help create a new and dynamic image for the concern. The account executive has asked you to submit a list of 100 possible names. The names must be five characters long. The first and fourth characters must be vowels (A, E, I, O, U). The second, third, and fifth characters must be consonants. Use **RND** and your knowledge of string variables to choose 100 possible new names for the company. *Hints:* Set up two strings, one containing the five vowels and one containing the 21 consonants. To select a vowel at random choose an integer from 1 to 5, using **RND**, and then use this integer in conjunction with the **MID$** function to pick a vowel from the vowel string. Use a similar approach to choose consonants at random.

8.16. Write a BASIC program that plays the game of "guess the number" as follows: Your program chooses the number to be guessed by selecting an integer at random in the range 1 to 1000. The program then types:

```
I have a number between 1 and 1000.
Can you guess my number?
Please type your first guess.
```

The player then types a first guess. The program responds with one of the following:

```
1. Excellent! You guessed the number!
   Would you like to play again?
   Please type "yes" or "no."
2. Too low. Try again.
3. Too high. Try again.
```

If the player's guess is incorrect, your program should loop until the player finally gets the number right. Your program should keep telling the player "Too high" or "Too low" to help the player zero in on the correct answer.

8.17. Modify the program of Problem 8.16 to count the number of guesses the player makes. If the number of guesses is less than 10, then print "You got lucky!" If the player guesses the number in 10 tries, then print "Ahah! You know the secret!" If the player makes more than 10 guesses, then print "You should be able to do better!" Why should it take no more than 10 guesses?

8.18. Parcel the program of Figure 8.12 into a subroutine that shuffles the deck and another subroutine that always deals the next card. Use these subroutines to shuffle the deck and deal a five-card poker hand. Then write the following additional subroutines:
(a) Determine if the hand contains a pair.
(b) Determine if the hand contains two pairs.
(c) Determine if the hand contains three of a kind (e.g., three jacks).
(d) Determine if the hand contains four of a kind (e.g., four aces).
(e) Determine if the hand contains a flush (i.e., all five cards of the same suit).
(f) Determine if the hand contains a straight (i.e., five cards of consecutive face values).

8.19. Use the subroutines developed in Problem 8.18 to write a program that deals two five-card poker hands, evaluates each hand, and determines which is the better hand.

8.20. Modify the program developed in Problem 8.19 so that it can simulate the dealer. The dealer's five-card hand is dealt face down so that the player cannot see it. The program should then evaluate the dealer's hand and, based on the quality of the hand, the dealer should draw one, two, or three more cards to replace the corresponding number of unneeded cards in the original hand. The program should then reevaluate the dealer's hand. (*Caution:* This is a very difficult problem!)

8.21. Modify the program developed in Problem 8.20 so that it can handle the dealer's hand automatically, but the player is allowed to decide which cards of the player's hand to replace. The program should then evaluate both hands and determine who wins. Now use this new program to play 20 games against the computer. Who wins more games, you or the computer? Have one of your friends play 20 games against the computer. Who wins more games? Based upon the results of these games, make appropriate modifications to polish up your poker playing program (this, too, is a difficult problem). Play 20 more games. Does your modified program play a better game?

8.22. Write a program that runs 1000 games of craps and answers each of the following questions.
(a) How many games are won on the first roll, second roll, . . ., twentieth roll, and after the twentieth roll?

(b) How many games are lost on the first roll, second roll, . . ., twentieth roll, and after the twentieth roll?

(c) What are the chances of winning at craps? (*Note:* You should discover that craps is one of the fairest casino games. What do you suppose this means?)

(d) What is the average length of a game of craps?

(e) Do the chances of winning improve with the length of the game?

8.23. (Knight's Tour) In the problems of Chapter 6 we developed a solution to the Knight's Tour problem. The approach used, called the "accessibility heuristic," generates many solutions and actually executes quite efficiently.

As computers continue increasing in power, we will be able to solve many problems with sheer computer power and relatively unsophisticated algorithms. Let us call this approach "brute force" problem solving.

(a) Use random number generation to enable the knight to walk around the chess board (in its legitimate L-shaped moves, of course) at random. The reader might observe here that this technique is unlikely to generate a full tour. Your program should run one tour and print the final chessboard. How far did the knight get?

(b) Most likely, the preceding program produced a relatively short tour. Now modify your program to attempt 1000 tours. Use a single-subscripted array to keep track of the number of tours of each length. When your program finishes attempting the 1000 tours, it should print this information in neat tabular format. Did you get any full tours? If not, then what was the best result?

(c) Most likely, the preceding program gave you some "respectable" tours but no full tours. Now "pull all the stops out" and simply let your program run until it produces a full tour. (*Caution.* This version of the program could run for hours on a powerful computer.) Once again, keep a table of the number of tours of each length, and print this table when the first full tour is found. How many tours did your program attempt before producing a full tour? How much time did it take?

(d) Compare the brute force version of the Knight's Tour with the accessibility heuristic version. Which required a more careful study of the problem? Which algorithm was more difficult to develop? Which required more computer power? Could we be certain (in advance) of obtaining a full tour with the accessibility heuristic approach? Could we be certain (in advance) of obtaining a full tour with the brute force approach? Argue the pros and cons of brute force problem solving in general.

8.24. In this problem you will develop several brute force approaches to solving the Eight Queens problem introduced in the Chapter 6 problems.

(a) Solve the Eight Queens problem, using the random brute force technique developed in Problem 8.23.

(b) Use an exhaustive technique, i.e., try all possible positionings of eight queens on the chessboard.

(c) Why do you suppose the exhaustive brute force approach may not be appropriate for solving the Knight's Tour problem?

(d) Compare and contrast the random brute force and exhaustive brute force approaches in general.

8.25. (Creative Writing) In this problem, you will develop an intriguing approach to creative writing.

(a) Write a program that produces a random sentence of the same form as

The boy went to the store.

Choose your nouns, verbs, prepositions, and articles from string arrays containing five or ten of each of these.

(b) Modify the preceding program to produce a short story consisting of several of these sentences. (How about the possibility of a random term paper writer!)

8.26. (Limericks) A limerick is a humorous five-line verse in which the first and second lines rhyme with the fifth, and the third line rhymes with the fourth. Using techniques similar to those developed in Problem 8.25, write a BASIC program that produces limericks. Polishing this program to produce good limericks is a challenging problem, but the result will be well worth the effort!

8.27. (Whodunnit?) Use the techniques developed in Problems 8.25 and 8.26 to produce a program that writes murder mysteries. Your program should develop several characters, their interrelationships, and their possible motives for perpetrating such a heinous crime. The reader should then be asked to guess who perpetrated the crime, and your program should divulge the answer.

8.28. (Simulation) In this problem you will recreate one of the truly great moments in history, namely the classical race of the tortoise and the hare. You will use random number generation to develop a simulation of this memorable event. The techniques developed here are best suited to use with reasonably fast display screens, but they will work with printers as well.

Our contenders begin the race at "square 1" of 70 squares. Each square represents a possible position along the race course. The finish line is at square 70. The first contender to reach or pass square 70 is rewarded with a pail of fresh carrots and lettuce. The course weaves its way up the side of a slippery mountain, so occasionally the contenders may lose ground.

There is a clock that ticks once per second. With each tick of the clock, your program should adjust the position of the animals according to the following rules:

Animal	Move Type	the Time	Percentage of Actual Move
Tortoise	Fast plod	50%	3 squares to the right
	Slip	20%	6 squares to the left
	Slow plod	30%	1 square to the right
Hare	Sleep	20%	No move at all
	Big hop	20%	9 squares to the right
	Big slip	10%	12 squares to the left
	Small hop	30%	1 square to the right
	Small slip	20%	2 squares to the left

Use variables to keep track of the positions of the animals (i.e., position numbers are 1-70). Start each animal at position 1 (i.e., the "starting gate"). If an animal moves left past square 1, move it back to square 1.

Generate the percentages in the preceding table by producing a random integer, i, in the range $1 <= i <= 10$. For the tortoise, perform a "fast plod" when $1 <= i <= 5$, a "slip" when $6 <= i <= 7$, or a "slow plod" when $8 <= i <= 10$. Use a similar technique to move the hare.

Begin the race by printing

```
BANG                    ! ! ! ! !
AND  THEY'RE  OFF        ! ! ! ! !
```

Then, for each tick of the clock (i.e., each repetition of a loop), print a 70 position line showing a letter "T" in the position of the tortoise and the letter "H" in the position of the hare. Occasionally, the contenders will land on the same square. In this case, the tortoise bites the hare and your program should print "OUCH!!!" beginning at that position. All print positions other than the "T," the "H," or the "OUCH!!!" (in case of a tie) should be blank.

After each line is printed, test if either animal has reached or passed square 70. If so, then print the winner and terminate the simulation. If the tortoise wins, print "TORTOISE WINS!!! YAY!!!" If the hare wins, print "Hare wins. Yuch." If both animals win on the same tick of the clock, then favor the turtle (the "underdog"). If neither animal wins, then perform the loop again to simulate the next tick of the clock. When you're ready to run your program, assemble a group of fans to watch the race. You'll be amazed at how involved your audience gets!

Chapter 9
Formatted Outputs

9.1 Introduction

An important part of the solution to any problem is the presentation of the results. In this chapter we discuss the features of the BASIC language that facilitate the presentation of the results of calculations in neat and orderly displays and printed reports.

Traditionally, powerful output formatting capabilities have been associated with commercial data processing applications. One of the most significant capabilities of the COBOL language, for example, is the use of the PIC clause to provide a precise "picture" of the format in which each output value is to appear.

The importance of formatted outputs has not been ignored in the more scientific languages such as FORTRAN. The WRITE under FORMAT control capabilities of FORTRAN provide for reasonably sophisticated output formatting.

9.2 The PRINT USING Statement

Precise output formatting is accomplished in BASIC with the *PRINT USING statement*. Every **PRINT USING** statement must reference an *image* (actually a character string) that describes the formats in which the output values are to appear. Images can be used to specify the following useful formatting capabilities:

1. Automatic *rounding* of numbers to an indicated number of decimal places.
2. Automatic *alignment* of a column of numbers with decimal points appearing one below the other.
3. Automatic *right justification of numeric output* (instead of the somewhat annoying left-justification, which occurs with the comma spacing character in normal **PRINT** statements).
4. Automatic *zero fill* to the right of the decimal point (to the indicated number of digits) so that numeric values for dollar amounts, for example, can be made to print in "everyday" format. The amount twenty-one dollars and fifty cents, which would ordinarily print as 21.5 in BASIC, can be made to print as 21.50 with the **PRINT USING** statement and an appropriate image.
5. *Insertion of blanks and other printing characters* at precise locations within a line of output.

The **PRINT USING** statement is written in one of the following formats:

1. **PRINT USING** string constant, list of items to be printed
2. **PRINT USING** string expression, list of items to be printed

Notice that each of these formats is identical, with the exception of the item immediately following the words **PRINT USING**. This item is the *image*, a character string that describes the form in which the list of items is to be printed.

The next section introduces integer image specifications and illustrates each of the two formats of the **PRINT USING** statement.

9.3 Integer Image Specifications

An integer is a whole number, such as 776 or 5 or 999,884, that contains no decimal point. To specify the image for printing an integer, the programmer writes a character string consisting of number signs (#). Each number sign indicates that a numeric digit (i.e., 0-9) is to occupy the indicated position of the printed line. Integers are printed right-justified, i.e., the units position is printed in the rightmost position of the "integer field" specified by the image. If an *integer image specification* is larger than the integer value to be printed, then the extra positions (to the left of the integer value) are set to blanks; these blanks are referred to as *leading blanks*.

Example 9.1 Integer image specifications
Write two different **PRINT USING** statements that will print the number 455 right-justified in an integer field designed to hold a maximum of ten digits. The number should print with seven leading blanks.

Discussion: We shall write two small BASIC programs (Figures 9.1 and 9.2) to illustrate the use of each of the forms of the **PRINT USING** statement presented in Section 9.2.

Figure 9.1 illustrates **PRINT USING** with a string constant image:

```
PRINT USING "##########"; 455
END
```

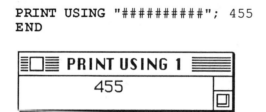

Figure 9.1 PRINT USING with a string constant image

Figure 9.2 illustrates **PRINT USING** with a string expression image:

```
LET a$ = "##########"
PRINT USING a$ ; 455
END
```

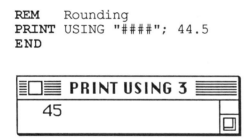

Figure 9.2 PRINT USING with a string expression image

9.4 More on Integer Image Specifications

It is often desirable to round a number to a certain number of decimal places. Rounding can be accomplished with the **PRINT USING** statement. When a number that is not an integer is printed with an integer-image specification, the number is *rounded* to the nearest integer, as shown in Figure 9.3. The **PRINT USING** statement specifies that the number 44.5 is to be printed in an integer-image specification containing four numeric digits. The number is rounded to 45 and printed. Note that the number is indeed right-justified within the four-digit field specified by the image in the **PRINT USING** statement.

```
REM    Rounding
PRINT USING "####"; 44.5
END
```

Figure 9.3 Rounding with PRINT USING

One problem that sometimes occurs in printing integers is that the integer image specification does not contain enough digits to hold the entire number being printed. Various versions of BASIC provide many different methods of coping with this situation. QuickBASIC prints the full number (even though the number is larger than the image) and precedes the number by a percent sign (%). Suppose, for example, as shown in Figure 9.4, that a BASIC program attempts to print the five-digit number 12345 using the integer image specification "####" (which contains spaces for only four digits).

In Figure 9.4, note that even though insufficient space has been provided for the number, the program still prints the complete number preceded by a percent sign. Ordinarily, a programmer provides enough space for all numbers to print properly. Thus, when the output of a program contains a percent sign preceding a numeric result, the programmer knows that the program contains an error.

```
REM    Insufficient space in format
PRINT USING "####"; 12345
END
```

```
≣☐≣ PRINT USING 4 ≣≣≣
%12345
```

Figure 9.4 Insufficient space in a format with PRINT USING

Of course, integers can be either positive or negative. Most versions of BASIC do not print the plus sign (+) if a number is positive but do print the minus sign (-) for negative numbers. The programmer must provide space for the minus sign to print for a negative number. This is done by simply providing an extra # at the left of the image to reserve space for the minus sign. If a number contains a sign and enough numeric digits to exceed the space provided in the image, then the complete number is printed, but with a preceding percent sign.

The program in Figure 9.5 contains an integer image specification that can handle either four numeric digits or three numeric digits and a sign. The first two values to be printed, 4444 and -444, both fit within the image specification. The last value, -4444, is too large to be printed by the "####" image because of the presence of the minus sign. Therefore, BASIC prints this value with a leading percent sign. If the programmer wishes to print a number as large as -4444 correctly, then the image "#####" may be used.

```
a$ = "####    ####    ####"
PRINT USING a$; 4444,  -444,  -4444
END
```

```
≣☐≣ PRINT USING 5 ≣≣≣
4444   -444   %-4444
```

Figure 9.5 Providing space for a minus sign with PRINT USING

One extremely important feature of the **PRINT USING** statement in BASIC is that numbers are printed right-justified. Thus, the programmer can cause numbers to print in the right-aligned column format that is so common in accounting reports. The program in Figure 9.6 illustrates how BASIC right-justifies numbers.

```
REM    Right justification of integers
a$ = "####"
PRINT USING a$; 1
PRINT USING a$; 12
PRINT USING a$; 123
PRINT USING a$; 1234
PRINT USING a$; 12345
END
```

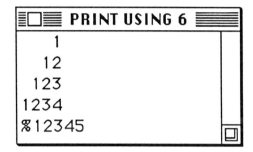

Figure 9.6 Right-justification of integers with PRINT USING

Each of the numbers is to be printed using an integer image specification of "####". This specification can accommodate at most a four-digit integer or a three-digit integer with a sign. Notice that the numbers 1, 12, 123, and 1234 all fit within the space provided by the "####" specification and that these numbers do indeed print right-justified. The number 12345 is too large for the "####" specification, so BASIC prints the full number with a leading percent sign.

9.5 Image Specifications: Some Notes and Observations

1. When a **PRINT USING** statement is executed, BASIC normally begins a new line of printed output. (This can be modified, for example, by ending a **PRINT USING** statement with a semicolon, in which case the next **PRINT USING** statement will continue printing on the same line.)

2. If the **PRINT USING** statement refers to a string variable image, the image appears on the line in which the string variable is assigned a value.

3. Many different BASIC statements in a single BASIC program may refer to the same string variable image.

4. If a **PRINT USING** statement contains more items to be printed than the corresponding image contains specifications, then the specifications are reused as often as needed until all items have been printed side by side.

9.6 Decimal Image Specifications

A decimal number is a number such as 33.5 or 657.987 that contains a decimal point. *Decimal image specifications* contain #'s and a decimal point. BASIC aligns a number to be printed with the decimal point in the decimal image specification. Numbers that are larger than the decimal image specification are printed, but with a leading percent sign. Unoccupied positions to the left of the decimal point are filled with (leading) blanks. Unoccupied positions to the right of the decimal point are filled with (trailing) zeros. Figure 9.7 illustrates how BASIC handles the alignment and printing of decimal numbers. Notice that decimal numbers which are larger than their corresponding decimal image specifications also print with leading percent signs.

```
REM    Decimal image specifications
a$ = "##.#"
PRINT USING a$; 3
PRINT USING a$; 3.4
PRINT USING a$; 3.44
PRINT USING a$; 33.44
PRINT USING a$; 333.44
PRINT USING a$; 333.444
PRINT USING a$; 33.444
END
```

```
====== PRINT USING 7 ======
 3.0
 3.4
 3.4
33.4
%333.4
%333.4
33.4
```

Figure 9.7 Decimal image specifications with PRINT USING

The decimal image specification "##.#" can accommodate two positions to the left of the decimal point and one position to the right of the decimal point. If a signed number is to be printed, then one of the two positions to the left of the decimal point is needed to hold the sign, so the largest negative number that can be printed with "##.#" is -9.9.

Decimal image specifications may be used in BASIC to round numbers to a specific number of decimal places, as is indicated in Figure 9.8. For example, the second PRINT USING statement provides for one position to the right of the decimal point. Thus, BASIC rounds the number 135.8647 to the tenths position and prints the number as 135.9. Note that the number is rounded only for printing purposes; the value of the variable remains unchanged.

```
REM    Rounding with PRINT USING
LET n = 135.8647
PRINT USING "###"; n
PRINT USING "###.#"; n
PRINT USING "###.##"; n
PRINT USING "###.###"; n
PRINT USING "###.####"; n
PRINT USING "###.#####"; n
END
```

```
≡☐≣  PRINT USING 8  ≣≣≣
136
135.9
135.86
135.865
135.8647
135.86470                    ▣
```

Figure 9.8 Rounding with PRINT USING

9.7 PRINT USING and E-Notation

E-notation is used to print either very large or very small numbers in BASIC. A decimal number immediately followed by the characters E+nn (or E-nn) means interpret the number in *scientific notation* as the number times 10 to the +nn power (or the number times 10 to the -nn power). For example, the number 1,500,000 may be expressed in E-notation as 1.5E+06, meaning 1.5 times 10 to the sixth power.

E-notation may be obtained by using four carets following a decimal image specification. BASIC fits as much of the number as it can to the decimal image specification and then determines an appropriate exponent to use. One of the #'s to the left of the decimal point is always used to hold the sign of the number even if the number is positive (in which case a leading blank is printed). The program in Figure 9.9 illustrates the use of E-notation with the **PRINT USING** statement.

```
PRINT USING "###.#^^^^"; 4444
END
```

```
≡☐≣  PRINT USING 9  ≣≣≣
44.4E+02
                          ▣
```

Figure 9.9 E-notation with PRINT USING

9.8 Comma Insertion with PRINT USING

Numeric values must frequently be "dressed up" when they are printed. The next several sections deal with various methods of improving the appearance of numeric values by inserting various special characters.

Commas may be inserted after every three decimal places automatically by placing a comma immediately to the left of the decimal point in the image referenced by the **PRINT USING** statement. Commas are particularly useful in assisting the reader to interpret the precise value of large numbers as indicated in Figure 9.10. Notice that the image contains a total of nine characters, namely eight #'s and one comma. BASIC automatically inserts the commas when the magnitude of the number being printed is large enough. The reader should note that the largest number that may be printed with the "########," image is 99,999,999. An attempt to print a larger number would cause a percent sign to precede the number.

```
REM    Edited numeric image specifications using the comma
PRINT USING "########,"; 1
PRINT USING "########,"; 10
PRINT USING "########,"; 100
PRINT USING " ########,"; 1000
PRINT USING " ########,"; 10000
END
```

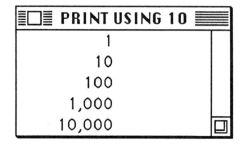

Figure 9.10 Comma insertion with PRINT USING

9.9 Insertion of Trailing Minus Signs with PRINT USING

In most business reports, negative amounts are printed with a *trailing minus sign*. For example, the number "minus forty-three" is printed as 43-. BASIC provides the programmer with the ability to specify insertion of trailing minus signs with the **PRINT USING** statement. The programmer merely places a minus sign to the right of the numeric image specification to indicate that the computer is to print a negative number with a trailing (instead of a leading) minus sign. Figure 9.11 illustrates the use of trailing minus signs in numeric image specifications.

```
REM     Edited numeric image specifications
REM     using the trailing minus sign
PRINT USING "####-"; 1
PRINT USING "####-"; -1
PRINT USING "####-"; 10
PRINT USING "####-"; -10
PRINT USING "####-"; 100
PRINT USING "####-"; -100
PRINT USING "####-"; 1000
PRINT USING "####-"; -1000
PRINT USING "####-"; 10000
PRINT USING "####-"; -10000
END
```

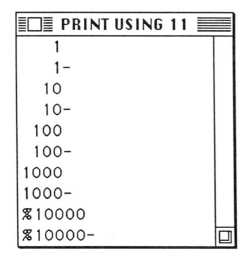

Figure 9.11 Insertion of trailing minus sign with PRINT USING

9.10 Insertion of Leading Asterisks with PRINT USING

We recall that BASIC prints numbers either right-justified or aligned around a decimal point in a decimal image specification. In both cases, if the image is larger than the number to be printed, BASIC fills the leftmost printing positions with blanks. In certain business applications, particularly those in which dollar amounts are printed, these leading blanks would make it relatively easy for someone to tamper with the value of the number by inserting digits in the blank spaces. To prevent such alteration, BASIC allows the programmer to specify that leading blanks in numeric amounts are to be replaced by asterisks (*'s). The programmer specifies leading asterisk insertion by replacing two #'s at the left of the image specification with asterisks as in Figure 9.12.

In numeric image specifications containing leading asterisks, the programmer may provide for the printing of negative values only with the trailing minus sign. If a trailing minus sign is not included in the image specification, then an attempt to print a negative value will cause an error message to be printed.

```
REM    Asterisk insertion for protecting numbers
PRINT USING "**##.##"; 1.25
PRINT USING "**##.##"; 12.5
PRINT USING "**##.##"; 125
PRINT USING "**##.##"; 1250
END
```

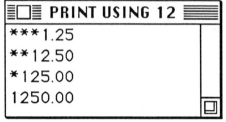

Figure 9.12 Insertion of leading asterisks with PRINT USING

9.11 Insertion of Floating Dollar Signs with PRINT USING

One way of protecting dollar amounts is to *"float" the dollar sign character* ($) so that no matter how large (or small) a value is the dollar sign always prints to the immediate left of the leftmost digit of the number. The programmer may specify that a particular number is to print with a floating dollar sign by replacing the leftmost two #'s in a numeric image specification with $'s, as in Figure 9.13.

```
REM    Floating dollar sign
PRINT USING "$$#.##"; 31.5
PRINT USING "$$#.##"; 27.9
PRINT USING "$$#.##"; 1.67
PRINT USING "$$#.##"; 111.2
END
```

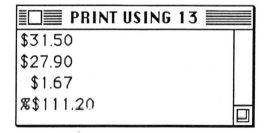

Figure 9.13 Insertion of floating dollar sign with PRINT USING

In numeric image specifications containing floating dollar signs, the programmer may provide for the printing of negative values with the trailing minus sign. If no trailing minus sign is present, then the program prints the minus sign before the floating dollar sign (see Figure 9.14).

The effects of leading asterisk insertion and the floating dollar sign may be combined by using the double asterisk dollar sign (`**$`). For example, the statement `PRINT USING "**$##.##; 3.67` will print `***$3.67`.

```
REM    Negative amounts with floating dollar sign
PRINT USING "$$#.##-"; -21.5
PRINT USING "$$#.##"; -21.5
END
```

```
████ PRINT USING 14 ████
$21.50-
%-$21.50
                        ▢
```

Figure 9.14 Floating dollar sign and negative amounts with PRINT USING

We are also able to print with a fixed dollar sign as Figure 9.15 demonstrates. This is done by replacing one # with a $.

```
REM    PRINT USING with fixed $
PRINT USING "$#####.##"; 3.45
END
```

```
████ PRINT USING 15 ████
$      3.45
                        ▣
```

Figure 9.15 PRINT USING with fixed dollar sign

9.12 String Image Specifications

Character string information may also be edited and printed with the `PRINT USING` statement. Figure 9.16 demonstrates the use of the exclamation point (!) as a string image specification. The exclamation point specifies that only the first character of the string is to be displayed on the screen.

Figure 9.17 demonstrates the use of the double backslash with spaces in between (\x-spaces\). This particular format specifies that the number of characters to be displayed is two plus the number of spaces between the backslashes (x-spaces). In Figure 9.17 there are two spaces between the backslashes.

```
REM    PRINT USING with !
a$ = "Computer"
PRINT USING "!"; a$
END
```

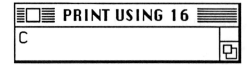

Figure 9.16 Using the exclamation point (!) string image specification

```
REM    PRINT USING with \\ with two spaces in between
a$ = "Computer"
PRINT USING "\  \"; a$
END
```

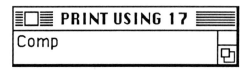

Figure 9.17 Using the double backslash with two spaces in between

Figure 9.18 demonstrates the use of the ampersand (&) as a string image specification. The ampersand specifies that the entire string of characters is to be printed without modification.

```
REM    PRINT USING with &
a$ = "Computer"
PRINT USING "&"; a$
END
```

Figure 9.18 Using the ampersand format character

Figure 9.19 demonstrates the use of the underscore (_) as a string image specification. The underscore specifies that the character immediately following it is to be printed as a literal character.

```
REM    PRINT USING with _
PRINT USING "##_!"; 12
END
```

```
≡□≣ PRINT USING 19 ≡≣≣
12!
```

Figure 9.19 Using the underscore format character

9.13 Printing Characters

Image specifications may contain two different types of characters:

1. *Format control characters*
2. *Printing characters*

Format control characters describe the forms in which output items are to be printed. The format control characters shown in Figure 9.20 have been discussed in this chapter. Each of the characters in an image that is not a format control character is called a *printing character*. Printing characters are essentially literals that print precisely as they are written in an image. Format control characters are generally replaced by output values when a **PRINT USING** statement is performed, whereas printing characters print exactly as they appear in an image.

#	a place for a numeric digit
.	a place for a decimal point
^^^^	replace with E-notation (E+nn) or (E-nn)
–	a place for a minus sign
,	a place for a comma to be inserted if needed
**	leading blanks to be replaced by *s
$$	leading blanks to be replaced by floating $
$	fixed dollar sign with leading blanks filling extra spaces
!	(exclamation point) prints the first character of a string
\x-spaces\	prints 2 + x-spaces characters
&	(ampersand) prints the entire character string
_	underscore prints the next character as a literal

Figure 9.20 Format control characters

Printing characters are useful for inserting literal information into a print line, as indicated by Figure 9.21. This program utilizes format control characters and printing characters to illustrate how *check protection* can be implemented with the **PRINT USING** statement. The second line of Figure 9.21 contains the words "Protected check amounts look like this." This is a good example of the use of printing characters.

```
REM    Illustrating the use of printing characters
LET f$ = "Protected check amounts look like this $**###.##"
PRINT USING f$, 1.50
END
```

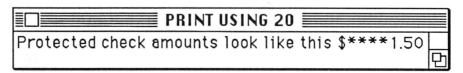

Figure 9.21 Inserting printing characters with PRINT USING

Concepts

alignment
ampersand (&) format character
backslash (\) format character
blank insertion
check protection
comma (,) format character
decimal image specification
decimal point alignment
decimal point (.) format character
double asterisk (**) format character
double dollar sign ($$) format character
E-notation
E+nn
E-nn
exclamation point (!) format character
fixed dollar sign
floating dollar sign
format character
four carets (^^^^)
image

integer image specification
leading asterisks
leading blanks
minus sign (-) format character
number sign (#) format character
percent sign (%) overflow character
PIC clause in COBOL
PRINT USING statement
printing character
protection of numeric amounts
right-justification
rounding
scientific notation
string image specification
trailing blanks
trailing minus sign
underscore(_) format character
WRITE under FORMAT
    control in FORTRAN
zero fill

Problems

9.1. Fill in the blanks in each of the following:
  (a) Precise output formatting is accomplished in the BASIC language with the _____ statement.
  (b) The character string that describes the formats in which the output values are to appear is called _____.
  (c) The process of aligning a numeric value on the right boundary of a print field is called _____.
  (d) An integer is a number such as 47 or 788 containing only the numeric digits and a sign but no _____.
  (e) If an integer image specification is larger than the integer value to be printed, then the extra positions (to the left of the integer value) are set to _____.

(f) The sign of a number may be either plus or minus. Most versions of BASIC generally print the _____ sign but suppress the _____ sign.

(g) What does BASIC do when a **PRINT USING** statement contains more values to be printed than it contains image specifications? _____.

(h) What does BASIC do when attempting to print a number that is larger than its corresponding image specification? _____.

(i) BASIC prints very large numbers and very small numbers using a special format called _____.

(j) Commas may be inserted in numbers by using _____ in the image referenced by the **PRINT USING** statement.

(k) In most business reports, negative amounts are printed with a _____.

(l) Asterisk insertion is generally used to _____ numeric amounts.

(m) A dollar sign that always prints to the immediate left of the leftmost digit of a number is said to _____.

9.2. Fill in the blanks in each of the following:
(a) Which characters are used in string image specifications to indicate
1. that the first character should be printed? _____.
2. that a specified number of characters should be printed? _____.
3. that the entire string should be printed? _____.

(b) The two different types of characters that may appear in an image specification are _____ and _____.

(c) The characters that are not format characters in an image are called _____.

(d) Printing characters are essentially _____ that print precisely as they are written in an image.

(e) A fixed dollar sign is indicated in a numeric image specification by inserting how many dollar signs? _____.

9.3. State which of the following are true and which are false:
(a) The importance of formatted outputs has been ignored in the more scientific languages such as FORTRAN.

(b) The BASIC statement

PRINT a,b,c,d,e

causes the values a, b, c, d, and e to print in column format with each value appearing right-justified in its print field.

(c) If the digits to the right of a decimal point are truncated, then that number is automatically rounded to the units position.

(d) Most versions of BASIC will not print a number if its value exceeds the size of the numeric-image specification.

(e) Whenever an image specification is reused, BASIC begins a new line of printed output.

9.4. State which of the following are true and which are false:
(a) One extremely important feature of the **PRINT USING** statement in BASIC is that numbers are normally printed left-justified.

(b) The dollar sign ($) always prints in a fixed position when dollar amounts are printed.

(c) Decimal image specifications may be used in BASIC to round numbers to a specific number of decimal places.

(d) The largest number that may be printed with the "#,###,###" image is 999999999.

(e) In most business reports, negative amounts are printed with a floating minus sign.

(f) The programmer may specify that a particular number is to print with a floating dollar sign by replacing the leftmost "#" in the image with a "$".

(g) Printing characters are generally replaced by output values when a **PRINT USING** statement is performed, whereas format control characters print exactly as they appear in an image.

9.5. Write a **PRINT USING** statement for each of the following:
  (a) Write a **PRINT USING** statement that will print the number 3456 right-justified in an integer field designed to hold a maximum of eight digits.
  (b) Write a **PRINT USING** statement that will round the value of variable x5 so that only the rounded integer part of x5 prints in an integer field designed to hold seven digits.
  (c) Write a **PRINT USING** statement that attempts to print a six-digit integer in an integer field designed to hold only four digits. How will BASIC perform such a statement?
  (d) Write a **PRINT USING** statement containing a single image specification designed to hold at most a five-digit positive integer. This statement should attempt to print the following series of values: 5,-5,55,-55,555,-555,5555,-5555,55555,-55555.
  (e) Write a **PRINT USING** statement containing three images designed to hold five-digit integers. The statement should print the values 55555, -6666, and 0.

9.6. Write a **PRINT USING** statement for each of the following:
  (a) Write a **PRINT USING** statement with a single image specification designed to hold a positive decimal number with two positions to the left of the decimal point and one position to the right of the decimal point. This statement should attempt to print the series of values: 5, 5.6, 5.66, 55.66, 555.66, 55.666.
  (b) Write a **PRINT USING** statement that will round a decimal number to the hundredths position. Provide for numbers with at most three printing positions to the left of the decimal point.
  (c) Write a **PRINT USING** statement that will print the value 5555555 using E-notation.

9.7. Write a **PRINT USING** statement for each of the following:
  (a) Write a **PRINT USING** statement with a single image specification designed to print numbers as large as 9999999 with comma insertion. This statement should attempt to print the numbers 7, 777, 77777, 7777777, 777777777.
  (b) Write a **PRINT USING** statement with a single image specification designed to print negative integers as large as -999999. Use the trailing minus sign feature. Print the following series of values: -8, -888, -88888, -8888888, -888888888.
  (c) Write a **PRINT USING** statement with a single image designed to print decimal amounts as large as 9999.99. Use the asterisk insertion feature to protect numbers smaller than 1000.00. Print the values 1000.00, 999.99.
  (d) Write a **PRINT USING** statement with a single image designed to print dollar amounts as large as 999.99. Provide for a floating dollar sign. Print the values .99, 1.50, 57.85, 972.98, 815.75, 6078.42.
  (e) Write a **PRINT USING** statement with a single image designed to print negative dollar amounts as large as $999.99-. Print the amounts -10.75, -698.75, and -8976.50 using a trailing minus sign.

9.8. Write a **PRINT USING** statement for each of the following:
  (a) Write a **PRINT USING** statement that will print the first character of "Basic".
  (b) Write a single **PRINT USING** statement that will print the first five letters of the word "Macintosh".
  (c) Write a **PRINT USING** statement that will print the entire word "specifications".

9.9. Write a **PRINT USING** statement that will print a protected check amount no greater than $999.99. Precede the check amount with the words "Pay to the order of John Doe." Print the amount 56.75. Use a fixed dollar sign and asterisk insertion to protect the check amount.

9.10. One important application of computers is in printing tabular information. Earlier chapters of this text have discussed table printing in detail. However, values within tables have been printed left-justified instead of right-justified as in most tables of numerical values appearing in published references. The **PRINT USING** statement in BASIC allows the programmer to specify that numeric values are to be right-justified.
  Write a BASIC program using the **PRINT USING** statement to prepare the following table of values:

X	X Squared	X Cubed
1	1	1
2	4	8
3	9	27
4	16	64
5	25	125
6	36	216
7	49	343
8	64	512
9	81	729
10	100	1000

Chapter 10
Sequential Files

10.1 Introduction

One of the most important functions of modern computers is the processing of large amounts of data. Indeed, the initials *EDP*, so often used to indicate computer processing, stand for *electronic data processing*. Computers store large amounts of data as *records* in neatly organized *files*. In this chapter, we explain how data files are created, updated, and processed by BASIC programs.

10.2 The Data Hierarchy

Ultimately, all data items processed by a computer are reduced to combinations of zeros and ones. This occurs because it is simple and economical to build electronic devices that can assume two stable states—one of the states represents a zero and the other represents a one. Thus, the impressive functions performed by computers essentially involve the manipulation of zeros and ones.

The smallest data item in a computer can assume the value zero or the value one. Such a data item is called a *bit* (short for "*b*inary dig*it*"—a digit can assume one of two values). Computer circuitry performs various simple bit manipulations such as examining a bit to see what value it contains, setting a bit to a particular value, reversing a bit, and so on.

It is too cumbersome for people to work with bits. Instead, people prefer to work with *decimal digits* (i.e., 0, 1, 2, 3, 4, 5, 6, 7, 8, and 9), *letters* (i.e., A through Z, and the lowercase letters as well), and *special symbols* (i.e., $, @, %, &, *, (,), -, +, ", :, ?, /, and many others). In computer parlance, digits, letters, and special symbols are referred to as *characters*. The set of all characters a person may use to write programs and represent data items on a particular computer is called that computer's *character set*. Since computers can process only ones and zeros, every character in the computer's character set is represented as a pattern of ones and zeros. People specify programs and data items as characters; computers then manipulate and process these characters as patterns of zeros and ones.

Just as characters are composed of bits, *fields* are composed of characters. A field is a group of characters that conveys meaning. A *numeric field* contains only digits. A person's age (such as "25") is an example of a numeric field.

An *alphabetic field* contains only letters. A person's last name (such as "Jones") is an example of an alphabetic field. Computer systems generally treat the *blank character* as a valid alphabetic character.

An *alphanumeric field* contains digits, letters, and blanks. A person's street address (such as "15 Foothill Road") is generally considered to be an alphanumeric field.

A *character field* may contain any combination of characters selected from the computer's character set. Thus, character fields may include digits, letters, and special symbols.

Data items processed by computers form a *data hierarchy* in which data items become larger and more complex in structure as we progress from bits to characters to fields, and so on.

A *record* is composed of several fields. In a payroll system, for example, a record for a particular employee might consist of the following fields:
1. Social security number (a numeric field)
2. Employee's name (an alphabetic field)
3. Employee's address (an alphanumeric field)
4. Hourly salary rate (a numeric field)
5. Number of exemptions claimed (a numeric field)
6. Year-to-date earnings (a numeric field)
7. Amount of federal taxes withheld (a numeric field), etc.

Thus, a record is a group of related fields. In the above example, each of the fields belongs to the same employee. Of course, a particular company may have many employees, and will therefore have a payroll record for each of its employees. A *file* is a group of related records. A company's payroll file contains one record for each of the company's employees. Thus, a payroll file for a small company might contain only 22 records, whereas a payroll file for a large company might contain 100,000 records.

The files created with the techniques of this chapter are automatically stored by the Macintosh on high-capacity disk storage devices. It is not unusual for a company to have many files, each containing millions of characters of information.

To facilitate the retrieval of specific records from a file, one field in each record is chosen as a *record key*. A record key identifies a record as belonging to a particular person or entity. In the payroll record described in this section, the social security number would normally be chosen as the record key.

There are many ways of organizing records within a file. The most popular type of organization is called a *sequential file* in which records are stored in order by the record key field. In a payroll file, records are usually placed in order by social security number. The first employee record in the file contains the lowest social security number, and subsequent records contain increasingly higher social security numbers. The vast majority of information stored in today's computer systems is stored in sequential files.

Most businesses utilize many different files to store data. For example, companies may have payroll files, accounts receivable files (listing money due from clients), accounts payable files (listing money due to suppliers), inventory files (listing facts about all the items handled by the business), and many other types of files. The sum total of all the files maintained by a particular organization is sometimes called that organization's *database*. A collection of programs designed to help an organization create and manage its database is called a *database management system* (DBMS).

10.3 Creating a Sequential File Using BASIC

The program and sample run of Figure 10.1 illustrate the creation of a simple sequential file that might be used in an accounts receivable system. This program inputs data for several clients of a company. For each client, the program obtains an account number, the client's name, and the client's balance (i.e., the amount the client still owes the company for goods and services received in the past). The data obtained for each client constitute a record for that client. The account number is used as the record key in this application; that is, the file will be created and maintained in account number order.

Now let us consider the more important statements of this program in detail. The statement

```
OPEN "status" FOR OUTPUT AS #1
```

names the file to be used by the program, and establishes a "line of communication" with the file. This program uses only one file, namely "status" which is created by the program.

Programs may process no files at all, a single file, or several files. Each file is named and given a different number in an OPEN statement. All other file processing statements refer to a file by the number (#1, #2, etc.) it was given in its OPEN statement. Files being created by a program are opened FOR OUTPUT. Existing files that are to be read by a program are opened FOR INPUT.

The program asks the user to enter the various fields for each record. The program of Figure 10.1 expects the user to type "eof" (meaning "end of file") as a user-chosen sentinel value to indicate when data entry is complete. (Note that the quotation marks around a string being input via an INPUT statement are optional.) Because the program also reads an account number and balance on each INPUT, the user supplies zeros for these values (when entering the "eof" line) to satisfy the INPUT. The statement

```
PRINT #1, account, ",", the names$, ",", balance
```

actually writes a record to the file "status". Notice that literal commas (", ") are also written to the file to separate the fields. The record may be retrieved at some later time by a program designed to read the file (see Section 10.4). The WRITE # statement performs the same task as PRINT #, but WRITE # automatically inserts commas between the fields of a record so no literal commas are needed.

After the user enters the sentinel value, the last PRINT statement writes the sentinel to the file. This sentinel will be used by the program that reads the file to recognize that it has reached the end of the file.

The CLOSE statement "closes" the file; this ensures that data will not accidentally be lost. The programmer must be careful to close each file used by a program as soon as it is known that the program will make no further references to the file.

Figure 10.1 also contains a sample run of our file creation program. In this run, the user enters information for five different accounts, and then signals that data entry is complete by typing 0, "eof", 0. Notice that the run does not show how the data records actually appear on the file. To verify that the file was created successfully, we shall now write and run a program to read the file and print its contents.

```
REM    Create a sequential file
OPEN "status" FOR OUTPUT AS #1
INPUT "Account, name, balance"; account, thename$, balance
WHILE thename$ <> "eof"
    PRINT #1, account, ",", thename$, ",", balance
    INPUT "Account, name, balance"; account, thename$, balanc(
WEND
PRINT #1, 0, ",", "eof", ",", 0
CLOSE #1
END
```

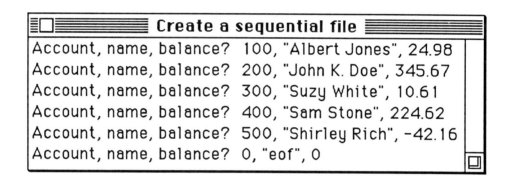

Figure 10.1 Creating a sequential file using BASIC

10.4 Obtaining Data from a Sequential File

Data are stored in files so that they may be retrieved for processing when needed. In the last section, we saw how to create a file. In this section, the techniques needed to reference the data in a file are presented.

The program and sample run of Figure 10.2 illustrate the reading of data from the sequential file created in Figure 10.1. This program reads records from the file "status" and displays the various fields from these records on the screen. The statement

```
OPEN "status" FOR INPUT AS #1
```

names the file referenced by the program, assigns the file **AS** #1, and states that the file will be used **FOR INPUT**. This program processes only the file "status" and refers to it throughout the program as #1. The statement

```
INPUT #1, account, thename$, balance
```

```
REM    Read from a sequential file
OPEN "status" FOR INPUT AS #1
PRINT "Account", "Name", "Balance"
INPUT #1, account, thename$, balance
WHILE thename$ <> "eof"
     PRINT account, thename$, balance
     INPUT #1, account, thename$, balance
WEND
CLOSE #1
END
```

Read a sequential file		
Account	Name	Balance
100	Albert Jones	24.98
200	John K. Doe	345.67
300	Suzy White	10.61
400	Sam Stone	224.62
500	Shirley Rich	-42.16

Figure 10.2 Reading data from a sequential file

reads a record from the file into the program. After this statement is performed, account will have the value 100, thename$ will have the value "Albert Jones," and balance will have the value 24.98. Then, each time the program performs the second INPUT statement, another record is read from the file and account, thename$, and balance each take on new values.

The WHILE statement determines when the end of file has been reached (i.e., there are no more records remaining in the file). When the file contains no more records, the file is closed and the run is complete.

10.5 Rereading Data from a Sequential File

To retrieve data from a sequential file in BASIC, a program must begin reading data from the beginning of the file, and must read every record until the desired data are found. In certain situations, it may be desirable to be able to process the data in a file several times (from the beginning of the file) during the execution of a program. The following example illustrates how to do this.

Example 10.1 Data retrieval for credit control

A company that maintains a file of customer balances has asked you to write a program that will retrieve account data from the file. Each record in the file (i.e., our file `"status"`) contains an account number, an account name, and the account's current balance.

Write a BASIC program that will allow the credit manager to obtain lists of those customers with zero balances (i.e., those customers who do not owe the company any money), credit balances (i.e., those customers to whom the company owes money because of overpayments of some type), and debit balances (i.e., those customers who owe the company money for goods and services received in the past).

Discussion: The program appears in Figure 10.3 and a sample run appears in Figure 10.4. The CLOSE/OPEN sequence near the end of the program causes the program to reposition to the beginning of the file each time a new request is made by the credit manager. The program displays a menu and allows the credit manager to enter three different options in order to obtain certain types of credit information. If a 1 is typed, the program produces a list of accounts with zero balances. If a 2 is typed, the program produces a list of accounts with credit balances. If a 3 is typed, the program produces a list of accounts with debit balances. A 4 is typed to terminate the run.

Concepts

alphabetic field
alphanumeric field
AS #
binary digit
bit
character
character field
character set
CLOSE statement
database
database management system
data hierarchy
DBMS
decimal digit
EDP
electronic data processing
end of a file

field
file
file name
FOR INPUT
FOR OUTPUT
INPUT # statement
letter
numeric field
OPEN statement
PRINT # statement
record
record key
sequential file
special symbol
WRITE # statement
zeros and ones

```
REM    Credit inquiry program
OPEN "status" FOR INPUT AS #1
PRINT "Enter request"
PRINT "     1-Means list accounts with zero balances"
PRINT "     2-Means list accounts with credit balances"
PRINT "     3-Means list accounts with debit balances"
PRINT "     4-Means end of run"
INPUT request
INPUT #1, account, thename$, balance
WHILE request <> 4
   IF request = 1 THEN
       PRINT "Accounts with zero balances are..."
       WHILE thename$ <> "eof"
          IF balance = 0 THEN
             PRINT account, thename$, balance
          END IF
          INPUT #1, account, thename$, balance
       WEND

       ELSEIF request = 2 THEN
          PRINT "Accounts with credit balances are..."
          WHILE thename$ <> "eof"
             IF balance < 0 THEN
                PRINT account, thename$, balance
             END IF
             INPUT #1, account, thename$, balance
          WEND

       ELSEIF request = 3 THEN
          PRINT "Accounts with debit balances are..."
             WHILE thename$ <> "eof"
             IF balance > 0 THEN
                PRINT account, thename$, balance
             END IF
             INPUT #1, account, thename$, balance
             WEND
   END IF
   INPUT "Enter request"; request
   CLOSE #1
   OPEN "status" FOR INPUT AS #1
   INPUT #1, account, thename$, balance
WEND
PRINT "End of run."
CLOSE #1
END
```

Figure 10.3 A credit data retrieval program

```
Enter request
   1-Means list accounts with zero balances
   2-Means list accounts with credit balances
   3-Means list accounts with debit balances
   4-Means end of run
? 3
Accounts with debit balances are ...
   100            Albert Jones        24.98
   200            John K. Doe        345.67
   300            Suzy White          10.61
   400            Sam Stone          224.62
Enter request? 1
Accounts with zero balances are ...
Enter request? 2
Accounts with credit balances are ...
   500            Shirley Rich       -42.16
Enter request? 4
End of run.
```

Figure 10.4 A sample run of the credit data retrieval program

Problems

10.1. Fill in the blanks in each of the following:
  (a) The initials EDP stand for _____.
  (b) Computers store large amounts of data as records in neatly organized _____.
  (c) Ultimately, all data items processed by a computer are reduced to combinations of _____ and _____.
  (d) The smallest data item a computer can process is called a _____.
  (e) In computer parlance, digits, letters, and special symbols are referred to as _____.
  (f) A group of related characters that conveys meaning is called a _____.
  (g) A field that may contain digits, letters, and blanks is called an _____ field.
  (h) A _____ is composed of several fields.
  (i) A _____ is a group of related records.
  (j) To facilitate the retrieval of specific records from a file, one field in each record is chosen as a _____.
  (k) The vast majority of information stored in today's computer systems is stored in _____ files.
  (l) The sum total of all the files maintained by a particular organization is sometimes called that organization's _____.
  (m) The _____ statement names a file to be used by a program.
  (n) The _____ statement should be performed when a program is finished referencing a file.
  (o) The _____ phase specifies that a file will be created by a program.
  (p) The _____ statement writes a record on a file.
  (q) The _____ statement reads a record from a file.

10.2. State which of the following are true and which are false:
  (a) One of the most important functions of modern computers is the processing of large amounts of data.
  (b) The impressive functions performed by computers essentially involve the manipulation of zeros and ones.
  (c) People prefer to manipulate bits instead of characters and fields because bits are more compact.

(d) People specify programs and data items as characters; computers then manipulate and process these characters as groups of zeros and ones.

(e) A person's zip code is an example of a numeric field.

(f) A person's street address is generally considered to be an alphabetic field in computer applications.

(g) Data items processed by a computer form a data hierarchy in which data items become larger and more complex as we progress from fields to characters to bits, etc.

(h) A record key identifies a record as belonging to a particular field.

(i) Most businesses store all of their information in a single file to facilitate computer processing.

(j) A collection of programs designed to help an organization create and manage its database is called a database management system.

(k) Files are always referred to by number in BASIC programs.

(l) When a programmer creates a file of records by using the PRINT # statement, the file is automatically saved by the program so that it will be available for future reference.

10.3. For each of the following, write only a single BASIC statement to accomplish the desired objective. Assume that each of these statements applies to the same BASIC program.

(a) Write a BASIC statement which states that the file "oldmast" will be treated as #1 and read by this program.

(b) Write a BASIC statement which states that the file "trans" will be treated as #2 and read by this program.

(c) Write a BASIC statement which states that the file "newmast" will be treated as #3 and created by this program.

(d) Write a single BASIC statement that reads a record from the file "oldmast." The record consists of an account number, a name, and the account's current balance.

(e) Write a single BASIC statement that reads a record from the file "trans." The record consists of an account number and a dollar amount.

(f) Write a single BASIC statement that writes a record on the file "newmast." The record consists of the same fields as the records of file "oldmast."

10.4. Problem 10.3 asked the reader to write a series of single BASIC statements. Actually, these statements form the core of an important type of file processing program, namely, a *file-matching* program. In commercial data processing, it is common to have several files in each system. In an accounts receivable system, for example, there is generally a master file containing detailed information about each customer such as the customer's name, address, telephone number, outstanding balance, credit limit, discount terms, contract arrangements, and possibly a condensed history of recent purchases and cash payments.

As *transactions* occur (i.e., sales are made and cash payments arrive in the mail), they are entered into a file. At the end of each business period (i.e., a month for some companies, a week for others, and a day in some cases) the file of transactions (called "trans" in Problem 10.3) is *applied* to the master file (called "oldmast" in Problem 10.3), thus *updating* each account's record of purchases and payments. After each of these updating runs, the master file is rewritten as a new file ("newmast"), which is then used at the end of the next business period to begin the updating process once again.

File-matching programs must deal with certain problems that do not exist in single-file programs. For example, a match does not always occur. A customer on the master file may not have made any purchases or cash payments in the current business period, and therefore no record for this customer will appear on the transaction file. Similarly, a customer who did make some purchases or cash payments may have just moved to this community, and the company may not have had a chance to create a master record for this customer.

Use the statements written in Problem 10.3 as a basis for writing a complete file-matching accounts receivable program. Use the account number on each file as the *record key* for matching purposes. Assume that each file is a sequential file with records stored in increasing account number order.

When a match occurs (i.e., records with the same account number appear on both the master file and the transaction file), add the dollar amount on the transaction file to the current balance on the master file, and write the "newmast" record. (Assume that purchases are indicated by positive amounts on the transaction file, and that payments are indicated by negative amounts.) When there is a master record for a particular account but no corresponding transaction record, merely write the master record to "newmast." When there is a transaction record but no corresponding master record, print the message "Unmatched transaction record for account number . . ." (fill in the account number from the transaction record).

10.5. After writing the program of Problem 10.4, write a simple program to create some *test data* for use in checking out the program of Problem 10.4. Use the following data:

Master file:

Account Number	Name	Balance
100	Alan Jones	348.17
300	Mary Smith	27.19
500	Sam Sharp	0.00
700	Suzy Green	-14.22

Transaction file:

Account Number	Dollar Amount
100	27.14
300	62.11
400	100.56
900	82.17

10.6. Run the program of Problem 10.4 using the files of test data created in Problem 10.5. Use the listing program of Section 10.4 to print a new master file. Check the results carefully.

10.7. It is possible (actually common) to have several transaction records with the same record key. This occurs because a particular customer might make several purchases and cash payments during a business period. Rewrite your accounts receivable file-matching program of Problem 10.4 to provide for handling several transaction records with the same record key. Modify the test data of Problem 10.5 to include the following additional transaction records:

Account Number	Dollar Amount
300	83.89
700	80.78
700	1.53

Chapter 11
Random Access Files

11.1 Introduction

In this chapter we will discuss *random access files*. To access a particular record of a sequential file, a program must begin with the first record of the file and read every record in succession until it finds the one it wants. Individual records of a random access file may be accessed directly without having to search through any other records. This makes random access files particularly useful in applications that require rapid access to individual facts. For example, an auto shop may want to determine very quickly if a particular part is in stock. Unfortunately, random access files can require considerably more complex programming than sequential files do.

Information in a random access file is stored in records, and all records are the same size. So, if we are creating a file for which no entry is longer than 28 bytes, then we must allocate 28 bytes for every record in the file. Since every record is the same length, the computer can quickly calculate the exact space at which a certain record will appear on the disk.

Random access files have other advantages as well. Unlike sequential files, we can add data to a random access file without destroying other information in the file. We can also change and delete data that has been stored previously without having to rewrite the entire file.

In this chapter we explain how to create a random access file, open the file, enter data, read the data both sequentially and randomly, update the data, and delete data no longer needed.

11.2 Creating a Random Access File

To create a random access file "CreditAccount" whose records are each 43 bytes long and which should be known as file #1, we would like to be able to write a statement such as

```
OPEN "CreditAccount" AS #1 LEN = 43
```

Actually, we must write a series of statements because of a special feature in Macintosh QuickBASIC that "gets in our way" (we will explain this in the Appendix). In particular, the file must first be created as a sequential file, then OPENed as a random access file as follows:

```
OPEN "CreditAccount" FOR OUTPUT AS #1
CLOSE #1
OPEN "CreditAccount" AS #1 LEN = 43
```

The first OPEN statement and the CLOSE statement create a sequential file on disk; the second OPEN statement opens the file for random access. The first two statements are only needed when creating a random access file; when opening a random access file that has already been created, only the second OPEN statement is required.

The OPEN statement for random access files differs from the OPEN statement for sequential files in two ways; there is no longer a mode specification such as INPUT or OUTPUT, and the phrase LEN = is new. If no mode is specified in the OPEN statement, the computer assumes that it is to open a random access file. The LEN defines the record length for the file. If the record length is not specified, a length of 128 bytes will be assumed.

The second OPEN statement above may have the alternate format

```
OPEN "R", #1, "CreditAccount", 43
```

where "R" stands for random access.

11.3   The FIELD Statement

The FIELD statement is used to define the lengths of the string variables within each record, and to reserve a *file buffer* in the computer's memory.

```
FIELD #1, 20 AS ln$, 15 AS frn$, 8 AS b$
```

tells the computer that for this file there are three variables in each record and that 20 bytes are for ln$, 15 bytes are for frn$ and 8 bytes are for b$. Notice that the total of all the bytes for the three variables is the same as the record length of 43 stated in the OPEN statement.

All data to be stored in a random access file must be in string form. Therefore, it is necessary to convert any numeric variables to string variables before entering them in the buffer. This will be discussed later in more detail.

11.4   The LSET and RSET Statements

LSET and RSET copy the information that will eventually be placed into a random access file to the *random file buffer* that was created in memory with the FIELD statement.

```
LSET ln$ = "Jones"
```

puts the string value "Jones" into the variable ln$ that was allotted twenty bytes of memory in the FIELD statement. Since "Jones" is five characters long, the LSET statement left justifies "Jones" within the string variable ln$ leaving 15 blanks to the right as follows:

```
"Jones              "
```

LSET fills the remainder of a string with trailing spaces if the string does not have enough characters to fill the maximum number of bytes allotted. By doing this, LSET always creates a string of exactly the correct length. If we enter a string that is too long for a variable as defined in the FIELD statement, both LSET and RSET truncate the extra characters from the right of the string.

RSET right justifies characters in a string field. The statement

```
RSET ln$ = "Jones"
```

therefore, would produce "   Jones" with 15 leading blanks.

11.5   The PUT # Statement

Once information has been stored in the random file buffer with LSET and/or RSET, we use PUT # to write the information from the buffer to the disk.

```
PUT #1, 7
```

works through channel number 1 to write the buffer to record number 7 of our random access file, namely "CreditAccount". If we use PUT # without the record number parameter, it will write the information to the next sequential record in the file.

11.6   Single-precision, Double-precision, Integer, and Long Integer Numbers

We will need to convert numbers back and forth between string and numeric formats when using random access files. QuickBASIC uses *single-precision numbers, double-precision numbers, integer numbers,* and *long integer numbers.* Calculations using single-precision numbers are accurate to seven significant digits and require four bytes of memory to be stored. Those using double-precision numbers are accurate to 15 digits and require eight bytes of memory to be stored. This is for the binary version of BASIC and varies slightly from the decimal version. Integers require two bytes of memory to be stored and are in the range -32,768 to 32,767. Long integers require four bytes of memory to be stored and are in the range -2,147,483,648 to 2,147,483,648. This is important to know specifically for the OPEN and FIELD statements at the beginning of our program so that we can allot the appropriate amount of space for each record and each variable.

We can specify at the beginning of our program that we would like all or some of the numeric variables to be of a certain type by using the DEFSNG, DEFDBL, DEFINT, or DEFLNG statements for single-precision numbers, double-precision numbers, integer numbers, and long integer numbers respectively.

```
DEFSNG a-f
DEFDBL g-l
DEFINT m-s
DEFLNG t-z
```

Each of these statements specifies that variables beginning with letters in the indicated ranges will be of the specific numeric variable types.

11.7   The MKS$, MKD$, MKI$ and MKL$ Functions

As stated earlier, all data to be written to a random access file must be in string format. Therefore, we must use the *make* functions, MKS$, MKD$, MKI$, and MKL$, to convert numeric data to string data. MKS$ is for single-precision numbers, MKD$ is for double-precision numbers, MKI$ is for integer numbers, and MKL$ is for long integer numbers. The statement

```
RSET b$ = MKD$(balance)
```

sets the string variable b$ to the string equivalent of the numeric variable balance; the value is right justified in the field reserved for b$. We may also use LSET, but RSET is better for numbers because it makes more sense to right justify them.

11.8   The CLOSE # Statement

A random access file is closed with the CLOSE # statement. For example,

```
CLOSE #1
```

will close channel number 1; no other input/output can occur through that channel unless it is reopened.

It is possible to close several channels at once. For example,

```
CLOSE #1, #3, #6, #7
```

```
REM    Initializing a random access file
DEFDBL a-z

OPEN "CreditAccount" FOR OUTPUT AS #1
CLOSE #1
OPEN "CreditAccount" AS #1 LEN = 43
FIELD #1, 20 AS ln$, 15 AS frn$, 8 AS b$
FOR record = 1 TO 1000
   LSET ln$ = "XXX"
   LSET frn$ = ""
   RSET b$ = MKD$(0)
   PUT #1
NEXT record
CLOSE #1
END
```

Figure 11.1 Initializing a random access file

closes channels 1, 3, 6, and 7. Once a file is opened, it should be closed when the reading or writing of data is completed.

The program of Figure 11.1 shows how to open a random access file, define the record fields, move data to the buffer, write data to the disk, and close the file. This program initializes the file "CreditAccount" by placing a last name (ln$) of "XXX", a first name (frn$) of "", and a balance (b$) of "0" in all 1000 records of the file (the choice of 1000 was purely arbitrary). We initialize the file so that when we use it later, we can determine whether or not each particular record already contains information.

The program of Figure 11.2 puts information into the file "CreditAccount". It works similarly to the initialization program except that it only puts information into specific records.

11.9   The CVS, CVD, CVI and CVL Functions

The *convert* functions, CVS, CVD, CVI, and CVL, are the opposites of the *make* functions. The convert functions convert numeric string data back to pure numeric data. CVS is used for single-precision numbers, CVD is used for double-precision numbers, CVI is used for integer numbers, and CVL is used for long integer numbers. The statement

```
balance = CVD(b$)
```

sets the numeric variable balance equal to the double-precision numeric equivalent of the string variable b$. Now we may perform calculations because we have a number rather than a string representation of a number.

```
REM   Writing data to a random access file
DEFDBL a-z

OPEN "CreditAccount" AS #1 LEN = 43
FIELD #1, 20 AS ln$, 15 AS frn$, 8 AS b$

PRINT "Enter ',,,' to end"
PRINT
PRINT "Enter account #(1 - 1000), last name, first name, balance"
INPUT record, lastname$, firstname$, balance
WHILE lastname$ <> ""
   LSET ln$ = lastname$
   LSET frn$ = firstname$
   RSET b$ = MKD$(balance)
   IF record < 1 OR record > 1000 THEN
      PRINT "Account number out of range"
      PRINT "Enter an account number between 1 and 1000"
      ELSE
         PUT #1, record
   END IF
   PRINT "Enter next record"
   INPUT record, lastname$, firstname$, balance
WEND
CLOSE #1
END


Enter ',,,' to end

Enter account #(1 - 1000), last name, first name, balance
?  737, Barker, Doug, 0.00
Enter next record
?  29, Brown, Fred, -24.54
Enter next record
?  396, Stone, Sam, 34.98
Enter next record
?  588, Smith, Dave, 258.34
Enter next record
?  133, Doe, John, 324.67
Enter next record
?  499, Dunn, Stacey, 314.33
Enter next record
?  ,,,
```

Figure 11.2 Writing data to a random access file

11.10 The GET # Statement

The **GET** # statement is used to copy a record from the disk to the random file buffer for reading into a program. For example, if we open `"CreditAccount"` on channel # 3 and use the statement

```
GET #3, 7
```

then the record number 7 will be copied from the file into the buffer. The **GET #** statement used without the record number parameter will copy the next sequential record from the file to the buffer.

11.11   The LOF Function

The **LOF** function returns the length of the file in bytes. Since the record length is known, the number of records may be determined by dividing the number of bytes by the length of each record in a statement such as

        numrecs = **LOF**(1) / 43

Thus, if there are 430 bytes in this file, then numrecs, the number of records, is ten.

11.12   The EOF Function

The **EOF** function is used to determine if the end of a file has been reached. When used with random access files, it returns the value *true* if a record that we try to access with **PUT #** or **GET #** is beyond the end of the file. The **EOF** function is often used in a **WHILE/WEND** loop of the following form:

        WHILE NOT EOF(1)

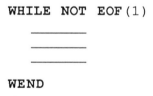

        WEND

The number after **EOF** specifies the channel through which we are accessing the file. The **WHILE/WEND** loop will continue as long as we are accessing records that are not beyond the end of the file.

The program of Figure 11.3 reads sequentially through every record in random access file "CreditAccount", checks each record to see if it holds information, and if it does, prints the information. The **LOF** function is used to find the number of records, the **CVD** function is used to convert a string variable back to a numeric variable, the **EOF** function is used to form a loop that ends when the end of the file is reached, and the **GET** # statement is used to move data from the disk into the random access buffer. This program is an example of reading a random access file sequentially.

```
REM    Reading a random access file sequentially
DEFDBL a - z
OPEN "CreditAccount" AS #1 LEN = 43
FIELD #1, 20 AS ln$, 15 AS frn$, 8 AS b$
u = 0
record = 1
numrecs = LOF(1)/43
LPRINT "There are "; numrecs; " records in this file"
GET #1, record
WHILE NOT EOF(1)
    lastname$ = ln$
    firstname$ = frn$
    balance = CVD(b$)
    IF LEFT$(lastname$,3) = "XXX" THEN
       u = u + 1
       ELSEIF LEFT$(lastname$,3) <> "XXX" THEN
          LPRINT record, lastname$; firstname$;
          LPRINT USING "#####.##"; balance
    END IF
      record = record + 1
    GET #1
WEND
LPRINT "There were "; u ;" unassigned records."
CLOSE #1
END
```

```
There are  1000  records in this file
29             Brown            Fred          -24.54
133            Doe              John          324.67
396            Stone            Sam            34.98
499            Dunn             Stacey        314.33
588            Smith            Dave          258.34
737            Barker           Doug            0.00
There were  994  unassigned records.
```

Figure 11.3 Reading a random access file sequentially

Example 11.1 Bank account program

Write a BASIC program that will keep track of and update the information of the bank's accounts, and will have the ability to add new accounts, delete accounts, and print out a listing of all the current accounts.

The program of Figure 11.4 gives us five options. Option 1 displays a listing of all the accounts. The subroutine Lineprinter is the same as Example 11.3 except that getting data from the disk is now a subroutine because it is used many times by different parts of the program. The following output would be obtained by choosing option 1:

```
There are  1000  records in this file
29              Brown           Fred            -24.54
133             Doe             John            324.67
396             Stone           Sam              34.98
499             Dunn            Stacey          314.33
588             Smith           Dave            258.34
737             Barker          Doug              0.00
There were  994  unassigned records.
```

Option 2 updates an account. The subroutine reads the inputted file number and checks to see if there is any information on it. It does this using the statement

IF LEFT$**(lastname$,3) = "XXX" **THEN

This statement checks to see if the left three characters of the variable lastname$ are "XXX". If so, then the record has no information. If there is, then the subroutine asks for the transaction amount, calculates the new balance, and rewrites the record to the file. If there is no information on the record, the subroutine indicates this and returns the original list of choices. Here is a typical output for option 2.

```
Enter the account# you wish to update?  499
499             Dunn            Stacey          314.33
Enter transaction amount (+ for charge, - for payment)?  -114.33
499             Dunn            Stacey          200.00
```

Option 3 adds a new account to the file. If we try to put new data in a record that already has information, the subroutine tells us the name of the person whose information is on the record and gives us the original list of five choices. The process of adding a new account in this subroutine is the same as that of Example 11.2. Here is a typical output for option 3.

```
Enter the account number(1 - 1000)?  671
Enter last name, first name, balance
?  McFuddle, Marcy, 335.81
671             McFuddle        Marcy           335.81
```

Option 4 lets us delete a record by first asking us for the file number and checking to see if the record holds any information. If there is no information on this record, the subroutine displays a message and then redisplays the original list of choices. If there is information, the subroutine reinitializes the record and confirms that the record has been deleted.

Option 5 terminates program execution.

```
REM    This program reads a random access file sequentially,
REM    updates data already written to the file,
REM    creates new data to be placed on the file,
REM    and deletes data already on the file.
DEFDBL a-z

OPEN "CreditAccount" AS #1 LEN = 43
FIELD #1, 20 AS ln$, 15 AS frn$, 8 AS b$

GOSUB Enterchoice
WHILE choice <> 5
    ON choice GOSUB Lineprinter,Updaterecord,Newrecord,Deleterecord
    PRINT
    GOSUB Enterchoice
WEND
CLOSE #1
END

Enterchoice:
    PRINT "Enter your choice"
    PRINT "1 - to print list of accounts on lineprinter"
    PRINT "2 - to update an account"
    PRINT "3 - to add a new account"
    PRINT "4 - to terminate an account"
    PRINT "5 - to end"
    INPUT choice
    RETURN

Lineprinter:
    PRINT "Now Printing"
    u = 0
    record = 1
    numrecs = LOF(1)/43
    LPRINT "There are "; numrecs; " records in this file"
    LPRINT "Account#       Last Name            First Name          Balance"
    GET #1
    WHILE NOT EOF(1)
        lastname$ = ln$
        firstname$ = frn$
        balance = CVD(b$)
        IF LEFT$(lastname$,3) = "XXX" THEN
            u = u + 1
          ELSEIF LEFT$(lastname$,3) <> "XXX" THEN
              LPRINT record,
              LPRINT USING "&"; lastname$, firstname$,
              LPRINT USING "#####.##"; balance
        END IF
        record = record + 1
        GET #1
    WEND
    LPRINT "There were "; u;" unassigned records."
    RETURN                                          continued
```

Figure 11.4 Bank account program (part 1 of 3)

continued

```
Updaterecord:
    INPUT "Enter the account# you wish to update"; record
    GOSUB Inputdata
    IF LEFT$(lastname$,3) <> "XXX" THEN
       PRINT record, lastname$; firstname$;
       PRINT USING "#####.##"; balance
       PRINT "Enter transaction amount(+ for charge, - for payment)";
       INPUT amount
       balance = balance + amount
       GOSUB Outputdata
       GOSUB Rereadrecord
    ELSEIF LEFT$(lastname$,3) = "XXX" THEN
          PRINT "This account# does not have any information on it."
    END IF
    RETURN

Newrecord:
    INPUT "Enter the account number(1-1000)"; record
    GOSUB Inputdata
    IF LEFT$(lastname$,3) = "XXX" THEN
       PRINT "Enter lastname, firstname, balance"
       INPUT lastname$, firstname$, balance
       GOSUB Outputdata
       GOSUB Rereadrecord
    ELSEIF LEFT$(lastname$,3) <> "XXX" THEN
          PRINT "This account# already holds information for ";
          PRINT firstname$; " "; lastname$
    END IF
    RETURN

Deleterecord:
    PRINT "Enter the account number that you would like to delete";
    INPUT record
    GOSUB Inputdata
    IF LEFT$(lastname$,3) = "XXX" THEN
       PRINT "This account# has no information."
       ELSEIF LEFT$(lastname$,3) <> "XXX" THEN
          lastname$ = "XXX"
          firstname$ = ""
          balance = 0
          GOSUB Outputdata
          PRINT "Account "; record; " has been deleted"
    END IF
    RETURN

Inputdata:
    IF record = 0 THEN PRINT "Bad record number": RETURN
    GET #1, record
    lastname$ = ln$
    firstname$ = frn$
    balance = CVD(b$)
    RETURN                                        continued
```

Figure 11.4 Bank account program (part 2 of 3)

continued

```
Outputdata:
   LSET ln$ = lastname$
   LSET frn$ = firstname$
   RSET b$ = MKD$(balance)
   PUT #1, record
   RETURN

Rereadrecord:
   GET #1, record
   lastname$ = ln$
   firstname$ = frn$
   balance = CVD(b$)
   PRINT record, lastname$; firstname$;
   PRINT USING "#####.##"; balance
   RETURN
```

Figure 11.4 Bank account program (part 3 of 3)

Concepts

channel
CLOSE #
CVD
CVI
CVL
CVS
DEFDBL
DEFINT
DEFLNG
DEFSNG
double-precision number
EOF
FIELD #
file buffer
GET #
integer number
LEN

LOF
LSET
MKD$
MKI$
MKL$
MKS$
OPEN
PUT #
random access
random access file
random file buffer
record
record number parameter
RSET
single-precision number

Problems

11.1. Fill in the blanks in each of the following
   (a) The _____ statement specifies the number of bytes to be reserved for each variable.
   (b) Random access files are generally stored on _____ devices.
   (c) The _____ statement is true when there are no longer any records to read in the file.
   (d) The _____ statement determines how may bytes are used by the file.
   (e) The _____ statement takes a disk record and places it into the random file buffer.
   (f) The three functions that change numeric variables into string variables are _____, _____, _____, and _____.
   (g) The _____ statement places data from the program into the random file buffer.
   (h) The functions _____, _____, _____, and _____ change the string equivalents of numeric variables into numeric variables.

(i)   The statement _____ specifies that all the variables beginning with the letters c-p are to be single-precision numbers.

11.2. For each of the following, write a single BASIC statement that accomplishes the desired task.
   (a)   Read a record from a file; place it in the random file buffer; use channel #4, record 18.
   (b)   Allot 30 bytes to a$, 15 bytes to b$, 10 bytes to c$, and 3 to d$. Use channel #2.
   (c)   State that the file "addresses" will be treated as #3 and read by the program.
   (d)   Write a single record to file #1 and record number 67.
   (e)   Right justify the variable g$ in the random file buffer.
   (f)   Close the files numbered 1 through 4.
   (g)   Convert the single-precision numeric variable money to the string variable m$ and left justify it in the random file buffer.

11.3. Write a series of statements that accomplish each of the following. Assume that the file is already open and has been fielded as follows: 15 AS a$, 15 AS b$, and 2 AS c$.
   (a)   Initialize the file "nameandage" so that there are 100 records with a$ = "unassigned", b$ = "", and c$ = "0".
   (b)   Input 10 last names, first names, and ages, and write them to the file.
   (c)   Update a record that has information in it, and if there is none tell the user "No info."
   (d)   Delete a record that has information by reinitializing that particular record.

11.4. You are the owner of a hardware store and need to keep an inventory that can tell you what tools you have, how many you have, and what the cost is for each one. Write a program that initializes the file "HardwareInventory" to one hundred records, lets you input the data concerning each tool, enables you to list all your tools, can delete a record for a tool that you no longer have, and lets you update any information in the file already. The catalog number should be the record number. Use the following information to start your file:

Record #	Tool Name	Inventory #	Cost
3	Electric sander	7	57.98
17	Hammer	76	12.99
24	Jig saw	21	11.00
39	Lawn mower	3	79.50
44	Leaf rake	13	14.89
56	Power saw	18	99.99
68	Screwdriver	106	6.99
77	Sledge hammer	11	21.50
83	Wrench	34	7.50

Chapter 12
The Mouse, Event Trapping, and Elementary Graphics

12.1 Introduction

The *mouse* helps us use windows, buttons, menus, and many other features of the Macintosh. This chapter explains how to determine the location of the mouse, if the mouse button was pressed and how many times it was pressed, and the coordinates of the starting and ending points of a drag if the mouse was dragged across the screen.

We also consider *event trapping* which allows a program to be processing statements while also waiting for, and responding to, unpredictable events (such as mouse clicks) to occur. Some elementary graphics capabilities are introduced.

12.2 The MOUSE(0) Function

The MOUSE(0) function determines whether or not the mouse has been clicked. The function can return values from -3 to 3. A value of 0 means that there has not been a mouse click, a 1 means that the mouse has been clicked once (since the last call to MOUSE(0)), a 2 means it has been clicked twice, and a 3 means it has been clicked three times. The values -1, -2, and -3 indicate the corresponding number of clicks and that the button has not yet been released after the last click. The statement

```
mouseclick = MOUSE(0)
```

saves the value of the MOUSE(0) function.

The program in Figure 12.1 waits for the mouse to be clicked. It then prints a value between -3 and 3 depending upon how many times the mouse was clicked and whether or not it was held. If the button is clicked three times and held on the last one, the program will end.

```
REM    Using the MOUSE(0) function
mouseclick = 0
WHILE mouseclick <> -3
   WHILE MOUSE(0) = 0
   WEND
   FOR x = 1 TO 2000
   NEXT x
   mouseclick = MOUSE(0)
   PRINT mouseclick
WEND
END
```

Figure 12.1 Using the MOUSE(0) function

12.3 The MOUSE(1) and MOUSE(2) Functions

The MOUSE(1) function finds the x coordinate of the pointer, and the MOUSE(2) function finds the y coordinate of the pointer. (The x coordinates extend from left to right on the screen, while the y coordinates extend from top to bottom.) These two functions do not give the coordinates of the pointer at the time they are executed; rather, they give the coordinates of the pointer when the last MOUSE(0) function was executed. If the MOUSE(0) function is executed right before MOUSE(1) and MOUSE(2) are executed, we will receive the exact coordinates of the mouse pointer (assuming that the mouse cannot be moved faster than the computer executes the three statements.)

```
xcoordinate = MOUSE(1)
ycoordinate = MOUSE(2)
```

By setting the functions equal to variables, the location of the pointer may be saved so that it can be used to plot a point, display text, or display a graphic on the screen where the pointer is. No click need be made to get values for MOUSE(1) and MOUSE(2).

The program in Figure 12.2 uses MOUSE(1) and MOUSE(2) and introduces two graphics statements, PSET and CIRCLE. A sample output of this program is shown in Figure 12.3.

```
REM    Using MOUSE(1), MOUSE(2), PSET, and CIRCLE
WHILE xcoordinate <= 490
   mouseclick = MOUSE(0)
   xcoordinate = MOUSE(1)
   ycoordinate = MOUSE(2)
   IF ycoordinate < 0 THEN ycoordinate = 0
   PSET (xcoordinate, ycoordinate)
   CIRCLE (xcoordinate, ycoordinate), .25 * ycoordinate
WEND
END
```

Figure 12.2 Using MOUSE(1), MOUSE(2), PSET, and CIRCLE

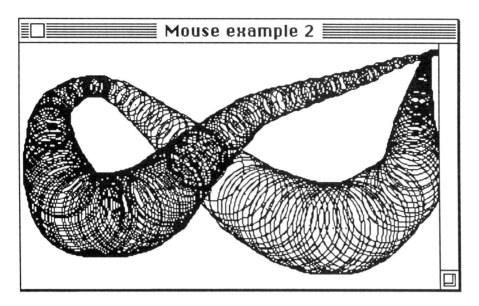

Figure 12.3 Output of program in Figure 12.2

This program uses the **MOUSE(1)** and **MOUSE(2)** functions to determine the coordinates of the mouse pointer frequently. The coordinates are then used to plot a point with the **PSET** statement and a circle with the **CIRCLE** statement. The **PSET** statement turns one pixel black at the point with coordinates xcoordinate and ycoordinate. The **CIRCLE** statement then draws a circle using the same coordinates as the center of the circle. The **CIRCLE** statement has the following form:

```
CIRCLE (xcoordinate , ycoordinate), radius, color
```

The first two parameters specify the location of the center of the circle. All measurements are in pixels, the dots that make up the screen. The color parameter, 30 for white or 33 for black, indicates the color in which the circle should be displayed. If no color is specified, the computer assumes black. The radius of each circle in the program of Figure 12.2 is set to one quarter of ycoordinate; this increases the size of the circle as the mouse moves toward the bottom of the screen. If xcoordinate is greater than 490 (the width of the output window from the left to the vertical scroll bar), the program ends.

12.4 Dragging the Mouse

Dragging the mouse occurs when we move the mouse while holding the mouse button. We can get the coordinates of the starting and ending points of the drag with the following four functions:

```
MOUSE(3)
MOUSE(4)
MOUSE(5)
MOUSE(6)
```

MOUSE(3) and MOUSE(4) return the x and y coordinates of the starting point of the drag, while MOUSE(5) and MOUSE(6) return the x and y coordinates of the ending point of the drag. To start a drag, the button on the mouse must be pressed and held. This enables us to get values for all four functions. It is not necessary to release the button to get values for MOUSE(5) and MOUSE(6). The program in Figure 12.4 introduces the LINE statement for drawing lines, and shows the effect of dragging the mouse.

```
REM    Dragging mouse and drawing lines
WHILE xendpoint < 490
    WHILE MOUSE(0) = 0
    WEND
    xstartpoint = MOUSE(3)
    ystartpoint = MOUSE(4)
    xendpoint = MOUSE(5)
    yendpoint = MOUSE(6)
    LINE (xstartpoint, ystartpoint)-(xendpoint, yendpoint)
WEND
END
```

Figure 12.4 Dragging the mouse and drawing lines

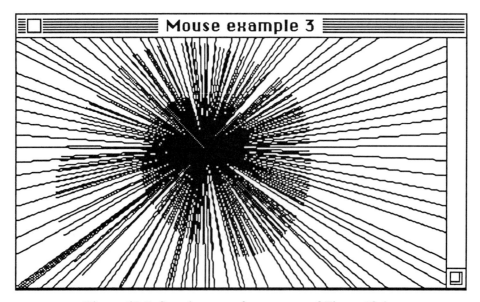

Figure 12.5 Sample output for program of Figure 12.4

The program begins in a loop where it waits for the mouse button to be pressed. It then finds the starting point of the drag, which remains constant while the button is held down, and it determines the changing ending points as the mouse is dragged. Each time a new end point is found, the program uses the LINE statement to plot a line from the starting point to that particular ending point (see Figure 12.5). The LINE statement has the following general form:

```
LINE (xstart, ystart) - (xend, yend), color, b or bf
```

The coordinates needed in this case are obtained by MOUSE (3), MOUSE (4), MOUSE (5), and MOUSE (6). Color 30 is for drawing in white and color 33 is for drawing in black. The *box parameter* (b) causes a rectangle to be drawn with the indicated coordinates specifying the opposite corners. The *box fill parameter* (bf) causes the rectangle to be filled with either white or black depending on the color parameter. If the color parameter is not specified, the computer assumes black. This program ends when the mouse is clicked in the vertical scroll bar or dragged into it. Figure 12.6 shows the effect of adding the box parameter to the line statement.

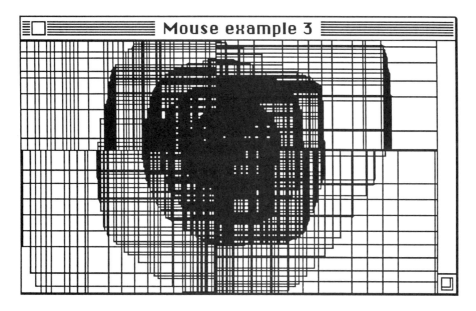

Figure 12.6 Dragging and using the box parameter

12.5 Event Trapping and the Mouse

Event trapping is a Macintosh feature that enables a program to determine that some action (or event) of interest to the program has occurred. In this and the next several chapters we shall investigate many common Macintosh events such as mouse clicks, menu selections, and the like.

There are four general statements that are related to event trapping. They include

```
ON event GOSUB ...
event ON
event OFF
event STOP
```

The purpose of these four statements is to control event trapping and cause appropriate subroutine transfers to process the events. The event trapping mechanism checks after each line of the program is executed to see if an event has occurred. When an event is detected, the program stops what it is doing, transfers to the subroutine to process the event, and returns to continue processing with the next statement in the program. For mouse event trapping, the word **event** is replaced with **MOUSE**. Each time a mouse event occurs, the program transfers control to the designated subroutine, processes the mouse event, most likely a mouse click, and returns to what it was doing before the event occurred.

Other types of events that can be trapped (and that are discussed in the remaining chapters) include **BREAK**, **DIALOG** (for windows, buttons, dialog boxes, and edit fields), **MENU**, and **TIMER**.

In order for the event trapping feature to be activated, the **ON event GOSUB** ... statement and the **event ON** statement must be used. Once an event occurs, either the **event OFF** or the **event STOP** statement should be used to turn off event trapping, or the computer will continue looking for an event between the execution of each program line. This could cause confusion if an event occurs while the previous event is being processed. With **event OFF**, events that occur are lost. With **event STOP**, the

```
REM    Event trapping with the mouse
ON MOUSE GOSUB Processmouse
MOUSE ON

PRINT "Press button 3 times and hold to end"
click = 1
WHILE click = 1
WEND
END

Processmouse:
   MOUSE OFF
   FOR x = 1 TO 1000
   NEXT x
   buttonclick = MOUSE(0)
   IF buttonclick <> -3 THEN
      IF buttonclick = 1 THEN
         PRINT "You pressed the button 1 time, and";
         ELSE
            PRINT "You pressed the button"; ABS(buttonclick);
            PRINT "times, and";
      END IF
      IF buttonclick < 0 THEN
         PRINT " you held it down."
         ELSE
            PRINT " you let it go."
      END IF
      click = 1
      ELSE
         PRINT "You pressed the button 3 times and held it."
         click = 0
   END IF
   MOUSE ON
   RETURN
```

Figure 12.7 Event trapping with the mouse

computer will remember if an event took place while the event trapping was turned off, and the appropriate subroutine transfer will occur when an **event ON** statement is executed. Thus **event OFF** disables event trapping, while **event STOP** suspends event trapping.

The program in Figure 12.7 is a simple event trapping program. It prints the number of times the mouse button was pushed and whether or not it was released. If the mouse button is clicked three times and held, the variable buttonclick will equal -3; this will terminate the program.

Example 12.1 A sample mouse program

Write a program using mouse event trapping and the **PSET**, **LINE**, and **CIRCLE** statements, that on one, two, or three clicks of the mouse will transfer control to a subroutine where the user can draw. One subroutine should plot points as the user moves the mouse around the screen, another should draw lines as the user drags the mouse around the screen, and the last should draw circles of changing size as the user moves the mouse. The program appears in Figure 12.8 and sample outputs are shown in Figures 12.9, 12.10, and 12.11.

Discussion: The program uses mouse event trapping to determine when the mouse button is clicked. Mouse activity causes the program to transfer control to the Processmouse subroutine where it determines the number of times the button was clicked; the program then transfers control to one of three drawing subroutines. If the button was clicked and held, the program ends. Each of the drawing subroutines returns to the Processmenu subroutine when the pointer moves into the vertical scroll bar at the right of the screen. The program may then be terminated by holding the mouse button down.

```
REM   Using mouse trapping and elementary graphics
ON MOUSE GOSUB Processmouse
MOUSE ON

PRINT "Press button and hold to end"
PRINT "Click once quickly to plot points as mouse is moved"
PRINT "Click twice quickly to draw lines ";
PRINT "as mouse is moved with button pushed"
PRINT "Click three times quickly to draw ";
PRINT "circles as mouse is   moved"
PRINT "Drag mouse to vertical scroll bar ";
PRINT "to end each type of drawing"
click = 1
WHILE click = 1
WEND
END                                        continued
```

Figure 12.8 Using mouse trapping and elementary graphics (part 1 of 2)

continued

```
Processmouse:
   MOUSE OFF
   FOR x = 1 TO 1000
   NEXT x
   buttonclick = MOUSE(0)
   IF buttonclick < 0 THEN
      click = 0
      CLS
      ELSEIF buttonclick > 0 THEN
         CLS
         ON buttonclick GOSUB Pointplot, Lineplot, Circleplot
         click = 1
      END IF
      RETURN

Pointplot:
   xcoordinate = 0
   WHILE xcoordinate <= 490
      buttonclick = MOUSE(0)
      xcoordinate = MOUSE(1)
      ycoordinate = MOUSE(2)
      IF ycoordinate < 0 THEN ycoordinate = 0
      PSET (xcoordinate, ycoordinate)
   WEND
   MOUSE ON
   RETURN

Lineplot:
   xendpoint = 0
   WHILE xendpoint <= 490
      WHILE MOUSE(0) = 0
      WEND
      xstartpoint = MOUSE(3)
      ystartpoint = MOUSE(4)
      xendpoint = MOUSE(5)
      yendpoint = MOUSE(6)
      LINE (xstartpoint, ystartpoint)-(xendpoint, yendpoint)
   WEND
   MOUSE ON
   RETURN

Circleplot:
   xcoordinate = 0
   WHILE xcoordinate < 490
      mouseclick = MOUSE(0)
      xcoordinate = MOUSE(1)
      ycoordinate = MOUSE(2)
      IF ycoordinate < 0 THEN ycoordinate = 0
      CIRCLE (xcoordinate, ycoordinate), .25 * ycoordinate
   WEND
   MOUSE ON
   RETURN
```

Figure 12.8 Using mouse trapping and elementary graphics (part 2 of 2)

Figure 12.9 Point plotting with mouse event trapping

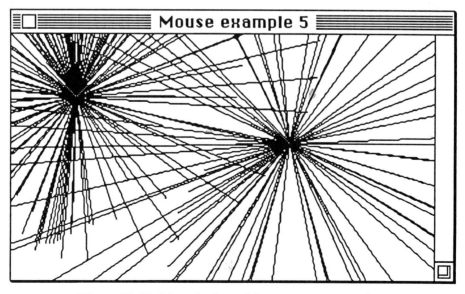

Figure 12.10 Line plotting with mouse event trapping

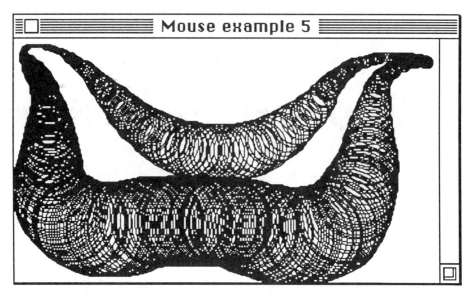

Figure 12.11 Circle plotting with mouse event trapping

Concepts

box fill parameter
box parameter
BREAK event trapping
CIRCLE statement
color parameter
DIALOG event trapping
disable event trapping
event trapping
LINE statement
MENU event trapping
Mouse
mouse event trapping
MOUSE(0) function

MOUSE(1) function
MOUSE(2) function
MOUSE(3) function
MOUSE(4) function
MOUSE(5) function
MOUSE(6) function
MOUSE OFF statement
MOUSE ON statement
MOUSE STOP statement
ON MOUSE GOSUB ... statement
PSET statement
suspend event trapping
TIMER event trapping

Problems

12.1. Fill in the blanks in each of the following.
  (a) The _____ statement turns on event trapping for the mouse.
  (b) The _____ statement returns values from -3 to 3 indicating mouse click activity.
  (c) The _____ function and the _____ function return the x and y coordinates, respectively, of the mouse pointer.
  (d) The four functions that return the x and y coordinates of the starting and ending points of a drag are _____, _____, _____, and _____
  (e) The _____ statement suspends mouse event trapping.
  (f) The four events (besides mouse events) that can be trapped with event trapping are _____, _____, _____, and _____.
  (g) The _____ statement disables mouse event trapping.

12.2. Write a single BASIC statement that accomplishes each of the following.
   (a) Set the the variable xcoordinate equal to the function that determines the x coordinate of the mouse pointer.
   (b) Set the variable ycoordinate equal to the function that determines the y coordinate of the mouse pointer.
   (c) Turn on mouse event trapping.
   (d) Turn off mouse event trapping. (Show two ways to do this.)
   (e) When a mouse event occurs, transfer control to the subroutine Processevent.
   (f) Set the variable xstart equal to a function that determines the starting x coordinate of a drag.
   (g) Set the variable yend equal to a function that determines the ending y coordinate of a drag.

12.3. Write a program that draws boxes with the first set of coordinates being the starting point of the drag and the second set of coordinates being each end point while the mouse button is held down. The program should end when the button is released.

12.4. Write a program that draws circles of random radii as the user drags the mouse around the screen. The program should end when the mouse pointer is dragged into the vertical scroll bar at the right of the screen.

12.5. Write a program that plots points of four pixel squares. The upper left corner of the square should be at the x and y coordinates of the mouse pointer. The program should end when the pointer is dragged into the vertical scroll bar.

12.6. Write a program that draws a rectangle that moves as the mouse moves. The program should erase the previous rectangle before the next one is printed. Do not use **CLS**. The program should end when the pointer enters the vertical scroll bar.

12.7. Write a BASIC program that uses the **CIRCLE** statement to draw concentric circles.

12.8. Write a BASIC program that uses the **LINE** statement to draw concentric squares.

12.9. Write a BASIC program that uses the **PSET** statement to plot random points on the screen.

12.10. Write a BASIC program that uses the **CIRCLE** statement to draw circles of random radii and centers on the screen.

12.11. Write a BASIC program that uses the **LINE** statement to draw random lines on the screen.

12.12. Write a BASIC program that uses the **LINE** statement to draw random lines from a fixed point on the screen.

12.13. Modify the program of Figure 12.8 so that the Pointplot subroutine only draws when the mouse button is held down.

12.14. Modify the program of Figure 12.8 so that the Circleplot subroutine only draws when the mouse button is held down.

Chapter 13
Menus

13.1 Introduction

In this chapter we consider how to create and use Macintosh *menus*. Menus can be found in virtually every piece of software for the Macintosh. They are used to select tasks to be performed such as opening and closing files, cutting material out of a file, ejecting disks, and the like. This chapter explains how to create menus, place choices in them, use menus effectively, and do event trapping with menus.

13.2 Creating a Menu

A menu is created by using a statement such as

```
MENU 3, 0, 1, "Meals"
```

This statement tells the Macintosh to put a menu named `Meals` onto the menu bar at the top of the screen along with the **File** menu and the **Edit** menu. The first parameter, in this case `3`, is the *menu number parameter*. It tells the computer in which of the ten available locations on the menu bar the menu should be placed. The BASIC default menus (**File**, **Edit**, **Search**, **Windows**, and **Run**) can be replaced with menus created by a BASIC program.

The second parameter, in this case `0`, is the *item number parameter*. It tells the computer that the title in this statement (`"Meals"`) is to be placed in 0th position, i.e., in the menu bar itself, of menu 3. If the item number parameter is greater than 0, the title is listed as an item within the menu number specified in that statement. It is possible to have item numbers ranging from 1 to 20 in any one menu.

The third parameter, in this case `1`, is the *state parameter*. A menu item can be in one of three different states, namely 0, 1, or 2. State 0 specifies that the item is to be disabled and dimmed, state 1 specifies that the item is to be enabled and black (which also means that it is selectable), and state 2 specifies the item is to be enabled and that there is to be a check preceding that item when it appears in the menu.

The fourth parameter, in this case `"Meals"`, is the *title parameter*. In the **MENU** statement in which the item number is zero, the title parameter specifies the title of the

238

menu. In the MENU statements in which the item number is greater than zero, the title parameter specifies the choice within the menu.

The MENU statement

```
MENU 3, 1, 1, "Hamburger        $0.79"
```

places "Hamburger $0.79" in the first slot of menu 3 labeled Meals and the item is to be selectable. There must be a separate MENU statement for every item in every menu.

```
REM    Starting a menu
MENU 3, 0, 1, "Meals"
MENU 3, 1, 1, "Hamburger        $0.79"
MENU 3, 2, 1, "Cheeseburger    $0.89"
MENU 3, 3, 1, "Chicken Parts $2.25"
MENU 3, 4, 1, "Fish Sandwich $1.69"

FOR counter = 1 TO 4000
NEXT counter
END
```

Figure 13.1 Starting a program with menus

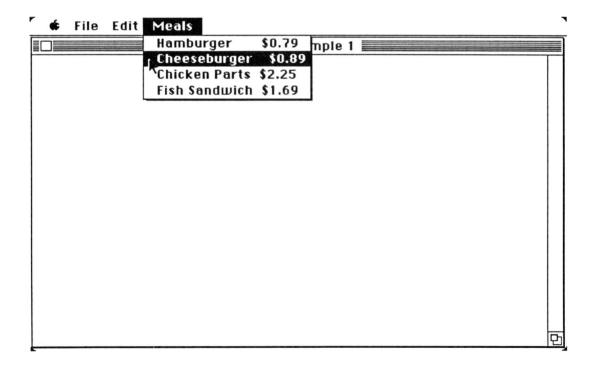

Figure 13.2 The "Meals" menu on the menu bar

The program in Figure 13.1 puts the menu Meals on the menu bar as shown in Figure 13.2. The FOR...NEXT loop simply displays the menu long enough to see it, because as soon as the program ends, the menu disappears from the menu bar. Try running this program, and you will notice that if you select the menu `Meals` it will become blackened and remain that way until it disappears. The menu can be unhighlighted by using a version of the MENU command to be discussed later, or by choosing another menu.

13.3 The MENU(0) Function

The MENU(0) function enables the computer to find out which menu has been chosen. The function returns a zero if no menu has been chosen or if a BASIC default menu has been chosen. The reason that MENU(0) does not return a 1 or 2 for a choice from the two default menus that appear when the program is run is that we cannot control the BASIC default menus through our programs. However, if we were to replace the default menus with our own menus, MENU(0) would indeed return a value of 1 or 2 for those menus.

If "`Meals`" is selected from the menu bar as in Figure 13.2, the MENU(0) function returns a 3, because the number of that menu was 3. The value of MENU(0) can only be read once, so if we wish to print its value, we should first assign it to a variable as in the statement

```
menunumber = MENU(0)
```

The program in Figure 13.3 waits as the counter varies from 1 to 4000. If you choose the menu before the counter finishes counting, the program prints "You chose menu number 3," but if no choice is made, the program prints "You chose menu number 0."

```
REM    Using MENU(0)

MENU 3, 0, 1, "Meals"
MENU 3, 1, 1, "Hamburger      $0.79"
MENU 3, 2, 1, "Cheeseburger   $0.89"
MENU 3, 3, 1, "Chicken Parts  $2.25"
MENU 3, 4, 1, "Fish Sandwich  $1.69"

FOR counter = 1 TO 4000
NEXT counter
menunumber = MENU(0)
PRINT "You chose menu number "; menunumber
END
```

Figure 13.3 Using MENU(0)

13.4 The MENU(1) Function

The MENU(1) function enables the computer to find out which item has been chosen from the menu whose number was found with MENU(0). The item number may be saved with a statement such as

        itemnumber = MENU(1)

which sets itemnumber equal to the value returned by MENU(1).

The program in Figure 13.4 uses the MENU(0) function and the MENU(1) function to determine which item was chosen from which menu. The program waits for a menu to be selected. When a menu is selected, the program prints the number of that menu and the number of the item selected. If a menu is chosen and no choice is made, the program does nothing. Notice that if an item from the Meals menu is chosen, the menu title becomes highlighted. If an item from the Drinks menu is chosen, the Meals menu returns to the normal state, and the Drinks menu becomes highlighted. The MENU statement without parameters "unhighlights" a menu that has been chosen.

```
REM     Combining MENU(0) and MENU(1)
MENU 3, 0, 1, "Meals"
MENU 3, 1, 1, "Hamburger      $0.79"
MENU 3, 2, 1, "Cheeseburger   $0.89"
MENU 3, 3, 1, "Chicken Parts  $2.25"
MENU 3, 4, 1, "Fish Sandwich  $1.69"
MENU 3, 5, 1, "Order Completed"

MENU 4, 0, 1, "Drinks"
MENU 4, 1, 1, "Cola           $0.99"
MENU 4, 2, 1, "Grape Soda     $1.09"
MENU 4, 3, 1, "Ginger Ale     $0.99"
MENU 4, 4, 1, "6-UP           $1.29"

PRINT "Choose 'Order Completed' from the Meals menu to end"
GOSUB Waitloop
itemnumber = MENU(1)
WHILE itemnumber <> 5
    PRINT "You chose menu number "; menunumber;
    PRINT ", and item number"; itemnumber
    GOSUB Waitloop
    itemnumber = MENU(1)
WEND
END

Waitloop:
    menunumber = 0
    WHILE menunumber = 0
        menunumber = MENU(0)
    WEND
    RETURN
```

Figure 13.4 Using **MENU**(0) and **MENU**(1) together

13.5 The MENU RESET Statement and Removing BASIC Default Menus

If we need more than the eight extra menus that BASIC normally allows us, we can replace the BASIC default menus simply by creating menus with the same numbers as the default menus.

The statements

```
FOR x = 1 TO 2
    MENU x, 0, 0, ""
NEXT x
```

erase the BASIC default menus from the menu bar. If we need to use the BASIC default menus again, we use the **MENU RESET** statement to put the default menus back on the menu bar.

The program of Figure 13.5 removes the BASIC default menus from the menu bar and replaces them with two menus, **Meals** and **Drinks**, as shown in Figure 13.6. Once a menu item has been selected and processed, the program uses the **MENU** statement to unhighlight the menu that was chosen. If **Order Completed** is chosen from the **Meals** menu, the program places the BASIC default menus back on the menu bar with **MENU RESET** and ends.

```
REM    Using menu and menu reset
FOR x = 1 TO 2
    MENU x, 0, 0, ""
NEXT x

MENU 3, 0, 1, "Meals"
MENU 3, 1, 1, "Hamburger       $0.79"
MENU 3, 2, 1, "Cheeseburger    $0.89"
MENU 3, 3, 1, "Chicken Parts   $2.25"
MENU 3, 4, 1, "Fish Sandwich   $1.69"
MENU 3, 5, 1, "Order Completed"

MENU 4, 0, 1, "Drinks"
MENU 4, 1, 1, "Cola            $0.99"
MENU 4, 2, 1, "Grape Soda      $1.09"
MENU 4, 3, 1, "Ginger Ale      $0.99"
MENU 4, 4, 1, "6-UP            $1.29"          continued
```

Figure 13.5 Using **MENU** and **MENU RESET** (part 1 of 2)

continued

```
PRINT "Choose 'Order Completed' from the 'Meals' menu to end"
   GOSUB Waitloop
   itemnumber = MENU(1)
   WHILE itemnumber <> 5
      PRINT "You chose menu number "; menunumber;
      PRINT ", and item number"; itemnumber
      MENU
      GOSUB Waitloop
      itemnumber = MENU(1)
   WEND
   MENU RESET
   FOR c = 1 TO 2000
   NEXT c
   END

Waitloop:
   menunumber = 0
   WHILE menunumber = 0
      menunumber = MENU(0)
   WEND
   RETURN
```

Figure 13.5 Using **MENU** and **MENU RESET** (part 2 of 2)

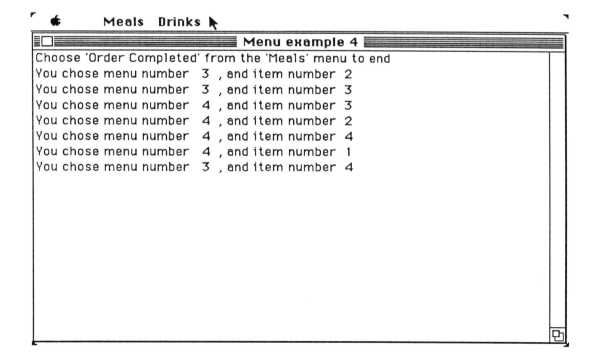

Figure 13.6 The menu bar without the BASIC default menus

13.6 Event Trapping with Menus

There are several statements associated with menu event trapping. These include

```
ON MENU GOSUB ...
MENU ON
MENU OFF
MENU STOP
```

The ON MENU GOSUB statement waits for a menu to be chosen, and when one is, the GOSUB passes control to a designated subroutine. This feature does not work unless it is enabled with the MENU ON statement. Once in the subroutine, event trapping should be either disabled with MENU OFF or suspended with MENU STOP. Doing this prevents the program from being interrupted while processing the subroutine. MENU OFF turns off menu event trapping and simply ignores any subsequent menu activity. MENU STOP remembers if a menu is selected while menu event trapping is disabled; when menu event trapping is enabled again with MENU ON it will acknowledge the menu choice made during the break in event trapping.

The program in Figure 13.7 uses event trapping to determine when a menu has been selected. Once a choice has been made, the program prints the menu number and item number that were selected and waits for another selection. The program is ended by choosing Order Completed from the Meals menu.

Example 13.1 A Fast Food Drive-up with Menus
Write a program that lets customers at a fast food drive-up window pull down menus for meals and drinks to select what they would like. After a customer finishes ordering, the program should total the customer's purchase and print the total price. Replace the BASIC default menus with blank menus and use menus numbered 3 and 4 for Meals and the Drinks.

The program of Figure 13.8 uses all the standard features of menus except the MENU OFF statement. The outputs of the program are shown in Figures 13.9, 13.10, and 13.11. The program begins by printing an opening message to the customer. The customer clicks the mouse to continue. The program then tells the customer how to stop ordering. Then the program simply waits in a loop until a selection is made from one of the menus. When a selection is made, it is processed in the ProcessChoice subroutine which then GOSUBs to the Meals subroutine or the Drinks subroutine depending on the menu selected. The program then returns to the loop to wait for another choice. When Order Completed is chosen from the Meals menu, the program prints the total purchase on the screen, and begins again for the next customer. If total = 0, the program ends.

This is an especially simple menu program and yet it is lengthy and complex. The reader should understand that menu programs with event trapping can easily be very large and complex indeed.

```
REM     Event trapping with menus

FOR x = 1 TO 2
   MENU x, 0, 0,  ""
NEXT x

MENU 3, 0, 1, "Meals"
MENU 3, 1, 1, "Hamburger        $0.79"
MENU 3, 2, 1, "Cheeseburger     $0.89"
MENU 3, 3, 1, "Chicken Parts    $2.25"
MENU 3, 4, 1, "Fish Sandwich    $1.69"
MENU 3, 5, 1, "Order Completed"

MENU 4, 0, 1, "Drinks"
MENU 4, 1, 1, "Cola             $0.99"
MENU 4, 2, 1, "Grape Soda       $1.09"
MENU 4, 3, 1, "Ginger Ale       $0.99"
MENU 4, 4, 1, "6-UP             $1.29"

ON MENU GOSUB ProcessChoice
MENU ON

PRINT "Choose 'Order Completed' from the 'Meals' menu to end"
donextperson = 1
WHILE donextperson = 1
WEND
END

ProcessChoice:
   MENU STOP
   menunumber = MENU(0)
   itemnumber = MENU(1)
   IF itemnumber <> 5 THEN
      LOCATE 6,1
      PRINT "You chose menu number"; menunumber;
      PRINT ", and itemnumber"; itemnumber
      MENU
      MENU ON
      ELSE
         donextperson = 0
         MENU
         MENU RESET
         CLS
         PRINT "Menu demo is finished"
         FOR x = 1 TO 2000
         NEXT x
   END IF
   RETURN
```

Figure 13.7 Event trapping with menus

```
REM    Fast food order program with menus

FOR x = 1 TO 2
    MENU x, 0, 0, ""
NEXT x

MENU 3, 0, 0, "Meals"
MENU 3, 1, 1, "Hamburger      $0.79"
MENU 3, 2, 1, "Cheeseburger   $0.89"
MENU 3, 3, 1, "Chicken Parts  $2.25"
MENU 3, 4, 1, "Fish Sandwich  $1.69"
MENU 3, 5, 1, "Order Completed"

MENU 4, 0, 0, "Drinks"
MENU 4, 1, 1, "Cola           $0.99"
MENU 4, 2, 1, "Grape Soda     $1.09"
MENU 4, 3, 1, "Ginger Ale     $0.99"
MENU 4, 4, 1, "6-UP           $1.29"

ON MENU GOSUB ProcessChoice
MENU ON

donextperson = 1
WHILE donextperson = 1
    CLS
    PRINT "Hi!  Welcome to Freddie's."
    PRINT "Please click the mouse "
    PRINT "to proceed."
    PRINT "            Thank you for coming."
    PRINT
    nothing = MOUSE(0)
    mouseclick = 0
    WHILE mouseclick = 0
        mouseclick = MOUSE(0)
    WEND
    CLS
    PRINT "Choose 'Order Completed' from the 'Meals' menu to end"
    PRINT
    GOSUB Initializevariables
    PRINT "Your order is:"
    MENU 3, 0, 1
    MENU 4, 0,1
    persondone = 0
    WHILE persondone = 0
    WEND
WEND
END                                    continued
```

Figure 13.8 Fast food order program with menus (part 1 of 3)

continued

```
ProcessChoice:
    MENU STOP
    menunumber = MENU(0)
    itemnumber = MENU(1)
    IF itemnumber <> 5 THEN
        ON menunumber - 2 GOSUB Meals, Drinks
        MENU
        ELSE
            GOSUB Endorder
    END IF
    RETURN

Endorder:
    MENU
    persondone = 1
    IF total <> 0 THEN
        CLS
        MENU 3, 0, 0
        MENU 4, 0, 0
        PRINT
        PRINT USING "That will be $$###.##"; total
        PRINT "Please pay at the window."
        PRINT "                    Come again."
        FOR x = 1 TO 7000
        NEXT x
        MENU ON
        ELSE
            donextperson = 0
            MENU RESET
            CLS
    END IF
    RETURN

Meals:
    SELECT CASE itemnumber
        CASE 1
            total = total + .79
            LOCATE 5, 1
            hamburger = hamburger + 1
            PRINT  hamburger, "Hamburger"
        CASE 2
            total = total + .89
            LOCATE 6, 1
            cheeseburger = cheeseburger + 1
            PRINT cheeseburger, "Cheeseburger"
        CASE 3
            total = total + 2.25
            LOCATE 7, 1
            chickenparts = chickenparts + 1
            PRINT  chickenparts, "Chicken Parts"
        CASE ELSE
            total = total + 1.69
            LOCATE 8, 1
```

Figure 13.8 Fast food order program with menus (part 2 of 3)

continued

```
                fishsandwich = fishsandwich + 1
                PRINT fishsandwich, "Fish Sandwich"        continued
        END SELECT
        MENU ON
        RETURN

Drinks:
    SELECT CASE itemnumber
        CASE 1
            total = total + .99
            LOCATE 5, 30
            cola = cola + 1
            PRINT cola, "Cola"
        CASE 2
            total = total + 1.09
            LOCATE 6, 30
            grapesoda = grapesoda + 1
            PRINT grapesoda, "Grape Soda"
        CASE 3
            total = total + .99
            LOCATE 7, 30
            gingerale = gingerale + 1
            PRINT gingerale, "Ginger Ale"
        CASE ELSE
            total = total + 1.29
            LOCATE 8, 30
            up6 = up6 + 1
            PRINT up6, "6-UP"
    END SELECT
    MENU ON
    RETURN

Initializevariables:
    itemnumber = 0
    hamburger = 0
    cheeseburger = 0
    chickenparts = 0
    fishsandwich = 0
    cola = 0
    grapesoda = 0
    gingerale = 0
    up6 = 0
    total = 0
    RETURN
```

Figure 13.8 Fast food order program with menus (part 3 of 3)

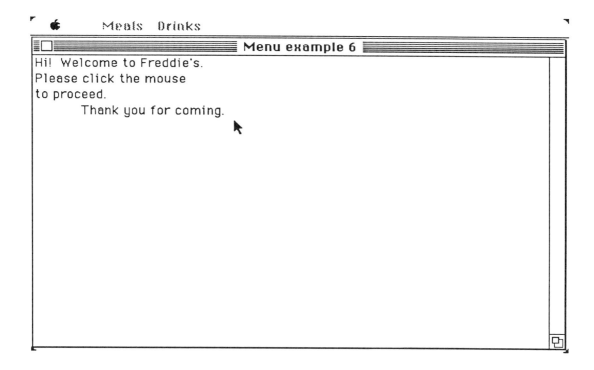

Figure 13.9 Freddie's Restaurant welcome message

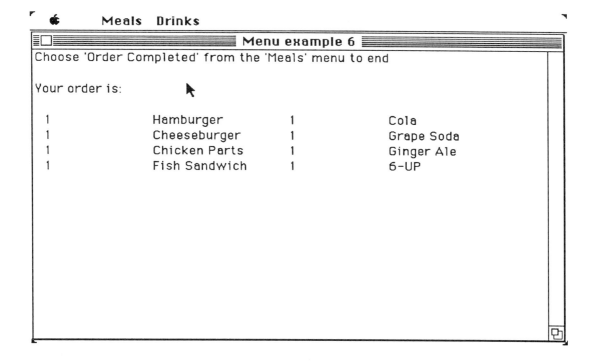

Figure 13.10 An order in progress

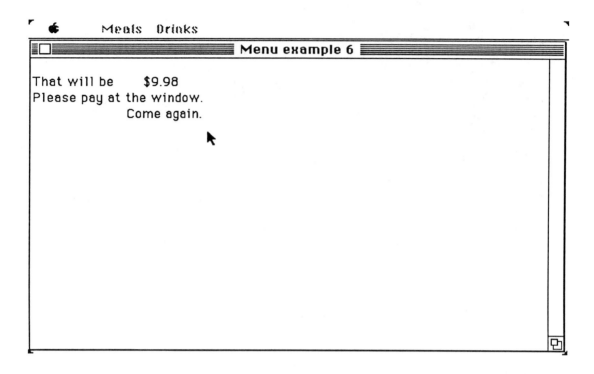

Figure 13.11 A completed order

Concepts

default menus	**MENU ON** statement
item number parameter in **MENU** statement	**MENU RESET** statement
menu	**MENU** statement
menu bar	**MENU** statement without parameters
menu event trapping	**MENU STOP** statement
MENU(0) function	**ON MENU GOSUB ...** statement
MENU(1) function	state parameter in **MENU** statement
menu number parameter in **MENU** statement	title parameter in **MENU** statement
MENU OFF statement	

Problems

13.1. Fill in the blanks in each of the following.

    (a) The _____ is where the titles of all the menus appear.

    (b) The _____ statement starts menu event trapping.

    (c) The _____ function determines which menu has been selected.

    (d) The _____ function determines which menu item has been selected.

    (e) The _____ statement returns the menu bar to the BASIC default menu.

    (f) There may be a maximum of _____ menus on the menu bar at once.

    (g) The _____ and _____ statements disable and suspend event trapping for menus.

    (h) The five BASIC default menus are _____, _____, _____, _____ , and _____.

    (i) The two BASIC default menus that appear when a program is run are _____ and _____.

13.2. Write a single BASIC statement that accomplishes each of the following.
- **(a)** Create the menu **Desserts** on the menu bar.
- **(b)** Make item 1 of the menu **Desserts** a **Banana split**.
- **(c)** Make item 2 of the menu **Desserts** an **Ice cream sundae**.
- **(d)** Make item 3 of the menu **Desserts** an **Orange sherbert**.
- **(e)** Dim the menu **Desserts**.
- **(f)** Dim only item 3 of the menu **Desserts**.
- **(g)** Erase item 3 from the menu **Desserts**.

13.3. Write a program that defines a dessert menu with ten items and their prices. Use a delay loop to give the person sufficient time to select the menu before the program ends.

13.4. Write a program using the menu created in Problem 13.3 that allows the user to make a choice. The program should then tell the user what item number was chosen and what the item was. The menu title should be unhighlighted after the choice.

13.5. Using event trapping and the menu created in Problem 13.3, write a BASIC program that allows the user to choose desserts. The program should provide a way for the user to stop making choices. It should then print the quantity of each dessert chosen and the total price of the order.

13.6. Incorporate the menu in Problem 13.3 into the example program at the end of the chapter. Use only four menu items in this menu.

13.7. (Airline Reservations System) At many airports today, travellers may select flights and reserve their seats by using automated reservation and ticketing systems. Write a BASIC program using random access files and menus that enables a traveller to select a seat on a single flight. The customer may choose smoking or nonsmoking, window seat or aisle seat, first class or tourist, near the wing or near the rest room, and so on. Your program should display menus with each of these options. As travellers reserve particular seats, print their tickets and indicate that those seats are no longer available. Include an option in your menus that allows a traveller to request a seating layout for the entire plane indicating which seats are occupied and which are available.

Chapter 14
Buttons

14.1 Introduction

Buttons are quite familiar in Macintosh applications. We use them, for example, each time we save or print a document. Button manipulation is not a regular feature of Microsoft BASIC. Rather it is unique to the Macintosh version of the language.

In this chapter we explain the three different types of Macintosh buttons and how to create them, how to use them, and how to do event trapping with buttons.

14.2 The BUTTON Statement

There is a single format for the **BUTTON** statement which includes five parameters as follows:

```
BUTTON  identification#, state, title, rectangle, type
```

This statement places a button on the screen; once on the screen, the button is automatically maintained by BASIC. For instance, if we close the output window and open it again, the button will still be there.

The *button identification parameter* gives BASIC a way to differentiate between the many buttons that may appear on the screen at once.

The *button state parameter* specifies how the button should be displayed on the screen. State 0 is for an inactive button that is dimmed, state 1 is for an active button that has not been selected, and state 2 is for an active button that has been selected.

The *button title parameter* enables us to label a button on the screen. For a type 1 button, the title is placed within the button; for type 2 and type 3 buttons the title is placed to the right of the button. Button types will be explained momentarily.

The *button rectangle parameter* indicates where to place the button on the screen, and how large the button should be. For type 1 buttons, this is the actual size of the rectangle with rounded corners, but for types 2 and 3, the rectangle defines an area large enough to include the button and its title. The coordinates of the rectangle are given in the form

```
(x1, y1) - (x2, y2)
```

These are the coordinates of the upper left and lower right corners of the rectangle, respectively.

The *button type parameter* specifies the button type. A type 1 button is called a *push button*, a type 2 button is called a *check box*, and a type 3 button is called a *radio button*. If the button type is not specified, then a type 1 button is assumed.

The program in Figure 14.1 places 9 buttons on the screen. Once defined, the buttons are maintained by the computer and cannot be removed unless they are closed or a new program is run. Figure 14.2 shows the output of the button display program.

```
REM    Displaying the three types of buttons
PRINT "      Meals                         Drinks"
BUTTON 1, 1, "Hamburger       $0.79", (5, 15)-(170, 30), 2
BUTTON 2, 1, "Cheeseburger    $0.89", (5, 35)-(170, 50), 2
BUTTON 3, 1, "Chicken Parts   $2.25", (5, 55)-(170, 70), 2
BUTTON 4, 1, "Fish Sandwich   $1.69", (5, 75)-(170, 90), 2
BUTTON 5, 1, "Cola            $0.99", (180, 15)-(345, 30), 3
BUTTON 6, 1, "Grape Soda      $1.09", (180, 35)-(345, 50), 3
BUTTON 7, 1, "Ginger Ale      $0.99", (180, 55)-(345, 70), 3
BUTTON 8, 1, "6-UP            $1.29", (180, 75)-(345, 90), 3
BUTTON 9, 1, "Order Completed", (30, 100)-(170, 120), 1
END
```

Figure 14.1 Displaying the three types of buttons

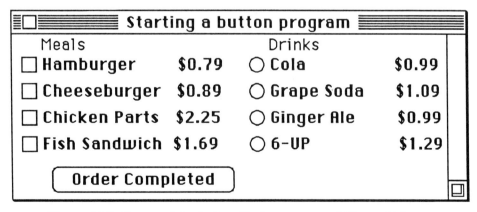

Figure 14.2 Output of the button display program of Figure 14.1

14.3 The BUTTON CLOSE n Statement

The **BUTTON CLOSE** n statement closes button number n. For example, the statement

```
BUTTON CLOSE 1
```

closes button number 1. This allows new information to be displayed on the screen. If this statement is not used, the button will remain on the screen and may interfere with any new output.

The program of Figure 14.3 puts 9 buttons on the screen for a few seconds then closes them and ends. Closing the buttons removes them from the screen. The **CLS** statement removes the headings "Meals" and "Drinks" from the screen.

```
REM    Displaying and then closing buttons
PRINT "      Meals                  Drinks"
BUTTON 1, 1, "Hamburger      $0.79", (5, 15)-(170, 30), 2
BUTTON 2, 1, "Cheeseburger   $0.89", (5, 35)-(170, 50), 2
BUTTON 3, 1, "Chicken Parts  $2.25", (5, 55)-(170, 70), 2
BUTTON 4, 1, "Fish Sandwich  $1.69", (5, 75)-(170, 90), 2
BUTTON 5, 1, "Cola           $0.99", (180, 15)-(345, 30), 3
BUTTON 6, 1, "Grape Soda     $1.09", (180, 35)-(345, 50), 3
BUTTON 7, 1, "Ginger Ale     $0.99", (180, 55)-(345, 70), 3
BUTTON 8, 1, "6-UP           $1.29", (180, 75)-(345, 90), 3
BUTTON 9, 1, "Order Completed", (30, 100)-(170, 120), 1

FOR x = 1 TO 12000
NEXT x

FOR n = 1 TO 9
   BUTTON CLOSE n
NEXT n
CLS
END
```

Figure 14.3 Displaying and then closing buttons

14.4 Determining and Changing the State of a Button

During program execution, it may be necessary to determine the state of a particular button. The statement

```
BUTTON(Id#)
```

returns the state of the button numbered Id#. The value returned by the **BUTTON** function may be used directly, or it may be saved in a variable for future use.

It may also be necessary to change the state of a button. For example, once a button has been selected, we may want to dim that button so it may not be selected again. This would be rather time consuming if we had to retype the entire button statement for that button each time we wanted to change the state, so there is a simple, two parameter statement that does this for us.

```
BUTTON  Id#, state
```

This statement changes the state of the button numbered Id# to the specified state.

14.5 The DIALOG(0) Function

The DIALOG(0) function is used to determine if any of a number of so-called *dialog events* has occurred. Dialog events include button activity, and window and edit field activity (see Chapter 15).

If a button has been pressed in the active window, then DIALOG(0) returns 1. DIALOG(0) returns 0 if there has not been a dialog event since the previous execution of DIALOG(0). As we will see in Chapter 15, DIALOG(0) returns values in the range 2 through 7 to indicate various events related to edit fields and windows; the appropriate processing for each of these values will be explained in Chapter 15.

The DIALOG(0) function is commonly used in a WHILE/WEND wait loop such as

```
buttonselect = 0
WHILE buttonselect = 0
    buttonselect = DIALOG(0)
WEND
```

or an IF/THEN statement such as

```
IF DIALOG(0) = 1 THEN ...
```

14.6 The DIALOG(1) Function

The DIALOG(1) function returns the identification number of the button that has been selected. The statement combination

```
buttonnumber = DIALOG(1)
ON buttonnumber GOSUB ...
```

directs the program to transfer control to the subroutine that handles processing for the button that was pushed. It is important to note that DIALOG(1) only works properly after DIALOG(0) has been executed.

The program in Figure 14.4 uses the DIALOG(0) and DIALOG(1) functions to determine whether or not a button has been pushed, and if one has, which one it was. If the Order Completed button is pushed, the program dims the buttons for several seconds, and then closes them one at a time. The output of Figure 14.4 appears in Figure 14.5; it shows a button that has been clicked and the button number that was chosen. An example showing dimmed buttons is presented later in this chapter.

```
REM     Using DIALOG(0) and DIALOG(1), and changing the button state
PRINT "        Meals               Drinks"
BUTTON 1, 1, "Hamburger      $0.79", (5, 15)-(170, 30), 2
BUTTON 2, 1, "Cheeseburger   $0.89", (5, 35)-(170, 50), 2
BUTTON 3, 1, "Chicken Parts  $2.25", (5, 55)-(170, 70), 2
BUTTON 4, 1, "Fish Sandwich  $1.69", (5, 75)-(170, 90), 2
BUTTON 5, 1, "Cola           $0.99", (180, 15)-(345, 30), 3
BUTTON 6, 1, "Grape Soda     $1.09", (180, 35)-(345, 50), 3
BUTTON 7, 1, "Ginger Ale     $0.99", (180, 55)-(345, 70), 3
BUTTON 8, 1, "6-UP           $1.29", (180, 75)-(345, 90), 3
BUTTON 9, 1, "Order completed", (30, 100)-(170, 120), 1

WHILE buttonnumber <> 9
   buttonselect = 0
   WHILE buttonselect <> 1
      buttonselect = DIALOG(0)
   WEND
   buttonnumber = DIALOG(1)
   LOCATE 9,1
   PRINT "You chose button number "; buttonnumber
WEND
FOR n = 1 TO 9
   BUTTON n, 0
NEXT n
FOR x = 1 TO 2000
NEXT x
FOR n = 1 TO 9
   BUTTON CLOSE n
NEXT n
CLS
END
```

Figure 14.4 Using **DIALOG**(0) and **DIALOG**(1), and changing the button state

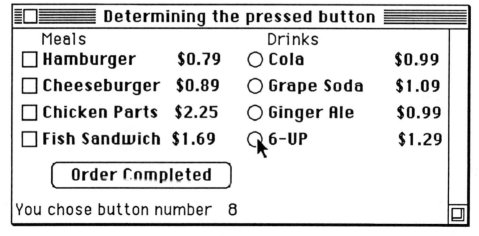

Figure 14.5 Output of the program of Figure 14.4

14.7 Event Trapping with Buttons

The four statements used for event trapping with buttons are

```
ON DIALOG GOSUB...
DIALOG ON
DIALOG STOP
DIALOG OFF
```

The ON DIALOG GOSUB statement waits for any of a series of Macintosh dialog events to occur. In this chapter we are concerned with button selections. In subsequent chapters, we shall deal with other types of events monitored by the ON DIALOG mechanism. For now we confine our attention to button selections as in Figure 14.6.

```
REM    A simple event trapping program with buttons
PRINT "      Meals                Drinks"
BUTTON 1, 1, "Hamburger      $0.79", (5, 15)-(170, 30), 2
BUTTON 2, 1, "Cheeseburger   $0.89", (5, 35)-(170, 50), 2
BUTTON 3, 1, "Chicken Parts  $2.25", (5, 55)-(170, 70), 2
BUTTON 4, 1, "Fish Sandwich  $1.69", (5, 75)-(170, 90), 2
BUTTON 5, 1, "Cola           $0.99", (180, 15)-(345, 30), 3
BUTTON 6, 1, "Grape Soda     $1.09", (180, 35)-(345, 50), 3
BUTTON 7, 1, "Ginger Ale     $0.99", (180, 55)-(345, 70), 3
BUTTON 8, 1, "6-UP           $1.29", (180, 75)-(345, 90), 3
BUTTON 9, 1, "Order Completed", (30, 100)-(170, 120), 1
ON DIALOG GOSUB Processbutton
DIALOG ON

donextperson = 1
WHILE donextperson = 1
WEND
END

Processbutton:
   DIALOG OFF
   buttonselect = DIALOG(0)
   buttonnumber = DIALOG(1)
   IF buttonnumber < 9 THEN
      LOCATE 9, 1
      PRINT "You chose button number "; buttonnumber
      DIALOG ON
   ELSE
      donextperson = 0
      FOR n = 1 TO 9
            BUTTON CLOSE n
      NEXT n
      CLS
      PRINT "Button demo finished"
      FOR x = 1 TO 2000
      NEXT x
   END IF
   RETURN
```

Figure 14.6 A simple event trapping program

The ON DIALOG GOSUB waits for a button to be selected, and branches off to the indicated button processing subroutine. Event trapping must be enabled with DIALOG ON in order for this to work. Once the program has branched to the processing subroutine, the event trapping feature should be suspended with DIALOG STOP or disabled with DIALOG OFF so that the processing subroutine is not interrupted. When the program is ready to wait for another selection, the event trapping should be turned on again with DIALOG ON.

The program in Figure 14.6 uses event trapping to determine if a button has been pressed, and, if so, which one. The output for this program is identical to that of Figure 14.5. If the **Order Completed** button is selected in this program, the buttons are all closed, and the message Button demo finished is printed.

Example 14.1   A fast food drive-up with buttons

Write a program that lets customers at a drive-up window press a push button to indicate that they are ready to order. After the button is pushed, it should be closed, and a menu using radio buttons and check boxes should appear along with a push button to press to finish ordering. As a customer orders, the program should display the order under the menu (use the **LOCATE** statement to position to the appropriate location on the screen before printing each item with the number of that item ordered). When the order is complete, the program should dim all the buttons and print the total price. After a short wait, the program should reinitialize the screen to prepare for the next customer. If the total price equals zero, i.e., if nothing was ordered, the program should close all the buttons and terminate.

The program is shown in Figure 14.7. Its various displays are shown in Figures 14.8, 14.9, and 14.10.

```
REM    Fast food button program
donextperson = 1
WHILE donextperson = 1
   GOSUB Initializevariables
   CLS
   PRINT "Hi!  Welcome to Freddie's."
   PRINT "Please press the order button"
   PRINT "When you are ready to order."
   PRINT "           Thank you for coming."
   BUTTON 10, 1, "Order", (30, 100)-(110, 120), 1
   buttonselect = 0
   WHILE buttonselect <> 1
      buttonselect = DIALOG(0)
   WEND
   BUTTON CLOSE 10
   CLS
   PRINT "     Meals                Drinks"
   BUTTON 1, 1, "Hamburger      $0.79", (5, 15)-(170, 30), 2
   BUTTON 2, 1, "Cheeseburger   $0.89", (5, 35)-(170, 50), 2
   BUTTON 3, 1, "Chicken Parts  $2.25", (5, 55)-(170, 70), 2
   BUTTON 4, 1, "Fish Sandwich  $1.69", (5, 75)-(170, 90), 2
   BUTTON 5, 1, "Cola           $0.99", (180, 15)-(345, 30), 3
   BUTTON 6, 1, "Grape Soda     $1.09", (180, 35)-(345, 50), 3
```
                                                          continued

Figure 14.7 Fast food button program (part 1 of 3)

continued

```
    BUTTON 7, 1, "Ginger Ale    $0.99", (180, 55)-(345, 70), 3
    BUTTON 8, 1, "6-UP          $1.29", (180, 75)-(345, 90), 3
    BUTTON 9, 1, "Order Completed", (30, 100)-(170, 120), 1
    ON DIALOG GOSUB Processbutton
    DIALOG ON
    persondone = 0
    WHILE persondone = 0
    WEND
WEND
END

Processbutton:
    DIALOG STOP
    buttonselect = DIALOG(0)
    buttonnumber = DIALOG(1)
    IF buttonnumber <> 9 THEN
        GOSUB Meals
        ELSE
            GOSUB Endorder
    END IF
    RETURN

Endorder:
    FOR n = 1 TO 9
        BUTTON n, 0
    NEXT n
    persondone = 1
    IF total <> 0 THEN
        CLS
        PRINT "     Meals                 Drinks"
        LOCATE 10, 1
        PRINT USING "That will be $$###.##"; total
        PRINT "Please pay at the window."
        PRINT "              Come again."
        FOR x = 1 TO 7000: NEXT x
        GOSUB Closebuttons
        DIALOG OFF
        ELSE
            donextperson = 0
            GOSUB Closebuttons
    END IF
    RETURN

Meals:
    SELECT CASE buttonnumber
        CASE 1
            LOCATE 10, 1
            total = total + .79
            hamburger = hamburger + 1
            PRINT hamburger, "Hamburger"
```

continued

Figure 14.7 Fast food button program (part 2 of 3)

```
        CASE 2                                      continued
            LOCATE 11, 1
            total = total + .89
            cheeseburger = cheeseburger + 1
            PRINT cheeseburger, "Cheeseburger"
        CASE 3
            LOCATE 12, 1
            total = total + 2.25
            chickenparts = chickenparts + 1
            PRINT  chickenparts, "Chicken Parts"
        CASE 4
            LOCATE 13, 1
            total = total + 1.69
            fishsandwich = fishsandwich + 1
            PRINT fishsandwich, "Fish Sandwich"
        CASE 5
            LOCATE 10, 30
            total = total + .99
            cola = cola + 1
            PRINT cola, "Cola"
        CASE 6
            LOCATE 11, 30
            total = total + 1.09
            grapesoda = grapesoda + 1
            PRINT grapesoda, "Grape Soda"
        CASE 7
            LOCATE 12, 30
            total = total + .99
            gingerale = gingerale + 1
            PRINT gingerale, "Ginger Ale"
        CASE 8
            LOCATE 13, 30
            total = total + 1.29
            up6 = up6 + 1
            PRINT up6, "6-UP"
    END  SELECT
    RETURN

Closebuttons:
    FOR n = 1 TO 9
        BUTTON CLOSE n
    NEXT n
    CLS
    RETURN

Initializevariables:
    hamburger = 0
    cheeseburger = 0
    chickenparts = 0
    fishsandwich = 0
    cola = 0
    grapesoda = 0
    gingerale = 0
    up6 = 0
    total = 0
    RETURN
```

Figure 14.7 Fast food button program (part 3 of 3)

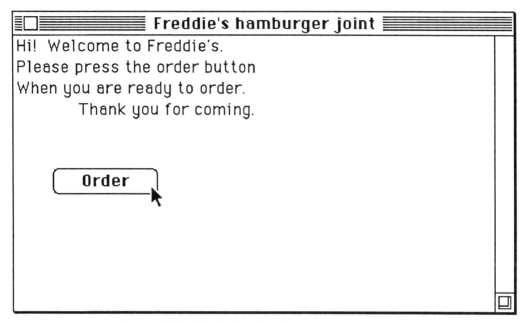

Figure 14.8 Displaying the first push button

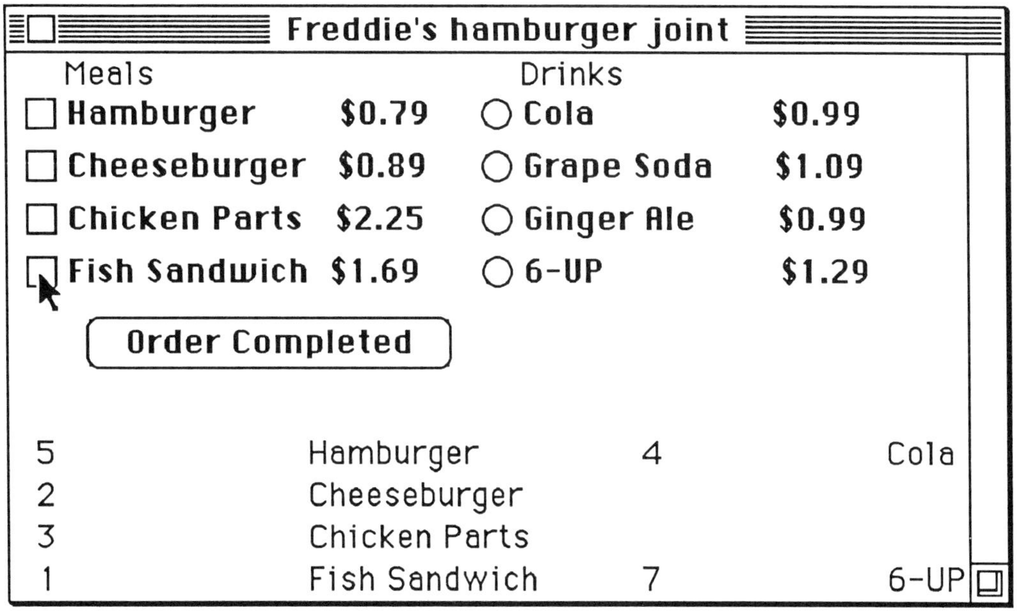

Figure 14.9 Displaying all three types of buttons

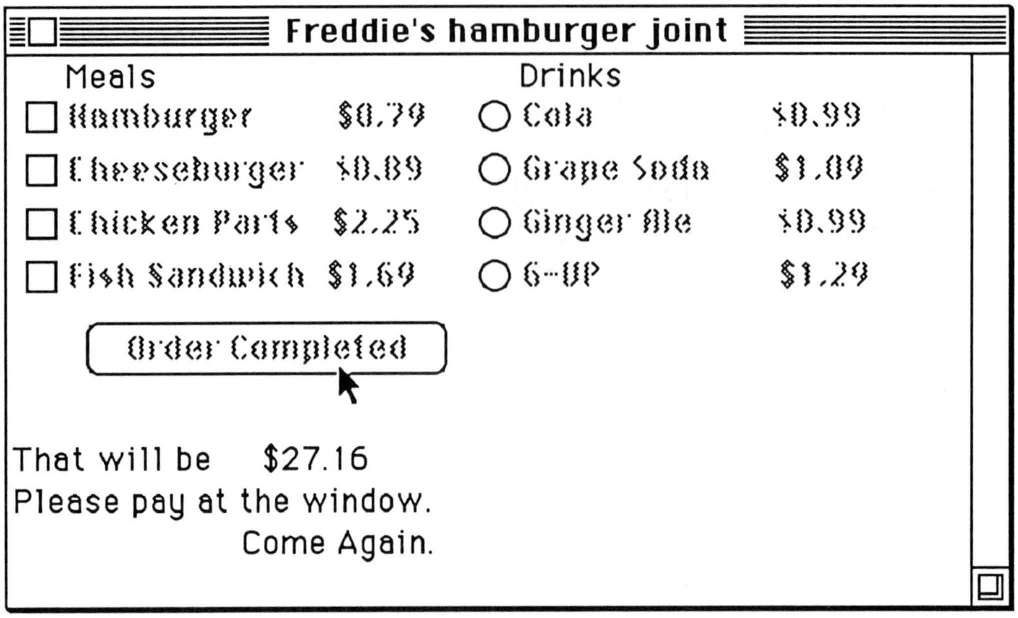

Figure 14.10 Display with all buttons dimmed

Concepts

button
BUTTON CLOSE n statement
button event trapping
BUTTON(Id#) function
BUTTON Id#,State statement
button identification parameter
button state parameter
BUTTON statement
button title parameter
button type parameter
check box

dialog events
DIALOG(0) function
DIALOG(1) function
DIALOG OFF statement
DIALOG ON statement
DIALOG STOP statement
LOCATE statement
ON DIALOG GOSUB... statement
push button
radio button

Problems

14.1. Fill in the blanks in each of the following.
    (a) The _____ function finds the number of the most recently pushed button.
    (b) The _____ statement is used to position to a certain point on the screen for the placement of text.
    (c) The _____ statement creates a button.
    (d) The _____ statement changes the state of a button.
    (e) The _____ statement disables event trapping for buttons.
    (f) The _____ statement enables event trapping for buttons.
    (g) The _____ function returns 1 if a button has been pushed or 0 if no button has been pushed.
    (h) The _____ statement suspends event trapping for buttons.

14.2. Write a single BASIC statement that accomplishes each of the following.
- **(a)** Create a push button with the title "Push".
- **(b)** Create a radio button with the title "Radio".
- **(c)** Create a check box with the title "Check".
- **(d)** Set the variable `buttonpush` equal to a function that determines whether or not a button has been pushed.
- **(e)** Disable event trapping of buttons.
- **(f)** Enable event trapping of buttons.
- **(g)** Set the variable `buttonnumber` equal to a function that determines what button number has been pressed.
- **(h)** Change the state of button number 1 to dimmed.
- **(i)** Suspend event trapping of buttons.

14.3. Modify the program in Figure 14.4 so that it displays the item name in addition to the button number.

14.4. Write a BASIC program that displays a list of tools and their prices to enable a customer to order tools. Each tool should have its own button. The program should use event trapping to wait for button selections to be made. It should print out the quantity of each tool purchased, the name of that tool, and the total price for the number of that tool ordered. When the customer is finished ordering tools, all the buttons should be dimmed, and the grand total should be printed. If the total is zero, the program should close all the buttons and end.

14.5. Look at any pocket calculator. Using buttons, create a screen-based calculator that completely simulates the operation of the pocket calculator.

14.6. Write a BASIC program with buttons that simulates a typewriter. As the user clicks a button, the program should display the character the button represents.

Chapter 15
Windows, Dialog Boxes,
and Edit Fields

15.1 Introduction

This chapter discusses how to use windows, dialog boxes, and edit fields in Macintosh BASIC programs. We consider the various **WINDOW** and **DIALOG** events that can occur, how to tell when they have occurred, how to refresh a window that has just been uncovered, and how to create and use edit fields.

15.2 Windows

There are seven different types of windows that can be created in Macintosh QuickBASIC, namely *document windows with or without grow boxes*, *document windows with zoom boxes*, *rounded corner document windows*, *bordered dialog boxes*, *plain dialog boxes*, and *shadowed dialog boxes* (see Figure 15.2). All seven types of windows may hold text and graphics.

15.3 The WINDOW Statement

The **WINDOW** statement displays a window on the screen. As many as sixteen windows may be displayed at once, but only one of these may be *active*. The **WINDOW** statement has four parameters as follows:

```
WINDOW  Id#, "title", rectangle, type
```

The *window identification number parameter* gives the computer a way of distinguishing between several different windows.

The *window title parameter* can only be displayed on document windows. If no title is desired, the " " notation is used to skip the title parameter, and nothing will appear in the title bar. For dialog box windows, the title parameter is omitted, but a comma must be used to skip the space where the title parameter would have appeared in the statement.

The *window rectangle parameter* gives the coordinates of the upper-left and lower-right corners of the window. With this parameter we have the ability to place a window anywhere on the screen and make it any size.

The *window type parameter* specifies the window type: 1 is for a document window with a close box and grow box, 2 is for a bordered dialog box, 3 is for a plain dialog box, 4 is for a shadowed dialog box, 5 is for a plain document window, 6 is for a rounded document window with a close box, and 7 is for a document window with close box, grow box, and zoom box. All document windows can be moved to different places on the screen by dragging the title bar (at the top of the window), window types 1, 6, and 7 can be closed by clicking the close box (at the upper left corner of the window), window types 1 and 7 can be resized by dragging the grow box (at the bottom right of the window), and by pressing the zoom box of window type 7 (at the upper right of the window), the window can be enlarged to the full screen. The program in Figure 15.1 displays the first four types of windows: the outputs are shown in Figure 15.2.

```
REM    Displaying the first four types of windows
WINDOW 1, "Document window", (30, 50)-(200, 100),1

WINDOW 2,, (30, 115)-(200, 165), 2
PRINT "Bordered dialog box"

WINDOW 3,, (215, 50)-(385, 100), 3
PRINT "Plain dialog box"

WINDOW 4,, (215, 115)-(385, 165), 4
PRINT "Shadowed dialog box"
```

Figure 15.1 Program that displays the first four types of windows

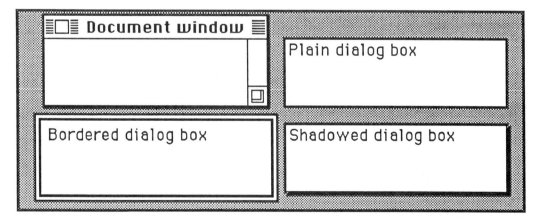

Figure 15.2 The first four types of windows

15.4 The WINDOW Statements

There are three other **WINDOW** statements in Microsoft QuickBASIC for the Macintosh, namely

```
WINDOW Id#
WINDOW OUTPUT Id#
WINDOW CLOSE Id#
```

The **WINDOW** Id# statement makes window number Id# active and *current*. This means that the window can accept input, display output, and respond to the mouse.

The **WINDOW OUTPUT** Id# statement causes window number Id# to become the *current output window* but not necessarily the active window. This means that the program can display output in another window without disturbing the active window. In order to use this statement, a **WINDOW** x statement must first be used to make window x active and current; then a **WINDOW OUTPUT** y must be used to make window y current.

The **WINDOW CLOSE** Id# statement may be used to close a window at any time. The window may be reopened by using the **WINDOW** Id# statement.

The program in Figure 15.3 makes window 1 active and current, then makes window 2 current instead, and prints the output in window 2 (Figure 15.4).

```
REM    Using the WINDOW statement
WINDOW 1, "Window 1", (40, 40)-(240,240), 1
WINDOW 2, "Window 2", (250, 40)-(450, 240), 1
WINDOW 1
WINDOW OUTPUT 2
FOR n = 1 TO 100 STEP 2
    CIRCLE (100,100), n
NEXT n
FOR x = 1 TO 10000
NEXT x
WINDOW CLOSE 1
WINDOW CLOSE 2
```

Figure 15.3 Using the **WINDOW** statements

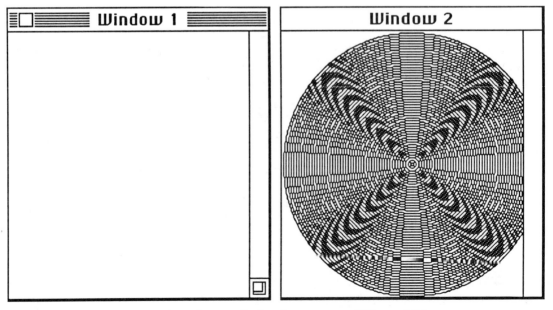

Figure 15.4 Screen display for program of Figure 15.3

15.5 The WINDOW Functions

Six WINDOW functions in QuickBASIC return various useful facts. These functions are WINDOW(0), WINDOW(1), WINDOW(2), WINDOW(3), WINDOW(4), and WINDOW(5).

The WINDOW(0) function returns the identification number of the active output window. If no output window is active, WINDOW(0) returns 0.

The WINDOW(1) function returns the identification number of the current output window. The current output window is the one in which the next print or graphics display will appear.

The WINDOW(2) function returns the width of the current output window in pixels, and the WINDOW(3) function returns the height of the current output window in pixels. These functions can be useful when we are looking to fit a certain output, either graphic or text, in a window. The WIDTH(string) function returns the width of a string in pixels. This combined with the WINDOW(2) function can help determine the length of a line of text or the width of an output window to help position text in the window.

The WINDOW(4) and WINDOW(5) functions return the x and y pixel coordinates, respectively, of the position in the current output window where the next character in a line of text will appear.

15.6 Refreshing Windows

We need to *refresh a window*, i.e., redisplay it, after having dragged something over the window and off again. We also need to refresh a window after clicking on it to make it active. The remainder of this section develops the large window refreshing demonstration program of Figure 15.8.

The PICTURE ON and PICTURE OFF statements must be placed around the program lines that create a picture. The picture may then be captured with the PICTURE$ function. The program in Figure 15.5 creates a picture and stores it in a string variable for future use.

```
REM    Recording a picture
WINDOW 1, "Example Window 1", (40, 40)-(240, 240), 1
PICTURE ON
FOR n = 1 TO 50
    x1 = INT(RND*200) + 1
    y1 = INT(RND*200) + 1
    x2 = INT(RND*200) + 1
    y2 = INT(RND*200) + 1
    LINE (x1, y1)-(x2, y2),,b
NEXT n
PICTURE OFF
graphic$(1) = PICTURE$
```

Figure 15.5 Recording a picture

Now our first picture is saved. (Keep in mind that there are actually two windows and two pictures in the demonstration program.) The next step is determining when the picture needs to be refreshed. This is done with the **DIALOG**(0) function whose possible values are

0	no event has occurred
1	a button was clicked
2	an inactive edit field was clicked
3	an inactive document window was clicked to make it active
4	the close box of a document window was clicked
5	a document window was dragged, thus uncovering another window
6	the Return key was pressed to accept data from an edit field
7	the Tab key was pressed to switch edit fields

Events 3 and 5 require that a window be refreshed. The program segment in Figure 15.6 checks for this.

```
WHILE waitloop <> 99
    windowevent = 0
    WHILE windowevent = 0
       windowevent = DIALOG(0)
    WEND
    IF windowevent = 3 OR windowevent = 5 THEN
       GOSUB Refreshwindow
       ELSEIF windowevent = 4 THEN
          waitloop = 99
    END IF
WEND
```

Figure 15.6 The waiting loop

The program enters the loop and waits for an event to occur. If the event is a 3 or a 5, the program refreshes the window in which the event occurred. If the event is a 4, the close box was clicked in one of the windows and the program terminates.

Finally, we consider the Refreshwindow subroutine shown in Figure 15.7.

```
Refreshwindow:
    windowrefresh = DIALOG(windowevent)
    WINDOW windowrefresh
    PICTURE, graphic$(windowrefresh)
    RETURN
```

Figure 15.7 Window refreshing subroutine

First the subroutine determines the window in which the event occurred by using **DIALOG**(windowevent). **DIALOG**(3) returns the number of the most recently selected output window, **DIALOG**(4) returns the number of the window whose close box was clicked most recently, and **DIALOG**(5) returns the number of the output window that needs to be refreshed. This information is then used to make the window active with **WINDOW** windowrefresh. The statement **PICTURE,** graphic$(windowrefresh) redraws the picture in the window. If you would like to scale a picture that has already been recorded, a set of rectangle coordinates can be added as follows:

```
PICTURE (xstart, ystart)-(xend,yend), graphic$(windowrefresh)
```

The new coordinates will cause the picture to be scaled to that size in the window. When the picture has been redrawn, the program waits for the next event. If the close box on one of the windows is clicked, the program ends. The program is shown in Figure 15.8. The two pictures produced by this program are shown in Figure 15.9. The effect of dragging one window on top of another is shown in Figure 15.10. The effect of clicking on a partially covered window and causing it to be refreshed is shown in Figure 15.11.

```
REM    Window refreshing program
WINDOW 1, "Example Window 1", (40, 40)-(240, 240), 1
PICTURE ON
FOR n = 1 TO 50
    x1 = INT(RND*200) + 1
    y1 = INT(RND*200) + 1
    x2 = INT(RND*200) + 1
    y2 = INT(RND*200) + 1
    LINE (x1, y1)-(x2, y2),,b
NEXT n
PICTURE OFF
graphic$(1) = PICTURE$

WINDOW 2, "Example Window 2", (250, 40)-(450, 240), 1
PICTURE ON
FOR n = 1 TO 50
    x = INT(RND*200) + 1
    y = INT(RND*200) + 1
    CIRCLE(x, y), n
NEXT n
PICTURE OFF
graphic$(2) = PICTURE$

WHILE waitloop <> 99
    windowevent = 0
    WHILE windowevent = 0
        windowevent = DIALOG(0)
    WEND
    IF windowevent = 3 OR windowevent = 5 THEN
        GOSUB Refreshwindow
        ELSEIF windowevent = 4 THEN
            waitloop = 99
    END IF
WEND
END

Refreshwindow:
    windowrefresh = DIALOG(windowevent)
    WINDOW windowrefresh
    PICTURE, graphic$(windowrefresh)
    RETURN
```

Figure 15.8 Window refreshing program

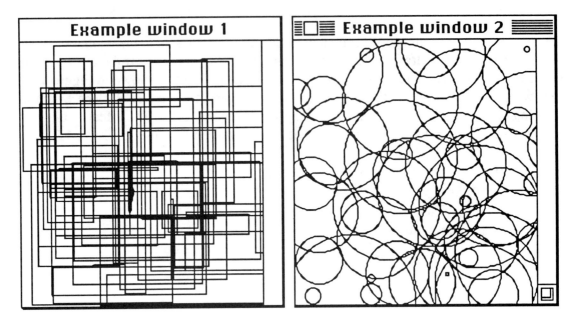

Figure 15.9 The two pictures produced by the program of Figure 15.8

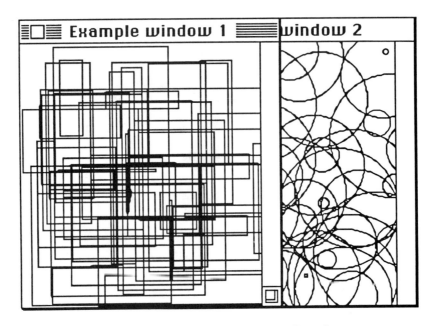

Figure 15.10 Dragging one window on top of another

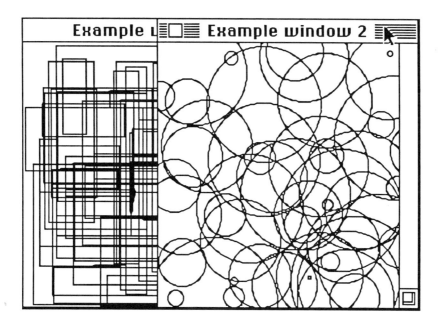

Figure 15.11 Clicking on a partially covered window and causing it to be refreshed

15.7 Using Windows as Dialog Boxes

The bordered dialog box, plain dialog box, and shadowed dialog box are all used by the Macintosh quite frequently to display error messages and to input information such as with the Save dialog box used when saving files. When inputting information, the dialog boxes often use edit fields as well as buttons. The next several sections explain how we program these features for use in BASIC programs.

15.8 The EDIT FIELD Statement

Edit fields in QuickBASIC offer the standard editing capabilities like cutting, pasting, and positioning the mouse and text, as well as the ability to press a button to enter information instead of having to press the return key.

The **EDIT FIELD** statement creates an edit field. The format is as follows:

```
EDIT FIELD Id#, Default, Rectangle
```

The identification number enables the Macintosh to distinguish between the different edit fields in a window. There may be any number of edit fields in a window; however, if an **EDIT FIELD** statement is executed with the identification number of a previous one, the latter edit field will replace the former.

The default is a string that will automatically appear in the edit field when the statement is executed. This is often used when the user's input can be anticipated. If for some reason this is not what the user would like to enter, the user can delete the default string and type new information. If no default string is desired, a "" (empty string) is typed instead. This leaves the edit field empty when it appears on the screen.

The rectangle parameter defines the size of the edit field and its location within the dialog box. The first set of coordinates defines the upper left corner; the second set of coordinates defines the lower right corner.

```
WINDOW 4,, (20, 60)-(300, 170), 2
EDIT FIELD 1, "This is an edit field", (20, 20)-(190, 35)
```

Figure 15.12 Creating an edit field

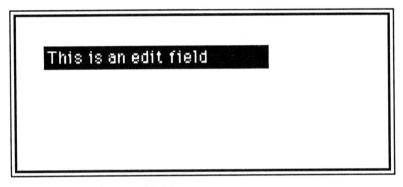

Figure 15.13

The program of Figure 15.12 creates the dialog box and edit field shown in Figure 15.13. Notice that the default string in the edit field is highlighted when the program is run, so the information in the edit field can be erased by hitting any key if this information is incorrect.

Now that we know how to create edit fields, let us consider how to monitor them and capture the information entered into them.

15.9 Using an Edit Field

Once an edit field has been created, control proceeds to the next executable statement in the program. We must, therefore, include a loop that waits for a dialog event. This is accomplished with the following statements.

```
WHILE DIALOG(0) <> 1 AND DIALOG(0) <> 6
WEND
```

Remember that dialog event 1 occurs when a button is pushed and dialog event 6 occurs when the Return key is pressed in an edit field. These two events are the normal ways in which information is entered through an edit field.

Next, the information must be assigned to a string variable. Information that is entered through an edit field is automatically stored in the EDIT$ function. This function, like the PICTURE$ function used in the window refreshing section, must be used for all information entered into an edit field. Therefore, in order to store this information for use in our program, we must save it in a string variable using a statement such as

```
entry$ = EDIT$(1)
```

The "(1)" after EDIT$ indicates the edit field from which the information to be assigned to entry$ is coming. We can also enter numeric data through an edit field, but the VAL function must be used to convert the data from string variable format to numeric variable format.

The program of Figure 15.14 begins with a default string in the edit field. We can type anything in the field and press the OK button, and it is printed in the document window as in Figure 15.15. We can also press the Return key on the keyboard and the information will be printed in the document widow. If the Done button is pressed, the program ends. The entry in an edit field does not have to fit inside the field, and the edit field can occupy more than one line. In both of these cases, the entry is a single line when printed on the screen.

```
REM    Using an edit field
WINDOW 2, "Output", (13, 175)-(293, 265), 1
WINDOW 4,, (20, 60)-(250, 140), 2
EDIT FIELD 1, "This is an edit field", (10, 10)-(180, 25)
BUTTON 1, 1, "OK", (20, 40)-(80, 65)
BUTTON 2 , 1, "Done", (90, 40)-(150, 65)

buttonnumber = 0
WHILE buttonnumber <> 2
   WINDOW 4
   dialogevent = DIALOG(0)
   WHILE dialogevent <> 6 AND dialogevent <> 1
     dialogevent = DIALOG(0)
   WEND

   buttonnumber = DIALOG(1)
   IF buttonnumber <> 2 THEN
      entry$ = EDIT$(1)
      WINDOW 2
      PRINT "The entry in the edit field was:"
      PRINT entry$
   END IF
WEND
END
```

Figure 15.14 Using an edit field

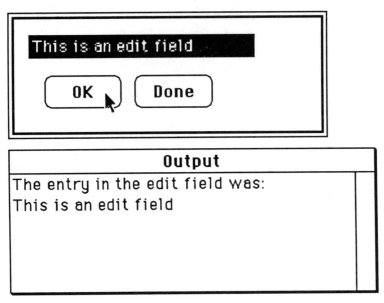

Figure 15.15 Using an edit field

Figure 15.16 presents an example of an edit field with more than one line; its display is shown in Figure 15.17. If an entry in a multiline edit field is too long for one line, it is automatically wrapped around to the next line.

```
WINDOW 4,, (20, 60)-(300, 170), 2
EDIT FIELD 1, "This is an edit field", (20, 20)-(190, 80)
BUTTON 1, 1, "OK", (200, 20)-(260, 45)
BUTTON 2 , 1, "Done", (200, 55)-(260, 80)
```

Figure 15.16 Multiline edit field

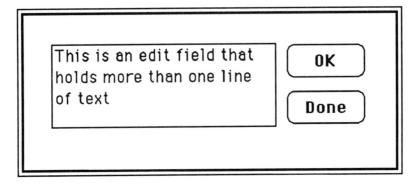

Figure 15.17 Display of a multiline edit field

In a dialog box with multiple edit fields, it is possible to shift between edit fields in two ways. The first is to click the mouse with the pointer in an edit field, and the second is to press the Tab key. A dialog event 7 occurs when the Tab key is pressed. Unfortunately, the computer will not automatically change edit fields for us, so we must program this ourselves. The program of Figure 15.18 demonstrates this capability; its display is shown in Figure 15.19.

```
REM    Edit fields with all edit features incorporated
WINDOW 2, "Output", (13, 186)-(305, 286), 1
WINDOW 4,, (20, 60)-(300, 155), 2
LOCATE 1, 3
PRINT "Last name"
EDIT FIELD 1, "", (20, 20)-(190, 35)
LOCATE 4, 3
PRINT "First name"
EDIT FIELD 2, "", (20, 70)-(190, 85)
BUTTON 1, 1, "OK", (200, 20)-(260, 45)
BUTTON 2 , 1, "Done", (200, 55)-(260, 80)
EDIT FIELD 1
numfields = 2
fieldnumber = 1

buttonnumber = 0
WHILE buttonnumber <> 2
   WINDOW 4
   dialogevent = DIALOG(0)
   WHILE dialogevent <> 6 AND dialogevent <> 1
      dialogevent = DIALOG(0)
      IF dialogevent = 7 THEN
         IF fieldnumber < numfields THEN
            fieldnumber = fieldnumber + 1
         ELSE
            fieldnumber = 1
         END IF
         EDIT FIELD fieldnumber
      END IF
   WEND

   buttonnumber = DIALOG(1)
   IF buttonnumber <> 2 THEN
      lastname$ = EDIT$(1)
      firstname$ = EDIT$(2)
      WINDOW 2
      PRINT firstname$;" "; lastname$
   END IF
WEND
END
```

Figure 15.18 Edit fields with all edit features incorporated

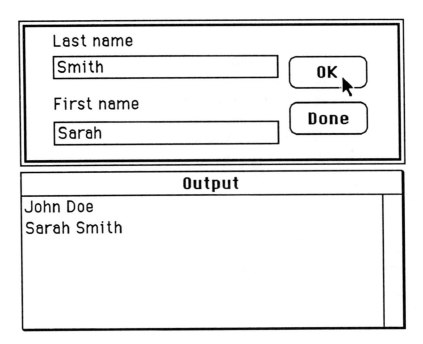

Figure 15.19 Display produced by Figure 15.18

This program to uses two edit fields to type a first and last name. We can switch between the fields using either the mouse or the Tab key, we can enter the data using either the OK button or the Return key, and we can use all the standard edit features including cutting, pasting, and placing the cursor anywhere within each edit field. The program is ended by pressing the Done button.

Concepts

active window
bordered dialog box
close box
current output window
DIALOG(0)
dialog box
document window
edit field
EDIT FIELD statement
EDIT$ function
grow box
PICTURE$ function
PICTURE OFF statement
PICTURE ON statement
PICTURE statement
plain dialog box
refresh a window
shadowed dialog box

VAL function
window
WINDOW CLOSE Id# statement
WINDOW(0) function
WINDOW(1) function
WINDOW(2) function
WINDOW(3) function
WINDOW(4) function
WINDOW(5) function
WINDOW Id# statement
window identification number parameter
WINDOW OUTPUT Id# statement
window rectangle parameter
WINDOW statement
window title parameter
window type parameter
zoom box

Problems

15.1. Fill in the blanks in each of the following.
   (a) The _____ statement makes a specified window active and current.
   (b) The _____ statement makes a specified window current.
   (c) A window is closed with the _____ statement.
   (d) The _____ function returns the number of the active window.
   (e) A way to enter information other than with an INPUT statement is with an _____.
   (f) When a picture is recorded, it is captured in the _____ function.
   (g) The _____ statement is used to create an edit field.
   (h) The _____ statement is used to create a window.
   (i) The _____ statement is used to turn on the picture recording capability.

15.2. Write a single BASIC statement that accomplishes each of the following.
   (a) Create an edit field with the default string "Edit Field."
   (b) Create a type 1 window of any size.
   (c) State that all output will go to window number 3.
   (d) Close window number 2.
   (e) Turn off the picture recording capability.
   (f) Set the variable `image$(1)` equal to a function that captures a recorded picture.
   (g) Set the variable `information$(1)` equal to a function that captures any information entered through an edit field.
   (h) Set the variable `windowevent` equal to a function that determines when an event has occurred.

15.3. Write a basic program that creates four different types of windows and places a picture in each one.

15.4. Write a BASIC program that creates two windows. Make one window active and the other current. Display circles of random size at random locations in the current window.

15.5. Write a BASIC program that creates a dialog box with two edit fields. The program should provide ways to switch between edit fields with the Tab key or the mouse, to enter data with a button or the Return key, and to terminate by pressing a button.

15.6. Write a BASIC program that creates two windows with an image for each window. The program should save these images and be able to refresh each window if it is uncovered or clicked to make it active.

15.7. Write a BASIC program that allows the user to input a person's name, address, and telephone number through edit fields in a dialog box. The program should then store the data in a random access file.

Chapter 16
QuickDraw

16.1 Introduction

QuickDraw is a series of commands that can be called out of the read-only memory (ROM) routines of the Macintosh for use in BASIC programs. These routines produce text and graphics quickly—hence the name QuickDraw. QuickDraw enables us to draw graphics such as rectangles, ovals, rounded rectangles, and other shapes. It can fill these shapes with patterns, invert the background pattern within a shape (i.e., change white pixels to black pixels and vice versa), paint a new pattern in a shape, and erase a shape from the screen. QuickDraw also allows us to draw with a pen of any width, height, and pattern. The statements PSET, CIRCLE, and LINE we have discussed are not part of QuickDraw; rather, they are regular commands in QuickBASIC.

     This chapter gives an overview of the QuickDraw routines. It explains how we can use different text fonts, text sizes, text faces, and text modes; how to enlarge the graphics pen and draw with a pattern; and how to draw certain popular shapes.

16.2 The CALL Statement

The QuickDraw routines are not written in BASIC; they are coded in machine language. Therefore, we need a statement that can transfer control from a BASIC program to the appropriate routine in the Macintosh's ROM. This is the CALL statement. By placing the CALL statement in front of the name of the QuickDraw function we would like to use, control is passed to the machine language routine and then returned to the BASIC program. The statement

```
CALL TEXTSIZE(9)
```

passes control to QuickDraw where the text size of text to be displayed is set to 9 point type. Now everything printed by this program will be in 9 point type until the text size is changed. The word CALL is optional; the previous statement can also be written as follows:

```
TEXTSIZE 9
```

278

This accomplishes the same task as with the **CALL** statement; however, this form can make it difficult to distinguish between QuickDraw statements and alphanumeric labels. When using this form, remember to eliminate the parentheses from the statement.

16.3 The CALL TEXT Statements

There are four **CALL TEXT** statements. They are

```
CALL TEXTSIZE(n)
CALL TEXTFONT(n)
CALL TEXTFACE(n)
CALL TEXTMODE(n)
```

Once one of these statements has been used, n remains the same until the next statement is executed. So, if **TEXTSIZE(12)** is executed, all output will be in 12 point type until another **TEXTSIZE** statement is executed.

The **CALL TEXTSIZE**(n) statement allows us to print text output in values of n from 2 point type to 127 point type. If a certain font size is not found on the BASIC disk, BASIC will scale a smaller font size to the desired size. Even multiples of a font size tend to look better than odd multiples.

The **CALL TEXTFONT**(n) statement can accept values of 0 to 11, 21, and 22 for n. These values correspond to different fonts on the Macintosh as follows.

0	Chicago
1	Geneva
2	New York
3	Geneva
4	Monaco
5	Venice
6	London
7	Athens
8	San Francisco
9	Toronto
10	Seattle
11	Cairo
21	Courier
22	Helvetica

Not all these fonts are on the BASIC disk because each font takes up a large amount of memory, and the larger font sizes require considerably more memory. You may need to use the Macintosh's *font mover* utility program to move a font to the BASIC disk if and when you need it. The Chicago, Geneva, and Monaco fonts are included on the BASIC disk. If you choose a font that is not present in the system, BASIC automatically substitutes the Geneva font.

The **CALL TEXTFACE**(n) statement enables us to choose how we would like to display output on the screen. The possible values are

```
0  Plain
1  Bold
2  Italic
4  Underlined
8  Outlined
16 Shadowed
32 Condensed
64 Extended
```

Several of these options may be combined by adding the values of the different effects we would like to combine. For example, if we wanted to print "Macintosh" in bold, underlined, and outlined, we would type

```
CALL TEXTFACE(13)
PRINT "Macintosh"
```

Notice that the only way to total 13 without repeating any face is by using the bold, underlined, and outlined faces $(1 + 4 + 8 = 13)$.

For **CALL TEXTMODE**(n), n can have values of 0 to 7. The values 0 to 3 correspond to

```
0  Copy
1  OR
2  XOR
3  BIC
```

The values 4 to 7 correspond to Not Copy, Not OR, Not XOR, and Not BIC respectively. The tables accompanying each of the mode descriptions give the four different combinations that are possible in mixing pixels and indicate the result of mixing them.

In the *Copy mode*, every word is surrounded by a small white box. Therefore, when in this mode, any text printed is overlaid on the background and it shows the white box surrounding it (unless of course the background is white), thus wiping out any background pixels. The following table shows the combinations of pixels and the final pixel for Copy mode. In the Copy mode, the final pixel is the same as the text pixel regardless of the background pixel.

Text pixel	Background pixel	Final pixel
black	white	black
black	black	black
white	black	white
white	white	white

In the *OR mode*, if either the text pixel or the background pixel is black, the final pixel is black. The pixel combinations for the OR mode are

Text pixel	Background pixel	Final pixel
black	white	black
black	black	black
white	black	black
white	white	white

In the *XOR mode*, if the text and background pixels are the same, the final pixel is white; otherwise it is black. The pixel combinations for XOR mode are

Text pixel	Background pixel	Final pixel
black	white	black
black	black	white
white	black	black
white	white	white

Finally, the *BIC (black is changed) mode* changes all the black pixels in the text to white before they are printed on the screen. It also makes previously white text pixels transparent, thus causing any black pixels in the background to show through.

Text pixel	Background pixel	Final pixel
black	white	white
black	black	white
white	black	black
white	white	white

The program in Figure 16.1 uses the various **CALL TEXT** statements to print text on several different backgrounds. The text is printed in the four available textmodes (Figure 16.2).

16.4 The MOVETO, LINETO, MOVE, and LINE Statements

The **MOVETO** statement works as if we combined the **LOCATE** and **PTAB** statements, but actually a bit better. It has the following form:

```
CALL MOVETO(x1, y1)
```

This statement moves the graphics pen to the pixel with coordinates (x1, y1). The pixel referenced is the lower left corner of the character that is to be placed there. This is better

```
REM    Using the CALL TEXT statements
CALL TEXTSIZE(24)
CALL TEXTFONT(1)
CALL TEXTFACE(8)
FOR x = 1 TO 100 STEP 1
      LINE (x, 0)-(x, 300)
NEXT x
FOR x = 101 TO 200 STEP 3
      LINE (x, 0)-(x, 300)
NEXT x
CALL TEXTMODE(0)
LOCATE 1,1
PRINT "Copy mode   Copy mode"
CALL TEXTMODE(1)
LOCATE 3,1
PRINT "OR mode   OR mode"
CALL TEXTMODE(2)
LOCATE 5,1
PRINT "XOR mode   XOR mode"
CALL TEXTMODE(3)
LOCATE 7,1
PRINT "BIC mode   BIC mode"
END
```

Figure 16.1 Using the CALL TEXT statements

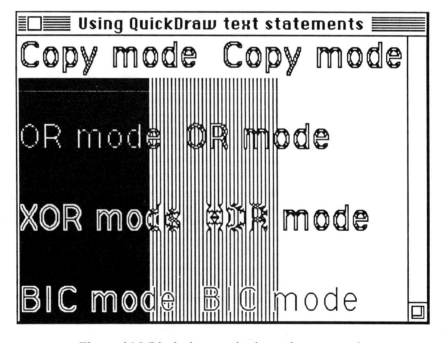

Figure 16.2 Displaying text in the various textmodes

than combining **LOCATE** and **PTAB** because **MOVETO** can specify a precise location on the screen, whereas the others can only specify screen location in terms of rows and columns like text.

The statement

```
CALL LINETO(x2, y2)
```

draws a line from the last point referenced to the point (x2, y2). If these two are combined, a line will be drawn from the point (x1, y1) to the point (x2, y2).

Both these statements use *absolute coordinates*, i.e., the coordinates referenced are the actual coordinates of points. The MOVE and LINE statements, however, use *relative coordinates*. Relative coordinates are coordinates that depend on the last point referenced.

```
CALL MOVETO(100, 100)
```

moves the graphics pen to the point (100, 100). The statement

```
CALL MOVE(20, 30)
```

moves the graphics pen from the point (100, 100) to the right 20 pixels and down 30 pixels. The final destination of the graphics pen after executing these two program lines is the point (120, 130). If we wanted to go up and to the left instead, both the coordinates in the MOVE statement would be negative. For example

```
CALL MOVE(-20, -30)
```

would move the graphics pen from (100, 100) to (80, 70).

The LINE statement works like the MOVE statement. After using the MOVETO statement, the statement

```
CALL LINE(-20, 30)
```

would print a line from (100, 100) to (80, 130).

The program in Figure 16.3 uses the four statements discussed in this section to draw a right triangle, and then prints the message "This is a right triangle." The output is shown in Figure 16.4.

```
REM    Using MOVETO, LINETO, MOVE, and LINE
CALL MOVETO(10, 10)
CALL LINETO(10, 100)
CALL LINE(90, 0)
CALL LINETO(10, 10)
CALL MOVE(0, 110)
PRINT "This is a right triangle";
END
```

Figure 16.3 The MOVETO, LINETO, MOVE and LINE statements

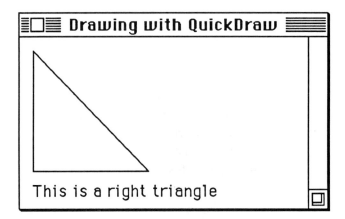

Figure 16.4 Drawing provided by QuickDraw statements

16.5 Changing the Size of the QuickDraw Pen

The *QuickDraw pen* draws all lines in QuickDraw. It draws the lines as thick as we like and in whatever pattern we like. The pen is referenced by its upper left corner. Anything printed with the pen is printed down and to the right of it. The default pen size is one pixel, but this may be changed with the **PENSIZE** statement.

> **CALL PENSIZE**(width, height)

With this statement, the pen size can be made as large as desired.

16.6 Drawing Patterns with the Pen

Not only can we change the size of the pen, but we can have the pen draw in a pattern rather than a plain black line. To do this though, we must first explain *hexadecimal numbers*.

When we define a pattern for the pen to draw in, we use an 8-by-8 pixel block as a basis for the entire pen whether the pen is larger or smaller. In this 8-by-8 block, every two rows translates to one hexadecimal number. The following is an illustration of an 8-by-8 block using 1 for black pixels and 0 for white pixels.

```
0 0 0 1 1 0 0 0
0 0 0 1 1 0 0 0
0 0 0 1 1 0 0 0
1 1 1 1 1 1 1 1
1 1 1 1 1 1 1 1
0 0 0 1 1 0 0 0
0 0 0 1 1 0 0 0
0 0 0 1 1 0 0 0
```

Each group of four digits (such as 0 0 0 1) is the binary representation of a four-pixel block. Every four-digit combination of ones and zeros is a letter or number in hexadecimal notation as in the following table.

Binary #	Hexadecimal	Binary #	Hexadecimal
0000	0	1000	8
0001	1	1001	9
0010	2	1010	A
0011	3	1011	B
0100	4	1100	C
0101	5	1101	D
0110	6	1110	E
0111	7	1111	F

Every four-digit binary code has a unique hexadecimal representation. Every hexadecimal number in QuickBASIC must have "&H" preceding the actual number. So the first pair of lines in the 8-by-8 pixel block is represented in hexadecimal format as &H1818, the second pair of lines is represented as &H18FF, the third pair of lines is represented as &HFF18, and the fourth pair is the same as the first, &H1818.

Now we must create an array to hold the hexadecimal number formation.

```
DIM crosspattern(3)
crosspattern(0) = &H1818
crosspattern(1) = &H18FF
crosspattern(2) = &HFF18
crosspattern(3) = &H1818
```

This set of statements dimensions the array `crosspattern` to hold the four hexadecimal values, and assigns these values to the elements of the array. The last statement we need to make the pen draw in our newly created pattern is

```
CALL PENPAT(VARPTR(crosspattern(0)))
```

This statement sets the pen to use the pattern we created. When the program is run, the Macintosh stores the array variables in order in memory. **VARPTR**, the variable pointer, creates a pointer to the location in memory where `crosspattern` resides. The pen can be restored to normal by using the **CALL PENNORMAL** statement.

The following statements make a pattern the same for the entire background.

```
CALL BACKPAT(VARPTR(crosspattern(0)))
CLS
```

These statements cause the background to be the same as the pattern we just designed.

The program in Figure 16.5 changes the pen size and creates a pattern for the pen. It allows the user to drag the mouse to draw, hold the button down to stop drawing, and press the button three times and hold it to terminate. Its display is shown in Figure 16.6.

16.7 The PENMODE Statement

As with the **TEXTMODE** statement, the **PENMODE** statement has Copy mode, OR mode, XOR mode, BIC mode, Not Copy mode, Not OR mode, Not XOR mode, and Not BIC mode. These modes are numbered from 8 to 15. The difference between the Copy and Not Copy modes is that the pattern pixels are reversed; all black pixels become white pixels and all white pixels become black pixels before being printed on the screen. The pixel combinations for the different pen modes are the same as those for the text modes. "Not" modes follow the same combination patterns as the regular modes. Copy mode is the default. The format for this statement is

```
CALL PENMODE(n)
```

PENMODE(8) and **PENMODE(12)** are the Copy and Not Copy modes, respectively. Like Copy of **TEXTMODE**, **PENMODE(8)** and **PENMODE(12)** cover any background pixels completely; the pattern is undisturbed on any background.

PENMODE(9) and **PENMODE(13)** are the OR and Not OR modes. In these modes, the pen pattern is laid over the background pattern. Black pixels in the background show through white pixels in the pen pattern, so if the entire background is black, the pen pattern will not be seen.

PENMODE(10) and **PENMODE(14)** are the XOR and Not XOR modes. In this mode, if the pixels of the pen pattern and the background are different, the resulting pixel is black. This mode is helpful in printing dark patterns on dark backgrounds because the pattern will turn light.

PENMODE(11) and **PENMODE(15)** are the BIC and Not BIC modes. In this mode, the black pixels in the pen pattern change to white and the previously white pixels become transparent; this lets black background pixels show through the pen pattern.

The program in Figure 16.7 displays the eight pen modes against three different backgrounds. It uses the **MOVETO** and **LINETO** statements to place the lines in the correct places. Its display is shown in Figure 16.8.

16.8 Drawing Shapes with QuickDraw

The basic shapes we can draw with QuickDraw include rectangles, ovals, rounded rectangles, and others. There are several features that apply to each of these shapes. We can draw them in any pen thickness and with any pattern, fill them with a pattern, invert

```
REM    Changing the pensize and drawing with a pattern
DEFINT a-z
DIM crosspattern(3)
crosspattern(0) = &H1818 : crosspattern(1) = &H18FF
crosspattern(2) = &HFF18 : crosspattern(3) = &H1818
PRINT "Drag mouse to draw"
PRINT "Click once and hold to stop drawing"
PRINT "Click three times and hold to end"
FOR x = 1 TO 7000: NEXT x
CLS
CALL PENSIZE(16, 16)
CALL PENPAT(VARPTR(crosspattern(0)))
mouseclick = MOUSE(0)
WHILE mouseclick <> -3
   x = MOUSE(1)
   y = MOUSE(2)
   CALL MOVETO(x, y)
   CALL LINE(0, 0)
   mouseclick = MOUSE(0)
   IF mouseclick = -1 THEN
      WHILE mouseclick = -1
         mouseclick = MOUSE(0)
      WEND
   END IF
WEND
END
```

Figure 16.5 Changing the pen size and drawing with a pattern

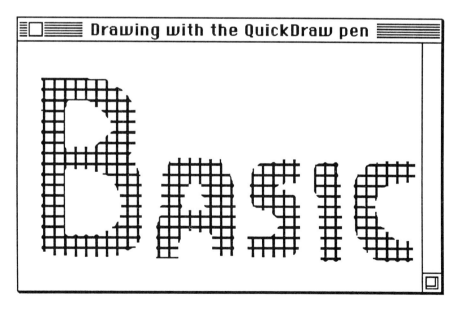

Figure 16.6 Drawing with a pattern

the background pattern inside them, paint them with different patterns, and erase them from the screen.

```
DEFINT a-z
DIM pattern(3)

pattern(0) = &H7789
pattern(1) = &H8F8F
pattern(2) = &H7798
pattern(3) = &HF8F8
CALL PENPAT(VARPTR(pattern(0)))
CALL PENSIZE(16,16)
FOR x = 101 TO 200 STEP 1
   LINE (x, 0)-(x, 300)
NEXT x
FOR x = 201 TO 300 STEP 5
   LINE (x, 0)-(x, 300)
NEXT x
FOR y = 0 TO 300 STEP 5
   LINE(201, y)-(300, y)
NEXT y

CALL MOVETO(1, 25)
PRINT "Copy Mode"
CALL PENMODE(8)
CALL MOVETO(101, 10)
CALL LINETO(400, 10)

CALL MOVETO(1, 50)
PRINT "OR Mode"
CALL PENMODE(9)
CALL MOVETO(101, 35)
CALL LINETO(400, 35)

CALL MOVETO(1, 75)
PRINT "XOR Mode"
CALL PENMODE(10)
CALL MOVETO(101, 60)
CALL LINETO(400, 60)

CALL MOVETO(1, 100)
PRINT "BIC Mode"
CALL PENMODE(11)
CALL MOVETO(101, 85)
CALL LINETO(400, 85)

CALL MOVETO(1, 125)
PRINT "Not Copy Mode"
CALL PENMODE(12)
CALL MOVETO(101, 110)
CALL LINETO(400, 110)

CALL MOVETO(1, 150)
PRINT "Not OR Mode"
CALL PENMODE(13)
CALL MOVETO(101, 135)
CALL LINETO(400, 135)
```

continued

Figure 16.7 Pen mode demonstration (part 1 of 2)

continued

```
CALL MOVETO(1, 175)
PRINT "Not XOR Mode"
CALL PENMODE(14)
CALL MOVETO(101, 160)
CALL LINETO(400, 160)

CALL MOVETO(1, 200)
PRINT "BIC mode"
CALL PENMODE(15)
CALL MOVETO(101, 185)
CALL LINETO(400, 185)

FOR n = 1 TO 10000 : NEXT n
END
```

Figure 16.7 Pen mode demonstration (part 2 of 2)

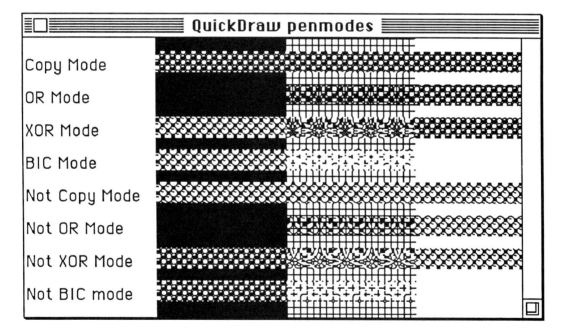

Figure 16.8 Display of QuickDraw pen modes

The five statements used in drawing rectangles are:

```
CALL FRAMERECT(VARPTR(rectanglecoords(0)))
CALL FILLRECT(VARPTR(rectanglecoords(0)),
    VARPTR(pattern(0)))
CALL PAINTRECT(VARPTR(rectanglecoords(0)))
CALL INVERTRECT(VARPTR(rectanglecoords(0)))
CALL ERASERECT(VARPTR(rectanglecoords(0)))
```

The first statement, **FRAMERECT**, draws a rectangle on the screen. The coordinates for the rectangle are stored in a four-element array. In this case `rectanglecoords(0)` through `rectanglecoords(3)` represent the top, left, bottom, and right boundaries respectively. The **VARPTR** statement tells the computer where to find these coordinates. This statement will draw the rectangle in the thickness and pattern that the graphics pen has been set for, or in the normal one-pixel-thick black line.

The second statement, **FILLRECT**, draws a filled rectangle. Two **VARPTR** statements are needed in this case; one is for finding the coordinates of the rectangle, and the other is for finding the pattern.

The **PAINTRECT** statement also gives us the ability to draw a rectangle that is filled with a pattern, but because this statement uses the graphics pen to fill the rectangle, it can also use the eight pen mode options that are available. The **FILLRECT** statement does not have this capability.

INVERTRECT is a simple statement that inverts every pixel in the current background pattern within the area of the rectangle defined. **ERASERECT** fills the rectangle with the current background pattern, thus erasing the rectangle.

These five statements remain the same for ovals except **RECT** is replaced with **OVAL** in each statement. In drawing with the **FRAMEOVAL** statement, a circle can be drawn by giving the coordinates of a square, and an oval from the coordinates of a rectangle. The following are the five statements used in drawing ovals:

```
CALL FRAMEOVAL(VARPTR(rectanglecoords(0)))
CALL FILLOVAL(VARPTR(rectanglecoords(0)),
    VARPTR(pattern(0)))
CALL PAINTOVAL(VARPTR(rectanglecoords(0)))
CALL INVERTOVAL(VARPTR(rectanglecoords(0)))
CALL ERASEOVAL(VARPTR(rectanglecoords(0)))
```

Drawing rounded rectangles is a bit more complicated as there are other parameters to consider. The five statements for drawing rounded rectangles are as follows:

```
CALL FRAMEROUNDRECT(VARPTR(rectanglecoords(0)),
    oval width, oval height)
CALL FILLROUNDRECT(VARPTR(rectanglecoords(0)),
    oval width, oval height, VARPTR(pattern(0)))
CALL PAINTROUNDRECT(VARPTR(rectanglecoords(0)),
    oval width, oval height)
CALL INVERTROUNDRECT(VARPTR(rectanglecoords(0)),
    oval width, oval height)
CALL ERASEROUNDRECT(VARPTR(rectanglecoords(0)),
    oval width, oval height)
```

The oval width and oval height parameters specify how rounded the corners should be. By making these two parameters the same, four ninety degree arcs of a circle replace the corners of the rectangle. The parameters could be for a tall and thin oval or a short and fat one, but the best results are when oval width and oval height are identical.

The program in Figure 16.9 uses each of the three QuickDraw frame statements twice to frame six different shapes on the screen. The screen display for this program is shown in Figure 16.10.

```
REM     Framing QuickDraw shapes
DEFINT a-z
DIM rect(3)
GOSUB Rectcoords
CALL FRAMERECT(VARPTR(rect(0)))
GOSUB Rectcoords
CALL FRAMERECT(VARPTR(rect(0)))
GOSUB Rectcoords
CALL FRAMEOVAL(VARPTR(rect(0)))
GOSUB Rectcoords
CALL FRAMEOVAL(VARPTR(rect(0)))
GOSUB Rectcoords
CALL FRAMEROUNDRECT(VARPTR(rect(0)), 70, 70)
GOSUB Rectcoords
CALL FRAMEROUNDRECT(VARPTR(rect(0)), 10, 10)
END

Rectcoords:
   FOR x = 0 TO 3
        READ rect(x)
   NEXT x
   RETURN

   DATA 10, 10, 120, 120
   DATA 130, 10, 170, 120
   DATA 10, 130, 120, 250
   DATA 130, 130, 170, 250
   DATA 10, 260, 120, 380
   DATA 130, 260, 170, 380
```

Figure 16.9 Framing QuickDraw shapes

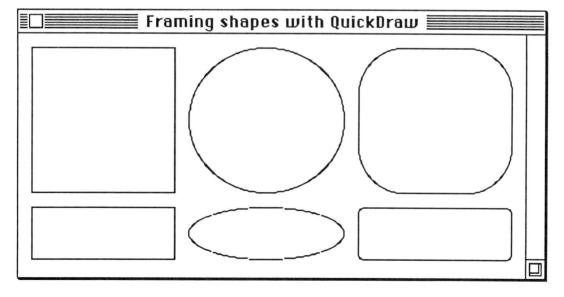

Figure 16.10 Framed shapes produced by QuickDraw

The program in Figure 16.11 uses the five oval statements to show how each one works. The screen display produced by this program is shown in Figure 16.12.

```
DEFINT a-z
DIM pat(3)
DIM coords(3)

GOSUB Pattern
CALL BACKPAT(VARPTR(pat(0)))
CLS
CALL PENSIZE(10,10)
GOSUB Pattern
CALL PENPAT(VARPTR(pat(0)))

coords(0) = 10 : coords(1) = 5 : coords(2) = 90 : coords(3) = 65
CALL FRAMEOVAL(VARPTR(coords(0)))

coords(0) = 10 : coords(1) = 70 : coords(2) = 90 : coords(3) = 130
GOSUB Pattern
CALL FILLOVAL(VARPTR(coords(0)), VARPTR(pat(0)))

coords(0) = 10 : coords(1) = 135 : coords(2) = 90 : coords(3) = 195
CALL PAINTOVAL(VARPTR(coords(0)))

coords(0) = 10 : coords(1) = 200 : coords(2) = 90 : coords(3) = 260
CALL INVERTOVAL(VARPTR(coords(0)))

coords(0) = 10 : coords(1) = 265 : coords(2) = 90 : coords(3) = 325
CALL ERASEOVAL(VARPTR(coords(0)))

CALL MOVETO(1, 110)
CALL TEXTMODE(0)
CALL TEXTFACE(1)
PRINT "  FRAME    FILL    PAINT    INVERT    ERASE    "

coords(0) = 130 : coords(1) = 10 : coords(2) = 160 : coords(3) = 40
CALL FILLOVAL(VARPTR(coords(0)), VARPTR(pat(0)))
CALL MOVETO(50, 150)
PRINT "  Fill Pattern   "

coords(0) = 130 : coords(1) = 200 : coords(2) = 160 : coords(3) = 230
CALL PAINTOVAL(VARPTR(coords(0)))
CALL MOVETO(240, 150)
PRINT "  Pen Pattern   "
END

Pattern:
   FOR p = 0 TO 3
      READ pat(p)
   NEXT p
   RETURN
   DATA &HDDFF, &H77FF, &HDDFF, &H77FF
   DATA &H8244, &H3944, &H8201, &H0101
   DATA &H7789, &H8F8F, &H7798, &HF8F8
```

Figure 16.11 Using the QuickDraw oval statements

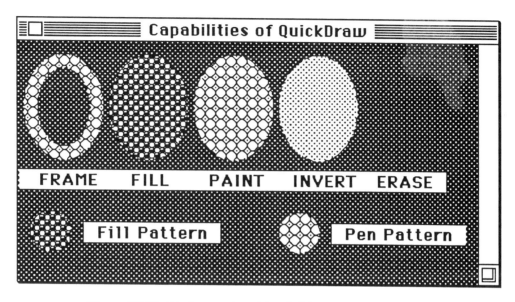

Figure 16.12 Display produced by QuickDraw oval statements

Concepts

absolute coordinates
background pixel
`BACKPAT` statement
BIC (black is changed) mode
binary numbers
`CALL` statement
Copy mode
`ERASEOVAL` statement
`ERASERECT` statement
`ERASEROUNDRECT` statement
`FILLOVAL` statement
`FILLRECT` statement
`FILLROUNDRECT` statement
font mover
`FRAMEOVAL` statement
`FRAMERECT` statement
`FRAMEROUNDRECT` statement
hexadecimal numbers
`INVERTOVAL` statement
`INVERTRECT` statement
`INVERTROUNDRECT` statement
`LINE` statement
`LINETO` statement
`LOCATE` statement
`MOVE` statement
`MOVETO` statement

Not BIC mode
Not Copy mode
Not OR mode
Not XOR mode
OR mode
`PAINTOVAL` statement
`PAINTRECT` statement
`PAINTROUNDRECT` statement
pen mode
`PENMODE` statement
`PENNORMAL` statement
`PENPAT` statement
pen pattern
pen pixel
`PENSIZE` statement
`PTAB` statement
QuickDraw
QuickDraw pen
relative coordinates
text face
text font
text mode
text pixel
text size
`VARPTR` statement
XOR mode

Problems

16.1. Fill in the blanks in each of the following.
   (a) The _____ statement is used to change the size of the pen.
   (b) The _____ statement accesses QuickDraw statements from the Macintosh read-only memory (ROM).
   (c) The _____ statement moves the pointer to an exact pixel on the screen.
   (d) The _____ statement can change the size of the type.
   (e) The _____ mode for text places a white box around the text.
   (f) The _____ mode makes originally white pixels "transparent," thus letting black background pixels show through.
   (g) A rectangle can be drawn and filled with the _____ statement.
   (h) An oval can be drawn with the _____ statement.
   (i) There are _____ different pen modes.
   (j) The _____ statement uses absolute coordinates to draw a line.
   (k) The _____ statement uses relative coordinates to locate a point.

16.2. Write a single BASIC statement that accomplishes each of the following.
   (a) Change the pen size to 5 pixels by 10 pixels.
   (b) Draw a rounded rectangle and fill it with the pen pattern. Make up a variable containing the coordinates of the rectangle.
   (c) Draw an oval.
   (d) Change the text mode to XOR mode.
   (e) Change the pen mode to Not BIC mode.
   (f) Move the graphics pen from wherever it is on the screen to the left 10 pixels and down 40 pixels.
   (g) Draw a line from wherever the graphics pen is on the screen to the point (400, 35).
   (h) Set the background pattern using a pattern that can be found with the variable pointer (**VARPTR**) and the variable `pattern1(0)`.
   (i) Erase a rectangle whose coordinates are found beginning with the variable `coordinates(0)`.

16.3. Write a BASIC program that prints several lines of text on the screen in 24 point type, shadowed face, Chicago font, and all four textmodes on a black background.

16.4. Write a BASIC program that makes the pen size 20 by 10. Create your own pattern for the pen. The program should have four different backgrounds across the screen and should print lines in the new pen size and pattern across these backgrounds. Use four of the eight pen modes.

16.5. Write a program that draws each QuickDraw shape. The program should display each shape separately with a subroutine. Use the same rectangle coordinates for all three shapes.

16.6. Write a program that displays the five QuickDraw possibilities for either the rectangle or the rounded rectangle. Label each one and display the pen pattern and the fill pattern; both should be labeled.

Chapter 17
Sights and Sounds

17.1 Introduction

In this chapter, we discuss QuickBASIC's music features and techniques of animation.

17.2 Animation

Animation can be performed with elementary graphics by drawing a figure, redrawing it in the background color to erase it, redrawing it in its new position, and continuing this process. This can be tedious with complex figures. The technique of animation we consider uses the *GET statement* to capture the figure, and the *PUT statement* to place the figure elsewhere on the screen.

The GET statement captures an area of the screen and stores it in an array. The PUT statement specifies this array when placing the picture on the screen again. The format for the GET statement is

```
GET (x1, y1)-(x2, y2), array
```

The coordinates specify a box that must be large enough to frame the picture. The array must be large enough to store the entire picture. To find the size of the picture in bytes, use the following formula

```
size-in-bytes = 4+((y2 - y1)+1) * 2 * INT(((x2 - x1)+16) / 16)
```

The number of array elements needed to store the image depends on whether the array is an integer array, single-precision array, or double-precision array. If the array that will store the picture is an integer array, the number of elements is `size-in-bytes/2`; if it is a single-precision array, the number of elements is `size-in-bytes/4`; if it is a double-precision array, the number of elements is `size-in-bytes/8`. When determining the number of array elements, if the quotient is not a whole number, round the number up. Once the size of the array has been determined, the array must be dimensioned appropriately. Use the following statement.

```
DIM array% (array-length)
```

The above statement represents an integer array of length `array-length`. If the array is a single-precision array, replace the percent sign (%) in the above statement with an exclamation point (!), and if the array is a double-precision array, replace the percent sign with a number sign (#).

The **PUT** statement places an image anywhere on the screen. The format for the **PUT** statement is

```
PUT (x, y), array, action
```

The `action` parameter is for one of five options including **PSET**, **PRESET**, **AND**, **OR**, and **XOR**. These have been described previously in Chapter 16.

We now have the pieces to build a simple animation program. The program in Figure 17.1 shows a ball that bounces around the screen. Depending on which `action` parameter is chosen, many interesting patterns may be formed. Outputs for the **XOR** option with `xdelta` and `ydelta` set to 2 are shown in Figures 17.2, 17.3, and 17.4.

```
REM A bouncing ball animation program
DEFINT a-z
PRINT "Size the output window, then click once to start."
PRINT "Click again to end."
WHILE MOUSE(0) <> -1
WEND
WHILE MOUSE(0) <> 0
WEND
CLS
xbound = WINDOW(2) - 32
ybound = WINDOW(3) - 32
DIM rect(4), ball(107)
rect(0) = 4
rect(1) = 4
rect(2) = 31
rect(3) = 31
CALL PAINTOVAL (VARPTR(rect(0)))
GET (0, 0) - (34, 34), ball
x = 0
y = 0
xdelta = 2
ydelta = 2
WHILE MOUSE(0) = 0
    x = x + xdelta
    y = y + ydelta
    IF x < -3 OR x > xbound THEN xdelta = -xdelta
    IF y < -3 OR y > ybound THEN ydelta = -ydelta
    PUT (x, y), ball, XOR
WEND
END
```

Figure 17.1 The bouncing ball animation program

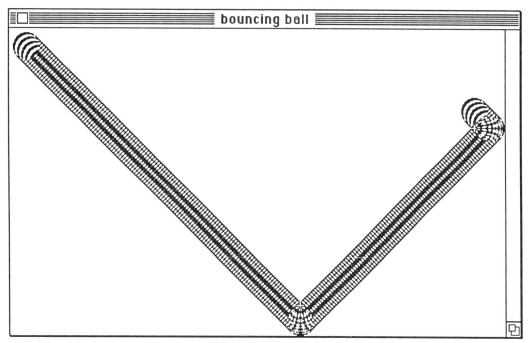

Figure 17.2 Beginning of the bouncing ball program

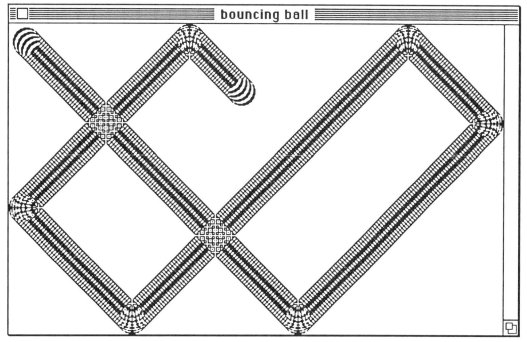

Figure 17.3 Screen display after several seconds

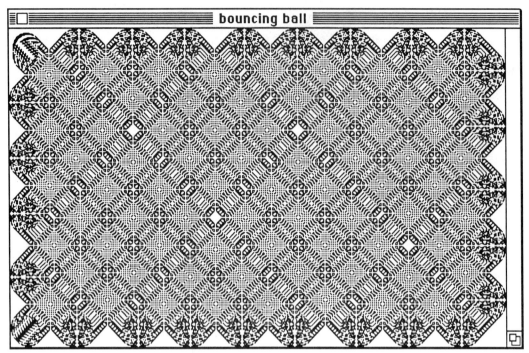

Figure 17.4 Bouncing ball program after the screen is filled

17.3 Music in QuickBASIC

Music in Microsoft Macintosh QuickBASIC consists of two statements, `SOUND` and `WAVE`, each of which has several features. The format for the `SOUND` statement is as follows:

```
SOUND frequency, duration, volume, voice
```

The frequency can be any number, and indicates the note that will be played. Figure 17.5 shows the frequency values for one octave.

Note	Frequency
C	523
D	587
E	659
F	698
G	784
A	880
B	988

Figure 17.5 The frequencies for one octave

To determine the frequency of the note C in the next higher octave, multiply the frequency (523) by 2; to determine the frequency of the note C in the next lower octave, divide the frequency by 2. The duration represents the length of time the note will sound. This number can be anywhere in the range 0 to 77. A duration of one second can be represented with the number 18.2. The volume is a number between 0 and 255 (0 being the lowest). The voice is a number between 0 and 3. This must be 0 if the system is in single-voice mode. The volume and voice parameters are optional. The program in Figure 17.6 plays notes up and down a one octave scale until the user clicks the mouse button.

```
REM    Program that plays up and down the scale
PRINT "Click the mouse button to end."
FOR x = 1 TO 7
   READ note(x)
NEXT x

WHILE MOUSE(0) = 0
   FOR y = 1 TO 7
      SOUND note(y), 5
   NEXT y
   FOR z = 6 TO 2 STEP -1
      SOUND note(z), 5
   NEXT z
WEND
END

DATA 523, 587, 659, 698, 784, 880, 988, 1046
```

Figure 17.6 A program that plays notes up and down one octave

The **WAVE** statement allows the user to define the shape of a sound wave for one of the four possible voices. The format for the **WAVE** statement is

WAVE voice, wavedefinition, phase

The voice parameter is the number of the voice being defined, and is in the range 0 to 3. The wavedefinition parameter can be either **SIN** or an integer array of at least 256 elements. Each element in the array represents the height of the wave at that point. The maximum height of the wave is the *amplitude*. The phase parameter indicates the subscript of the first array element to be used in the **WAVE** statement; it defaults to 0 if omitted. If a voice other than 0 is used, the wavedefinition parameter is required.

The **WAVE** statement does not actually produce a sound when it is executed in the program. The **SOUND** statement described previously plays the sound in the voice specified by the user at the end of the statement. The program in Figure 17.7 defines several voices and allows the user to choose which will be used to play up and down the scale.

```
REM    Program that plays several different sounds
RANDOMIZE  TIMER
DIM wave1%(255), wave2%(255), wave3%(255), wave4%(255), wave5%(255)
GOSUB Formwaves
FOR n = 1 TO 7
   READ note(n)
NEXT n

WHILE NOT done%
   CLS
   PRINT "Enter the number of the sound you would like"
   PRINT "1 - Sine wave"
   PRINT "2 - Noise"
   PRINT "3 - Sawtooth"
   PRINT "4 - Square wave"
   PRINT "5 - Triangle wave"
   PRINT "6 - End"
   INPUT number
   SELECT CASE number
      CASE 1
         WAVE 0,wave1%
      CASE 2
         WAVE 0,wave2%
      CASE 3
         WAVE 0,wave3%
      CASE 4
         WAVE 0,wave4%
      CASE 5
         WAVE 0,wave5%
      CASE ELSE
         done% = -1
   END SELECT
   IF NOT done% THEN
      FOR y = 1 TO 7
         SOUND note(y), 5
      NEXT y
      FOR z = 6 TO 1 STEP -1
         SOUND note(z), 5
      NEXT z
   END IF
WEND
END

DATA 523, 587, 659, 698, 784, 880, 988, 1046

Formwaves:
   pi = 3.14159
   stepsize = 2*pi/256
   FOR a = 1 TO 2*pi STEP stepsize
      wave1%(x%) = 100*SIN(a*10)
      x% = x% + 1
   NEXT a
   FOR b = 0 TO 255
      wave2%(b) = INT(256*RND-128)
   NEXT b
```
continued

Figure 17.7 Program that plays scales in several different voices (part 1 of 2)

continued

```
    FOR c = 255 TO 0 STEP -1
        wave3%(c) = c - 128
    NEXT c
    FOR d = 0 TO 127
        wave4%(d) = 127
        wave4%(255 - d) = -128
    NEXT d
    FOR e = 127 TO 0 STEP -1
        f = 2 * e
        wave5%(e) = f - 128
        wave5%(255 - e) = f-128
    NEXT e
    RETURN
```

Figure 17.7 Program that plays scales in several different voices

Concepts

amplitude	phase
animation	**PUT** statement
duration	scale
frequency	**SOUND** statement
GET statement	sound wave
image	voice
note	volume
octave	**WAVE** statement

Problems

17.1. Write a single statement to accomplish each of the following.
   (a) Play a single note.
   (b) Play the notes C,D,E,F,G,A, and B.

17.2. Write a program that allows the user to press the letter corresponding to the notes A through G and plays that note. The program should end when the user clicks a button labeled "END".

17.3. Write a program that plays notes randomly. The notes should be from several octaves.

17.4. Modify the program in Figure 7.1 so that it plays the song "The Twelve Days of Christmas" as it prints the words on the screen.

17.5. Modify the program in Figure 7.4 so that it plays the song "Old MacDonald Had A Farm" as it prints the words on the screen.

17.6. Write a program that lets two humans play tic-tac-toe. Your program should display a blank tic-tac-toe board on the screen and fill in large Xs and Os as each player indicates his or her moves. Your program should terminate when someone wins and should print the winner's name; or it should terminate if the game is a draw.

17.7. Write a BASIC program that displays and prints sheet music corresponding to the music compositions you produced with the program of Problem 12.8.

17.8.   Write a Jumping Jacks program using animation that creates three frames as shown above, and alternates them appropriately to simulate Jumping Jacks.

17.9.   Write a Jumping Jacks program that shows much smoother movement than the one created in Problem 17.8.

17.10. Write a program that lets two users play checkers. Your program should move the checkers to the designated squares and redisplay the board after each move. You may wish to add animation and music so that the checker gradually glides to the new square, and appropriate sounds are used to indicate a simple moving, taking a piece, "kinging," and so on.

17.11. Write a generalized music composition program that enables a person to enter a song at the keyboard. Your program should allow the user to specify all aspects of the music that QuickBASIC can handle. Your program should save the music composition on a disk file. When you want to play the piece you've composed, your program should read the composition from disk to primary storage and play the piece. Experiment with the various musical effects available on your computer.

17.12. Modify the Towers of Hanoi program you wrote in problem 5.26 to display a picture of the towers. As your program determines which disk to move next, you should show the actual disk moving from one tower to another.

17.13. Modify the craps program of Chapter 8 to display the rolling dice on the screen. Use sound to add a little flair.

17.14. Modify the simulation program you wrote in Problem 8.28 in which you simulated the classical race of the tortoise and the hare. Pull out "all the stops!" Use every technique you can reasonably incorporate to liven up the simulation. Show the actual animals. Use animation. Let the clouds roll by. Let the sun move across the sky. Use music to play the *Star Spangled Banner* before the race begins. Then play the trumpet refrain used at the Kentucky Derby. When one of the contenders wins, play *Happy Days Are Here Again*!

Appendix

A.1 Introduction

This appendix contains explanations of several powerful features of Microsoft's QuickBASIC that were not discussed in the main text.

A.2 Compiling QuickBASIC Programs

A program that is fully compiled (see Chapter 1) executes faster than one run directly from the QuickBASIC environment. This is because the program is completely translated to machine language, the natural language of the computer, whereas in the QuickBASIC environment each line of the program is translated as the program executes.

There are seventeen different compiler options in QuickBASIC. The following is a listing and brief description of each option.

Compile

- `Include MBPCs & MBLCs` - This option instructs the compiler to include library resources and/or user created resources in the compiled program. This is a default option.
- `Include The Runtime Code` - When this option is selected, the MBRL run-time library is included in your application. This makes your application capable of running on a system which does not have the QuickBASIC run-time libraries on the disk. This is a default option.
- `Make All Arrays Static` - This option makes all arrays in your program static (meaning the arrays have been allocated memory previous to execution, and this memory cannot be deallocated during execution).
- `Generate 68020 Code` - Generates compiled code for a Macintosh with the 68020 microprocessor. Produces fatal error if this option is selected and the 68020 microprocessor is not present in the Macintosh.
- `Generate 68881 Code` - Generates compiled code with calls to the 68881 math coprocessor. Produces fatal error if this option is selected and the 68881 math coprocessor is not present in the Macintosh.
- `Create Program List File` - Causes compiler to create a compiler listing. This listing has the same name as the program with the `lst` extension.
- `Create Error List File` - Causes errors during compilation to be printed in the compiler listing. These errors are otherwise displayed on the screen.
- `Generate Symbol Table` - Creates a symbol file for use with debugging programs. This option should only be used when you have a debugger which requires this file.

`Save Before Compiling` - Saves the program file before compiling. This is a default option.

`Launch After Compiling` - Runs the program after it is compiled. This is a default option.

Runtime

`Check Arrays & Overflow` - Causes compiler to generate compiled code which checks array boundaries and overflow conditions during execution. This option slows program execution, but is helpful during the debugging process, and can be omitted once the program has been completely debugged.

`Use Default Window` - This option must be selected unless your program creates its own window. This is a default option.

`Use Default Menu` - This option must be selected unless your program creates its own menus. This is a default option.

`Process Runtime Events` - This option is required if your program uses event trapping.

`Ignore Breaks (CMD .)` - Ignores the command-period key combination to break program execution.

`Disable File Not Found Dialog` - Disables the file search dialog box to allow error trapping of the `File not found` error.

`Use Long Addressing` - This option is necessary when compiling extremely large programs. Compile your program without it first, and if this option is necessary, QuickBASIC will display an error message stating that the option should be selected.

A.3 Include Files and the $INCLUDE Metacommand

Include files are text files with source code that can be reused in separate programs. For instance, if you are writing programs that work on the same random access file, an include file could be created that opens the random access file and defines the file buffer. This include file could then be incorporated into all your programs. This reduces the time it takes to write programs and eliminates typing errors. Include files may not contain `$INCLUDE` metacommands.

An include file must be saved in text format. To do this, first type the file, then choose the **Save As** option from the **File** menu in QuickBASIC, and specify that the file should be saved in **Text** format. Save the file, and it will be ready to be included in other files with the *$INCLUDE metacommand*.

The format for the `$INCLUDE` metacommand is

```
REM $INCLUDE "filename"
```

Metacommands must appear in a **REM** statement. When using `$INCLUDE`, be sure to place it in an appropriate part of the program because, when the program is compiled, all statements in the include file are placed into the program at the location of the `$INCLUDE` metacommand.

A.4 Debugging

QuickBASIC provides several debugging capabilities to help you complete your program "bug free." The `Trace All` option of the `Run` menu allows the user to follow the flow of the program. `Trace All` causes the current statement in the program to be highlighted as the program executes. To use this option, select it, then run the program. In order to make the best use of this feature, resize the output window with the grow box in the bottom right corner of the window, and place the output window adjacent to the list window. This allows you to watch both the output and the program simultaneously. If the program executes "too quickly," select the `STEP` option instead; one statement is executed each time this option is selected and the program pauses until the option is selected again (the program need not be running to use this option).

When QuickBASIC encounters an error, it automatically prints an error message, and places a box around the statement in which the error is located. This is the simplest form of debugging, but can prove to be quite helpful.

Breakpoints can be set to stop the program execution at any time. This is helpful when you are trying to follow the values of specific variables. The command bar can be used to display the values of these variables in the output window by typing `PRINT` and the variable name, and pressing the Return key. The command bar can also be used to change the values of variables in the context of the program. Program execution can then be continued with the `Continue` option in the `Run` menu.

A.5 QuickBASIC Menus

This section lists all the menus and menu options in QuickBASIC. Each of these options is described in depth in the Microsoft QuickBASIC manuals.

`File` menu

New - clears the current program from memory, and gives a fresh list window so the user may enter a new program.

Open - clears the current program from memory, and loads the program selected by the user.

Close - closes the currently active window.

Save - saves the current program to disk under the current file name. If the current program has not yet been saved, the Save As dialog box appears.

Save As - saves the current program to disk with the filename and specifications given by the user.

Page Setup - allows the user to input information pertaining to the paper size, print formats, and page orientation.

Print - sends program to be printed on the printer.

Transfer - allows the user to open another application without first quitting QuickBASIC.

Quit - leaves QuickBASIC and returns to the Macintosh Desktop.

`Edit` menu

    `Undo` - cancels the last command performed.

    `Cut` - removes the selected text and places it on the clipboard.

    `Copy` - copies the selected text and places it on the clipboard.

    `Paste` - inserts the contents of the clipboard at the current cursor position.

    `Clear` - deletes the selected text.

`Search` menu

    `Find` - locates the specified text.

    `Find Next` - locates the specified text using the last text searched for by any of the Search commands.

    `Find Selected Text` - locates the text currently selected in the List window.

    `Find Definition` - locates the given subprogram, label, or user-defined function definition.

    `Find Insertion Point` - displays the part of the program where the cursor is currently located.

    `Change` - allows the user to input text to be searched for and replaced with replacement text.

    `Jump To` - opens a dialog box in which a line of code is entered. QuickBASIC then moves to this line of code upon selection of the menu choice.

    `Get Info` - provides syntax and usage information on the QuickBASIC keyword currently containing the cursor.

    `Set Info` - allows the user to change or add information displayed with `Get Info`.

    `Set Bookmark` - allows the user to mark a point of interest in the program.

    `Clear Bookmark` - clears a bookmark which was previously set. This option can only be used directly after a `Set Bookmark` or `Next Bookmark` command.

    `Next Bookmark` - moves to the portion of the program containing the next bookmark.

`Windows` menu

    `Command` - makes the Command window active.

    `List` - makes the List window active.

    `Output` - makes the Output window active.

`Run` menu

    `Run Program` - runs the current program.

    `Continue` - restarts execution after the program has been stopped.

    `Step` - executes the program one statement at a time, and stops after each statement.

    `Breakpoint On/Off` - Sets or removes a breakpoint from the current statement. Execution of the program stops upon encountering a breakpoint.

    `Trace All` - turns on tracing. When this option is selected, QuickBASIC highlights each program statement as it is executed.

    `Options` - displays a dialog box containing the list of compiler options.

Compile - compiles the program into an application which can be run from the Macintosh Desktop.

Compile As - Allows the user to enter a file name before compiling the program.

A.6 Other Features

The SHARED statement allows a subprogram access to variables in the calling program without those variables being passed as arguments to the subprogram.

The COMMON statement allows the definition of global variables for chaining with other programs.

The CHAIN statement transfers control from the current program to another program. The first program stops running, and the second program is loaded into memory and executed. This is useful if you have several programs that are run successively so you do not need to run each program separately.

A.7 A Summary of Additional QuickBASIC Statements

(See *Microsoft QuickBASIC: BASIC Language Reference*)

Array related

ERASE statement - removes dynamic arrays from memory.
LBOUND statement - returns the lower bound (smallest available subscript) for the indicated dimension of an array.
OPTION BASE statement - declares the default lower bound for array subscripts.
UBOUND statement - returns the upper bound (largest available subscript) for the indicated dimension of an array.

Device related

LPOS function - returns the current position of the line printer's head within the printer buffer.
VARPTR function - return the address of a variable.

Directory related

CHDIR statement - changes the default location to the specified volume and/or folder.

Files related

`FILES` statement - prints the names of the files on the specified volume, or indicates whether a specified file exists.

`FILES$` function - displays the standard file dialog box, and allows the user to select a file.

`INPUT$` function - reads a string of characters from the keyboard or specified file.

`KILL` statement - deletes a file from disk.

`LOAD` statement - loads a file from disk into memory.

`LOC` function - returns the record number of last record read or written in random access files, or the number of bytes written to or read from a sequential file.

`MERGE` statement - appends specified file to program currently in memory.

`NAME` statement - changes the name and/or type of a disk file.

`RESET` statement - closes all open files.

`SYSTEM` statement - terminates program execution, closes all open files, and returns control to the Finder.

Memory related

`CLEAR` statement - reinitializes all program variables, closes files, and sets stack size.

`FRE` function - returns the amount of available memory.

`PEEK` function - returns the byte stored at a specified memory location.

`PEEKL` function - returns the four bytes stored at a specified memory location.

`PEEKW` function - returns the two bytes stored at a specified memory location.

`POKE` statement - writes a byte into a memory location.

`POKEL` statement - writes four bytes into a memory location.

`POKEW` statement - writes two bytes into a memory location.

Miscellaneous

`BEEP` statement - sounds the speaker.

`CONT` statement - continues the program after a `STOP`.

`ERR` statement - returns the error code of a runtime error.

`ERL` statement - returns the line number of the line in which the error occurred.

`ERROR` statement - simulates the occurrence of a BASIC error, or allows the user to define error codes.

`RUN` statement - restarts the program currently in memory, or executes a specified program.

`STOP` statement - terminates program execution and closes all files.

`SYSTEM` function - returns information about the system.

`TRON/TROFF` statements - traces the execution of program statements.

Numeric conversions

`CDBL` function - converts a numeric expression to a double-precision number.

`CINT` function - converts a numeric expression to an integer by rounding the fractional part of the expression.

`CLNG` function - converts a numeric expression to a long (4-byte) integer by rounding the fractional part of the expression.

`CSNG` function - converts a numeric expression to a single-precision value.

CVDBCD, CVSBCD functions - return binary format numbers from a random access file string containing a decimal format number.

HEX$ function - returns a string that represents the hexadecimal value of the decimal argument *expression*.

MKDMBF$, MKSMBF$ functions - return a random access file string that represents the decimal form of a binary number.

OCT$ function - returns a string representing the octal value of the decimal argument.

Screen related

CSRLIN function - returns the current line (row) position of the text cursor.

LCOPY statement - sends a copy of the screen to the Macintosh printer.

POINT function - reads the color number of a pixel from the screen.

POS function - returns the current horizontal position of the text cursor.

PRESET statement - plots a point at the specified location. The default color is white.

SCROLL statement - scrolls a defined area in the output window.

WIDTH statement - assigns an output-line width to a file or device.

String related

INKEY$ function - returns one character read from the keyboard, or the null string if no character has been typed.

SADD function - returns the address of the specified string expression.

SPACE$ function - returns a string of spaces of length *n*.

SPC function - skips *n* spaces in a PRINT statement.

STR$ function - returns a string representation of the value of a numeric expression.

STRING$ function - returns a string whose characters all have a given ASCII code or whose characters are all the first character of the string expression.

UCASE$ function - returns a string expression with all letters in upper-case.

VAL function - returns the numeric value of a string of digits.

Bibliography

Microsoft QuickBASIC For Apple Macintosh Systems: User's Guide, Microsoft Corporation, Redmond, Washington, 1988.

Microsoft QuickBASIC For Apple Macintosh Systems: BASIC Language Reference, Microsoft Corporation, Redmond, Washington, 1988.

Index

A

ABS function, 84
Absolute coordinates, 283
Absolute value, 84
Accounting reports, 190
Accounts payable, 205
Accounts receivable, 205, 206
Active button, 252
Active window, 255, 266, 267, 305
Ada, 6
Add a new record to a file, 222
Addition, 2, 25–28
Addition program, 19
Address of an argument, 93
Administrative section of computer, 2
Airline reservations system,
Algebraic expressions, 25
Algebraic sign function, 84
Algebraically inconsistent, 23
Algorithm, 37, 38, 42, 43, 51, 73, 141
Alignment of column of numbers, 187
Alphabetic field, 205
Alphanumeric field, 205
Alphanumeric label, 279
ALU (arithmetic and logic unit), 2
American Standard Code for
    Information Interchange, 149
Ampersand, 199
Ampersand format character, 198
Amplitude, 299
AND, 76, 145, 296
AND logical operator, 76
Animation, 295, 296, 302
Annual interest rate, 68
ANSI (American National Standards
    Institute), 7
Apl (application), 96
Apostrophe for remarks, 22
Apple, 1, 5, 7
Apple Macintosh, 1
Apple menu, 8
Application, 96, 307
Arcs of a circle, 290
Area of a circle, 88
Area program for arbitrary number of
    parcels, 70
Area program with READ/DATA, 69
Argument, 93
Argument of a function, 83
Arithmetic and logic unit (ALU), 2
Arithmetic average, 113

Arithmetic calculations, 25
Arithmetic expression, 30, 65, 88
Arithmetic mean, 26
Arithmetic operators, 25
Arrangements of a five letter word,
    146, 147
Array, 93, 103
Array boundaries, 304
Array formal parameter, 93
AS, 207, 218
ASC function, 156
ASCII, 149, 150
Assembler, 4
Assembly language, 4, 5
Asset, 72
Asterisk (*), 25
Asterisk insertion, 196, 197
Asterisk for multiplication,
At random, 167
Athens font, 279
ATN function, 84
Automatic variable, 92
Average, 113
Averaging calculation, 44

B

Back up, 9
Background pattern, 278
Background pixel, 280, 286
BACKPAT, 285
Backslash, 197
Backspace key, 13
Bank account program, 221, 223
Banner printing program, 164
Bar chart, 110
Base string, 152
BASIC, 5, 7
BASIC expressions, 25
Batch, 2
Batch of data,
Batch processing, 2, 3
BEEP statement, 308
BIC mode, 280, 281, 286
Binary number, 309
Binary operator, 77
Binary QuickBASIC, 11
Binary version, 7
Bit, 204
Blaise Pascal, 6
Blank character, 205
Blank disk, 9

Block IF/THEN/ELSE statement, 41
Body of a loop, 42, 65, 66
Bohm, C., 39
Bold text, 280
Boot, 7
Bordered dialog box, 264, 265, 271
Bouncing ball animation program, 296
Bowling scorekeeper, 165
Box fill parameter, 231
Box parameter, 231
BREAK, 232
Breakpoint, 305
Breakpoint ON/OFF, 306
Bubble sort, 111
Buffer, 216
Business-related problems, 166
Button, 227, 232, 254, 271
Button activity, 255
BUTTON CLOSE n statement, 253
Button display program, 253
BUTTON function, 254
Button identification parameter, 252
Button rectangle parameter, 252
Button selection, 257
Button state parameter, 252
BUTTON statement, 252
Button title parameter, 252
Button type parameter, 253
Buttons, 252
Byron, L., 6

C

Cairo font, 279
Calculation, 22
Calendar, 165
CALL BACKPAT, 285
CALL ERASEOVAL, 290
CALL ERASERECT, 289
CALL ERASEROUNDRECT, 290
CALL FILLOVAL, 290
CALL FILLRECT, 289
CALL FILLROUNDRECT, 290
CALL FRAMEOVAL, 290
CALL FRAMERECT, 289
CALL FRAMEROUNDRECT, 290
CALL INVERTOVAL, 290
CALL INVERTROUNDRECT, 290
CALL INVERTRECT, 289
CALL LINETO, 283
CALL PAINTOVAL, 290
CALL PAINTRECT, 289
CALL PAINTROUNDRECT, 290
CALL PENMODE, 286
CALL PENNORMAL, 285
CALL PENPAT, 285
CALL PENSIZE, 284
CALL statement, 92, 278, 279
CALL TEXT, 279, 281, 282
CALL TEXTFACE, 279, 280
CALL TEXTFONT, 279
CALL TEXTMODE, 279, 280
Call TEXTSIZE, 278, 279
Calling a subroutine, 88

Calling program, 93
Capture a figure, 295
Car towing agency, 86
Card dealing program, 180, 181
Card shuffling and dealing simulation, 176
Caret (^), 25, 193
CASE ELSE, 74
CDBL function, 308
Central processing unit (CPU), 2
CHAIN statement, 307
Chaining, 307
Chance, 167
Change, 306
Channel number, 216, 217, 219, 220
Character code, 149
Character field, 205
Character set, 149, 204
Character string, 199
CHDIR statement, 307
Check amount in words, 142
Check array boundaries, 304
Check box, 253, 258
Check protection, 162, 199
Checkers, 302
Chicago font, 279
Chip, 1
CHR$ function, 156
CINT function, 308
Circle, 229, 233
Circle plotting, 236
CIRCLE statement, 228, 229, 278
Ciphertext, 163
Class average on a quiz, 42, 43
Clear, 306
CLEAR statement, 308
Clear Bookmark, 306
Click the close box, 265
Click the mouse, 8, 10, 13, 233, 244
Click twice, 15
Clicking on a partially covered window, 271
Clipboard, 14
CLNG function, 308
Close a button, 258
Close a file, 206, 308
Close a window, 266
Close box, 8, 13, 265, 268
Close option, 11
Close option in File menu, 305
CLOSE # statement, 217
CLOSE statement, 206
Closing a file, 238
CLS statement, 285
COBOL, 6, 187
Coder, 163
Color number, 309
Color parameter, 231
Column, 85, 118
Column format, 30
Column skip, 30
Column subscript, 119
Column tabs, 30
COMIT, 131
Comma(,), 30, 199

Comma insertion with PRINT USING, 194
Comma spacing character, 187
Command, 306
Command bar, 9, 10, 305
Commercial applications, 6
Commercial data processing, 187
COMMON statement, 307
Comparing character strings, 148, 149
Compendium of more advanced string manipulation exercises, 159
Compile, 307
Compile As, 307
Compile option, 13, 96
Compiler, 5
Compiler listing, 303
Compiler options in QuickBASIC, 303
Compiling features, 13
Compiling QuickBASIC programs, 303
Complex condition, 76
Compound interest with FOR/NEXT, 67
Computation, 1
Computer, 1
Computer program, 1
Computer programmer, 1
Computer programming, 3
Condensed text, 280
Condition, 31, 39, 40, 41, 49, 74, 75
Conditional transfer of control, 31, 32
Constant, 25
CONT statement, 308
Continue, 306
Continue option, 13
Continue option in the Run menu, 305
Control panel, 8
Control structure, 38, 39, 55
Control variable, 64, 65, 66, 67
Conversational computing, 20
Convert functions, 218
Coordinates of the Mouse pointer, 229
Coprocessor, 303
Copy, 14, 306
Copy a part of a program, 14
Copy a variable, 93
Copy mode, 280, 286
Correct program, 91
COS function, 84
Cosine, 84
Cost of an asset, 26
Counter, 30, 44, 51, 54, 64
Counter-controlled looping, 42, 43, 54, 62, 64
Counter-controlled loops, 63
Counting loops, 66
Courier font, 279
CPU (central processing unit), 2
Craps, 174, 302
Create a sequential file, 207, 215
Creating a file, 214
Creating an edit field, 272
Creative writing program,
Credit balances, 209
Credit control, 209
Credit data retrieval program, 211

Crossword puzzle generator, 166
Cryptography, 162
CSNG function, 308
CSRLIN function, 309
Cube, 30
Current output window, 266, 267
Cursor, 10, 14, 309
Cursor in, 13
Cut, 238, 271, 276, 306
Cut option, 14
CVD function, 218, 220
CVDBCD, 309
CVI function, 218
CVL function, 218
CVS function, 218
CVSBCD function, 309

D

Dartmouth College, 5
Data, 2
Data analysis, 113
DATA list, 70
DATA list pointer, 70, 72, 133
Data processing, 204
DATA statement, 68, 69, 71, 72, 75, 133
Data hierarchy, 204, 205
Database, 205
Database management system, 205
DATE$ function, 85
Dates in various formats, 161
Dealing a deck of cards, 161
Debit balance, 209
Debug, 13, 91
Debugging, 171, 303, 304, 305
Decimal alignment,
Decimal digit, 204
Decimal fraction, 66
Decimal image specifications, 192, 193, 195
Decimal places, 187
Decimal point, 199
Decimal QuickBASIC, 11
Decimal version, 7
Decision symbol, 48, 49
Decision-making command, 30, 73
Decoder, 163
DEF command, 87
DEF statement, 88
Default color, 309
Default menus, 238, 240, 242, 243
Default string, 272, 273
DEFDBL statement, 217
DEFINT statement, 217
DEFLNG statement, 217
DEFSNG statement, 217
Deleting text, 13, 14
Delimiter, 21
Depreciation, 26, 72
Desktop, 7, 11, 15, 96, 305, 307
Destructive readin, 24
Development time, 39
DIALOG, 232

DIALOG (window event), 268
Dialog box, 11, 12, 14, 232, 264, 272, 275, 304, 306
Dialog event, 255, 257, 272
Dialog event 1, 272
Dialog event 6, 272
Dialog event 7, 275
DIALOG event, 264
DIALOG (0) function, 255, 268, 272
DIALOG (1) function, 255
DIALOG (3), 268
DIALOG (4), 268
DIALOG (5), 268
DIALOG OFF statement, 258
DIALOG ON statement, 258
DIALOG STOP statement, 258
Diamond symbol, 48
Digit, 22
Dim a button, 254, 255, 258
DIM statement, 105, 106, 108, 118, 137, 285
Dimension, 105
Dimensioning an array, 295
Direct access, 214
Directory, 307
Disabled and dimmed, 238
Disk, 8, 215, 219
Disk storage, 205
Display, 3, 20
Display a graphic, 228
Display text, 228
Divide and conquer, 82
Division, 2, 25, 26
Document a program, 20, 29
Document window, 264, 273
Double-precision array, 295, 296
Double-precision number, 216, 217, 308
Double-subscripted array, 118, 119
Double asterisk dollar sign (**$), 197
Double backslash, 197, 198
Drag the grow box, 265
Drag the mouse, 8, 14, 227, 229, 230, 233, 286
Dragging the title bar, 265
Draw a circle, 229, 233
Draw a filled rectangle, 290
Draw a rectangle, 290
Drawing, 233
Drawing lines, 230
Drawing shapes with QuickDraw, 286
Drawing with a pattern, 287
Drive button, 11
Dummy value, 43
Dunning letters, 166
Duration, 298
Duration of a sound, 299
Dynamic arrays, 307
Dynamic variable, 96

E

E-notation, 199
E-notation with PRINT USING, 193

EBCDIC, 149, 150
Edit a program, 13
Edit field, 232, 264, 271, 272, 273, 274, 275
Edit field activity, 255
EDIT FIELD statement, 271
Edit menu, 14, 238
Edited numeric image specifications, 195
EDIT$ function, 273
EDP, 204
Eject, 15
Eject a disk, 11, 15, 238
Eject button, 11
Electronic data processing, 204
Element of an array, 103
Element of chance, 167
Elementary graphics, 227, 233, 295
ELSEIF statement, 41
Enable event trapping, 258
Enabled, 238
Enabled and black, 238
Encoder, 163
END, 90
END command, 21
End of data, 62
End of file, 206, 208
End SUB, 92
Ending point of a drag, 229, 230
Engineering applications, 7
English-like abbreviations, 4
Enlarge a window, 265
EOF function, 206, 220
Equal sign, 23
Equation of a straight line, 27
EQV (equivalence) logical operator, 77
Erase a shape, 278
ERASE statement, 307
Erase text, 14
ERASEOVAL, 290
ERASERECT routine, 289
ERASEROUNDRECT, 290
ERL statement, 308
ERR statement, 308
Error codes, 308
Error message, 14
ERROR statement, 308
Error trapping, 304
Evaluation from left to right, 25
Even, 86
Event OFF, 231, 232, 233
Event ON, 231, 232, 233
Event STOP, 231, 232, 233
Event trapping, 227, 231, 232, 233, 244
Event trapping with buttons, 252, 257
Event trapping with menus, 238, 244
Events, 227, 231, 232
Examination results, 53
Exclamation point (!), 197, 199, 296
Exclamation point (!) string image specification, 198
Execute a program, 21
Exit SUB, 92
EXP function, 84

Exponential function, 84
Exponentiation, 25, 26, 27, 28
Exponentiation subprogram, 92
Extended Binary Coded Decimal
    Interchange Code, 149
Extended text, 280

F

Face of a clock, 165
Factorial, 93–96
Fall into a subroutine, 90
False, 32, 39, 40
Fast food button program, 258
Fast food order program with menus,
    246
Fibonacci series, 101
Field, 204, 205, 206
FIELD statement, 215, 216
File, 8, 204, 205, 208
File buffer, 215, 216, 219, 304
File creation, 206
File menu, 8, 11–15, 305
File processing, 206
FILES statement, 308
FILES$ function, 308
FILLOVAL, 290
FILLRECT, 289, 290
FILLROUNDRECT, 290
Final value of loop counter, 63–66
Financial applications, 7
Find, 306
Find Definition, 306
Find Insertion Point, 306
Find Next, 306
Find Selected Text, 306
Finder, 308
Fini, 153
First refinement, 54, 178
FIX function, 84
Flipping a coin, 167
Fixed dollar sign, 199
Floating dollar sign, 196–199
Flow of control using subroutines, 89
Flowchart, 46, 47, 72
Flowchart symbols, 46
Flowcharting, 46
Flowcharting template, 51
Flowcharting the FOR and NEXT
    statements, 66
Flowlines, 46, 49, 51
FN, 87
Folder, 8
Font, 278, 279
Font mover, 279
Food drive-up with menus, 245
FOR statement, 63, 64, 65, 67, 70
FOR/NEXT, 66, 68, 73, 74
FOR/NEXT structure, 64
FOR INPUT, 207
FOR OUTPUT, 218
Formal parameter, 88, 91, 93
Format control characters, 199

Format printed outputs, 21
Formatting, 187
FORTRAN, 5, 6, 131, 187
Frame a picture, 295
Frame statements, 291
FRAMEOVAL, 290
FRAMERECT routine, 289, 290
FRAMEROUNDRECT, 290
Framing QuickDraw shapes, 291
FRE function, 308
Frequency, 298
Frequency of a note, 299
Function definition, 87, 88
Function name, 87, 88

G

Game of chance, 174
Game of craps, 174
Game playing with computers, 176
General-purpose programming
    language, 7
Geneva font, 279
Get Info, 306
GET statement, 295
GET # statement, 219, 220
Global variables, 307
Good programming practice, 30, 43,
    105, 109
GOSUB statement, 31, 88, 89, 90, 91
GOTO, 32, 38
GOTO elimination, 39
GOTO-less programming, 39
Graph information, 110
Graphical representation of an
    algorithm, 46
Graphics, 227, 228, 233, 278, 295
Graphics pen, 278, 281, 283, 290
Greatest common divisor (GCD), 101
Greatest integer not greater than, 84
Grow box, 264, 265, 305

H

Hard disk, 7
Hardware, 1
Headings, 30
Helvetica font, 279
Hexadecimal numbers, 284
Hexadecimal value, 309
HEX$ function, 309
High-level language, 4, 5, 131
Highest level of precedence, 25
Highlight a menu, 241
Histogram, 110, 114

I

IBM, 5, 6
Icon, 7, 8, 9, 15
IF command, 30
IF/THEN selection structure, 40

IF statement, 31, 63, 73
IF/THEN/ELSE, 40, 55
IF/Then statement, 38
Image, 187, 188, 296
IMP (implication) logical operator, 77
Inactive button, 252
Inactive document window, 268
Include files, 304
$ Include metacommands, 304
Increment, 63, 65
Increment of control value, 64
Increment of loop counter, 63
Indentation, 39, 40
Infinite loop, 42
Information, 2
Initial value of control variable, 64
Initial value of loop counter, 63
Initial value, 30, 63, 65, 66
Initialization phase, 45
Initialize, 30
Initialize a numeric array to zero, 105
Initialize numeric variables to zero, 43
Initializing a random access file, 218
Initializing an array to zeros, 105
INKEY$ function, 309
Innermost set of parentheses, 25
INPUT command, 20, 21, 22
Input device, 2
INPUT statement, 48, 69
INPUT statement, 68
Input-output device, 3
Input/Output symbol, 48, 49, 72
Input unit, 2
INPUT$ function, 308
Insert text, 14
Insertion of blanks, 187
INSTR function, 152
Insufficient space in a format, 190
INT function, 84, 86
INT intrinsic function, 85, 169, 170
Integer, 85
Integer array, 295, 296
Integer image specifications, 188, 189,
    190
Integer number, 216, 217
Integer part, 86
Interaction, 69
Interactive computing, 20
Interest, 67
Interest rate, 68
Internal numeric code representations of
    characters, 149
Internal representation of numbers, 66
International Morse Code, 163
Interpret, 96
Interrupt a program, 244
Intrinsic function, 82, 83, 88, 91
Inventory, 205
Inventory control, 174
Inventory simulation model, 176, 177
Invert the background pattern, 278
INVERTOVAL, 290
INVERTRECT, 289, 290
INVERTROUNDRECT, 290
Invoking a subroutine, 88

IPL/V, 131
Italic text, 280
Item number, 239
Item number parameter, 238

J

Jacopini, G., 39
Job, 2, 3
Jump To, 306
Jumping Jacks, 302

K

Kemeny, J., 5
Kentucky Derby, 302
Keyboard, 2, 10
KILL statement, 308
Kurtz, T., 5

L

Label, 31
Last-in-first-out (LIFO) order, 90
LBOUND statement, 307
LCOPY, 309
Leading asterisk, 162, 195
Leading asterisk insertion, 197
Leading blanks, 188, 192, 199
Leading percent sign, 192
LEFT$ function, 152, 222
Left-justification, 187
Left-to-right order, 27
LEN, 215
Length of a file, 220
LET command, 21, 22
LET statement, 30, 48, 69
Letter, 22, 204
Level of refinement, 44
Life of an asset, 26
LINE, 223, 278
LINE INPUT command, 156
Line plotting, 235
Line printer, 307
LINE statement, 230, 283
LINETO, 283
LISP, 131
List, 103, 306
List window, 10, 11, 13, 14, 305
Literal, 22, 30, 132, 198, 199
Literal comma, 206
Load, 3, 305, 307
LOAD statement, 308
LOC function, 308
Local variable, 91, 92
LOCATE, 282
Locate text, 14
LOCATE statement, 258, 281
Location name, 23
Location value, 23
LOF function, 220
LOG function, 84

Logical decision, 1
Logical operators, 75, 76, 77, 145
Logical unit, 2
London font, 279
Long integer number, 216, 217
Loop, 31, 44, 62, 64, 68
Loop counter, 62, 64, 65
Looping with a loop counter, 64
Loop termination, 42, 65
Looping, 28, 29, 42, 54, 62
Looping phase, 45
Looping with FOR/NEXT, 64
Lovelace, A., 6
Lowercase letters, 23, 204
LPOS function, 307
LPRINT, 20
LSET statement, 215, 216

M

M by n array, 118
Machine-dependent, 4
Machine-independent, 5
Machine language, 4, 5, 278, 303
Machine language instruction, 4
Macintosh, 1, 5, 7
Macintosh BASIC, 22
Macintosh desktop, 7, 11, 96
Main program, 88, 89, 91, 92, 96
Main storage, 2, 3
Make functions, 217, 218
Manufacturing section of the computer,
    2
Marlowe, C., 159
Math coprocessor, 303
Mathematical calculations, 82, 83
Mean, 26, 113, 114, 115, 117
Meaningful variable names, 22
Median, 113, 114, 115, 117
Menu, 227, 238, 238
MENU, 232, 242, 243
Menu bar, 8, 238, 239, 243
Menu event trapping, 244
MENU (0) function, 240, 241
MENU (1) function, 241
Menu number parameter, 238
MENU OFF statement, 244
MENU ON statement, 244
MENU RESET, 242, 243
Menu selection, 231
MENU statement, 239
MENU STOP statement, 244
MERGE statement, 308
Message, 22
Metric conversion, 166
Microprocessor, 303
Microprocessor, 303
Microsoft, 1, 5, 7
Microsoft QuickBASIC, 1
Microsoft Macintosh QuickBASIC, 7
MID$ function, 145, 146, 151
Minimal BASIC, 7
Minus sign, 199

MKDMBF$ function, 309
MKD$ function, 217
MKI$ function, 217
MKL$ function, 217
MKSMBF$ function, 309
MKS$ function, 217
Mode, 113, 114, 116, 117
Mode specification, 215
Module, 82
Monaco font, 279
Morse code, 163
Morse, S., 163
Mouse, 8, 11, 227, 232
MOUSE, 232
Mouse activity, 233
Mouse button, 9, 11, 227, 229, 230,
    233
Mouse click, 227, 231, 232
Mouse event trapping, 232, 233, 235,
    236
MOUSE (0) function, 227, 228
MOUSE (1) function, 228, 229
MOUSE (2) function, 228, 229
MOUSE (3) function, 230, 231
MOUSE (4) function, 230, 231
MOUSE (5) function, 230, 231
MOUSE (6) function, 230, 231
Mouse pointer, 8, 229
Mouse trapping, 233
MOVE, 283
MOVETO statement, 281–283
Moving text, 14
Multiline edit field, 274
Multiline format, 40
Multiple line IF/THEN/ELSE
    statement, 41
Multiplication, 2, 25–28
Multiprogramming, 2, 3
Multitasking, 6
Music, 295, 298, 302
Music composition program, 302

N

Name, 23
Name of a loop counter, 63
Name of an array, 103
NAME statement, 308
Narrative flowchart, 47, 48, 49, 53, 56
Natural language of a computer, 4, 303
Natural logarithm, 84
Negative amounts with floating dollar
    sign, 197
Neat tabular format, 73, 105, 106, 107
Negative step, 65, 66
Nested FOR/NEXT, 178
Nested FOR/NEXT loop, 110, 113
Nested FOR/NEXT statement, 119
Nested parentheses, 25, 27, 28
New option, 11
New option in File menu, 305
New York font, 279
Next Bookmark, 306

NEXT statement, 63, 65
Nondestructive readout, 24
Nonrecursive, 94
NOT, 76
NOT BIC mode, 286
NOT COPY mode, 286
NOT logical operator, 77
NOT OR mode, 286
NOT XOR mode, 286
Null, 92
Number sign, 296
Numeric image specification, 196, 197
Numeric code representations, 150
Numeric data, 218
Numeric digit, 199
Numeric field, 204
Numeric image specifications, 195
Numeric string data, 218
Numeric variable, 22, 23, 30, 220

O

Octal, 309
Octave, 298, 299
OCT$ function, 309
Odd, 86
"Old MacDonald Had a Farm", 137,
    139, 301
ON DIALOG GOSUB, 258
ON DIALOG statement, 257
ON event GOSUB, 231, 232
ON MENU GOSUB, 244
On-time delivery of systems, 39
Open a file for random access, 215
Open a window, 14
Open FOR INPUT, 206
Open option, 8, 11
Open option in File menu, 305
Open statement, 206, 215
Operator, 25
Operator precedence, 25, 26, 28
Opinion poll, 108, 113
OPTION BASE statement, 307
Options, 13, 306
OR, 76, 296
OR logical operator, 76
OR mode, 280, 286
Order in which the steps are to be
    performed, 46
Out of data, 72
Outlined text, 280
OUTPUT, 218
Output, 306
Output device, 2
Output formatting, 187
Output unit, 2
Output window, 9, 10, 11, 252, 305
Oval, 278
Oval height parameter, 290
Oval statements, 292, 293
Oval symbol, 48, 51
Oval width, 290
Overflow conditions, 304

P

Page Setup option in File menu, 305
Paint a pattern, 278
PAINTOVAL, 290
PAINTRECT, 289, 290
PAINTROUNDRECT, 290
Pair of parentheses, 25, 28
Paradise Island Casino, 167
Parallelogram symbol, 48, 72
Parentheses, 25
Pascal, 6
Pass by reference, 93, 94
Pass by value, 93, 94
Passed argument, 93
Paste, 271, 276, 306
Paste option, 14
Pattern of ones and zeros, 204
Payroll, 205
PEEK function, 308
PEEKL function, 308
PEEKW function, 308
Pen, 278
Pen mode, 286, 289
Pen mode demonstration, 288
Pen pattern, 285
Pen size, 286, 287
PENMODE, 286
PENNORMAL, 285
PENSIZE, 284
PENSIZE statement, 284
Percent sign, 192, 296
Perfect number, 100
Perform a program, 21
Period, 22
Permutations, 145
Personal computer, 1, 5
Phase parameter, 299
PIC clause, 187
Picture, 268
PICTURE, 268, 269
PICTURE OFF statement, 267
PICTURE ON statement, 267
PICTURE$ function, 267, 273
Piecework payroll example, 73
Pig Latin, 152, 153
Pixel, 229, 267, 280, 281, 283, 286,
    309
Plain dialog box, 264, 265, 271
Plain document window, 265
Plain text, 280
Plaintext, 163
PL/1, 6, 131
Plot a line, 230
Plot a point, 228
Plus sign (+), 190
POINT function, 309
Point of a drag, 229
Point plotting, 235
Pointer, 70, 228
Points of the compass, 165
POKE statement, 308
Poll, 108
Polynomial, 27, 28
Poor programming practice, 66

Popping a stack, 91
POS function, 309
Position in a window, 267
Position number, 118
Position number of array element, 103
Power down the computer, 15
Precedence, 25, 26, 27, 28
PRESET statement, 296, 309
Primary storage, 2
Prime integer, 101
Principal, 68
PRINT command, 20, 21
Print delimiters, 21
Print option, 11
Print option in File menu, 305
Print positioning, 85
Print statement, 13, 30, 48
PRINT USING statement, 187, 188
Printed reports, 187
Printer, 20, 309
Printing, 2
Printing a calendar, 165
Printing characters, 199
Printing characters with PRINT
    USING, 199
Printing dates in various formats, 161
Printing histograms, 110
Printout, 2, 3
Probability, 167
Procedure, 37
Process symbol, 48
Program control, 38
Program flowchart, 47, 49, 52, 53, 57
Program label, 31
Program readability, 55
Programmer-defined function, 82, 87,
    91
Programming, 1
Programming language, 3
Protected check amounts, 199
PSET statement, 228, 229, 223, 278,
    296
Pseudocode, 38, 39, 40, 41, 51, 54,
    55
Pseudocode algorithm, 43
PTAB statement, 281, 282
Pull down menus, 244
Punched card, 2, 3
Push, 91
Push button, 253, 258
PUT statement, 295, 296
PUT # statement, 220

Q

Quadratic equation, 27
Question mark, 22
QuickBASIC, 1, 7, 9, 11, 14
QuickBASIC environment, 303
QuickBASIC window, 15
QuickDraw, 278, 284, 291
QuickDraw frame statements, 291
QuickDraw oval statements, 292, 293
QuickDraw pen, 284

QuickDraw pen modes, 289
Quit, 14
Quit option, 11
Quit option in File menu, 305
Quotation marks, 22, 72, 131, 133,
    206

R

Radio button, 253, 258
Random, 167
Random access, 215
Random access buffer, 220
Random access file, 214, 216, 218,
    219, 304, 308, 309
Random file buffer, 215, 216, 219
Random number, 84
RANDOMIZE, 171
RANDOMIZE statement, 171
RANDOMIZE TIMER, 171
Randomizing die-rolling program, 172
READ statement, 68, 70
READ/DATA statements, 69, 73, 74
Readability, 20, 40, 45, 55
Reading a random access file
    sequentially, 220, 221, 223
Reading data from a sequential file,
    207, 208
Read-only memory (ROM), 278
Receiving section of the computer, 2
Record, 204, 205, 206, 207, 208, 219
Record key, 205
Record length, 215, 220
Record number, 216, 220
Recording a picture, 267
Rectangle, 278, 290
Rectangle symbol, 48, 231
Rectangle with rounded corners, 252
Recursion, 93, 95
Recursive factorial subprogram, 95
Recursive program, 96
Recursive subprogram, 93, 95, 96
Redraws a picture in a window, 269
Refinement, 178, 180
Refinement process, 44
Refresh a window, 264, 267
Relational operator, 32, 75, 77, 148
Reliable software system, 93
REM command, 20
REM statement, 22, 29, 304
Remark, 20
Repeatability, 171
Repetition, 39, 42, 49, 62
Repetition structure, 41, 49
Replacement, 23
Rereading data from a sequential file,
    208, 209
Reserved word, 11
RESET statement, 308
Restart a program, 13, 308
RESTORE command, 133
RESTORE statement, 72
RETURN, 88, 89, 90, 91
Return key, 10, 11, 20, 268, 273, 276

Return location, 89, 91
Reuse instructions, 29
Right-aligned column format, 190
RIGHT$ function, 152
Right-justification of integers, 191
Right-justification of numeric outputs, 187
Right-justified, 189, 190, 195, 217
RND (x), 170
RND function, 84, 85
RND intrinsic function, 167
Roll a six-sided die, 167, 168, 170, 302
ROM, 278
Roman numerals, 164
Root of a quadratic equation, 27
Round up, 86
Rounded corner document window, 264, 265
Rounded rectangle, 278, 290
Rounding, 85, 187, 189, 192
Rounding with PRINT USING, 193
Roundoff errors, 7
Row, 118
RSET statement, 215, 216, 217
Rules of operator precedence, 25, 26, 28
Run a program, 13, 14, 15, 21
Run menu, 13, 96
Run option, 13
Run Program, 306
RUN statement, 308
Runtime error, 308

S

SADD function, 309
Salvage value of an asset, 26, 73
Same level of precedence, 26
San Francisco font, 279
Save, 11
Save As, 11, 12
Save As dialog box, 305
Save As option in File menu, 305
Save button, 11, 14
Save dialog box, 271
Save option, 12
Save option in File menu, 305
Scale, 299, 300
Scale a picture, 269
Scaling, 168, 170
Scaling factor, 168, 173
Scientific notation, 193
Scope of a loop, 42, 65
Screen, 20
Scroll bar, 233
SCROLL statement, 309
Search menu, 14
Search string, 152
Seattle font, 279
Second degree polynomial, 27, 28
Second refinement, 45
Security copies, 9
Seed, 171
SELECT/CASE statement, 73, 74, 141

Selectable, 238, 239
Selection, 39, 49
Selection structure, 39, 40, 50, 54
Semicolon, 191
Semicolon print separator, 21
Sentinel value, 43, 44, 45, 62, 206
Sentinel-controlled loop, 44
Sentinel-controlled looping, 45, 62
Separator, 133
Sequence, 39, 49
Sequence structure, 39, 44, 50
Sequential file, 205, 206, 214, 308
Set bookmark, 306
Set info, 306
SGN function, 84
Shadowed dialog box, 264, 265, 271
Shadowed text, 280
Shakespeare, W., 159
SHARED Statement, 307
Sharing, 3
Shift, 169
Shifting, 169, 170
Shifting value, 173,
Shipping section of the computer, 2
Side effect, 91, 93
Sights and sounds, 295
Signal value, 43
Signed integer portion, 84
Silicon, 1
Simple conditions, 75, 77
Simulation, 161, 176
Simulation model, 174
Simulation of the game of craps, 175
SIN function, 84
Sine, 84
Single-precision array, 295, 296
Single-precision number, 216, 217
Single-user batch processing, 3
Single-voice mode, 299
SLIP, 131
SNOBOL, 131
Software, 1
Software projects, 39
Songwriting program, 161
Sorting, 113
Sorting an array, 111
Sound, 295, 308
SOUND, 298
Sound wave, 299
Source code, 304
SPACE$ function, 155, 309
SPC function, 309
Speaker, 308
Special symbols, 204
Spelling phrases backwards, 151
SQR function, 83, 84
Square, 30
Square root, 83, 84
Stack, 90, 91
Starting point of a drag, 230
State of a button, 254
State parameter, 238
Statement, 20
STATIC, 92, 116
Static arrays, 303

Step, 13, 65, 67, 306
STEP option, 305
STEP portion of the FOR statement, 64
Stepwise refinement, 53, 176, 178
Stop, 13
STOP statement, 308
Storage unit, 2
Storage location, 23, 24
Stored program, 3
STR$ function, 155, 309
Straight-line depreciation, 26, 72, 73
Straight-line form, 25, 27
String, 4, 22, 72, 131, 132
String array, 137
String concatenation, 155
String constant image, 188
String constants, 131, 132
String expression image, 188, 189
String image specifications, 197,
String manipulation, 131, 148
String representation of a number, 218
String value, 131, 132, 133
String variable, 72, 92, 132, 133, 220, 273
String variable image, 191
String variable name, 132
STRING$ function, 155, 309
Structured flowcharting, 46, 51
Structured programming, 6, 7, 19, 37, 39, 40
SUB, 92
Subprogram, 82, 83, 91, 93, 114
Subprogram call, 95
Subprogram definition, 92
Subroutine, 82, 83, 88, 89, 90, 91, 222
Subscript, 103, 118
Subtraction, 2, 25, 26
Summarizing the results of an opinion poll, 108
Summation with FOR/NEXT, 67
Supercomputer, 1
Survey data analysis, 113–117
Symbol file, 303
Symbols, 46
System clock, 171
System folder, 7
SYSTEM function, 308
SYSTEM statement, 308
Swap statement, 113

T

TAB function, 85
Tab key, 268, 275, 276
Table, 30, 103, 118
Tabular information, 29
TAN function, 84
Task, 2, 3
Telephone number word generator, 160
Terminal, 3
Terminate a Macintosh session, 15
Terminate program execution, 308
Terminating condition, 41, 62, 95

Termination phase, 45
Termination symbol, 48
TEXT, 281
Text analysis, 159
Text cursor, 309
Text format, 304
Text manipulation, 159
Text modes, 286
Text pointer, 13
TEXTFACE, 280
TEXTMODE, 280, 282, 286
TEXTSIZE, 278
The PUT # statement, 216
Tic-tac-toe, 301
TIME$, 85
TIMER, 232
Timesharing, 2, 3, 5
Title line of a table, 30
Title parameter, 238
Top-down, stepwise refinement, 44, 53, 54, 176, 178
Toronto font, 279
Tortoise and the hare simulation, 302
Totaler, 43, 44
Totaling the elements of an array, 108
Towers of Hanoi, 101, 302
Trace All option, 13, 305, 306
Trailing minus sign, 194, 195, 197
Trailing minus sign insertion with PRINT USING, 194
Trailing spaces, 216
Trailing zeros, 192
Transfer of control, 31, 32, 38, 39, 90
Transfer option, 11
Transfer option in File menu, 305
Translate, 4, 96
Translation, 3
Translator program, 4
Trigonometric cosine, 84
Trigonometric sine, 84
Trigonometric tangent, 84
TRON/TROFF statements, 308
True, 32, 39, 40
Truncate, 216
Truth table, 77
"Twelve Days of Christmas", 133, 134, 158, 301
Two-letter words, 143, 144
Types of windows, 265

U

UBOUND statement, 307
UCASE$ function, 309
Unary operator, 77
Unconditional transfer of control, 31, 89
Underlined text, 280
Underscore (_) as a string image specification, 198
Undo, 306
United States Department of Defense (DOD), 6
Unhighlight a menu, 241

Unpredictable events, 227
Unstructured approach, 19
Update an account, 222
Uppercase letters, 23
User-friendly language, 38
Useful life of an asset, 72

V

VAL function, 155, 273, 309
Value, 23, 24
Value of an element, 103
Value separator, 133
Variable, 20, 25, 30, 41, 49, 54, 69
Variable name, 22, 23
Variable pointer, 285
VARPTR function, 285, 289, 290, 307
Venice font, 279
Vertical scroll bar, 231, 233
Voice, 298, 299
Voice parameter, 299
Volume, 298
Volume parameter, 299

W

Wait for a dialog event, 272
Warehouse section of the computer, 2
WAVE, 298, 299
Wavedefinition parameter, 299
WEND, 42
WHILE/WEND, 42, 55, 66, 139
WIDTH (string) function, 267
WIDTH statement, 309
Window, 8, 9, 227, 232, 264, 265, 268
WINDOW, 264
Window activity, 255
WINDOW CLOSE Id#, 266

WINDOW (0) function, 267
WINDOW (1) function, 267
WINDOW (2) function, 267
WINDOW (3) function, 267
WINDOW (4) function, 267
WINDOW (5) function, 267
WINDOW Id#, 266
Window rectangle parameter, 265
Window refreshing, 268, 269
WINDOW OUTPUT Id#, 266
WINDOW statement, 265
Window type parameter, 265
Windows menu, 14
Word arrangements, 146, 160
Word equivalent of a check amount, 162
Word processing, 131, 161
WRITE # statement, 206
WRITE under FORMAT control in FORTRAN, 187

X

XOR, 296
XOR (exclusive OR) logical operator, 77
XOR mode, 280, 281, 286

Y

Yes button, 14

Z

Zero fill, 187
Zeroth column, 118
Zeroth (0th) element of an array, 105
Zeroth row, 118
Zoom box, 264, 265